THE NOBLEST TRIUMPH

Property and Prosperity
through the Ages

Tom Bethell

St. Martin's Griffin
New York

For Donna, with all my love

ISBN 0-312-22337-4

Library of Congress Cataloging-in-Publication Data
Bethell, Tom.
   The noblest triumph : property and prosperity through the ages /
  Tom Bethell.
      p. cm.
  Includes bibliographical references and index.
  ISBN 0-312-21083-3 (cloth) 0-312-22337-4 (pbk)
   1. Property.   2. Right of property—Economic aspects.   I. Title.
HB711.B477 1998
330.1'7—dc21   98-6010
                                                          CIP

Design by Acme Art, Inc.

First published in hardcover in the United States of America in 1998
First St. Martin's Griffin edition: September 1999
10 9 8 7 6 5 4 3 2 1

CONTENTS

ACKNOWLEDGMENTS

I owe a debt of gratitude to many. Year after year, I was able to return to the Hoover Institution for months at a time. My particular thanks to John Raisian, the director of the institution, who kindly invited me back, and to Tom Henriksen, the head of the media fellow program, whose help was indispensable. I cannot imagine that, anywhere in the world, there is a think tank better than Hoover, where they give you an office and leave you alone. Right next door is Stanford University's Green Library, which must be just about the world's best. Between earthquake and flood, its stacks became my haunts. The law library is a short walk away. What more could a fellow want?

My thanks to Robert Hessen, who kept me informed of new articles in the field, and who knew what I had in mind, if not on paper. Many thanks also to those at Hoover who read chapters or made helpful suggestions: Martin Anderson, Arnold Beichman, Mikhail Bernstam, Bill Evers, Seymour Martin Lipset, Guity Nashat, Alvin Rabushka, Peter Robinson, Henry S. Rowen, Abraham Sofaer. Hoover is well colonized by economists, and it was my privilege to discuss some of the ideas in the book with them; notably Aaron Director, Robert J. Barro, Gary S. Becker, Douglass C. North, and Sherwin Rosen. But I do not wish to impute to them the agreement with my conclusions, and I alone am responsible for any errors.

Richard L. Stroup and Jane S. Shaw of the Political Economy Research Center in Bozeman invited me to Montana, read chapters and made excellent suggestions, which I hope have found their way into print. Others who kindly read chapters include Lowell Harriss, Donald Leal, Paul Heyne and the late Murray Rothbard. Particular thanks are due to the Manhattan Institute's Walter Olson, whose critical reading of two chapters inspired some hasty revision. I have also had many stimulating discussions with Fred Smith and his team at the Competitive Enterprise Institute

I first became aware of economic analysis in 1974, when I read the alternating columns of Milton Friedman and Paul Samuelson in *Newsweek*. I found that I could always understand Friedman whereas Samuelson baffled me. What was this machine called "the economy," and this "aggregate demand" of which there was either too little or too much? Friedman wrote about individual incentives, which always made sense. Price controls created shortages; thus the energy crisis. The supply side movement came a few years later. Its origin was simple. Inflation had unjustly moved people into higher income tax brackets, and I remember the exhilarating discussions about marginal effects, tax rates and revenues, prices and quantities, with George Gilder, Jeff Bell, Paul Craig Roberts, Arthur Laffer, Bruce Bartlett, Howard Segermark and others. At just the right moment, Ronald Reagan was elected.

The belief was that tax rates were too high everywhere, in the Third World as well as the First. Eventually, however, I decided that most countries were crippled by something more fundamental. The legal and political foundations that are essential to economic growth had never been properly laid in the first place. That is where this book begins. But those 1970s discussions were its progenitor. If Hoover was my graduate school, supply-side was my Econ 101.

I worked on the book in intervals between writing many magazine articles. My thanks to the *American Spectator*'s Bob Tyrrell; to Wladyslaw Pleszczynski for his support; and to William F. Buckley, Jr., for his generosity. I have also benefited from discussions with Joe Sobran on the subjects raised in this book. I would particularly like to thank Jim Bovard, who read and recommended the manuscript at a crucial juncture. Michael Flamini's enthusiasm came just in time, and his small team at St. Martin's Press, particularly the painstaking work of Alan Bradshaw and Bill Berry, refute the notion that editing is a dying art. Finally, many thanks to John and Bea Smalley, and to Carlotta Maurice, Bay Area property owners.

INTRODUCTION

IN THE SPRING OF 1990, the World Bank held a series of lunch-hour talks on subjects related to bank business but not normally on its agenda. Gabriel Roth, a bank consultant, had asked me to speak and my topic was the relationship between property rights and economic development. Perhaps 50 staff assistants from both the World Bank and the International Monetary Fund were present. I said that if the countries they deal with want to achieve the level of development that has been reached by the United States and a few other countries, they would have to adopt legal regimes that give security to private property. It would be understandable if some countries preferred to retain their traditional character, or to avoid the ceaseless striving and upheaval that accompanies the free-market system. But they should be clear about both means and ends. If it was real growth and modernization that they wanted, then tinkering with the levers of macroeconomic policy—here a little fiscal stimulus, there a little monetary restraint—would not do the job. Their legal and political systems would have to be brought more closely into line with those of the Western world.

World Bank professionals are nothing if not courteous, and they responded to my remarks with what might be called polite puzzlement. Questions were skeptical. My sense was that many of them disagreed, without saying so openly. Specialized agencies of the United Nations, such as the World Bank and the International Monetary Fund, are supposed to be apolitical and must be cautious about advocating political reform. Without portfolios of loans outstanding, they are dependent on the goodwill of their host governments, most of whom would not countenance drastic change. To complicate matters, the World Bank has historically been a statist institution, its loans usually supporting government-directed projects. The legal regime of private property, on the other hand, is antithetical to state power.

But there was more at issue than political pragmatism. To some present, the necessity of private property seemed to be a genuinely unfamiliar recommendation. Perhaps incomprehension was the polite mode of disagreement. But some also seemed eager to pursue the subject and to learn more about the connection between private property and economic development. The experience planted a seed of this book.

After the Berlin Wall fell, and the Soviet Union ceased to exist, the long-neglected subject of property became a lively topic of discussion. A wide-ranging book on the subject seemed needed, because the institution of private property, in which power is decentralized and the rule of law is dominant, has been one of the most important institutions of Western civilization. Books had been written on the Takings Clause of the Fifth Amendment, on the eminent domain power, on patents and copyrights, on the effects of state ownership on the environment. Aspects of the broader topic had been put under a microscope. What was needed was a wider-angled book on property and its consequences.

The image of a lens often occurred to me. Property was the lens through which seemingly unrelated events could be examined. Because it had been hidden away in the intellectual attic, it could perhaps bring a wide range of issues into focus now. Some of the questions dealt with here include the prosperity of empires, the decline of Rome, the rise of Great Britain, the failure of communes, the nineteenth-century famine in Ireland, the materially backward state of the Arab world, the modern-day drought in California, the extent of deserts, the destruction of rain forests, the endangered status of wild animals and, most recently, the rise of interest in intellectual property.

Property sprawls awkwardly across a dozen disciplines. Law, economics, history, political philosophy, moral philosophy, anthropology, sociology and psychology are only the most important, and no doubt I have omitted a few. For that reason, a general book on property more or less has to be written by a non-specialist. Amateurs rush in, no doubt, where experts fear to tread. The area that I have mostly concentrated on is the overlapping zone of law and economics, and the light that this sheds on history.

Economic analysis is like a suspension bridge. It can have all the fancy engineering you want, but at some point it must reach down to the solid rock of law and secure political institutions. Works of economic history, however, often disregard the political and legal foundations of the societies under examination. Economic outcomes are thought to be satisfactorily explained by economic data. Growth is a function of "capital formation," for example. But capital is a highly derivative abstraction, a mere cable on the suspension bridge. Is the whole structure embedded in the solid foundations of secure property rights, enforceable contracts, an independent judicial system? Until very recently, economists have paid little attention to these questions. Perhaps the old name, *political economy,* should be restored. This is not to imply that the delicate balance of supply and demand can be overcome by a combination of goodwill and sheer political force. Rather, the bow to politics makes explicit the indispensable foundation of economics.

Karl Marx and Friedrich Engels played a crucial role in changing our understanding of political economy. Economic relations are the causal *infra-*

structure of society, they argued, law and politics are mere *superstructure*. In large measure this reversed cause and effect, but it was highly influential all the same. Marx's far better known attack on private property looked ideological by comparison. The claim that economic relations determined legal relations aroused less suspicion, and many economists were happy to agree that their field enjoyed an independence comparable to that of physics and mathematics. (And, as we shall see in chapter 2, the Marxian claim has just enough truth in it to complicate the picture.)

My thesis, then, is that when we put law back in its proper place, antecedent to economy, and make legal relations the true bedrock upon which the bridge of economic analysis must be placed, we can look at many historical events through new eyes. The great explanatory hypothesis of history then becomes: When property is privatized, and the rule of law is established, in such a way that all including the rulers themselves are subject to the same law, economies will prosper and civilization will blossom. Of the different possible configurations of property, only private property can have this desirable effect.

I

FIRST THINGS

ONE

THE BLESSINGS
OF PROPERTY

FALL FROM GRACE

OVER ONE HUNDRED YEARS AGO, the institution of private property fell into intellectual disrepute. That is the great historical fact that we must face at the outset. No doubt some of the skeptics among my World Bank audience were quietly thinking that eighteenth-century ideas are a little passé at the end of the twentieth century. Property's fall from grace was gradual, beginning early in the nineteenth century. But with the *Communist Manifesto* the war on property became overt, and finally it became respectable. Property in the abstract was then viewed disparagingly by Western intellectuals for many decades. The form that this most commonly took was neglect.

In the 1950s, when Encyclopaedia Britannica Inc. published its *Great Books of the Western World,* property was not among the 102 topics in its index of "great ideas." Arnold Toynbee overlooked property in his 12-volume *Study of History.* Elsewhere, his comments showed that he saw no important difference between public and private property.[1] William H. McNeill's *Rise of the West* and Oswald Spengler's *Decline of the West* alike found property dispensable. Fernand Braudel's three-volume *Civilization and Capitalism, Fifteenth to Eighteenth Century,* paid scant attention to property or law; as did *A History of Civilizations,* by the same author. Noting that the cause of Europe's rise has long intrigued scholars, Paul Kennedy, in his *Rise and Fall of the Great Powers,* attributed it not to political institutions but, more materialistically, to geography. Europe had escaped central domination largely because there are "no enormous plains over which an empire of horsemen could impose its swift dominion."[2]

In academic circles in recent decades, John Locke's justification of private property—that people deserve to own what they labor to create—has been scrutinized with a degree of suspicion that would have impressed the apologists of the Stuart tyranny, with whom Locke was in contention.[3] Although they extend over hundreds of pages, the arguments of the modern-day anti-Lockeans are vain, for the case for private property would be just as strong if he had never lived. That case is borne of human nature, not seventeenth-century philosophy.

In the all-important realm of constitutional law, 50 years ago "the U.S. Supreme Court interred property rights in the constitutional graveyard," the political scientist Dennis J. Coyle has written.[4] By the mid-1930s, economic rights were no longer thought deserving of constitutional protection. Between 1928 and 1974, the Court refused to hear a single zoning case. In the area of psychology, Professor Richard Pipes of Harvard reports, a child-psychology researcher "expressed surprise that as of 1980 'there has been almost no empirical work, and no systematic theoretical work, on the psychology of possession—on the origins and development of individual possessiveness.'"[5] This, Pipes added, a century after William James had suggested that the psychological implications of ownership were potentially considerable.

In economics, best-selling textbooks by Paul Samuelson and others either skirted questions of ownership or relegated them to a paragraph under the rubric of "capitalist ideology."[6] Since World War II, almost all such texts have argued that a more rapid growth could be attained with state ownership than with private property. The University of California at Los Angeles economist Armen Alchian found that the fields of economics, as listed in the Directory of the American Economic Association in the mid-1970s, included no field "on Property, Entitlements, or Rights." Government, nonprofit and communal property were treated as if they were "no different in their effects than stereotyped private property rights."[7] In graduate studies, property rights were for a long time an "untouchable area" for doctoral theses, according to the economist Steven Cheung.[8] In his graduate studies in the 1970s, the Harvard economist Robert Barro heard nothing at all about property rights.[9] Robert Solow of the Massachusetts Institute of Technology, winner of the Nobel Prize in economics in 1987, said: "I still believe the institution of private property has to keep proving itself." He referred to Proudhon's "insight" that "property is theft."[10]

The economists' neglect is noteworthy. Starting with Adam Smith, the most influential treatises on political economy, as economics was then called,* were

---

*"Economy" originally referred to those decisions made by a family with respect to wealth. "Political economy," first used in the eighteenth century, expanded the analysis to nations. Adam Smith wrote that the "progress of opulence in different ages and nations" had given rise to "different systems of political oeconomy, with regard to enriching the people." Not until the late nineteenth century did *political economy* became *economics*. Alfred Marshall's *Principles of Economics* (1890) was the first major treatise to abandon the older phrase. This change coincided with the use

written at a time when property was so highly regarded that defending it seemed superfluous. Private property was deemed "sacred." The English economists of the classical period did not analyze the legal institutions upon which their reasoning was predicated. It is hardly an exaggeration to say that by the time property came under attack, in the mid-nineteenth century, economists had written very little in its defense. Private property "was assumed and taken for granted, without investigation, by the nineteenth-century economists," wrote John R. Commons in The *Legal Foundations of Capitalism*.[11] It has also been taken for granted much more recently—and by those for whom economic development is a professional concern.

THE BLESSINGS OF PRIVATE PROPERTY

The many blessings of a private-property system have never been properly analyzed, probably because of this peculiar history. It is a vast subject, and an introduction of this nature can only outline those benefits. But there are four great blessings that cannot easily be realized in a society that lacks the secure, decentralized, private ownership of goods. These are: liberty, justice, peace and prosperity. The argument of this book is that private property is a necessary (but not a sufficient) condition for these highly desirable social outcomes.

Of these, the relationship between liberty and property is by now fairly well understood. Leon Trotsky long ago pointed out that where there is no private ownership, individuals can be bent to the will of the state, under threat of starvation.[12] The Nobel Prize–winning economist Milton Friedman has said that "you cannot have a free society without private property."[13] Yet this elementary truth was not understood a hundred years ago, when intellectuals began to think of private property as a dispensable institution. It was the practical experience of Communism that made all the difference. Those who lived under its tyranny soon understood that without property rights, all other rights mean little or nothing. Angels and spirits surely do not need property, but human beings have not yet attained that incorporeal state.

Private property is a compromise between our desire for unrestricted liberty and the recognition that others have similar desires and rights. It is a way to be free, "and yet secure from the freedom of others," as the American University law professor James Boyle has written.[14] Privacy these days is a much

---

of mathematical tools to help resolve a number of problems, thereby conferring prestige upon economics by associating it with science rather than politics. Most economists since have not wanted to return to the older association. But the crucial importance of political and legal institutions to economic life suggests that "political economy" really is preferable.

admired good, and American courts have discovered a right to it in the penumbras and emanations of the Constitution. Yet it is obvious that privacy cannot be attained without an anterior respect for private property.

Rights are held against the state, and property is an important bulwark against state power. Ownership in a society that protects and respects property will tend to be unequal, to be sure, and for over a hundred years property has been represented as an *expression* of power; but like all genuine rights, property rights protect the weak against the strong. Some early arrivals in the United States marveled that smallholders were as secure in their possession as the rich were in theirs. ("The law of the land is so constituted, that every man is secure in the enjoyment of his property," a group of German settlers in Maryland said in 1763. "[T]he meanest person is out of reach of oppression from the most powerful."[15]) Recent immigrants have been delighted to find that you can buy property in the United States without paying bribes. The call for secure property rights in Third World countries today is not an attempt to help the rich. It is not the property of those who have access to Swiss bank accounts that needs to be protected. It is the small and insecure possessions of the poor. This key point was well understood in the first and best of the social encyclicals of the Catholic Church. In *Rerum Novarum* (On the Condition of the Working Classes), published in 1891, Pope Leo XIII wrote that the "fundamental principle of Socialism, which would make all possessions public property, is to be utterly rejected because it injures the very ones whom it seeks to help."[16]

The institution of private property also plays a key role in establishing justice in a society. This is one of the most important arguments in its favor, yet the connection between private property and social justice has rarely been made, mainly because social justice has been equated with the distribution of already existing goods. Inequality is equated with injustice. Nonetheless, a private property regime makes people responsible for their own actions in the realm of material goods. Such a system therefore ensures that people experience the consequences of their own acts. Property sets up fences, but it also surrounds us with mirrors, reflecting back upon us the consequences of our own behavior. Both the prudent and the profligate will tend to experience their deserts. Therefore, a society of private property goes some way toward institutionalizing justice. As Professor James Q. Wilson has said, property is a "powerful antidote to unfettered selfishness."[17]

Property is also the most peaceable of institutions. In a society of private property, goods must be either voluntarily exchanged or laboriously created. As long as such ownership is protected by the state, goods cannot easily be taken by force. Furthermore, a society with legal institutions that encourage the creation of wealth poses a diminished threat to the wealth of neighbors. In contrast, mutual raiding parties will flourish in adjacent societies with communal ownership. Private property also allows a country to become rich enough to defend itself against aggressive neighbors, thereby reducing the likelihood of conflict.

Private property both disperses power and shields us from the coercion of others. It enables us to formulate our own plans and to use the information that is uniquely in our heads. It leaves us free to act without interference, within our own autonomous spheres. People are not only permitted to make their own plans, but to a considerable degree are obliged to do so. Nonetheless, in most countries the trend for much of the twentieth century has until recently been in the reverse direction. Power has been centralized almost everywhere, and property frequently nationalized. Where this was carried to an extreme—in the centrally planned economies of the Communist countries—a few "master brains" at the center were supposed to plan for everyone. Most people were thereby reduced to servile status. That is why all such countries turned out to be tyrannical. The state was at war with the natural inclinations of the people.

Prosperity and property are intimately connected. Exchange is the basic market activity, and when goods are not individually owned, they cannot easily be exchanged. Free-market economies, therefore, can only be built on a private property base. Property rights are "the fundament of a market economy," as Daniel Yergin and Joseph Stanislaw note in *The Commanding Heights*.[18] By the same token, a knowledge of existing property rules in a society is a prerequisite of economic analysis, and the effects of such rules ought to be made explicit in economic theory. Private ownership permits people to "evaluate" what they own and (in both the everyday and the financial sense) to "realize" that value. It enables them to decide how much to ask, or to bid, for the good in question.

This connection, between prosperity and private property, has only been recently accepted. For a long time, many people thought that centrally directed and planned economies could improve upon the free-market system. But it turned out that non-owners employed by the state could not successfully substitute their own commands for the vast multiplicity of market judgments and exchanges. The belief that planners could do this, thereby achieving the same outcome as that produced by private ownership (or a better outcome, because supposedly more just), was the key economic delusion of socialism.

THE LENS OF PROPERTY

Seen through the lens of property, the continued and unanticipated preeminence of the West in the half century since World War II becomes understandable. Those countries that enjoyed well-developed private property before disenchantment set in have continued to enjoy real economic growth. But the new nations of the postcolonial period, experimenting with untried methods, have experienced failure. After the Soviets came to power, misleading economic statistics obscured the real (and dismal) results of Communism. This error continued for decades. For a long time, therefore, it seemed that the Marxian criticism of private property (that it was little more than an expression of class interest) had been validated. The central-planning system seemed to be working well without it. Property's true role in economic life was thereby masked. For if, as America's best-selling economics textbook claimed as recently as 1987, "the Soviet growth rate has generally exceeded that of the United States in the post–World War II period as a whole,"[19] how could anyone claim that private property was indispensable for economic growth?

Today, it seems probable that the gross domestic product (GDP) of the Soviet Union and its satellites were exaggerated by as much as a factor of ten. One example should suffice. The *Statistical Abstract of the United States,* published by the Department of Commerce, includes a table comparing GDP per capita in different countries. In 1989, the year the Berlin Wall fell, per capita income was said to be higher in East Germany ($10,330) than in West Germany ($10,320). The same table also alleged that East Germany's GDP per capita in 1980 was higher than Japan's.[20] No one even tries to defend these figures today.

The problem was not just statistical credulity. Development economists and elites had failed to grasp the true institutional requirements of economic growth. To some extent these requirements are still not understood. For example, the repeated call for "democracy" abroad suggests that Western political institutions have not been analyzed much beyond the obligation to hold elections periodically. But democracy, like economy, must have its foundations. It is not something that can be set down, naked and exposed, on the unprepared terrain of anarchy or tyranny. That is not the foundation upon which democracy developed in the Western world itself, and there is no reason to expect that it will suffice for the Third World either.

In 1996, the *Economist* called attention on its cover to the "mystery of economic growth."[21] Its persistently lopsided nature had for years been a considerable embarrassment to the "models" of economists. Something had been forgotten along the way. We can now see that it was private property and the rule of law. We are only just beginning to realize that the institutional structure of capitalism is not as "natural" as some have thought. It has proven much more difficult to replicate than was anticipated. Its consequences—the material outcome that we see around us—we take for granted. Few understand the antecedent legal substratum or its evolution. The Peruvian writer Hernando de Soto tells an amusing story of his inability to find someone (anyone) who could explain to him the legal foundations of Western economies.[22] Eventually he concluded that no such person existed.

The welfare states of the Western world were built on the premise that property, particularly in its income form, was no longer sacred. It could be taken from some and given to others—to the advantage of all. The latter would enjoy it more than the former would miss it. This rearrangement was assumed to be both virtuous and efficient. The rich would be relieved of the temptation to excess and the poor would be relieved of their poverty. Meanwhile the "laws" of economics would ensure that the poor countries would catch up with the rich ones. The factors of production, capital in particular, would be more efficacious in the former than in the latter. Therefore the wealth of nations would converge. But it hasn't worked out that way.

The use of legal and political institutions as an explanatory device can be pursued only so far however. I argue, for example, that Britain was the first country in Europe to develop the correct (prosperity-encouraging) system outlined above. In this fashion Britain's great success and influence beginning in the eighteenth century can be explained. It is much harder to explain *why* this happened in Britain and not elsewhere. (Actually, Holland seems to have beaten Britain, but soon made a fatal error: taxes were set too high and the country became uncompetitive. But why the Dutch made this mistake and the British did not remains a mystery.) Again, why did the British surrender their lead in the twentieth century? One can point to statutory changes that increased regulation and decreased competition. But one cannot easily answer the question: Why did the governing class forget what it once knew? We are seeing a comparable amnesia in the United States today.

Vital to the prosperity-encouraging system was the great discovery of equality before the law. This is what the Romans did not have and what the British were rapidly moving towards. It is the most important single discovery of Western law, enshrined in the American Declaration of Independence. By the same token, discarding the presumption that people are sufficiently equal to be treated as such by the law, as is beginning to happen in the United States, is a grave error of policy. If not corrected it will give rise to great tensions and conflict and will be highly destructive.

Underlying everything said here is an assumption of approximate individual equality around the globe. Economic development in the world has of course been very unequal, but so have the relevant legal systems. All those countries that have advanced far ahead of others have enjoyed free, competitive markets, in which the appropriate incentives were established by law. Therefore the "theory" here is that, were all nations to enjoy the same legal and political infrastructure, they would also, eventually, enjoy comparable levels of economic development, irrespective of race. This theory might ultimately be falsified. Ethnic differences may be shown to have a noticeable, or even a considerable, effect. But the egalitarian theory should at least be given a hearing. It is suggestive that residents of legally oppressive countries do become much more productive when they move abroad. The Indians, classified by caste and relatively unproductive in India but not elsewhere, are a striking example. Clearly, they have been oppressed by their laws, not by their genes. The same applies to the Irish.

Intriguingly, a new field called law and economics, introduced in the 1970s, has become influential in legal circles. Its most tireless exponent, Richard A. Posner, almost single-handedly contrived to turn it into a movement. He had many interesting things to say, and by a roundabout method the new field did in the end help to restore property to economics departments. Still, there was something odd about the whole exercise. Even though Posner himself is a lawyer—he was appointed a federal appeals court judge in 1981 and he remains on that court today—law and economics was an imperialist exercise by economists, who were making claims about the impact of economics upon the law; more specifically, about the underlying rationale for the common law. Posner's startling claim was that economic efficiency was a surrogate for justice. The more fundamental claim, that economic life is itself dependent on the legal regime, was not entirely neglected, but it was given little emphasis.

Posner relished the idea that there was an objective and measurable thing called efficiency, and that it could be used to resolve the moral perplexities of the law. Old debates could be settled at last without recourse to the subjective claim that my "ought" is worthier than your "ought." This was all very intriguing, and controversial, and it stimulated a vast literature. Bruce Ackerman of Yale University Law School called law and economics "the most important thing that has happened in legal thought since the New Deal," even the most important development in legal education "since the birth of Harvard Law School."[23] The subject is addressed in chapter 20.

PROPERTY AND PROGRESS

Property's eclipse coincided with the reign of the idea of progress. There was an important connection between the two: throughout history, most people have realistically been resigned to living in what might be called the Present Imperfect. As a result of the Fall, it was widely accepted, human nature was flawed. For this reason property was regarded as a necessary, although perhaps not an ideal, institution. The *particular* division of goods was neither ordained of God nor a necessary reflection of natural justice. But *some* division had to be accepted, if peace and harmony were to be preserved. That was the view of Saint Thomas Aquinas among others. It would be nice if we were perfect beings who could get along without the rules, boundaries and sanctions of ownership. But until that time came, property would be indispensable.

Before Edward Gibbon published *The Decline and Fall of the Roman Empire,* a better condition of society was usually visualized as a restoration of a Golden Age. Philosophers and poets looked back wistfully to an Eden before the Fall. Goods were held in common, yet people somehow still lived in peace. There was harmony without property. Jean-Jacques Rousseau, so modern in so many ways, was one of the last to propose such an age of primal innocence. Earlier, Seneca had described a time when "it was impossible for any man to have more or less than another; all things were divided among them without discord . . . Not yet had the miser, by hiding his wealth away unused, deprived others of the very necessities of life."[24] He quoted Virgil's description of a time when

> No ploughman tilled the ground,
> No fence dividing field from field was found;
> When to the common store all gains were brought,
> And earth gave freely goods which none had sought.

At the time of the French Revolution, or shortly before it, something new arose. What might be called the Future Perfect began to replace nostalgia for the past. The imperfection of human nature was conceded, but now was thought to be only temporary. A greater human perfection was to be expected in the future. This lay at the heart of the idea of progress—a new idea in the world, and a dangerous one. At exactly the same time, a number of thinkers began to harbor serious doubts about property. We begin to see in print such phrases as "the existing institution" or the "present system" of property. Because something better could be imagined, the existing system suddenly seemed defective. Therefore it should be changed—perhaps even abolished. Still others believed that, whether we liked it or not, change was on its way. And of course it was.

Until that time, anyone who suggested that the existing system of property should be changed had to contend with this objection: alternative rules of ownership, although perhaps desirable, were not feasible because incentives would be undermined. Private property, apparently, was the only arrangement that encouraged people to work hard. Communal living had been tried, but did not seem to work. Communards would start out amicably enough, happy to share and share alike, but within a year or two would end in bitter arguments. Then they would divide up or "privatize" the commune and go their separate ways. (In chapter 9, we see that this happened to Robert Owen's commune in Indiana.)

Now there was a hopeful rejoinder: Progress. Man had been selfish in the past, to be sure, and still was (in the Present Imperfect). But the future would be different—the Future Perfect. Human nature could not be changed? Don't be too sure. One day, man's moral evolution would triumph over original sin. And at that point private property would no longer be necessary. The new vision, in which society was to be built anew on different foundations, bringing forth a New Man, was for intellectuals greatly energizing. A real hope for the future replaced a merely poetic wistfulness about the past. Optimism replaced nostalgia.

What was the origin of this belief that human nature could be reformed? Richard Pipes of Harvard has made the interesting suggestion that an important role was played by John Locke.[25] This is paradoxical, for he was also the great defender of property rights. Arguably, nonetheless, he both laid the groundwork for the modern defense of property and for the later attack on it. His *Essay Concerning Human Understanding* (1689)[26] pointed the way toward the belief that human nature could be remade. Contradicting the doctrine of "innate ideas," Locke argued that all our knowledge and understanding was derived from sensory experience. The initial state of the mind was simply "white paper, void of all characters, without any ideas," he thought.[27]

Locke here opened the door to a number of very modern ideas, among them a thoroughgoing materialism. (He was himself agnostic on that point, believing that "we shall never be able to know whether any mere material being thinks or no.") But there was something else: by controlling the inflooding sense data, he hinted, the content of our minds could be manipulated. "If it were worth while," he wrote, "no doubt a child might be so ordered as to have but a very few, even of the ordinary ideas, till he were grown up to a man."[28]

Locke's *Essay* was published in France in 1700, where it had its greatest influence. Its possibilities were soon recognized by the *philosophes* of the Enlightenment. Among them was Claude Helvetius, whose De *l'esprit* (translated as *Essays on the Mind*) was published in 1758. "Locke has opened the road to truth," wrote Helvetius, who immediately saw the implications. If what we think is a function of the impressions we receive, then by legislation we can control what people learn and know. And so people can be improved. Not by religion, he added. For "it is not on religion, nor on what is called morality, . . . but on legislation alone, that the vices, the virtues, the power and the felicity of a people depend."[29] By manipulating what we today would call the "learning environment," people could be molded this way or that. In fact, he proclaimed, education could do anything. ("L'education peut tout!") In indoctrination, and in reeducation camps, these ideas were carried to their logical conclusion in the twentieth century.

The founder of Russian Marxism, G. V. Plekhanov, included an admiring essay on Helvetius in his *Essays in the History of Materialism*. "In applying the principle of 'physical sensation' he showed himself to be the most consistent and logical of the eighteenth-century materialists," Plekhanov wrote.[30] As it happened, his essay was written in 1895, in Geneva. In that same year and city he met and befriended a like-minded revolutionary—Vladimir Ilyich Lenin.

Helvetius's belief that human nature could be reformed by legislation was "one of the most revolutionary ideas in the history of political thought," wrote Richard Pipes, who seems to have been the first to take note of Helvetius's role as intermediary between Locke and Lenin. "By extrapolation from an esoteric theory of knowledge, a new political theory is born with the most momentous practical implications."[31] The new task of politics, then, was to make men virtuous.

For over a thousand years, in the Western world, the institution of property had been upheld by the doctrine of the Fall of Man, which was thought to have embedded a flaw deep within human nature. The new belief that mere legislation could make all the difference to this natural imperfection would have seemed absurd and childish, not to say impious and heretical, to the old thinkers. But once these revolutionary new ideas began to spread, as they did after the French Revolution, property came under attack. If human nature could be changed so easily, after all, then the old argument—that it was futile to try to reform something that had been put there by God—began to look merely reactionary.

Private property had been criticized before, and it had been defended at least since the time of Aristotle. But the onslaught of the nineteenth-century socialists— Godwin, Owen, Marx and others—was unprecedented in its intensity. The result was that property came under attack before it had been properly analyzed or defended. Cicero and others had put in a few good words for it in their day. Locke himself had defended the division of goods originally intended for all: individual labor justified removing it "out of that common state Nature left it in."[32] David Hume had defended the existing distribution of property—an argument that naturally appealed to those who had inherited large estates.[33] Sir William Blackstone set forth a mass of property-related legal rules a generation later.[34] But when the Marxian attack came, there was no one ready to warn of the disastrous consequences that would flow from the abolition of private property.

The socialist claim that production would actually increase without private property in the means of production admittedly seemed outlandish, yet more and more people began to say just that. Because human nature had given rise to property, the strange idea took hold that the abolition of property would stimulate the reform of human nature. This fallacy helped legitimize the harsh changes soon implemented by the Bolsheviks. Now began their 70-year attempt to organize life without private property. Something close to a taboo against discussing the institution of property took hold and retained its power in this period. The hopeful experiment had been launched, with the Soviet Union as its laboratory.

Enthusiasts would go over to "the future" and bring back optimistic reports. "Putty is exactly like human nature," George Bernard Shaw wrote on his return in 1931. "You can twist it and pat it and model it into any shape you like; and when you have shaped it, it will set so hard that you would suppose that it could never take any other shape on earth."[35] He added that the Soviet government "has shaped the Russian putty very carefully . . . and it has set hard and produced quite a different sort of animal." At the end, in 1991, Boris Yeltsin spoke of the Soviet experience precisely as an experiment.[36] He wished only that it had first been tried on a smaller scale.

In the years ahead, the growth of world population will only increase the importance of private property. If population doubles in the next century, privatization will be inescapable for all. When population was small in relation to territory, as it once was in North America, it did not matter that land was used communally and therefore wastefully. There was enough left over to prevent what Garrett Hardin called the tragedy of the commons. The same was true in Africa until recently. But if population growth continues, and if living standards are to be sustained, let alone improved, the whole world will have to be privatized before too long.

Normally it is said that if population trends continue, starvation will result, resources will be depleted, and the environment ravaged. But private property solves all these problems. It is in the thinly populated countries, where property is communal by custom or controlled by the state—Somalia, Ethiopia and Sudan, for example—that we have seen the worst of famine and environmental destruction. Countries that do not enjoy secure and transferable private property will certainly remain backward, however. That is because human nature is everywhere the same.

The great error of Enlightenment thinkers and of more recent philosophers was to imagine that human transformation would be a straightforward business. But human nature proved to be more intractable, and property less dispensable, than was imagined. This has given rise to a good deal of disappointment. In its more radical manifestations, the environmental movement today is probably an expression of disenchantment with the intractability of human nature. If mankind will not improve, then nature must at least be spared the depredations of so disappointing a creature. In *Earth in the Balance,* Vice President Al Gore was still hoping for a "wrenching transformation of society."[37] But all that belongs to the past. No one talks seriously about "progress" any more, or believes that a "new man" can be conjured into existence by mere legislation.

TWO

PROPERTY, LAW
AND ECONOMY

THE IDEA OF PROPERTY is instinctively understood. Animals who mark territorial boundaries "define" property rights. Barking dogs "enforce" them. Despite this elemental quality, a concise definition of property has always eluded lawyers, and for once this is not meant as a criticism of lawyers. In its details, property admits of endless shading, compromise and complexity. As soon as a simple definition is proposed, exceptions and new distinctions will suggest themselves. Historically, however, property has been thought to describe a legal or customary relationship between a *person* and a *thing*. The thing may be physical or abstract. Particular people with property rights to the thing in question enjoy legally enforceable claims. Giles Jacob's *New Law Dictionary,* frequently consulted by eighteenth-century lawyers, defined property as "the highest right a man can have to anything"; in his *Commentaries on the Laws of England,* Sir William Blackstone (1723-1780), the first professor of English law at Oxford (or any university), defined property as "that despotic dominion that one man claims and exercises over the external things of the world, in total exclusion of the right of any other individual in the universe."[1]

In the twentieth century, it became conventional to describe property as a "bundle of rights." In an influential essay published in 1961, Prof. Tony Honore of Oxford University, an expert on Roman law, analyzed in detail the different sticks in the bundle. The most important are the rights to use the thing and to exclude others from doing so, to alter its physical configuration, to enjoy its fruits, including its income, and, not least, to transfer the title of ownership to another. Honore added that ownership means much the same thing in different legal systems. When we say of someone that he owns an umbrella, there is great similarity between what this means in England, France, Russia or any other modern country:

> Everywhere the "owner" can, in the simple, uncomplicated case, in which no other person has an interest in the thing, use it, stop others using it, lend it, sell it, or leave it by will. Nowhere may he use it to poke his neighbor in the ribs or to knock over his vase. Ownership, dominium, propriete, Eigentum, and similar words stand not merely for the greatest interest in things in particular systems but for a type of interest with common features transcending particular systems.[2]

In the U. S. Supreme Court's ruling in *Pruneyard Shopping Center v. Robins* (1980), Justice William Rehnquist noted that the right to exclude other people is "one of the essential sticks in the bundle of property rights."[3] In the last 30 years, this metaphor has become widespread, although it is not clear who invented it. It may well have been Roscoe Pound, dean of the Harvard Law School from 1916 to 1936, who used it in the last volume of his five-volume treatise on jurisprudence.

Since Roman times, property has been the most important subdivision of the field of law. Under the classification of *things,* it is the major category in the sixth-century synopsis of Roman law known as the *Institutes* of Justinian. The law of *persons* is the other important category, describing the legal status of different groups, chiefly citizens, slaves and freedmen. The same division still prevailed in the eighteenth century, which may be thought of as the heyday of property. By then, however, the law of persons was becoming vestigial; while the law of things had become relatively far more important.

With the American Law Institute's *Restatement of the Law of Property,* however, we come to an earnest attempt to revise the understanding of property. Organized in 1923, the American Law Institute marshaled "expert opinion" and an array of law school deans in an attempt to present "an orderly statement of the general common law of the United States."[4] It was primarily an academic exercise. The institute's work may be seen as a quiet attempt to influence the Anglo-American legal tradition, developed in courtroom practice, by introducing more academic and Continental elements, developed in the law schools.

In its (fruitless) attempt to develop a definition of property, the institute placed great reliance on the work of a young Yale law professor named Wesley Newcomb Hohfeld (1879-1918), who in the years after 1913 produced a treatise called *Fundamental Legal Conceptions as Applied in Judicial Reasoning.* One of his main points was that legal relationships can exist only between people. Because "things" can neither bring nor defend lawsuits, they cannot be recognized at law. And this in turn cast doubt on the old understanding of property as a relationship between a person and a thing. Being a good Hegelian, he believed that everything had its "opposite" or correlative, and so he argued that one person's right was another person's duty, one person's power was another's liability, and so on. His special terminology and his mirror maze of correlatives and opposites enlightened some but it also confused others, and without the support of the American Law Institute it probably would have faded away, along with other Hegelian schemes of classification.[5]

Roscoe Pound early on questioned Hohfeld's whole argument. Hohfeld replied that he would have to "rethink the whole subject and rewrite it."[6] But he died soon thereafter, without having done so. Since then his ideas have been kept alive primarily in the "Basic Terminology" chapter of the law school property treatise, *Powell on Real Property.*[7] (Richard R. B. Powell of Columbia University Law School for many years headed up revisions of the American Law Institute's property restatement, and is said to have been "the dean of American property lawyers.")[8]

It seems, however, that the institute's oft-quoted summary, that "legal relations in our law exist only between persons. There cannot be a legal relation between a person and a thing or between two things,"[9] has very little relevance to our understanding of what property is. To think otherwise is to confuse the particular case with the general definition. You do indeed need a plaintiff for a judge to decide who owns exactly what in a particular dispute; but you don't need a plaintiff to arrive at a general definition of property.

Hohfeld has since been feted in the footnotes, living on in academic circles as the enlightened precursor to modern skepticism about property. Professor Bruce Ackerman was on the mark when he wrote in his *Private Property and the Constitution* (1977): "I think it is fair to say that one of the main points of the first-year Property course is to disabuse entering law students of their primitive lay notions regarding ownership. They learn that only the ignorant think it meaningful to talk about owning things free and clear of further obligation. Instead of defining the relationship between a person and 'his' thing, property law discusses the relationships that arise between people with respect to things. More precisely, the law of property considers the way rights to use things may be parceled out amongst a host of competing resource users."[10]

A bundle of rights can, of course, be unbundled. That is to say, property rights can be divided up. One person can own a building and others can rent it. Some have construed this ability of property to become unbundled as the "disintegration" of property. Prof. Thomas Grey of Stanford University Law School, for example, wrote that supplanting the old "thing-ownership conception of property has the ultimate consequence that property ceases to be an important category in legal and political theory." In fact, he added, it tends to "dissolve the notion of ownership."[11] But this was incorrect, surely. Things continue to be owned, and property remains an important category in legal and political theory.

The easy separability of the sticks in the bundle turns out to be one of the most useful features of property. If it really were subject to an all-or-nothing rule, so that estates could not be divided, trusts could not be split off, and buildings and automobiles could not be rented, we would live in a much less convenient world. Leases, for example, allow tenants to enjoy some incidents of ownership without obliging them to incur the costs and responsibilities of full ownership. The divisibility of property rights makes social arrangements more flexible, allowing the various incidents, or "sticks," to be purchased and enjoyed by those who value them most highly. To appreciate the point, one only has to think of the convenience of time-sharing arrangements for vacation condominiums.

The divisibility of property rights has been understood for centuries. Nineteenth-century authors noted that a piece of land might be tilled by one person, used as a right of way by another, grazed by the cattle of a third, held as a security for debt by a fourth; yet possibly none of these would be thought of as the owner. Nonetheless, all these rights can revert to a single person. This capacity of rights to be separated and then reunited in a single individual is a crucial feature of property. As Sir William Markby pointed out a hundred years ago, ownership "is no more conceived as an aggregate of distinct rights than a bucket of water is conceived as an aggregate of separate drops."[12]

What is vitally important is that the owner must be allowed to retain control over the terms under which the "separation" of the sticks occurs. If state authorities can themselves seize some of the incidents of ownership, then property really is undone. Where draconian rent-control laws exist, for example, nominal owners may be left with little more than the responsibility to make repairs to "their" buildings. Under such conditions, rental markets will be ruined. In the western states of the United States, water use-rights have long been compulsorily separated from other incidents of water ownership. This has caused a tremendous waste of a valuable commodity, as shown in chapter 18.

When we look at the ancient categories of law, we can see that until the twentieth century the tendency of Western history has been to minimize the legal distinctions of persons and simultaneously to elaborate upon the divisions of property. In the millennium following the Fall of Rome, distinctions of status were slowly removed from the law. In fact, the transformation of law in the Western world since Roman times has tended toward the substitution of a single legal person for unequal legal classes; we may call this the democratizing tendency. This change more than any other also laid the groundwork for the emergence of the free-market, or "capitalist," economy in the West. The twentieth century, however, has seen an ominous reversal. There has been a far-reaching attempt to restore the legal distinctions of persons, complete with classes, privileges and disabilities. Increasingly, laws make allowances for such characteristics as race, gender and ethnicity. At the same time, there has been an attempt to undermine the law of things; to delegitimize property, to deconstruct it, to abolish it, or expropriate it, at the least to redistribute it.

Since about the mid 1980s, there has been a partial counterattack. Certainly there has been a restoration of interest in property. With the takings clause of the Fifth Amendment as his weapon, Prof. Richard Epstein of the University of Chicago Law School argued in *Takings* (1985) that most income-redistribution programs since the New Deal have been unconstitutional.[13] In 1987, Professor Honore revised his 1961 article describing the sticks in the bundle of property rights. By the later date, he had concluded that ownership is the "most important legal conception" in Western culture. In the earlier version, he said merely that it was "one of the characteristic institutions" of Western culture. In the intervening decades, property had come to seem increasingly important to him—as indeed it had for many others in that same period.[14]

A further milestone occurred in 1993, with the publication of a major article entitled "Property in Land" by Yale University law professor Robert C. Ellickson. Property can be understood to embody a set of "default rules," or a "Blackstonian package of entitlements," he proposed. A single individual owns in perpetuity a territory demarcated by horizontal boundaries, with absolute rights to use and abuse the land, to exclude would-be entrants and to transfer the whole or any part of it to anyone by sale, gift or bequest. In practice, he added, Anglo-American custom and law have usually generated a less absolute set of rights called the "fee simple," with provisions against the imposition of nuisance on neighbors.[15]

LAWYERS AND THE LAW OF PROPERTY

A society without property rights would hardly need lawyers. Not for nothing was the phrase "Soviet lawyer" understood to be an oxymoron. Justinian's *Digest* is overwhelmingly concerned with property issues. Nonetheless, the disfavor into which property fell in the twentieth century sometimes extended to the legal profession. One reason for this is that everyday practitioners of the law have little occasion to reflect upon something as abstract as the role of property in society. Lawyers have a particular and practical interest. To enforce a contract on behalf of a client, for example, they need to know exactly which law, which court, and which witnesses might help to achieve a satisfactory resolution. If a client has died without leaving a will, lawyers may be called upon to deal with problems raised by competing claimants or creditors. They can discharge this duty satisfactorily by becoming expert in the law's details and exceptions; they do not need to spend time thinking about how the law of property is rooted in a need to provide a secure basis for the acquisition, enjoyment and transfer of wealth.

The lawyer's interest may be contrasted with the economist's, which is quite different. Economists are not concerned with particular people or the particular channels through which wealth may flow. In disputes over wills or contracts, for example, economists do not mind which address the money is sent to. But they should know the answer to this more general question: Can contracts be enforced at all? If not, they are dealing with a society in which wealth cannot easily change hands. Since economics is mostly *about* the exchange of goods, it can be predicted that such a society will be economically primitive. In the case of the intestate client, it matters not to the economist whether sons, daughters or guardians inherit. But it does matter that wealth can be bequeathed predictably to chosen recipients. Estates cannot (from the economist's perspective) just be looted or swallowed up by the state, because both outcomes would adversely affect the willingness of people to create the wealth in the first place.

Another ancient division of the law helps us to understand the changed legal position of property in the twentieth century: the distinction between public and private law. Disputes can arise between private citizens (as in divorce, for example) or in public cases in which the state itself represents the interest of all citizens (criminal law is the most obvious example). Property law was long considered to belong to the realm of private law. In fact, it was thought to constitute the heart of private law. Property itself was contrasted with government. "I consider that it is a true and received division of law into *ius publicum* and *ius privatum*," said Francis Bacon, "the one being the sinews of property, and the other of government."[16]

But in the late nineteenth century, a momentous change took place. The law of property became less and less a private matter, and more and more a public one. The old impediments to the private transfer of property were much reduced by such innovations as property registers and improved surveying methods. Time, expense and huge fees to conveyancers and lawyers were thereby saved. Simultaneously, however, taxes and regulations were greatly increased, and the former security of property was partly undermined. As conveyancing became routinized, legal skill was increasingly redirected from the private to the public realm. Professor F. H. Lawson of Oxford University noted in his *Introduction to the Law of Property* (1958):

> A solicitor acting for his client in purchasing a house may take comparatively little trouble over the investigation of title—which belongs entirely to private law—knowing from past experience that the title is almost

certainly good; he will, however, be extremely careful to find out whether public law imposes awkward restrictions on use. Similarly, whereas the old convey-ancers were anxious to draw their settlements in such a way as to carry out a purely family policy and within the four corners of it to protect each person concerned against possible encroachments on the part of the rest, their successors are willing to quite a great extent to trust those persons to behave decently towards each other, if only they can protect all of them against the big bad wolf, the tax-levying state.[17]

ECONOMISTS AND THE LAW OF PROPERTY

Broadly speaking, there are three configurations of property rights: private, communal and state. Private property decentralizes ownership, conferring upon an individual or individuals the rights to use some good and to exclude others from doing so. It is understand that in a free society there will be thousands or millions of such owners. They can sell their property rights to others and retain the proceeds. With communal property, the rights to some good are shared in an undefined fashion, by a definite or an indefinite number of people. Air and oceans are communal, and so was most of the U.S. land mass before the arrival of Europeans. Within a family, many goods are usually treated as communal, as they are in communes, of course. With the third configuration, state property, the managers who control access to it are employed and salaried by the state and legally cannot profit from the disposal of such state assets. Normally, in fact, such assets are not for sale at all, although they may occasionally be sold to the private sector. If so, the proceeds are expected to go to the public treasury, not into the pockets of state employees.[18]

Modern societies usually include a mixture of the different forms of property rights. The "optimal mix," as Richard Epstein has pointed out, depends upon the nature of the good.[19] It is not necessary to adhere to either the Marxian or the libertarian dogma. As the Romans long ago recognized, some goods are naturally managed by the state—those that are needed to provide for the common defense, for example, or for administering justice and enforcing the law. Such goods are natural monopolies, and their private provision runs into the difficulty that nonpayers cannot easily be excluded from sharing in their benefits. So their private provision can be achieved only with difficulty, if at all. But most goods (as the Romans agreed) are best owned privately.

These three configurations of ownership establish quite different incen-tives. In fact, they can be thought of as "programming" individuals to behave in different ways. Since they encourage different types of behavior, the structures of ownership established by law and custom should be of great interest to economists. Economics can be defined as the study of the choices that people make with respect to goods of value. Until recently, however, economic theory has paid little attention to the structure of the laws and to the differing incentives engendered by different legal regimes.

The late Mancur Olson, the author of *The Logic of Collective Action,* examined the very uneven levels of economic growth in different parts of the world, and he argued that the diversity of legal regimes is central to this outcome. The neglect of that diversity by economists has a simple explanation, he said: parochialism. Starting with Adam Smith, all the leading economists came from just those countries where the essential legal preconditions for real economic advance did exist. So they took them for granted. This was a "tremendous oversight," Olson admitted. "Economics developed, loosely speaking, in a particular type of society, namely democratic societies with secure rights and independent judiciaries, so people haven't bothered to think about these things very much in economics."[20]

It seems, then, that if we are to understand economic behavior in a society, we must first know, at least in outline, the laws of the society. Economists have sometimes tended to think that the reverse was the case: that the economy itself would shape the law. Which view is correct? The truth is that the influence flows in both directions, but the former—the influence of law over economy—is by far the more important. A river's current can reshape its banks, but, more fundamentally, topography determines the course of a river. Nonetheless, the idea that economics affects the law, as the current shapes the banks, has historically been the more influential among economists. It was entertained, at least, by Adam Smith, and promoted by Karl Marx. Let us examine the idea more closely.

Changes in technology will bring about changes in relative prices, and increasingly valuable goods may need increased legal protection as a result. It is likely that the law will indeed be changed in response to such economic forces. We have seen just such a change in recent years in the realm of intellectual property (see chapter 19). More fundamentally, though, the banks guide the stream: the existing structure of law steers the behavior of economic actors. This is the direction of influence that needs a more detailed examination.

A baseball analogy may help. The game is highly constrained by its rules, and the play can be understood only in light of these rules. At the same time, the rules themselves sometimes may be changed in response to long-term trends in the play. The pitcher's mound was lowered a few years ago because it was believed that pitchers had become too dominant. Here was a case where the play changed the rules. But to understand what is happening on the field on a given day, one must first know the rules as they are now. If a foreign visitor who has never seen or heard of baseball goes to a ballpark, and he wants to understand what is going on, someone must first tell him the rules. That they evolved historically over the decades is true, but that is something he can study later if he wishes. The key point is that, on the field in front of him, the rules are the "infrastructure" upon which the play is based.

By the same token, in the real world of economic life, if we are to understand what is and is not happening in a particular country, we must first know the rules—the relevant laws of that society. As the businessman and writer Hernando de Soto concluded after a lengthy search for an explanation of economic backwardness in Peru and in the Third World more generally, the law has long been the "missing ingredient" in economic discourse.[21] It is what the frustrated economic development experts had failed to study.

Most decisions with respect to wealth are not directly coerced by laws. In the same way, the outcome of a game of baseball is not determined by its rules. But the play, both within the economy and the ballpark, is constrained by them. The law is a structure of restraint, setting the boundaries within which people may pursue their respective interests. They are steered toward one choice and away from another by their knowledge of what is legal and what is illegal, what is rewarded and what is penalized. Until we know some of the more important features of the legal structure of a society, all our attempts to predict how its people will behave economically are unlikely to be accurate.

To some economists, the need for laws securing property may have seemed too obvious to mention. It may be that laws against theft and robbery are so universal that it is superfluous to stress their necessity. But there are many intermediate conditions. We do not live in a world in which property is either fully respected or nonexistent. If laws against robbery are on the books but are only haphazardly enforced, as in some parts of American inner cities today, for example, this would be sufficient to discourage economic activity there. Supply-side enthusiasts were criticized some years back for suggesting that a capital-gains tax cut would be sufficient to create busy enterprise zones, when the more basic problem was that it wasn't safe to go into these areas at all.

In some Third World countries, even though there are laws against theft, government officials can expropriate goods without penalty, thereby enriching themselves. Under such circumstances, as in the former Zaire, economic growth probably cannot occur. Or consider the effect of tax rates that are confiscatory. They, too, will discourage economic behavior. In short, there are many gradations between "secure" and "insecure" property. As we have seen, property can be shaved and sliced and split apart. The various ways in which this may happen, with or especially without the owners' consent, are directly relevant to our expectations of economic performance.

One might expect, therefore, that much effort would have been devoted to specifying the legal rules that should be in place before the economic game can be efficiently played, and to studying the economically relevant laws that are in place in different countries. Diverse laws and levels of enforcement will differentially affect the ways people use their resources and talents. In recent years, the Fraser Institute of Vancouver, B.C., together with leading economists including Milton Friedman, Gary S. Becker and Douglass C. North, launched just such a project (see chapter 21). Earlier, however, little attention was paid to the infrastructure of law. The World Bank, the International Monetary Fund and the United Nations keep track of the performance of different economies, but until recently they have done so with little regard to the underlying diversity of legal rules. It is as though baseball were played in a hundred countries and an international organization kept detailed records of the statistics, while ignoring the point that the strike zone was large in some countries and small in others, that three strikes put you out in some lands while two or six strikes were used in others; that fielders used gloves in some countries, not in others, and so on.

An important reason for this neglect is that for a long time there was no consensus as to the relationship between the rules and the play. In fact, the influence of legal institutions on economic performance was contested by economists. If anything, there was a consensus that state ownership led to more rapid economic growth than private ownership. "Measured Soviet real GNP has grown more rapidly over the long run than have most of the major market economies," Paul Samuelson wrote in the thirteenth (1989) edition of his famous textbook, even as the Berlin Wall was coming down.[22] One winner of the Nobel Prize in economics said in the 1960s that the structure of property rights has no effect on people's behavior.[23] Ultimately, this opinion was in line with the dominant neoclassical theory, which for over a hundred years had avoided specifying the institutional rules that encourage economic productivity.

The best-known economist to have criticized this vacuum at the heart of economic theory is Douglass North of Washington University in St. Louis. With Robert W. Fogel, he won the Nobel Prize in economics in 1993—and here was another landmark in intellectual life. In his Stockholm lecture, North observed that if we want to know why some economies develop and others do not, neoclassical theory is an "inappropriate tool." Economists have given mathematical precision to their theories, he said, but they have completely ignored "the incentive structure embodied in institutions." Among the most important of these is a system of "efficient property rights." By that he meant private property.[24]

"The neoclassical model doesn't say anything about property rights," North earlier told an interviewer. "It doesn't say anything about socialism versus capitalism, nor does it make any reference to the institutions of capitalism or socialism."[25] In his Structure and Change in Economic History, he pointed out that neoclassical theory incorporated no institutions except for a disembodied market.[26] It was believed that as different economies strove to become more efficient, they would tend to converge under pressure from the law of diminishing returns. But North lost faith in this idea, and criticized it in 1990:

> The central puzzle of human history is to account for the widely divergent paths of historical change. How have societies diverged? What accounts for their widely disparate performance characteristics? After all, we all descended from primitive hunting and gathering bands. This divergence is even more perplexing in terms of standard neoclassical and international trade theory, which implies that over time economies, as they traded goods, services and productive factors, would gradually converge. [But we find instead that] the gap between rich and poor nations, between developed and undeveloped nations, is as wide today as it ever was, and perhaps a great deal wider than ever before. What explains this divergence? . . . The evolutionary hypothesis advanced by [Armen] Alchian in 1950 would suggest that ubiquitous competition would weed out inferior institutions and reward by survival those that better solve human problems.[27]

He was forced to abandon the idea that legal institutions themselves evolve in response to the dictates of efficiency. Persistently stagnant economies put too much strain on the theory. Eventually, he concluded that rulers simply "devised property rights in their own interests." We shall examine the concept of efficiency in economics in chapter 20. Considered in isolation from the law, it turns out to have no definite meaning. It is difficult to define it as anything other than the result of free-market exchange between private owners. The idea that different economies, starting out in a Hobbesian state with no laws, will under the pressure of efficiency evolve in a convergent direction must be abandoned. It is as unlikely as believing that if people in different parts of the world who had never heard of baseball were given bats and balls, and were asked to devise a game with nine people on each side, they would all end up playing baseball by American rules.

THE DYNAMO AND THE INTERNET

How did it come about that the crucial role of the law disappeared from view? There seems not to have been any decisive moment, but at some point in the late nineteenth century, economists suddenly felt confident that the old axioms of law were no longer relevant to their inquiries. Stanley Jevons, one of the founders of neoclassical theory, was by the 1880s opposed to "any theory of eternal fixed principles or abstract rights."[28] In place of laissez faire, a new presumption arose in favor of positive legislation intended to abolish undesirable conditions.

Poverty, for example, was thought to be a consequence of low wages, which in turn could be abolished by minimum-wage laws. The conservative A. V. Dicey noted in 1905 that "the rapidity with which collectivist legislation now makes way excites astonishment."[29] A great gulf had opened up between the old Benthamite liberalism and the new "democratic collectivism."

Economists, confined to the role of bystanders by the doctrine of laissez faire, were about to become policymakers. Their hands were at last on the levers of policy and power. Law was sometimes openly disparaged by Western academics. The principle that public authorities ought not to have wide discretionary powers was "a rule of action for Whigs and may be ignored by others," said Ivor Jennings, who taught constitutional law at the University of London in the 1930s. He asserted that "the law is that the law may at any moment be changed."[30]

The new economic statistics played an important role. Averaged and aggregated, individuals and their incentives disappeared from view. The Keynesian theory, proposed in 1936 and swiftly embraced by the profession, was devoid of all political institutions or postulates about property. It was a theory about economic activity that depended for its fulfillment upon . . . economic activity itself. It needed no external lever to move the world. Supply, the production of useful goods, was a function, simply, of demand. A multiplicity of exchanges was reimagined as a system of hydraulic circulation. The "income stream" drove "the economy," which was conceived of now as a great dynamo, using Depression-era technology as a model. Government spending conveniently added to the force of the income stream. Private savings, though, were drawn off into a "sump" and reduced the force turning the dynamo. In consequence, saving was discouraged by a tax policy that in part remains in place to this day.

Once people accepted the notion of an economy as a hydraulic organism, controllable from the center by economists adjusting the fiscal or monetary levers of policy, it became inappropriate to think of individual people and businesses as autonomous centers of decision. In a kind of misapplied Copernicanism, the national government became the center of the economic solar system. Economists were empowered to fine-tune its natural power, and property could be ignored. Independently acting human agents seemed to be in conflict with the very idea of a scientifically controllable economic machine. The fall of the Soviet Union, however, brought with it a sense that the Keynesian conception of the economy was, if not wrong, at least out-of-date; that a Depression-era theory was increasingly irrelevant in an Internet-driven world.

THE FREE-RIDER PROBLEM

INTRODUCTION

ANTHROPOLOGISTS TELL US that no society has existed without rules of property. But the rules themselves may vary considerably. As we have seen, there are three basic property configurations. In analyzing the merits of private property, we will consider its rivals in turn. In this part, communal property is analyzed. Communalism is an arrangement in which people share the rights to some good but their individual shares are not defined. Their identities may be specified, and they may decide to exclude outsiders. If a communal good is open to all without restriction, it is logically equivalent to an absence of property rights. On the other hand, if communal owners apportion consumption to work done, or "run a tab" on members, they are already on their way to converting communal to private property.

When the Pilgrims arrived in Massachusetts in 1620, they established a society with communal property—Plymouth Colony. But within three years they privatized their property. Between those two events, the Pilgrims fully experienced communalism's great problem: it sets up a system of rewards and punishments that puts the welfare of the community on a collision course with human nature. This problem of communalism is sometimes known as the free-rider problem. Among other defects, it gives rise to what Garrett

Hardin has called "the tragedy of the commons."[1] If, after experiencing the free-rider problem, communal property is privatized, the
change can be experienced by community members as the restoration of justice.

THREE

PLATO'S CONCEIT: PROPERTY AT JAMESTOWN AND PLYMOUTH

JAMESTOWN

"THE FOURE AND TWENTIETH DAY we set up a Crosse at the head of this River, naming it Kings River, where we proclaimed James King of England to have the most right to it." So wrote George Percy, of the English colonists' first days in Jamestown, Virginia. James I had recently signed a peace treaty with Spain, and soon thereafter a joint-stock company, called the Virginia Company, was formed in London. In May, 1607, three small ships sailed up the James River, in what is now Tidewater Virginia. Of the 104 people who had left London, all but 38 were dead within six months of arriving in Virginia, even though the country was fertile and in many ways hospitable. There were mussels and oysters, "turkie nests and many Egges," many fruits, "as Strawberries, Mulberries, Raspberries and Fruits unknown"; meadows "great and large," "great store of Deere both Red and Fallow." The soil was "good and fruitfull."[1]

With a modicum of industry, the colonists should have been able to survive satisfactorily. True, they were beset by Indians, "creeping upon all foure from the Hills like Beares, with their bowes in their mouthes." And there were fearful outbreaks of disease. "Our men were destroyed with cruell diseases," Percy wrote. But for the most part, "they died of meere famine." He added: "There were never Englishmen left in a forreigne Countrey in such miserie as we were in this new discovered Virginia."[2]

The Virginia Company's finances were reorganized, and ships, with 500 new recruits, sailed across the Atlantic in the summer of 1609. One, carrying the deputy governor, was shipwrecked on Bermuda, where life turned out to be so pleasant that many were reluctant to leave. Their instincts were correct. Most did rejoin the Jamestown remnant, but catastrophe followed: the "starving time."[3] Within six months, the population was reduced from about 500 to 60.[4] When spring came, the survivors decided to return to England. They had actually embarked when a stray ship carrying new colonists, including the governor, Lord De La Warr, or Delaware, sailed up the James River. Encouraged by these reinforcements, the survivors stayed on.

One eyewitness wrote of the starving time: "So great was our famine, that a Savage we slew and buried, the poorer sorte tooke him up againe and eat him; and so did divers one another boyled and stewed with roots and herbs." He continued: "It were too vile to say, and scarce to be beleeved, what we endured: but the occasion was our own, for want of providence, industrie and government, and not the barrennesse and defect of the Countrie, as is generally supposed."[5]

The first man in authority to see what was wrong was Sir Thomas Dale, who had served in military campaigns in the Netherlands. He arrived in Virginia as high marshal in May, 1611.[6] It is recorded that on his arrival, settlers were playing bowls in the streets—this just one year after the starving time. In extenuation, historians point out that Dale arrived on a Sunday. But Ralph Hamor, the secretary of the colony at that time, recorded that bowling was "daily and usual."[7]

The colonists were indolent because most of them were indentured servants, expected to toil for seven years and contribute the fruits of their labor to the common store before becoming freemen.[8] They had not paid for their passage, and it was by their labor that they were supposed to repay the company. According to Philip Bruce's *Economic History of Virginia in the Seventeenth Century,* "the settlers did not have even a modified interest in the soil, or a partial ownership in the returns of their labor. Everything produced by them went into the store, in which they had no proprietorship. . . . " As a result, the colonists were naturally disposed "to idle over their tasks, or to avoid the performance of these tasks altogether, and it was observed that those who were most honest and energetic by nature, were comparatively indolent and indifferent in attending to their duties in the field."[9]

All this was changed by Thomas Dale. He was praised in London for introducing into the colony a strict penal code, known as the "Lawes Divine, Morall and Martiall." More importantly, he also introduced private property. The following passage, written by Ralph Hamor, appeared in "The True Discourse of the Present Estate of Virginia," published in England in 1615: "Sir Thomas Dale hath taken a new course throughout the whole colonie . . . and this it is, he hath allotted to every man in the colonie, three English acres of cleere Corne ground, which every man is to mature and tend, being in the nature of farmers . . . and they are not called unto any service or labour belonging to the

Colonie, more than one month in the yeere, which shall neither be in Seed time, or in Harvest, for which, doing no other dutie to the Colonie, they are yeerely to pay into the store two barrels and a halfe of Corne. . . ."[10]

A workable incentive system was put in place. Private property was established and, as we might say today, a "flat tax" was levied ("community service" was one month in the year, and the tax was a predictable measure of corn). The year in which Dale made this change was not recorded, but it was almost certainly 1612 or 1613. He left Virginia permanently in 1616, on the ship that returned to England with the Indian princess Pocahontas and her husband John Rolfe, who had introduced the cultivation of tobacco into Virginia.[11] Rolfe himself said that, with private property, people could henceforth sit under their own trees "in safety, gathering and reaping the fruits of their labors with much joy and comfort."[12]

The new incentives brought swift changes. "With all his forcefulness," the Virginia historian Matthew Page Andrews wrote, "Dale could not have overcome the general inertia arising from the initial Crown-devised policy of joint possession. . . . As soon as the settlers were thrown upon their own resources, and each freeman had acquired the right of owning property, the colonists quickly developed what became the distinguishing characteristic of Americans—an aptitude for all kinds of craftsmanship coupled with an innate genius for experimentation and invention."[13]

Shortly after Rolfe, Pocohontas and Thomas Dale arrived in England, Lord Carew wrote to his fellow Virginia stockholder Sir Thomas Roe: "The worst of that plantation is past, for our men are well victualled by there owne industrie, but yett no proffitt is retourned."[14] Sir Edwin Sandys, the treasurer of the Virginia Company, knew that something had changed in the New World, but he attributed the new prosperity to the severity of Dale's penal code rather than the incentives of ownership. Building upon earlier foundations "with great and constant severity," Sandys wrote, "[Dale] has reclaimed almost miraculously those idle and disordered people, and reduced them to labour and an honest fashion of life."[15]

Here we see something that we shall encounter time and again: the failure to grasp the true role played by private property in economic life, and the attribution of its advantages to some other cause; in this instance, the use of severity.

Another disincentive to industry in early Jamestown was that the colony was conceived more as a base camp from which indigenous, preexisting wealth could be captured than as a permanent settlement within which new wealth could be created. In a "True and Sincere Declaration," winning "poore and miserable soules, wrapt under unto death in almost invincible ignorance" was the stated purpose of the colony.[16] But the thought of capturing the wealth of others had also crossed the colonists' minds. In this respect, however, Virginia turned out to be a disappointment.

"We chanced in a lande even as God made it," William Simmonds wrote in an account published in 1612, explaining why everything had (to date) gone wrong. "We found only an idle, improvident, scattered [indigenous] people, ignorant of the knowledge of gold, or silver, or any commodities, and carelesse of anything but from hand to mouth, but for baubles of no worth; nothing to encourage us but what accidentally we found nature afforded." By contrast, the Spanish in Mexico had a comparatively easy time of it. They had arrived in a place that providentially afforded "victuall at all times," and where the people had learned the use of gold and silver. Consequently, they were able to profit from "spoile and pillage," and not "the labours of their owne hands."[17]

Dale's decision to give each man in Jamestown a three-acre plot of land led to a swift increase in production. By 1616, John Rolfe wrote: "Whereas heretofore we were constrayned yearly to go to the Indians and intreate them to sell us corne, which made them esteeme verie basely of us—now the case is altered; they seeke to us—come to our townes, sell their skin from their shoulders, which is their best garments, to buy corne—yea, some of their pettie Kings have this last yeare borrowed four or five hundred bushells of wheate, for payment whereof, this harvest they have mortgaged their whole countries, some of them not much less in quantitie than a shire in England."[18]

The colonists had accidentally discovered something that even today is poorly understood: Private property is the most peaceable of institutions, encouraging its owners to cultivate their own gardens and do so productively, rather than to organize into armies and raid the storehouses of neighbors. Adjacent tribes will almost certainly be in a state of conflict if neither has instituted private property, and so will neighboring countries whose economies are centrally owned (as in feudal times) or centrally planned (as in the twentieth century). By 1616 the English colonists were beginning to enjoy the fruits of property. Their native American neighbors, lacking the institution, were mortgaging "their whole countries" to obtain these fruits.

PLYMOUTH

Jamestown had been underwritten by the English aristocracy. They put up most of the money, and they also lost a good deal of their investment. By contrast, the expedition to Massachusetts was more of a freelance venture. Noblemen were not among the "adventurers" as the investors were called. Moreover, it is likely that the Plymouth investors in the end more than made their money back. James I knew about the proposal to found the Massachusetts colony, and the investors did obtain a "patent," or charter, to form their "particular plantation." But from the first, there was no thought of capturing gold or profiting from the labor of native Americans. When the patent was granted, in 1620, the king asked how the colonists proposed to make a living. "By fishing," said the petitioner, Robert Naunton. "So God have my soul," King James is reported to have replied. "'Tis an honest trade. 'Twas the Apostles own calling!"[19]

Desiring to practice their religion as they wished, the Pilgrims had emigrated in 1609 from England to Holland, then the only country in Europe that permitted freedom of worship. They found life in Holland to be in many respects satisfactory. But war with Spain was a constant threat, and the Pilgrims did not want their children to grow up as Dutchmen. They longed to start afresh in "those vast and unpeopled countries of America, which are fruitful and fit for habitation, being devoid of all civil inhabitants," as William Bradford would later write in his history, *Of Plymouth Plantation*. There, they could look forward to "laying some good foundation, or at least to make some way thereunto," for propagating and advancing "the gospel of the kingdom of Christ."[20]

Born in Yorkshire in 1590 and 30 years old when he arrived in the New World, Bradford became the second governor of Plymouth (the first died within weeks of the *Mayflower*'s arrival) and was the most important figure in the early years of the colony. He recorded in his history the key passage on the property relations in Plymouth, and the way in which they were changed.[21] His is the only surviving account of these matters.

The Pilgrims knew about the early disasters at Jamestown, but the more adventurous among them were willing to hazard the Atlantic anyway. First, however, they sent two emissaries from Leyden to London, John Carver and Robert Cushman, who sought permission from Sir Edwin Sandys to found the plantation.[22] This was granted, but finding investors was a problem. Eventually Carver and Cushman wrote back to Holland, reporting success. The chief investor (of a syndicate) turned out to be a London ironmonger named Thomas Weston, who ever afterward has received a bad press from historians. He is thought to have been unscrupulous and usurious, and it is true that he harassed the colonists as soon as they arrived in the New World, scolding them for not showing a profit immediately. He would also ship over fresh recruits without warning.[23]

In Weston's defense, however, we should remember that he and his 50-odd investors were taking a big risk in putting up the equivalent of hundreds of thousands of dollars in today's money. The big losses in Jamestown had scared off most "venture capital" in London. The exact amount invested in the *Mayflower* expedition has never been established, but Weston and his investors were paid off with a lump sum of £1,800 in 1648 (approximately $300,000 in today's money). The historian Samuel Eliot Morison estimates that "the cost of the *Mayflower*'s voyage, including ship hire, victuals and outfit, can hardly have exceeded 1,500 pounds."[24]

Those waiting for news in Leyden were concerned that their agents in London would, in their eagerness to find investors, agree to unfavorable terms. Carver and Cushman were admonished "not to exceed the bounds of your commission." They were particularly enjoined not to "entangle yourselves and us in any such unreasonable [conditions as that] the merchants should have the half of men's houses and lands at the dividend, and that persons should be deprived of the two days in a week agreed upon, yea every moment of time for their own Particular."[25]

Eventually, however, Carver and Cushman did accept terms stipulating that at the end of seven years everything would be divided equally between investors and colonists. In Morison's summary: "A family of husband, wife and three children who had worked seven years would get exactly the same dividend as a capitalist who had invested about $250." Some historians do claim that those who came over on the *Mayflower* were exploited by capitalists. In a sense, they were. But of course they came voluntarily, a point made by Cushman in one of his letters back to Holland. "[D]o they put us upon it, do they urge or egg us? Hath not the motion and resolution been always in ourselves?"[26]

The colonists had hoped that the houses they would build would be exempt from the division of wealth at the end of seven years; in addition, they sought two days a week in which to work on their own "particular" plots (much as collective farmers later had their own private plots in the Soviet Union). The Pilgrims would thereby avoid servitude. But the investors refused to allow these loopholes. The relevant documents disclosing the reasoning of Weston & Co. have not survived, but almost certainly they worried that if the Pilgrims—3,000 miles away and beyond the reach of supervision—owned their own houses and plots, the investors would find it difficult to collect their due. How could they be sure that the faraway colonists would spend their days working for the company if they were allowed to become private owners? With such an arrangement, rational colonists would work little on "company time," but would reserve their best efforts for their own gardens and houses. Such private wealth would be exempt when the shareholders were paid off. Only by insisting that all accumulated wealth was to be "common wealth," or placed in a common pool, could the investors feel reassured that the colonists would be working to benefit everyone, including themselves.

Those waiting in Leyden objected to this arrangement on the grounds that it was "contrary to the advice of politics," or political theory—a reference either to Aristotle's *Politics* or to Jean Bodin's *Six Books of a Commonweale,* translated from French into English in 1606 and brought to America on the *Mayflower.* If the Pilgrims were not permitted private dwellings, "the building of good and fair houses" would be discouraged, they wrote back to London. Robert Cushman was thus caught in a crossfire between profit-seeking investors in London and his worried Leyden brethren, who accused him of "making conditions fitter for thieves and bondslaves than honest men."[27]

Cushman responded with an artful case for common ownership: "[O]ur purpose is to build for the present such houses as, if need be, we may with little grief set afire and run away by the light. Our riches shall not be in pomp but in strength; if God send us riches we will employ them to provide more men, ships, munition, etc. You may see it amongst the best politics that a commonweal is readier to ebb than to flow, when once fine houses and gay clothes come up. . . . Brethren, look to it, that make profit your main end; repent of this, else go not lest you be like a Jonas to Tarshish."[28]

Common ownership would also "foster communion" among the Pilgrims, he thought (wrongly). Having held discussions with the investors, Cushman wanted to close the deal. And the investors seem to have been unyielding. So Cushman tried to persuade his brethren not to worry about the property arrangements. Those still in Leyden remained unconvinced and unreconciled to the terms, but there was little they could do. Many had already sold their property in Holland and so had no bargaining power. Bradford makes it quite clear that the terms were unsatisfactory. Their agents in London had "presumed to conclude with the merchants on those terms, in some things contrary to their order and commission and without giving them notice of the same; yea, it was concealed lest it should make any further delay. Which was the cause afterward of much trouble and contention."[29]

It is worth emphasizing all this because it is sometimes said that the Pilgrims in Massachusetts established a colony with common property in emulation of the early Christians. Not so. It is true that their agent Cushman used arguments that were calculated to appeal to Christians—in particular warning them against the perils of prosperity—in order to justify his acceptance of unpopular terms. No doubt he felt that a bad deal was better than none. But the investors themselves unquestionably had profit in mind when they insisted upon common property. The Pilgrims went along because they had little choice.

The Pilgrims may have been "exploited," but a greater source of hardship was the harsh environment of the North American continent. This needs to be stressed, given the tendency to regard the wealth of the United States as a product of "abundant natural resources," and the equally erroneous association of the *Mayflower* and those who arrived in it with the idea of privilege.

The *Mayflower* arrived at Cape Cod in November, 1620, with 101 people on board. About half of them died within the first few months, probably of scurvy, pneumonia and malnutrition. One who died was William Bradford's young wife, Dorothy May, who either jumped or fell overboard and drowned in Provincetown Harbor before the *Mayflower* even arrived at Plymouth. Along with other historians, Morison speculates that she took her own life, "after gazing for six weeks at the barren sand dunes of Cape Cod."[30] It is not easy for us to grasp the hardships that the first settlers to this country experienced, even in New England, where the native American Indians were relatively friendly. "When the *Mayflower* dropped anchor in Provincetown Harbor on November 11, the prospects for successful settlement seemed grim," George D. Langdon wrote in *Pilgrim Colony*.

> From the ship the Pilgrims looked upon a wilderness that reached to the edge of the sea. Uncertain as to who or what prowled through the gloom, they knew that the nearest English settlement was hundreds of miles to the south, that no one could help them in the forthcoming struggle to survive. They had no homes to live in, no fort to defend them, no docking facilities to receive them. Moreover, although only one passenger had died on the voyage, confinement for eleven weeks in crowded living conditions, the meager shipboard diet, and an inability to stay dry had already undermined their health. Many of them were now coughing, and in the five weeks the *Mayflower* lay at Provincetown, four perished, including William Bradford's wife.[31]

In the spring of 1621, the *Mayflower* returned to England with its hired crew—but no cargo for the investors. A second vessel, the *Fortune,* arrived at Plymouth in November, 1621, bringing 35 new colonists. It returned immediately with a cargo of beaver skins, but was intercepted by French pirates. The vessel returned to London with empty holds in February, 1622. The *Charity* and the *Swan* reached Plymouth Colony that summer, bringing 60 newcomers with them. By the spring of 1623, the population of Plymouth can have been no larger than 150. But still the colony was barely able to feed itself. On one occasion newcomers found that there was no bread at all, only fish, or a piece of lobster, and water. "So they began to think how they might raise as much corn as they could, and obtain a better crop than they had done, that they might not still thus languish in misery," Bradford wrote in his key passage on property. He continues as follows (and this is the complete text, as edited by Samuel Eliot Morison, with modernized spelling):

> At length, after much debate of things, the Governor (with the advice of the chiefest amongst them) gave way that they should set corn every man for his own particular, and in that regard trust to themselves; in all other things to go on in the general way as before. And so assigned to every family a parcel of land, according to the proportion of their number, for that end, only for present use (but made no division for inheritance) and ranged all boys and youth under some family. This had very good success, for it made all hands very industrious, so as much more corn was planted than otherwise would have been by any means

the Governor or any other could use, and saved him a great deal of trouble, and gave far better content. The women now went willingly into the field, and took their little ones with them to set corn; which before would allege weakness and inability; whom to have compelled would have been thought great tyranny and oppression.

The experience that was had in this common course and condition, tried sundry years and that amongst godly and sober men, may well evince the vanity of that conceit of Plato's and other ancients applauded by some of later times; that the taking away of property and bringing in community into a common-wealth would make them happy and flourishing; as if they were wiser than God. For this community (so far as it was) was found to breed much confusion and discontent and retard much employment that would have been to their benefit and comfort. For the young men, that were most fit and able for labour and service, did repine that they should spend their time and strength to work for other men's wives and children without any recompense. The strong, or man of parts, had no more in division of victuals and clothes than he that was weak and not able to do a quarter the other could; this was thought injustice. The aged and graver men to be ranked and equalized in labours and victuals, clothes, etc., with the meaner and younger sort, thought it some indignity and disrespect unto them. And for men's wives to be commanded to do service for other men, as dressing their meat, washing their clothes, etc., they deemed it a kind of slavery, neither could many husbands well brook it. Upon the point all being to have alike, and all to do alike, they thought themselves in the like condition, and one as good as another; and so, if it did not cut off those relations that God hath set among men, yet it did at least much diminish and take off the mutual respects that should be preserved amongst them. And would have been worse if they had been men of another condition. Let none object this is men's corruption, and nothing to the course [ownership arrangement] itself. I answer, seeing all men have this corruption in them, God in His wisdom saw another course fitter for them.[32]

In the "common course," then, Governor Bradford reports that the community was afflicted by an unwillingness to work, by confusion and discontent, by a loss of mutual respect and by a prevailing sense of slavery and injustice. And this among "godly and sober men." Therefore the land they worked was converted into private property, which brought "very good success." The colonists immediately became responsible for their own actions (and that of their immediate families), not for the actions of the whole community. Bradford's comments about washing clothes and dressing meat suggest that more than land was privatized. Knowing that the fruits of his labor would benefit his own family and dependents, the head of each household was given an incentive to work harder. He could know that his additional efforts would help specific people who depended on him. Under the arrangement of communal property he might reasonably suspect that any additional effort might merely substitute for the lack of industry of others. And these "others" might well be able bodied, too, but content to take advantage of the communal ownership by contributing less than their fair share.

Langdon argues that the condition of early Plymouth was not "communism," but "an extreme form of exploitative capitalism in which all the fruits of men's labor were shipped across the seas."[33] In this he echoes Morison, who claims that "it was not communism that was abolished, but a very degrading and onerous slavery to the English capitalists that was somewhat softened."[34] Notice that this does not agree with the dissension that Bradford reports, however. It was between the colonists themselves that the conflicts arose, not between the colonists and the investors in London. Morison and Langdon conflate two separate problems. On the one hand, it is true that the colonist did feel "exploited" by the investors, because they were eventually expected to surrender to them an undue portion of the wealth they were trying to create. It is as though they felt that they were being "taxed" too highly by their investors—at a 50 percent rate, in fact.

But there was another problem, separate from the "tax" burden. Bradford's comments make it clear that common ownership demoralized the community far more than the "tax." It was not Pilgrims laboring for investors that caused so much distress, but Pilgrims laboring for other Pilgrims. Common property gave rise to internecine conflicts that were much more serious than the transatlantic ones. The industrious (in Plymouth) were forced to subsidize the slackers (in Plymouth). The strong "had no more in division of victuals and clothes" than the weak. The older men felt it disrespectful to be "equalized in labours" with the younger men.

This does suggest that a form of communism really was practiced at Plymouth in 1621 and 1622. No doubt this equalization of tasks was thought (at first) the only fair way to solve the problem of who should do what work in a community where there was to be no individual property: if everyone was to end up with an equal share of the property at the end of seven years, everyone should presumably do the same work throughout those seven years. The problem that inevitably arose was the formidable one of policing this division of labor. How to deal with those who did not pull their weight?

The Pilgrims had encountered what is called the free-rider problem. As we shall see, it is difficult to solve without dividing property into individual or family-sized units. And this was the course of action that William Bradford wisely took. It "had very good success" because it ensured that workers would reap the fruits of their industry, whether they worked much or little. This in turn made the system self-policing. All colonists were made responsible for their own behavior; family heads also assumed responsibility for the welfare of their own family members. In short, the division of property established a proportion or "ratio" between act and consequence. Human action is deprived of rationality without it, and work will decline sharply as a result.

William Bradford died in 1657, having been reelected governor nearly every year. Among his books, according to the inventory of his estate, was Jean Bodin's *Six Books of A Commonweale,* a work that criticized the utopianism of Plato's *Republic.*[35] In Plato's ideal realm, private property would be abolished or curtailed, and most inhabitants reduced to slavery, supervised by high-minded, ascetic guardians. Bodin said that Plato "understood not that by making all things thus common, a Commonweal must needs perish; for nothing can be public where nothing is private." Such a society, Bodin wrote, would also be "against the law of God and nature," which forbids us to desire "anything that another man's is."[36] (Bodin also said in his enormous tome that communal property was "the mother of contention and discord," and that a commonwealth based on it would produce "many absurdities."[37])

Bradford felt that, in retrospect, his real-life experience of building a new society at Plymouth had both confirmed Bodin's judgment and had exposed "that conceit of Plato's." Property in Plymouth was further privatized in the years ahead. The housing, and later the cattle, were assigned to separate families, and provision was made for the inheritance of wealth. The colony flourished, Plymouth Colony was absorbed into the Commonwealth of Massachusetts, and in the prosperous years that lay ahead, nothing more was heard of "the common course and condition."

FOUR

THE LOGIC OF THE COMMONS

WHEN PROPERTY IS COMMUNALLY OWNED, there is no "mine" or "thine" by intention. Everything is "ours." This is likely to create dissension, as it did at Plymouth Colony. The lack of ratio between effort and reward "was thought injustice." Such an outcome may be expected when members have rights to equal shares in the product of a community. Those who contribute little will enjoy a free ride at the expense of those who work hard. We recognize the free-rider problem, even if we don't know its name. A group dividing the check equally at a restaurant will encounter it. Those ordering expensive items will come out ahead. Separate checks are the solution—the equivalent of privatization.

The problem notoriously arises in a shared apartment. In the Soviet Union, where several families were often pushed into a single flat, it was greatly magnified. "The word 'neighbors' has a sinister connotation in the context of the communal apartment," Andrei Sinyavsky wrote in *Soviet Civilization* (1988). "Good relations are rare. More often one's neighbors are hostile, dangerous, alien, in one's way. Any molehill becomes a mountain, any trifle a catastrophe. The suspicion and hatred breed gossip, slander, scandals, fights and denunciations. The Communist brotherhood is transformed into the most terrible civil strife." Sinyavsky quoted from Zoshchenko's "Summer Respite" (1929), a Soviet-era story based on a communal dispute over who owed what on the electric bill. Nine families shared one meter:

> At the end of the month, one has to calculate the consumption. Which of course
> leads to serious misunderstandings, if not to blows. So fine, you say: go by the

light bulbs. But one conscientious tenant turns on his light for five minutes, the time it takes to undress or kill a flea. Another tenant chews and chews on something till midnight with the light on. Refuses to turn it off. . . . There was one tenant, a loader, who literally went off his head because of this. He stopped sleeping and spent all his time ascertaining who was reading algebra at night and who was fixing himself something hot to eat. . . . He literally did not sleep nights and ran inspections every minute. Ducking in here, ducking in there.[1]

The larger the group, the more insoluble the problem. If there are one hundred members in a commune, one who stops working is still entitled to 99 percent of what he received before. Unless this is addressed by the strict supervision of labor, the ownership arrangement will impoverish the community in short order, and historically has done so. We may think that the real problem is precisely that each member is guaranteed an equal share of the total output; but notice that if this sharing agreement is removed, and the members simply reassure one another that they may take from the common store "sufficient for their needs," there will be a further breakdown. Until that moment, commune members have an incentive to show up for work late. After it, they have good reason to appear at the common store early.

The communal setting, in which well-defined property rights are missing, introduces perverse incentives and encourages greed, selfishness, idleness, suspicion and a brooding sense of injustice, even among members who joined with good moral training (as William Bradford claimed was the case at Plymouth). For centuries, idealists have dreamed that individuals living communally could be inspired to work hard, even while understanding that others might take advantage of them. But a spirit of self-sacrifice is essential for such a regime, and most communards don't realize that is what will be required of them. It is particularly difficult for families to submit to such a regime, because a family is itself a mini-commune and raising children already involves self-sacrifice. As Plymouth showed, people draw the line at making additional sacrifices for other people's children.

Admittedly, communal property has not been the undoing of the traditional family, even though nonproductive children enjoy a free ride at the expense of their parents. But the circumstances are special. Family ties are strong enough to defuse the sense of injustice that is so corrosive when free riding occurs in more distantly related groups. Small children are in any event helpless, and parents don't mind being "exploited" by them. Even so, parental policing becomes indispensable as children grow up. Furthermore, families are small enough to make such policing possible. In a family of four with two children, there is one cop per potential robber.

The problems of communal ownership are sufficient to explain why tribal life anywhere in the world will always be economically marginal. A tribe may be thought of as a group of people connected by family-like relations, but large enough to make it impracticable for the head of the tribe to police those outside his immediate circle. For this reason, free riding will be endemic. In 1833, a writer named John Wade summarized the effects of communal ownership on tribal life. In his *History of the Middle and Working Classes,* a long-neglected minor classic, he wrote:

> The tribal member is neither free nor secure; he is the slave of every member of his tribe stronger than himself, and may be sacrificed to his lust, his anger or revenge. Sustenance, under which is included food, clothing and lodging, is not less precarious than freedom and security. The rights of property not being recognized, no one can possess any thing which he can call his own; if he cultivate a plot of ground, he cannot be sure he will be allowed to reap the produce; if by superior toil and ability in hunting and fishing, he lay up a stock of provisions, he cannot be certain he will not be compelled to share them with a stranger; where things are in common, spoliation is not robbery, it is only partnership: hence there can be no industry, no provision for the future; the gratification of immediate wants is the sole object of exertion, and any thing beyond this is an unprofitable, because it is an unsafe, accumulation.[2]

The logic of the commons was set down on paper, apparently for the first time, shortly before Wade's book appeared. William Forster Lloyd made the case in his *Two Lectures on the Checks to Population,* given at Oxford University in 1832. When people agree to labor jointly, he said, and the result of their labor becomes common property, only a fraction of any increase of that exertion will benefit those who work harder. With many partners, "the motive for economy" vanishes entirely. "The future is struck out of the reckoning," he added, when the constitution of society is such as to "diffuse the effects of individual acts throughout the community at large, instead of appropriating them to the individuals by whom they are respectively committed."[3]

A remarkable amnesia ensued, corresponding to the period of property's intellectual eclipse. Lloyd's central idea was forgotten everywhere. Then, in the 1960s, two influential articles appeared, independently and within little over a year of one another, on the same subject. First, "Toward A Theory of Property Rights," by Harold Demsetz, an economist then at the University of Chicago, was published in the *American Economic Review* in 1967. Then Garrett Hardin, a professor of human ecology at the University of California, published "The Tragedy of the Commons" in *Science* in 1968. It was reprinted over 50 times within the next decade.[4]

Demsetz examined anthropological findings on the development of private property among the Montagne Indians in Quebec. Private property was highly unusual among such tribes. A traveler's account from the 1630s gave no indication of private property among the Montagne; nor did an account by a Jesuit who lived with the same tribe in 1647. The Montagne hunted only for food, and for the few furs needed by their own families. But by the eighteenth century, evidence of territorial hunting and trapping arrangements by individual families began to be seen. Separate areas were appropriated for small groups to hunt exclusively. Ownership of beaver houses was established by blazoning them with individual marks. Families practiced conservation and retaliated against trespassers.

Why did the Montagne develop private property in beavers? The arrival of Europeans had increased the value of beaver furs, which now could be traded for novel goods. Beaver hunting increased. Communal ownership of beavers then posed a problem: because individuals could not control hunting by others, it was in no one's interest to preserve the stock of animals. Individuals had an incentive to capture as many as they could, because the benefits from the pelts were privatized. But the cost, in the dwindling number of beavers, was borne by the entire tribe. This was a formula for the eventual extermination of beavers.

Establishing private property had costs. Collective curtailment of hunting was difficult to achieve, because holdouts would continue as before; in fact, they would benefit from the restraint of others. Even if an agreement were reached, policing it would be costly. Tribesmen would have to spend their time monitoring the activities of everyone else. Fences would have been impossibly expensive. Thus the "theory" mentioned in Demsetz's title was simply that privatization will not occur unless the benefits exceed the costs. With the arrival of fur traders, that is exactly what happened. The increased value of the pelts gave tribesmen the incentive to establish private hunting grounds.

The problem with this theory—and it bedevils law and economics generally—is that it is difficult or impossible to quantify the costs and benefits. So the theory is not really testable. If our assessment that the benefits exceed the costs is arrived at merely by observing that the hunting grounds are privatized, and there is no other way of telling, then the theory is circular. Nonetheless, Demsetz's analysis was important in that it drew economists' attention to the important effects that different ownership arrangements have on incentives, and on the costs involved in changing that arrangement.

"The Tragedy of the Commons" looked at the same problem from a different angle. Garrett Hardin was primarily concerned with the stimulus that communal property supposedly gives to population, and the effect of that on the environment. In an unbounded terrain, large families will be the rule because individuals foraging on communal land can privatize the benefits and "externalize" the costs of their activities. Given a small enough population, admittedly, the common ownership of property is workable. It did not much matter how American frontiersmen disposed of their waste. "Flowing water purifies itself every ten miles,"[5] Hardin's grandfather would say; and this was true enough for the small population of his day. But as population increases, the natural processes of recycling become overloaded, "calling for a redefinition of property rights." If this does not ensue, the "tragedy of the commons" inevitably follows:

> Picture a pasture open to all. It is to be expected that each herdsman will try to keep as many cattle as possible on the commons. Such an arrangement may work reasonably satisfactorily for centuries, because tribal wars, poaching and disease keep the numbers of both man and beast well below the carrying capacity of the land. Finally, however, comes the day when the long-desired goal of social stability becomes a reality. At this point, the inherent logic of the commons remorselessly generates tragedy. As a rational being, each herdsman seeks to maximize his gain. Explicitly or implicitly, more or less consciously, he asks, "What is the utility *to me* of adding one more animal to my herd?"[6]

Since the herdsman gains the full benefit of adding one more animal (because he keeps the milk and meat for his own family), but imposes the cost of grazing on all other herdsmen (whose pasture becomes more denuded with each new animal), the herdsman decides to add another animal to his herd. And then another. "But this is the conclusion reached by each and every rational herdsman sharing a commons." Therein lies the tragedy. All are locked into a system that rewards the very actions that eventually will destroy the resources upon which all depend.

Hardin added that this had been vaguely understood for a long time, "perhaps since the discovery of agriculture or the invention of private property in real estate."[7] The tragedy could be averted "by private property or something formally like it," he conceded. But he was not interested in such solutions. His later writings made it clear that he would rather curtail population forcibly than solve the problem by instituting private property. In his essay "Property Rights: The Creative Reworking of a Fiction," he argued that property as a "concept" had changed over the years, and it should be redefined once more, "giving some sort of standing in court to the lilies, the trees, and all the other glories of nature."[8] In due course, the Endangered Species Act did in effect give legal standing to some 950 species. But its unintended consequence, as we shall see in chapter 19, was to further jeopardize some of these species.

More recently, Hardin's conflation of an open access "free-for-all" and a limited-access, regulated commons has been criticized. The former does lead unavoidably to tragedy (it is conceded), while the latter can be managed. A number of writers, notably Elinor Ostrom in *Governing the Commons* (1990), Glenn Stevenson in *Common Property Economics* (1991), and Matt Ridley in *The Origins of Virtue* (1996), have made the argument.[9] It is true that communal lands can be regulated, and the permissible number of sharers or users can be specified. The number of sheep on a moor can be agreed to by all shepherds ("stinting"); the right to cut trees in communal woods can be allocated among the owners, to avert overexploitation. But these self-imposed regulations make communal property workable by going a long way toward privatizing it. When the right can be sold to someone outside the original collective—for example, the right to graze sheep on a moor—it has been individualized and one of the most important features of private property has been co-opted. A case could be made for taking the final step and formally privatizing the property with title deeds.

It was originally believed that, with many partners instead of a single owner, common property would circumvent the need for overseers. They were thought to be more an expression of ruling-class exploitation than of real economic necessity, borne of human weakness. When everyone was a partner, it was thought, all would pull together for the enterprise and throw the profits into a common pot. When workers became communal owners, however, they often stopped working. To solve the problem of idle co-owners, managers were found to be more necessary than ever. A commune, it turned out, resembled nothing so much as an army in which all the privates had been elevated to the rank of general.

"A key advantage of individual land ownership is that detecting the presence of a trespasser is much less demanding than evaluating the conduct of a person who is privileged to be where he is," Robert Ellickson of Yale has commented. "Monitoring boundary crossings is easier than monitoring the behavior of persons situated inside boundaries. For this reason, managers are paid more than night watchmen."[10] In fact, managers are among the highest-paid members of society, security guards among the lowest. Even dogs can distinguish strangers, and like fences, they do not have to be paid at all.

IDEOLOGICAL AND TECHNICAL ORIGINS

The free-rider problem arises when property rights are not well defined. That is the essence of the problem. But two very different sets of circumstances can give rise to it. In communes, the question "Who has a right to what?" is left deliberately vague as a matter of ideological preference. In sharp contrast are cases in which confining benefits to those who pay for them is technically difficult to achieve. The former situation awaits a renovation of philosophy, or of human nature; the latter, an improvement of technology. Or it may be insoluble, in which case government action may be called for.

Philosophically based communes are difficult to preserve, but the historical experience has been that they can work under special conditions. Membership must be small enough that members know one another personally. They must also be imbued with religious zeal or enthusiasm, imparting the necessary spirit of self-sacrifice. Celibacy is probably also required, implying that members do not have children and are not already divided up into separate families. Under these stringent conditions, the free-rider problem can be overcome. The commune established in the early nineteenth century by George Rapp, and purchased by the early socialist Robert Owen, was a striking example, as we shall see. Catholic, Orthodox and Buddhist monasteries with communal property have survived for hundreds of years.

It is said that the Hutterites, a sect of Anabaptist Protestants who moved to the United States in the 1870s, have falsified the celibacy requirement. Combining monogamous marriage and community of property, their numbers increased from 800 to about 28,000 in little over a century. They live in farming communities on both sides of the Canadian border, mainly in the Dakotas, Alberta and Manitoba. A high birthrate (about 9 children per family) allows them to withstand defections to the outside world. Married couples have small apartments but little privacy—others can enter without knocking. Only personal articles are held as private property. Dining is communal, and women in the course of the day are mostly separated from men. As a colony approaches about 150 people, it is divided and a new one is hived off. The Hutterites speak a German dialect, and by banning radio and television they have mostly succeeded in keeping the outside world at bay.[11] But their very uniqueness, and the strictness of their rule, point to the great difficulties involved. They are the exception that illuminates the rule.

The Israeli kibbutzim attempted to achieve much the same goal. At first it seemed that they had succeeded. Martin Buber called the kibbutz "the only socialist experiment that did not fail."[12] As recently as the early 1980s, Amos Elon could still say that the kibbutzim had realized, "with greater success than had been possible elsewhere, a utopian society, which, on a limited scale, still expresses some of the noblest aspirations of mankind."[13] By 1989, however, the 3 percent of the Israeli population then living on the kibbutz had accumulated debts exceeding $4 billion.[14] These were absorbed by the state, even as new debts mounted. A small number of the kibbutzim (17 out of 277 in the early 1990s) are religious, and some think that they could have endured without subsidies. But politics dictated that the finances of all kibbutzim, secular and religious, be intermingled.[15] This increased the lobbying power of the kibbutz sector generally. In the end, then, the massive state subsidies invalidated the experiment for all.

As to the free-rider cases that arise from technical difficulty, we only have to think of such common-pool resources as ocean fisheries and subterranean wells. Roads, broadcast signals, lighthouse beams and national defense are goods with related qualities. As the name suggests, broadcasting capitalizes on the public nature of electromagnetic waves by reaching a wide audience, and relies on advertising to pay the bills. With the support of fund-raising appeals, listener-supported radio stations dispense with the latter; but they, too, receive subsidies, and so their situation is analogous to that of the kibbutzim. (Radio station WETA in Washington, D.C., 60 percent listener-supported, reported in 1998 that 90 percent of listeners don't pay.)

Goods that cannot easily be confined to paying customers are called (by economists) public goods. National defense is the best example. Because a national defense system will protect those who don't pay for it, a privately financed defense system will immediately run into the free-rider problem. As a matter of both justice and practical politics, therefore, the government intervenes and taxes are levied from all to pay for such goods. Police, and a system of public justice, are subject to the same constraints. If privately furnished, they would work well for nonpayers. In fact, the concept of public goods usefully delineates those activities that are appropriate to government. If the good in question really is indispensable, and the market cannot easily provide it, then a proper role for government is indicated. It's worth noting that the goods traditionally supplied by the minimal state—military, police and justice system—do correspond to the economist's conception of public goods.

The advance of technology is meanwhile tending to make it easier for the market to provide an ever increasing range of goods; that is, for private owners to furnish them. Road building has with reason been a government activity for a long time, mainly because the cost of collecting fees from road users has been high. The private purchase of right of way also runs into the problem that holdouts can command monopoly prices. But digital technology is reducing the cost of collecting tolls, and if, in the years ahead, clogged freeways are not cleared by user fees (collected by road scanners "reading" prepaid magnetic strips on cars and deducting a toll) then ideology will surely have trumped technology.

Earlier technological advance also made privatization easier. Demsetz suggested that the American Indians of the Great Plains did not privatize their hunting lands as those in Quebec had done because Plains animals need to roam over large areas to find sufficient grazing. Fencing would have been prohibitively expensive. "Like oil in a common pool or the sperm whale on the high seas, buffalo were a 'fugitive resource,' the mobility of which made property rights (and therefore sound management) unattainable," the economists James Gwartney and Richard Stroup wrote. "Only the later fencing of the range solved the problem, after most buffalo had already been destroyed by both Indians and whites."[16] The invention of barbed wire, patented by Joseph Glidden in 1873, made this possible. It greatly reduced the cost of fencing, possibly saving the buffalo from extinction. As long as the animal remained communal property (or not owned by anyone), the logic of the commons worked inexorably to its disadvantage. The same problem exists today with the tiger, the elephant and the rhinoceros.

It is increasingly understood that when "free," naturally provided goods—clean air, ocean fish, continental forests, wild animals—are treated as though they belong to everyone, and private-property rules are either shunned or thought impracticable, then the good in question will be overutilized, polluted, or (in extreme cases) ruined or obliterated entirely. World population and the ability of modern fleets to catch and sell fish have risen more rapidly than the ability of fish stocks to reproduce in the ocean. Catches increased almost five-fold from 1950 to 1990, and in 1993 the UN Food and Agriculture Organization estimated that it cost $92 billion to capture a worldwide fish haul worth considerably less than that—$72 billion. Thirteen of 17 major ocean fisheries were said to be depleted or in serious decline.[17]

There is a growing recognition that property mechanisms can alleviate or solve such problems. Air pollution can be controlled by giving emission permits to smokestack industries within a given air basin, and allowing these permits to be traded voluntarily. Those who value them highly will buy them from those who value them less highly. Emission trading was incorporated into the global climate-change conference at Kyoto, Japan, in 1997. As to fisheries, the solution now used by Iceland and New Zealand is to issue fishing quotas (a certain percentage of the overall permitted catch) to each vessel owner. These quotas can then be traded at whatever price the market will bear, encouraging owners to operate economically, with long time-horizons. Under the old, devil-take-the-hindmost regime, fishing vessels would race each other to corner the earliest and biggest catch, harming everyone in the long run.

The applicability of such property rules to communal goods, where for physical reasons they seemed difficult or impossible to implement, was not obvious (and some environmentalists still oppose them). Necessity, provoked by growing populations and a commensurate strain on the commons, no doubt accounts for the change in outlook. But it is also a sign of the growing prestige of property that analysts in the policy arena are willing to advocate "property rights" solutions in so many words. In the past, the phrase "property rights" would probably have been used to impugn or delegitimize such solutions.

DISLOCATED MORAL AMBITION

Harold Demsetz's analysis became well known for a barbarous phrase. He pointed out that the most important effect of establishing private property is to "achieve a greater internalization of externalities." An externality is an economic benefit or cost that is transferred, without consent, compensation or reward, to others in the neighborhood. The word seems to have been first used by the economist Paul Samuelson in 1958.[18] Before that, the underlying idea was discussed by the economist A. C. Pigou in 1920. Although important in economic thought, it seems to have eluded description until the twentieth century.

Air pollution is the most cited example of a "negative" externality—one that imposes costs on others. "Smoke in large towns," Pigou wrote, "inflicts a heavy uncharged loss on the community, in injury to buildings and vegetables, expenses for washing clothes and cleaning rooms, expenses for the provision of extra artificial light, and in many other ways." Unjustly, the factory "externalizes" the costs of its pollution by depositing it on the neighborhood, instead of incurring the cost of installing scrubbers or burning cleaner fuel.[19]

But externalities can also be positive—Disneyland is a favorite example. When the amusement park was built in Anaheim in the 1950s, the surrounding land, mostly undeveloped, became much more valuable. Because Disney did not own it, the company inadvertently enriched those surrounding owners. In a sense, the Disney executives miscalculated, because they could not be compensated for their unintended philanthropy. In the 1970s, when Disney World was built in Florida, they avoided that mistake, buying options on the surrounding land before anyone knew what was going on. This allowed the company to benefit from the side effects of its own investment.

The pollution example may really have been more misleading than instructive. It has been cited time and again, but the costs associated with the famously smoking chimney have never been measured. They are no doubt offset by the gift of uncompensated benefits to the area, such as the stimulus to further business enterprise. Plant-closing laws imply that factories are viewed more positively than negatively today. The polluting factory of the textbooks may have prevented us from crediting the beneficial externalities of property. When value is created where it did not exist, it will tend to "radiate" additional value beyond its own boundaries. The first successful casino-hotel in Las Vegas externalized economic goods to the open air nearby, to the good fortune of those who came next. When Hewlett and Packard started up in their famous garage in Palo Alto, they launched not just a company but Silicon Valley.

Because the existence of externalities can be regarded as a "defect" of private property, there has sometimes been a tendency to think of them as an argument against it. But of course the problem of externalities is far more serious in a society of communal property. A man who is sensitive to noise will be able to screen out most sound pollution with walls. But if he is required to live on an open plain, without walls, he will be far more exposed. Most of the time, private property has the great advantage that it does concentrate the consequences of people's actions upon themselves. Communal property never does.

The free riding that communal property encourages is widespread throughout human society because it is reasonable to accept or use things of value in situations where commensurate obligations are not imposed, or are difficult to enforce. "Don't look a gift horse in the mouth" is the guiding maxim in such cases. The production of economic goods is unavoidably arduous. "Free" goods are therefore irresistible. Furthermore, consumption (or the satisfaction that derives from it) is unavoidably private. So the free-rider problem is a byproduct of human nature. Someone who balks at working all day to create something when it can be taken away by another who does no work, is demonstrating not the vice of selfishness but the faculty of reason.

It is at this point that we encounter an apparently deep ideological division in humanity. Faced with the evidence that the communard works less hard because he knows that what he creates will not be his, and because he knows that at the end of the day he will receive equal rations anyway, some will acknowledge that such behavior is "only human." Or they will concede that he was "behaving rationally given the incentives he faced." Others will take a less resigned view of the matter. Believing the communal arrangement to be morally superior, they will be disposed to regard the idle or opportunistic communard as reformable—by persuasion, exhortation and education. He must be persuaded to rise to the moral challenge that has been created.

Those in the first group will also believe that the lazy communard's behavior can be changed. What is essential, they will say, is a mechanism that establishes a proper ratio between effort and reward, or satisfaction. If he is going to work less, he will have to suffer the consequences himself; he will have to receive less. If he works harder, he must be permitted to capture the benefit, too. Either way, he will be encouraged to produce more. The mechanism that achieves this result is private property. The advocate of communal property seems to believe that precisely because private property creates such strong material incentives, it undermines the moral challenge; no longer will the individual be obliged to reform his nature by suppressing his ego and abjuring his selfishness. The mundane considerations of gain, not the nobler aspirations toward improvement and self-sacrifice, will be his guide.

It is above all a dislocated moral ambition—perhaps a religious impulse transferred to the secular setting—that seems to drives the opponents of private property. The communal impulse is an attempt to impose the condition of religious life onto the secular world. David Horowitz, later governor of the Bank of Israel, recalled his 1920s commune in the Galilee as "a monastic order without God."[20] The early Christian fathers argued that, by nature, the goods of the world were meant to be shared in common. But original sin, and the Fall of Man, made private property a necessary, although an imperfect, institution. Probably, then, those who sought to abolish private property never accepted the doctrine of original sin, but retained other aspects of the religious worldview. Yet when the incentives of a communal arrangement are mistakenly embedded in a worldly context, the result is the opposite of what was sought. The morality of the people is undermined. Selfishness, far from being discouraged, is rewarded.

ROMAN AND COMMON LAW: STATUS TO CONTRACT

INTRODUCTION

The two most famous empires in history were the Roman and the British, and both enjoyed economies that were in their day the most advanced in the world. At the institutional heart of both was a well-developed system of law: civil law in Rome, common law in Britain. The latter is believed to have evolved largely independently of the former. Both systems provided a higher level of protection to private property than did the surrounding nations with which they were in contention. As a result, both prospered. Empire was a luxury they could afford. The question that must concern us is the relationship between law and economy. What were the characteristic and defining legal arrangements of these societies and how did they contribute to, or perhaps detract from, the wealth of empire?

Roman law to a very considerable extent was preoccupied with questions of property and its disposition, exchange and bequest. In the great compilation of Roman law known as the *Corpus Juris Civilis*, completed in A.D. 533, an attempt was made to set forth the bewildering variety of circumstances in which legal disputes between parties might arise.[1] The majority involved issues of property. In fact, the work— "the most important and influential collec-

tion of secular legal materials that the world has ever known,"
according to Professor Alan Watson of the University of Pennsylvania—should remind us that property is the major category of law.[2]

Private property was not "absolute" in Roman law, but the
whole Roman system incorporated a serious property-related
defect. The hierarchy of rights, as later developed in western Europe,
was incorrectly ordered in Rome. For most subjects (not citizens),
the rights of life and liberty were subordinated to the rights of
property. Talking about the division of "things" into corporeal and
incorporeal, for example, the legal scholar Gaius said that examples
of "corporeal things" include "land, a slave, a garment, gold . . ."[3]
Slaves were property, and without doubt this contributed to the
downfall of the empire. Roman society was bedeviled by its breakdown into classes of unequal legal status.

The common law of England, in the centuries following the
Norman Conquest, introduced crucial new elements. The law itself
was supreme, and both the king and agencies of government were
expected to conform their actions to legal rules of courts. Juries
decided issues of fact. Above all, the law was not so much a
statement of principles as it was an accretion of instances that were
discovered in real proceedings. It was the preserve of the practi-
tioner more than the philosopher; it emerged from the courthouse
rather than the law school. Decisions were based on all the particular circumstances that emerged in proceedings, and they were
expected to control the future judgment of courts in similar cases:
judges were expected to respect precedent.

Within this framework, many of the principles that had
guided the adjudication of property disputes in Rome remained
essentially unchanged. But real-life plaintiffs, defendants and witnesses presenting themselves in front of judges and juries had the
effect of breaking down the old distinctions of status. All men were
seen to be equal before the law. This was not only in conformity with

natural justice, but turned out to have momentous economic consequences. The new equality of status stimulated the freedom of contract and the rise of an exchange economy. The transmission of property became increasingly "horizontal"—from seller to buyer—and decreasingly "vertical"—from father to son. Because entrepreneurial talent is by no means confined within hereditary lines, the control and disposition of wealth was democratized. Material wealth was acquired by those who, by virtue of their labor and ingenuity, merited it rather than inherited it.

FIVE

ROMANS AND COUNTRYMEN

THE FIRST GREAT EFFLORESCENCE OF PRIVATE PROPERTY occurred in the Greco-Roman world. Some may consider this a materialistic way of looking at early civilization, but the institution of property, which became more advanced in Roman society than in any other part of the known world, yielded essential zones of privacy in which liberty and individualism could flourish. It helped to generate the wealth and leisure that enabled Greek and Roman citizens to pursue literature, philosophy and the arts. A further point, little examined by the historians of antiquity, is that just as Roman property was a stimulus to wealth, so this wealth put the Roman legions at a comparative military advantage over their neighbors and adversaries.

"No prior legal system had ever known the notion of an unqualified private property," the historian Perry Anderson has written. "Ownership in Greece, Persia or Egypt had always been 'relative,' in other words conditional on superior or collateral rights of other authorities or parties."[1] The idea that principles of law were superior to authority and force, that justice was "blindfolded" and (ideally) indifferent to persons, was something new to antiquity. Beyond the Roman perimeter, either a collectivist tyranny or a subsistence-level communalism generally prevailed.

In his *Decline and Fall of the Roman Empire*, Gibbon noted that the direct route taken by the roads of the Roman Empire showed "little respect for the obstacles either of nature or private property."[2] From dead-straight roads one can indeed deduce authoritarian rule. But in the places where these roads went it is unlikely that there were many property lines anyway. In *De Bello Gallico*, Julius Caesar recorded that he found among the Germans "no separate estates or private boundaries."[3] Unable themselves to produce any surplus wealth, such states were primarily organized to capture it from their neighbors.

The monarchs of pre-Roman Egypt claimed for themselves a monopoly of the land, leasing it out in small plots to an enslaved peasantry that lacked security of tenure and was subject to forced labor. To the east, the monarchs of Asia enjoyed unlimited personal power; here was the oriental despotism characterized by Montesquieu and later discussed by Marx.[4] In many cases, the king declared himself owner of all the lands in his realm. Agriculture was thereupon neglected, industry ruined, and nothing repaired or improved, Montesquieu noted. Everything was taken from the earth, and nothing restored to it: "The whole country becomes a desert." An equality of sorts was nonetheless to be found in such regimes—all subjects were equally oppressed. In such despotic regimes, Montesquieu said, "There are no laws; the judge is himself his own rule."[5]

In ancient Greece, agricultural land was at first controlled and shared by various clans and for a long time worked communally. Slowly, it was converted to private ownership. At the beginning of the sixth century B.C., the Athenian lawgiver Solon established a new constitution that gave a further impetus to the separation of property. If a man died without heirs, his property had hitherto reverted to the clan; henceforth, he might bequeath it to anyone. Under Solon's Removal of Burdens, Aristotle tells us, existing debts were canceled, "whether owing to private persons or the state."[6] Those who had earlier been enslaved for debt were set free. Getting wind of his intentions, some of Solon's friends bought tracts of land with borrowed money, and duly profited from the general forgiveness. Thus arose new fortunes, later "supposed to have been of immemorial antiquity," Aristotle wrote. At last, we are in a world that we begin to recognize.

Some of the arguments about property heard in our time can be found in the writings of Plato and Aristotle. In his ideal society, described in *The Republic*, Plato argued that members of the ruling or guardian class should not have any property of their own beyond personal essentials. They were to live in barracks, like soldiers. He seemed to have in mind an austere but fully empowered civil service; an elite born to rule. From taxes levied on the workers, they would receive a fixed and modest income. "Neither should they have a private house or store closed against anyone who has a mind to enter; their provisions should be only such as are required by trained warriors."

Greedy rulers had ruined Greek cities in the past, Plato believed. Preventing them from owning property should restore them to the path of virtue and idealism. In the nineteenth century, this idea found its echo in the belief that reconstructed rules of ownership would improve human nature. With property held in common, Plato argued, the guardians "will not tear the city to pieces by differing about 'mine' and 'not mine,' each man dragging any acquisition which he has made into a separate house of his own, where he has a separate wife and children and private pleasures and pains; but all will be affected as far as may be by the same pleasures and pains because they are all of one opinion about what is near and dear to them, and therefore they all tend towards a common end."[7]

Plato's student Aristotle disagreed with his teacher. In his *Politics,* he speculated as to the "proper system of property" for citizens living under an ideal constitution. "Is it a system of communism, or one of private property?"[8] Communal or commune-istic arrangements of the type proposed by his teacher tended to cause "a good deal of trouble," he pointed out. Aristotle anticipated Plymouth Colony when he wrote: "If they do not share equally in work and recompense, those who do more work and get less recompense will be bound to raise complaints against those who get a larger recompense and do little work."[9]

When a large number of people are in a position to say "'mine' of the same object," he noted, the result cannot be harmonious. "What is common to the greatest number gets the least amount of care. Men pay most attention to what is their own; they care less for what is common; or at any rate they care for it only to the extent to which each is individually concerned. Even when there is no other cause for inattention, men are more prone to neglect their duty when they think that another is attending to it."[10] On the other hand, when people have their separate spheres of interest, "there will not be the same ground for quarrels, and the amount of interest will increase, because each man will feel that he is applying himself to what is his own."[11]

These remarks, constituting perhaps the earliest "economic" analysis of property arrangements, have deservedly been emphasized, sometimes with the implication that there is not much new under the sun: the problems of property were long ago dissected by the ancients. Aristotle himself made a related point when he said that if Plato's recommendations had been practical, they would already have been put into effect. "It would not have gone unnoticed if they had been really good," he wrote. "Almost everything has been discovered already...."[12]

Most of Aristotle's comments on property were on the moral rather than the economic plane, however. Private property enables us to be generous in helping friends in need. Such liberality would be impossible "under a system of excessive unification of the state." We can only be generous if things are ours to give. He made this important and prescient criticism of the Platonic scheme:

> Legislation such as Plato proposes may appear to wear an attractive face and to argue benevolence. The hearer receives it gladly, thinking that everybody will feel towards everybody else some marvellous sense of fraternity—all the more as the evils now existing under ordinary forms of government (lawsuits about contracts, convictions for perjury, and obsequious flatteries of the rich) are denounced as due to the absence of a system of common property. None of

these evils, however, is due to the absence of communism. They all arise from
the wickedness of human nature. Indeed, it is a fact of observation that those
who own common property, and share in its management, are far more often at
variance with one another than those who have property in severalty.[13]

Aristotle's preference was for a scheme of private property ("for property
ought to be generally and in the main private"), the benefits of which should be
shared with the poor. This was the scheme already in existence in a number of
states—Sparta, for instance; and it was also the system advocated in Plato's last
work, the *Laws*. Here Plato conceded that although some form of communism
might be morally superior, something more practical was needed for men as
they are. Citizens should own equal portions of the land, to be worked by
privately owned slaves. Strict rules of inheritance and child bearing would
ensure that this equality persisted through the generations.

In his ideal state (found in book 7 of the *Politics*), Aristotle proposed that
only citizens should own property; laborers or "mechanics" would not qualify
either as owners or citizens.[14] As for the farming population, it "ought by rights
to be one of slaves or barbarian serfs," and of course they wouldn't be allowed
to own property either. But no one should lack subsistence, and so he
recommended a welfare system called "common tables," with the right of eating
at these tables open to all.[15] In order to provision them, territory would have to
be set aside as public property.

The whole system of Greek (and later, Roman) thought was vitiated by
the acceptance of slaves as property. In states such as Sparta, Aristotle tell us,
"men use one another's slaves, and one another's horses and dogs, as if they
were their own."[16] He admired the generosity more than he questioned the
slavery. Some people were slaves by nature, he believed—"barbarians" (non-
Greeks) in particular. Those who farmed the land should "ideally" be slaves,
although, to reduce the risk of insurrection, they should not be drawn from a
single stock.[17] He also saw the economic advantage of promising slaves their
emancipation—it gave them an incentive to work harder.

The notion of rights, in the sense of limits imposed by human nature upon
what the state should in justice do, seemed not to have existed in Greek political
thought. Society was unquestioningly divided into classes—slaves, mechanics,
freedmen, citizens—who labored under varying degrees of civil disabilities.
According to some estimates, slaves in Attica outnumbered the freeborn citizens.

PROPERTY IN ROME

Essentially the same legal and social arrangements prevailed in Rome. Written,
as opposed to customary, Roman law is thought to have begun with the Twelve

Tables, promulgated around 450 B.C. The laws were publicly displayed on twelve tablets, in response to protests that judges' rulings were obscure because the laws were known only orally. The contents of the Twelve Tables have survived only in fragments, but elements of them, such as Table III, suggest that property was not to be trifled with. Where debt was admitted, 30 days was allowed for payment, after which the debtor could be brought before the magistrate. If no one then came forward to guarantee payment, "the creditor may take the debtor away with him and bind him with thongs or fetters, the weight of which shall not be more than 15 pounds."[18]

The *Corpus Juris Civilis* included excerpts from the Twelve Tables. One demonstrated minute attention to property: "A rule of the Twelve Tables provides that nobody can be compelled to remove another's beams set into his house; instead he must pay double the timber's value under the claim called the action for beams-set-in. 'Beams' includes all materials which go into the building of a house."[19] The provision was designed to stop buildings from being demolished.

Almost a thousand years elapsed between the first promulgation of the Twelve Tables and Justinian's *Institutes* (a synopsis of the larger work), and our knowledge of early Roman law is sparse. No surviving legal text contains a Roman definition of ownership.[20] But it is impossible to read about life in the Roman Republic without concluding that property was more respected than liberty and more secure than life. Sallust complained that property took precedence over other rights.

Although the law permitting the enslavement of debtors and their children was later modified, cases occurred as late as the fifth century A.D. Until the time of Hadrian, the head of the family enjoyed the power of life and death over his family. Fathers could convert their own children into property and "alienate" them by selling them into slavery.[21] A thief caught in the act could become the slave, hence the property, of the man he had robbed. As the Roman Republic expanded, more territory was captured and more prisoners were enslaved. Slavery, Justinian's *Institutes* noted, "makes a man the property of another," but (by that time) the writer had the grace to add, "contrary to the law of nature."*

In *The Ancient City* (1864), the French scholar Numa Fustel de Coulanges proposed an interesting theory about the Roman reverence for property. It is worth repeating even though his scholarly reputation has declined.

---

*In his *Italian Manpower*, P. A. Brunt estimates that in 225 B.C. there were some 4.4 million free persons in Italy and 600,000 slaves. By 43 B.C. there were perhaps 4.5 million free and 3 million slaves. "Nothing like this had ever been seen in the Ancient World before," Perry Anderson writes in *Passages From Antiquity to Feudalism* "The full potential of the slave mode of production was for the first time unfolded by Rome. . . . The predatory militarism of the Roman Republic was its main lever of economic accumulation." P. A. Brunt, *Italian Manpower 225 B.C.–A.D. 14* (London: Oxford Univ. Press, 1971), 121-5; Anderson, *Passages,* 62.

Actual reverence was the key, he thought. The idea of private property had been reinforced by the Roman religion, which presupposed a multiplicity of household gods and was centered on the family. The decentralization of divinity encouraged the separation of property. The perpetuation of the family, through the veneration of its deceased members, tended to perpetuate that same hallowed ground. The altar and hearth belonged to the dead as much as to the living. The altar could not easily be moved, and was to be maintained not just for a lifetime but for as long as the family endured. Ancestors were buried in a field nearby, and around it an enclosure was fixed. And so a portion of the soil became consecrated as the perpetual property of each family.

Men who were fixed by their religion to one spot, which they believed it their duty not to quit, Fustel wrote, "would soon begin to think of raising in that place some solid structure. The tent covers the Arab, the wagon the Tartar; but a family that has a domestic hearth has need of a permanent dwelling. The stone house soon succeeds the mud cabin or the wooden hut. The family did not build for the life of a single man, but for generations that were to succeed each other in the same dwelling."[22] In short, it was religion, not law, that first guaranteed the right of property.

In the early cities, dwellings were brought nearer together, but still were not contiguous; "in no case could two houses be joined to each other; a party wall was supposed to be an impossible thing," Fustel wrote. "The same wall could not be common to two houses; for then the sacred enclosure of the gods would have disappeared. At Rome, the law fixed two feet and a half as the width of the free space." Communal property was thereby avoided.

Later, the sociologist Emilio Durkheim stood Fustel on his head and argued that it was the social structure that shaped religious belief rather than the reverse. Obviously it is difficult to decide which came first. Nonetheless, Fustel's argument is of interest to the student of property. An obvious prediction follows from it. One would expect that property could more easily be secured than alienated. After all, it belonged not just to the living, but also "to those who are dead, and to those who are yet to be born." Among the Hindus, Fustel claimed, property was also founded upon religion and was indeed inalienable. In ancient Greece and Rome, he argued, "everything leads us to believe" that property was inalienable.[23]

He does not back up the claim, however. True, Aristotle tells us in his *Politics* that the legislator "very rightly made it improper to buy or sell any land belonging to a Spartan citizen."[24] And he gives one or two more examples. By the time of the Roman Republic, however, it is certain that Roman property was frequently sold. Cicero tells us that if a family sold the field in which its tomb was situated, it nonetheless retained an "easement" to reach the tomb, in order to perform the ceremonies of worship.

Most property was presumed to be private. The legal authority known as Gaius thought that things that were subject to human right "in most cases belong within someone's property." But things may also be public, belonging "corporately to the whole community." Among the things considered to be public, according to the legal scholars cited in the *Digest,* were sacred or religious temples; flowing water, river banks and the seashore; stadiums and theaters, city walls and gates. The unstated principle guiding the resolution of property disputes was the belief that the law was an instrument of peace. With its help, people could resolve disputes amicably. Incidentally, therefore, they could also lead productive lives.[25]

Professor Moses Finley of Cambridge has noted the monumental indifference of extant Roman sources to the questions about property that interest us today. Absent from the sources are "any data or statements about the size and range of landholdings" in the Roman Empire. It's not just that we don't have such information. Finley believes that no one at the time did either (other than what individuals knew of their own holdings). The study of the distribution of property in ancient Rome is a puzzle with few pieces. A few registers of property have survived on inscriptions and papyrii. One, from Veleia in northern Italy, early in the second century A.D., lists the value of 47 estates, 46 of them in private hands. Another is from a town in southern Italy, another from Egypt.[26] "Almost all of the registers point unequivocally to heavy aggregation of property in the hands of the rich," R. P. Duncan-Jones wrote.[27]

This may be close to a tautology, for land and what was grown on it was the principal source of wealth (and this would generally hold true until the Industrial Revolution). Cicero rightly accused a tribune named Philippus of demagoguery for recommending agrarian reform on the grounds that "there were not in the state two thousand people who owned any property." But plainly a small minority did own disproportionately. The principal means of transferring landed wealth was inheritance and marriage. But thanks to war and high mortality, land changed hands more frequently than this would imply; one estate near Cicero's in Tusculum had at least 5 owners in 50 years. Elizabeth Rawson has concluded that "the Roman landowners' relation to his land was much less emotional than that of the English landed gentleman [of the eighteenth and nineteenth centuries]"—a rebuke to Fustel's theory.[28] Considering a site near Anzio as a shrine for his deceased daughter Tullia, Cicero worried that it might not long remain hallowed "in view of the many changes of ownership in the countless years to come." He hoped to preserve it as consecrated ground "so long as Rome remains Rome," and he felt that "open ground," rather than private property, improved his chances of doing so.[29]

Members of the senatorial class would often own several estates, preferably not too far from Rome; rarely did they rent in the country. At the time of the Republic, senators were not allowed to own land at all in the provinces (a chance remark by Cicero is our sole source for this). "Surely, if it had been possible to own land, Pompey would have owned half the east and the patrician Claudii most of the rest," Rawson adds. Urban property was frequently rented both to upper and lower classes. Leases began on July 1, and rent was due at the end of the rental period—a good indication of the owners' confidence that tenants would pay up.[30] Tenants in the building could sue the original owner if he sold to a new owner who then tried to disregard existing leases. In general, it seems, contract ruled.[31]

Investment in urban dwellings was discouraged by the risk of fire. A famous anecdote from the mid-second century A.D. tells of friends accompanying the rhetor Antonius Julianus up the Cispian Hill just as a large *insula,* or apartment block, caught fire. One of the party observed that while the returns to urban property were great, the risks were greater. If there were something "to prevent the houses of Rome from burning so readily," he said, "I assure you I would have given up my estates in the countryside and purchased urban property."[32] According to Plutarch, the vastly wealthy M. Licinius Crassus became rich by buying "most of Rome" literally at fire-sale prices.[33] But Plutarch's account is not coherent. He implies that Crassus bought buildings while they were actually burning. If Crassus really did become enriched by such purchases, he presumably was lucky to have avoided future fires himself.

Valuable property such as land, houses, slaves and farm animals were said to be *res mancipi,* meaning that their transfer to another owner required a ritual, or court procedure. If the original owner's title was unclear, then the new owner's title "ripened" (in the case of real estate) after two years' unchallenged possession. At the end of that time, the new owner was vested with full ownership. "Proof of title was therefore reasonably simple in Roman law," according to the historian John Crook. "There was no need to go back to title deeds of the distant past, for all you needed to prove was undisturbed control for the relevant short period, and the nature and genuineness of the transaction by which you had acquired."[34] Such a system no doubt gave rise to the saying that possession is nine-tenths of the law.

Rural property distributed to citizens by the state was surveyed; boundary lines were marked out, traces of which can still be seen from the air. The errors of surveyors were subject to litigation. The resulting "cadaster," or publicly recorded survey, was drawn out on paper and incised on bronze; one copy was kept locally and one in Rome. Large sections of a map of a district in Gaul from the Emperor Vespasian's time have survived, engraved in stone. Rivers and roads are marked, and the acreage of private land and Roman public land are indicated.[35] In the Roman province of Egypt, where the dry climate preserved a more abundant supply of papyrus records, the Ptolemaic monopolies gave way to private enterprise, and state land was privatized. Egypt had a pedantic system of land registration, whereas elsewhere in the empire the conveyance of property was not usually registered until the next full census.

Roman citizens enjoyed considerable, but not absolute, control over private property. After the fire of A.D. 64 destroyed 10 of the 14 districts of Nero's Rome, rebuilding was carefully regulated. "Street-fronts were of regulated alignment, streets were broad, and houses built round courtyards," Tacitus wrote. "Their height was restricted, and their frontages protected by colon-nades."[36] Some 50 years earlier, according to Tacitus, the Senate passed sumptuary laws. "The use of gold plate for private entertainments was prohibited, and so were the silk clothes into which male costume had degenerated."[37]

The law of property routinely made allowances for the inconveniences that owners might cause their neighbors, confirming our belief that the law of property was unusually well developed. The legal scholar Ulpian believed that there was no legal recourse against one owner whose property blocked the "ancient light" of another.[38] But a more recent examination has shown that, in fact, the law was not so indifferent to the rights of those who had built first.

Servitudes, or easements, were routine, as Justinian's *Digest* shows: "Suppose I sell part of my estate and make it a term of the contract that I am to have the right to channel water across that part to the rest of my estate, and suppose that the prescribed period elapses without my constructing a water-course. I do not lose any right, as there is no channel for the water to flow through. In fact, my right remains unimpaired. However, if I had made a watercourse and not used it, I would lose my right."[39]

In another example, the law of trespass was ameliorated to allow the gathering of fruit fallen onto a neighbor's ground; and a right of passage had to be given to someone who could not otherwise reach his property from the road. One owner might have to tolerate his neighbor's wall overhanging his own property by a few inches; plaintiffs could avail themselves of a law of nuisance to prevent a neighbor from emitting excessive smoke; and so on. But these supposed rebukes to the unbridled individualism of Roman law only increase our respect for it, because they show that owners were not permitted to be disdainful of their neighbors; the law of property was sufficiently well developed to permit neighbors to live at peace.

To what extent did the state interfere in the private lives and property of individuals? In his *Law and Life of Rome,* Crook writes that "a free Roman's house was his castle, his labor not directed, his children not appropriated for purposes either secular or religious, and his movement and change of domicile unrestricted." Municipal laws obliged owners to maintain roads at the bound-aries of their property, prevented burials or cremations within the city, and restricted what could be spent on funerals. Property could be confiscated as punishment for crimes or pulled down to create firebreaks or to facilitate the Auspices. Sometimes, it might be taken for eminent domain—making way for an aqueduct, for example. "If owners were powerful men they might stop a project—not qua owners but qua powerful men," Crook adds. "Or a tactful person like Augustus might prefer to restrict his new forum rather than demolish too many of the humble dwellings of the plebs. The state normally came to arrangements with owners."[40]

THE GRACCHI

In the long sweep of Roman history, we find a conflict about property at a critical juncture. It famously involved the brothers Gracchi—Tiberius and Caius—who were members in good standing of the Roman nobility. Like all property disputes, it indirectly tells us more about the society in which it arose than a merely legalistic understanding of property would suggest.

In 137 B.C., Tiberius Gracchus was on his way to the wars in Numantia (in Spain) when he noticed that the farms of Tuscany were being worked by slaves instead of citizens. Few yeoman farmers could be found at all. In subduing the rest of Italy and subordinating it to Rome, the Romans had captured not only territory, but more and more slaves. Part of this new land was given to soldiers and colonists. But other parts, laid waste by war, became public land (ager publicus). Rome decreed that those willing to work this land could in effect own it if they paid a tax on their produce. The idea was to give the Italians, then considered "the most laborious of peoples," a stake in the land and so ensure that they would be fruitful and multiply.

This hadn't worked out, however. The public land had increasingly fallen into the hands of the rich, who absorbed adjacent strips of their poorer neighbors' allotments, and so ended up with large estates (latifundia) instead of moderately sized ones. Moreover, poor farmers increasingly found they had to sell their land to those who already had plenty of it. This was the bad situation that Tiberius Gracchus, a tribune of the plebs, proposed to change with an agrarian reform law in 133 B.C. With the people crowding around the hustings, he said: "The savage beasts in Italy have their dens, their places of rest and refuge, but the men who bear arms, and risk their lives for the safety of their country, enjoy nothing more than the air and the light. And having no houses and settlements of their own, they must wander from place to place with their children."

Much earlier, in 367 B.C., an agrarian law had stipulated that no one could own more than about 330 acres of public land. Over time, however, that limit had been circumvented. The wealthy obtained an excess by conveying it to their relatives and using other people's names. Tiberius Gracchus now proposed to restore this old law, except that the permitted acreage would be doubled on average. The remainder was to be divided among the poor by elected commissioners. In short, it was an early land reform scheme. A good deal of already privatized property would be redistributed.

As the time for a vote in the Forum approached, Gracchus made various arguments: Was it not right to divide the common property among the people? Was not greater consideration due citizens than slaves? Were not those who served in the army worth more respect? Did not a stake in the land give owners a stake in the public interest? The Romans had gained most of their territory by conquest, he argued, and hoped to occupy the rest of the habitable world; but the nation's security was now at stake. There was a question whether they would continue to have the manpower to fight those wars. For their part, the rich were indignant: they had already paid their neighbors for the lands they now owned; their wives' dowries had been spent on improving it; the land had been made over to their daughters as dowry, as moneylenders could attest by showing loans made on the security. The poor meanwhile reproached the rich for employing slaves, instead of freedmen or citizens, to work their land.

The proposed law was about to be read to the Assembly when another tribune, Octavius, representing the landowners, interposed his veto, causing a delay. But within a few days he was voted out of office for opposing the will of the people. At that point the agrarian law was ratified. Three commissioners were appointed to see that the land was properly divided. They were Gracchus himself, his brother Caius, and his father-in-law, Claudius Appius.

Passage of the law made Gracchus popular. Crowds escorted him as though he were the founder of Italy. Meanwhile, the landowners fought back. As the elections of the tribunes approached, they came up with a plan to depose Gracchus, who was already making new campaign promises—reducing the time of military service, for example, and granting the right of appeal against judges' rulings. Voting began, and the first two tribes duly pronounced for Gracchus. But then the rich objected: It was not lawful for the same man to succeed himself in office. (Gracchus had either forgotten about term limits, or the rich had just thought of it.)

The following day, voting was to take place at the temple on the Capitoline Hill. There Gracchus continued to be obstructed by supporters of the wealthy. He gave a prearranged signal and fighting began. He and many of his supporters were killed; all the bodies were thrown into the Tiber. This was said to have been the first violent civil conflict in the history of the Roman Republic—beginning a series of events later known as the Roman Revolution. Caius Gracchus in turn also tried to bring about reforms—raising the age of military service to 17, dividing the public lands among the poor, giving Italians the same voting rights as the Romans. But he, too, was slain, 12 years after Tiberius.

Reading this account, one might at first suspect anachronism. It seems to be a twentieth-century interpretation of ancient events. It all sounds so familiar—something out of Latin America, perhaps: agrarian reform, greedy landlords, *latifundia,* popular reformers seeking to right old wrongs who in turn are killed by rich landowners. But every detail of the above account is taken from the two ancient sources who tell us most of what we know about the Gracchi—the historians Plutarch and Appian. Plutarch wrote his *Lives* at the beginning of the second century A.D., Appian's history was written a decade or two later.[41]

Both are unmistakably sympathetic to the Gracchi (unlike Livy and Cicero). But Plutarch and Appian also make it clear that a serious problem really was developing in the expanding republic. Ultimately it stemmed from a defect in the Roman constitution itself. The wealthy indeed had a critical advantage over their poorer neighbors, and it wasn't just a matter of money. The problem was that they could work their estates with slave labor.

Smallholders could not compete with this because property owners were qualified—that is, obliged—to serve in the Roman legions. This compelled them to be away from home, sometimes for several years at a time. On the other hand, slaves were not allowed to serve in the army because it was not considered safe to arm them. Even as these events unfolded, a revolt involving perhaps 100,000 slaves had lasted for several years in Sicily. Normally, free labor will be more than a match for slave labor, but in the Roman republic the free labor was often absent (on military campaigns), even as the slaves were toiling on the *latifundia.* The economic effect was comparable to a severe tax on the middle class that the wealthy could escape.

In attempting to correct the injustice by redistributing the land, Gracchus perhaps missed its real cause, which was slavery, compounded by a conscription that amounted to temporary enslavement. But slavery and conscription were too central to the Roman way of life to be candidates for abolition, perhaps even for discussion. It's worth noting the harm the property qualification evidently did. It gave small farmers who did not want to spend ten years or more in the Roman legions a real incentive to sell their holdings "and disappear once more into the slums of the City, and from the register of *assidui,*" in the words of a modern historian.[42] (*Assidui* were "those settled on the land" with the property qualification to bear arms.)

The need for military recruits also explains why, in the Gracchan reform, the newly distributed plots were to be inalienable in perpetuity. Unable to sell them, the new owners would always be eligible for the draft. This made military, but not economic, sense. It is possible, in fact, that Gracchus's real purpose was not the restoration of the yeoman farmer at all, but the bolstering of the Roman legions. His proposal made more men available for military service and ensured that they stayed that way. The new owners would have had a strong incentive to sell if their ownership "qualified" them for something as arduous and dangerous as military service.

In his *Economic Survey of Ancient Rome,* Prof. Tenney Frank said that during the Gracchan period down to the year 118 B.C., "individual allotments of small plots were made to a large number of poor citizens (perhaps 50,000 to 75,000), largely urban proletariat."[43] Since the plots were inalienable for several years, he added, "it is likely that many of the urban settlers learned to farm and remained, but our sources insist that after permission to sell was given the number of small plot-holders tended to diminish rapidly." If serving in the army was the price of ownership, smallholders declined to pay. The need for manpower persisted, and within a generation the Roman general and consul Gaius Marius abolished the property qualification for conscription. Julius Caesar later doubled the pay for those on active service, and veterans also received cash bounties on discharge;[44] Augustus provided allotments of land for demobilized soldiers, and finally conscription was abolished under the emperor Tiberius.

Whatever the real goal of the Gracchi, the maldistribution of property in Italy became their pretext for action. We shall meet this pattern again—agrarian reform that addresses the easily understood problem of distribution but fails to address a graver underlying problem. We may even regard it as a general rule that whenever the redistribution of land is proposed, real problems do exist—problems that are almost certainly more fundamental than the distribution itself. The circumstance that some people have more money (and therefore more land) than others is not in itself likely to do harm, or to endure, as long as there are no underlying legal disabilities that perpetuate the inequality. But if such legal disabilities do exist, *they* are what should be reformed. If they are not, the maldistribution will recur and persist even after attempted redistributions.

Cicero thought that putting such power in the hands of tribunes of the people such as Gracchus led only to mischief and strife—"planting the spear in the forum" and placing the citizens' property "under the auctioneer's hammer."[45] He called for the restoration of the aristocratic order that had been losing power in "a complete revolution of the state" ever since the Gracchi. As for the equalization of property, it was nothing but a policy of ruin. "For the chief purpose in the establishment of constitutional state and municipal governments was that individual property rights might be secured." It was in the hope of safeguarding their possessions that men had sought the protection of cities in the first place. Even those who expected to become popular by redistributing property find they have miscalculated. "For he who has been robbed of his property is their enemy; he to whom it has been turned over actually pretends that he had no wish to take it."[46]

Rule by a privileged class was good for all, Cicero argued. As a member in good standing of that elite, his comments are easily discounted as self-serving. In

De Officiis, nonetheless, he set forth the proper relationship between citizen and state, and was perhaps the first ever to do so. The officeholder, he wrote, "must make it his first care that everyone shall have what belongs to him and that private citizens suffer no invasion of their property rights by act of the state."[47]

Within the Roman system, however, that was not a sufficient recommendation. "Citizens" were a privileged subset of the population. In the second century B.C., perhaps no more than one in four men in Italy was a citizen of Rome. It is axiomatic that any system that permits some people to control the lives of others who are at a legal disadvantage cannot be just; it is also unlikely to be productive. Although the Roman respect for law was great, the ideal feature of law was absent. That is the requirement that it apply equally to all. Physical law—the law of gravity, for example—has this egalitarian character, and human law should aspire to it. But Rome was above all a society of classes: citizens, freemen, freedmen, "peregrines," slaves. With slaves increasing in number as Roman dominion expanded, the adverse effects of a law that was "contrary to the law of nature" (as Justinian's *Institutes* had noted) was bound to make itself felt.

Although Cicero identified with the old order and defended it despite its flaws, it is to his credit that he saw what the law should ideally look like. As far as we know, at that point nothing comparable to his adumbration of natural law had ever been written. It was published in *De Re Publica,* in 54 B.C. This law is of universal application, it is unchanging and everlasting, he wrote. It cannot be altered, repealed or abolished: "We cannot be freed from its obligations by senate or people, and we need not look outside ourselves for an expounder and interpreter of it. And there will not be different laws at Rome and at Athens, or different laws now and in the future, but one eternal and unchangeable law will be valid for all nations and all times, and there will be one master and ruler, that is, God, over all, for he is the author of this law. . . ."[48]

In his *Laws,* written two years later, Cicero says that no single thing is so like another "as all of us are to one another." The shared characteristics of human nature entitle us all to equal respect from the law. A single definition applies to all men—sufficient proof that "there is no difference in kind between man and man; for if there were, one definition could not be applicable to all." Reason, which alone raises us above the beasts and enables us to draw inferences and solve problems, "is certainly common to all of us."[49]

But the essential transformation still had not occurred, and would not until the idea took hold that "all men are created equal." It took a long time for this to happen, and the country in which it had the greatest impact on legal institutions was a remote outpost of the Roman Empire that Cicero would not have taken seriously. But it, too, acquired an empire; one that eventually rivaled Rome's.

SIX

THE ENGLISH LEAD

"THE MOST BEAUTIFUL PHAENOMENON"

THE CONSTITUTIONAL HISTORIAN HENRY HALLAM marveled in 1818 that the "long and uninterruptedly increasing prosperity of England" was "the most beautiful phaenomenon in the history of mankind."[1] How was it to be explained? The advantage could hardly be found in climate, soil or geography. Yet nowhere else had "the benefits that political institutions can confer been diffused over so extended a population." He concluded that the key lay in "the spirit of its laws, from which, through various means, the characteristic independence and industriousness of our nation have been derived." For that reason, the British constitution ought to be, "to inquisitive men of all countries, far more to ourselves, an object of superior interest."

Alexis de Tocqueville said much the same thing in *L'ancien régime* (1856). Writing about England, he asked: "Is there any single country in Europe in which the national wealth is greater, private property is more extensive, more secure, more varied in character, society more settled and more wealthy?" He, too, credited the legal system. He was particularly impressed that the "system of caste," or legal distinctions between classes, had been "effectively destroyed."[2]

Much more recently, Alan Macfarlane opened his book on *The Origins of English Individualism* (1978) with a challenge that echoed Hallam's. "If we could understand why the 'industrial revolution' occurred first in England and what caused it," he wrote, "we might be able to encourage economic growth elsewhere."[3] Because it is perhaps the best documented of all nations in the world over the last six hundred years, England more easily than any other country can help us to understand how an agricultural society turned into an industrial one. So, he asked: "Why did the industrial revolution occur first in England? When did England start to be different from other parts of Europe? In what, principally, did that difference consist?"

By the end of his book, he still had not quite located the "origins" of his book's title. But he studied the issue through the lens of property; and he saw that his questions resolve themselves into questions of law. He refreshingly claimed at one point: "It is very obvious that historians are quite unable to explain in purely economic terms why industrialization occurred."[4] On his final page, he shared the suspicion of Montesquieu that England's advantage lay in a political system in which the land law and law of inheritance created private property: no "group" or collectivity owned the land.

Now comes David S. Landes, professor emeritus of history and economics at Harvard, who asks the same question in *The Wealth and Poverty of Nations*: "Why did Britain do it and not some other nation?" He lists the political institutions that would ideally equip a society "to pursue material progress and general enrichment," including "secure rights of private property" prominently among them. But he neglects the relevant legal history. In *The Unbound Prometheus* (1969), however, Professor Landes had shown more interest in such questions. There, he noted that hedged and restricted property rights had evolved into full ownership—"full in the sense that the various components of ownership were united in the person or persons of the possessor." Property had become more secure, and Europeans had learned to deal with one another "on the basis of agreement rather than of force."[5] Contract between nominal equals had replaced personal bonds between superior and inferior. It is to the law that we must turn.

Frederic W. Maitland, the preeminent historian of English law, playfully but half seriously suggested in his inaugural lecture as Downing Professor at Cambridge (1888) that the "feudal system" was not so much a medieval reality as an early essay in comparative jurisprudence,[6] introduced into England by "that learned and laborious antiquary, Sir Henry Spelman."[7] Reading his Continental law books, Spelman, who died in 1641, had discovered family likenesses between European and English law, and the idea that there was a system common to all nations of the West immediately appealed to him, as it did to other Englishmen. Maitland next speculated that the feudal system had attained its "most perfect development" in the middle of the eighteenth century—in the work of the legal scholar William Blackstone. In his "easy attractive manner," his volumes on English law "popularized and made orthodox" Spelman's innovation. A few simple principles were used to explain the "mass of medieval law" in England.

But since Blackstone's time we have learned and unlearned many things, Maitland continued. We have discovered vast differences as well as resemblances between English and Continental law. England might be said to be either the most, or the least, feudalized; William the Conqueror may as easily be said to have suppressed the feudal system as to have introduced it. Maitland records his surprise that Sir Edward Coke, in his voluminous works summing up the English law of the later Middle Ages, includes "no word about the feudal system." He had no notion of a system common to the nations of Europe. In fact, Maitland writes, we do not hear of the feudal system in English law until feudalism itself has ceased to exist.[8]

Feudal land law has always been said to be the essence of the property system: the tenant held "of" his lord, who in turn was tenant of a higher lord, all the way up the feudal hierarchy to the king—the owner of all the land. But this was not explicit in the law. The great authorities of English law, Glanville in the twelfth century, Bracton in the thirteenth, never put it into words. "They never state as a noteworthy fact that all land is held of the king." In a bow to orthodoxy, Maitland adds that they didn't need to: it went without saying. Still, it is an omission that is "very remarkable in Bracton's great treatise. His general learning about property he draws from the Roman books, and propounds in the language of Roman law. The ultimate tenant of the land, the lowest freeholder in the feudal scale, is the owner of the land, he has *dominium rei, proprietatem,* he is *proprietarius. . . .*"[9]

Maitland falls into line in the end, accepting the consensus view, but of course the suggestion that the feudal system perhaps really wasn't the same in England—that it was perhaps a retrospective theory that made everything easier to understand—is provocative and interesting for anyone looking for some deep-rooted difference between English institutions and those on the Continent.

In the usual view, the feudal economic order existed uniformly across western Europe, including Britain, until the sixteenth century. Production was for use rather than exchange. Property rights were often communal and always conditional. The tenant stood in a subordinate relation to a higher lord, all the way up to the king. Communities were small, isolated and stable. "The hurrying, scattering generation of today can hardly imagine the immovable stability of the village of past centuries, when generation after generation grew from cradle to grave in the same houses," Eileen Power wrote in *Medieval People,* giving the usual interpretation.[10]

It is visualized as a static world, dominated by family ties, local custom, unequal status, different classes, suzerainty and vassalage, fealty, homage, and noblesse oblige. Protection was offered in exchange for service, or goods in kind. The feudal economy is thought of as a chessboard on which few moves (that is, economic exchanges) are made: Property is controlled by kings, queens, bishops and knights. Most players are of lowly estate—pawns. They know their place and stand ready to sacrifice themselves for the king if necessary. Status defines the rules of the game.

In this view, land was rarely bought or sold. Robert Heilbroner and Lester Thurow have suggested this useful analogy for understanding feudal property: The feudal lord "would no more have thought of selling a portion of his ancestral estates to a neighboring lord than the governor of Connecticut would think of selling off a few counties to the governor of Rhode Island. . . . The idea that one's productive property was an asset, worth a certain price and producing a certain income, was as foreign to pre-market society as the idea, today, that shares of common stock should be considered a family heirloom to be handed down from generation to generation."[11]

Our understanding of the next development in the story—the emergence of capitalism itself—has been strongly influenced by Karl Marx and Max Weber. Cash and its twin, capital, reared their ugly heads. Money rents replaced feudal service, wage labor emerged, the market economy grew, exchange linked isolated communities. The proletariat, Marx tells us, "was hurled," "was expropriated," "was dragged," was "suddenly and forcible torn"; the passive construction of the language mirrored the Marxian idea that abstract forces, including "historical movement" itself, were the mainsprings of history.[12] A new "ethic" was abroad in the land, a Protestant ethic, legitimizing accumulation as never before.

It seems likely, though, that Marx's spotty research amid the vast array of available records did little more than validate his own preconceived theory. Lending support to Maitland's conceit, Alan Macfarlane believes that parish and manorial records show that "England was as 'capitalist' in 1250 as it was in 1550 or 1750."[13] Developed markets and both geographical and social mobility existed by the earliest of these dates. The law had given rise to individual, as opposed to group or family, ownership, and these changes had occurred far earlier than most researchers have realized—perhaps in the twelfth century. Farm and family were separated, land was bought and sold, and "full private ownership was established." Rational accounting and the profit motive were widespread. In choosing England as their prime example of the transition from precapitalist to capitalist society, Marx and Max Weber had in fact selected "a singular and peculiar example."

The law, at any rate, is where we should look. If unusual legal features are found in England and not elsewhere, that may be regarded as suggestive, and perhaps sufficient to account for the later economic difference between England and other countries. Why the necessary legal changes did not arise in other countries is a much more difficult question to answer. In any event, we do immediately encounter a most important distinction. Writing in 1612, Sir John Davies, attorney general for Ireland, commented that England's customary law

is the most perfect and most excellent, and without comparison the best, to make and preserve a Commonwealth. For the written Laws which are made either by the Edicts of Princes, or by Councils of Estates, are imposed upon the subject before any Triall or Probation made, whether the same be fit and agreeable to the nature and disposition of the people, or whether they will breed any inconvenience or no. . . . [On the other hand, the English had] made their own laws out of their wisdome and experience (like a silk-worm that formeth all her web out of her self onely), not begging or borrowing a form of a commonweal, either from Rome or from Greece, as all other Nations of Europe have done. . . .[14]

Furthermore, the most basic principle of law—that it is supreme and all must obey it—was taken more seriously in England than elsewhere in Europe. Henry Bracton, a judge at the time of Henry III who wrote the most important legal treatise of the Middle Ages, asserted that "the king must not be subject to any man, but to God and the law; for the law makes him king. Let the king therefore give to the law what the law gives to him, dominion and power; for there is no king where will, and not law, bears rule." Not only were God and the law superior to the king, he said, but so too were his council of earls and barons. For "if the king were without a bridle, that is, the law, they ought to put a bridle upon him."[15]

THE COMMON LAW

The key feature of English law in its formative period in the twelfth and thirteenth centuries is that it was made by judges, not by legislatures, philosophers or kings. The English common law—the phrase implies general or nationwide law, common to the whole country—was made from the ground up, unlike statute law. It was the outcome of masses of judicial decisions that determined the rights of persons who had brought particular actions before the courts. Outside the realm of criminal law, the most important area, as in Rome, was the adjudication of property disputes. Judges had maneuvering room to recognize novel features of each case, thereby allowing the law to adapt to differing circumstances, but normally were expected to subordinate their own will to precedent; they followed the same rule that had been adopted in similar cases in the past.

A body of rules built by slow accretion allows wisdom and knowledge to accumulate. The costs and pitfalls of alternative rulings made in earlier generations are likely to be forgotten with time. This is the main argument for conserving whatever has lasted for a long time: the costs of making changes are not likely to be understood at some remove. Accepting that precedents existed for good reasons, even though those reasons may no longer be understood in detail, introduced a measure of judicial humility into the law (often since construed as blind deference). The law was discovered gradually, not invented suddenly.

The task of the judge was to find out what the law was, and to do so independently of the will of the king. Still, there was no "independent judiciary," we may be surprised to learn. Judges were expected to be apolitical, but in the thirteenth century and for centuries thereafter they held office at the king's pleasure. There appears also to have been some competition of jurisdiction. If willing to pay the fees, suitors could bring their cases to the king's Courts of Common Pleas. As judges were paid out of these fees, they had a financial interest in attracting legal business away from the older manorial courts. This perhaps gave them an incentive to strive for a more perfect justice.[16]

It is sometimes said that the substance of justice emerged from the evolved procedure—from the process "due." Under the influence of Christianity, trial by jury replaced trial by combat. Suitors could contest their right to their freeholds without exposing themselves to the hazards of battle. Just as all were equal in the eyes of God, so it began to be recognized that all should be equal before the law. The courts, in which suitors appeared personally and pleaded their cause, made it easier to appreciate this important truth.

Rights were protected in practice, not proclaimed on parchment. Theories of rights were subordinated to real remedies. Common law judges "fixed their minds far more intently on providing remedies for . . . averting definite wrongs, than upon any declaration of the Rights of Man," A. V. Dicey remarked.[17] It was understood that prolonged tenure gave a prescriptive right to ownership. (Roman law had accepted the same principle.) By the fifteenth century, common-law judges were securing the rights of "villeins" if their tenancy was to be found copied into court rolls. The "copy" served as the early equivalent of a title deed; and those so listed were called "copyholders." By the early seventeenth century, about one-third of all land in England was held in copyhold tenure. Gradually it became inheritable, and copyhold became freehold.

Evolving judicial rules might later be enshrined in statutes, or they might remain unwritten. General legislation was thought of as a formal restatement of law already discovered. Its advantage was one of abridgment, summarizing earlier judicial findings. As late as the seventeenth century, it could still be questioned in England whether Parliament could pass laws inconsistent with the common law.

"It appears in our books, that in many cases the common law will controul Acts of Parliament, and sometimes adjudge them to be utterly void," Sir Edward Coke wrote in the seventeenth century. "For when an act of Parliament is against common right and reason, or repugnant, or impossible to be performed, the common law will controul it, and adjudge such Act to be void."[18]

The feature of law that is most conducive to the modern market system is equality before the law. It was inherent in what Bracton said about the king's relation to the law: He was expected to obey it. Just as we are all equally subject to physical law, so we should all ideally be subject to the same human law. This requirement gives a restrained character to law, for if lawmakers must obey what they impose on others, the law cannot easily have a dictatorial character. Where equality before the law is a reality, the security of property will not be far behind. It will emerge in the interstices of this "golden rule." For if what one person can do to another is limited to what can be done to him, the security and privacy of all will be respected and transactions will be by consent. But if one can coerce another by virtue of his superior "station" or office, then the pursuit of compromise and agreement will probably be dispensed with in favor of force.

Historically, the most important obstacle to the establishment of such a rule of law has been the division of people into legally separate classes. From an early time, however, such distinctions were not as marked in England as elsewhere. By the thirteenth century, free men were the norm, privilege and disability exceptional. Serfdom, an inherited status, admittedly curtailed liberty. Criminal law protected serfs in life and limb, but not in liberty or security of possession. Serfdom was not the same as slavery, however. It was a relationship between serf and his lord only; in relation to all others the serf enjoyed the rights of liberty. "When compared with the contemporary law of France or at any rate of Germany," Pollock and Maitland wrote in *The History of English Law,* "our law of status is poor: in other words, it has little to say about estates or ranks of men."[19] All free men, including the nobility, were in the main equal before the law. Pollock and Maitland commented on this point:

> A conquered country is hardly the place in which we should look for an equality, which, having regard to other lands, we must call exceptional. Yet in truth it is the result of the Conquest, though a result that was slowly evolved. The compiler of the Leges Henrici [an early book of English law] would willingly have given us a full law of ranks or estates of men; but the materials at his command were too heterogeneous: counts, barons, earls, thegns, Norman milites, English radknights, vidames, vavassors, sokemen, villeins . . . a text writer can do little with this disorderly mass.
>
> But a strong king can do with it what he pleases; he can make his favor the measure of nobility; they are noble whom he treats as such. And he does not choose that there shall be much nobility. Gradually a small noble class is formed, an estate of temporal lords, of earls and barons. The principles that hold it together are far rather land tenure and the king's will than the transmission of noble blood. Its members have political privileges which are the counterpart of political duties; the king consults them, and they are bound to attend his summons and give him counsel. They have hardly any other privileges. During the baron's life his children have no privileges; on his death only the new baron becomes noble.[20]

Hallam noted the same thing, calling it "a prominent and characteristic distinction between the constitution of England and that of every other country in Europe." Wherever else you looked—France, Spain, Germany—the nobility formed a hereditary class distinguished from ordinary freemen by legal privilege. The French ranged their people under three divisions, noble, free and servile; the British have "no generic class, but freedom and villenage." The purchase of land held by knight-service had always been open to all freemen. There was a virtual equality of rights among all the commoners of England. Hallam added this remarkable comment:

> There is no part, perhaps, of our constitution so admirable as this equality of civil rights; this *isonomia,* which the philosophers of ancient Greece only hoped to find in democratical government. From the beginning, our law has been no respecter of persons. It screens not the gentleman of ancient lineage from the judgment of an ordinary jury, nor from ignominious punishment. It confers not, it never did confer, those unjust immunities from public burdens, which the superior orders arrogated to themselves upon the continent. . . . It is, I am firmly persuaded, to this peculiarly democratical character of the English monarchy, that we are indebted for its long permanence, its regular improvement, and its present vigor. It is a singular, a providential circumstance, that, in an age when the gradual march of civilization and commerce was so little foreseen, our ancestors, deviating from the usages of neighboring countries, should, as if deliberately, have guarded against that expansive force which, in bursting through obstacles improvidently opposed, has scattered havoc over Europe.[21]

Maitland and Hallam surely identified here the element of law that stimulated England's commercial lead and economic primacy, even though no one was thinking in such "economic" terms when the key principle gained strength. Equality before the law was the prerequisite for an exchange economy. We may summarize centuries of legal change by saying that the great transformation that had taken place since the demise of the Roman Empire was not that the law of property had changed so much, but that the law of persons had changed a great deal.

The triumph of the common law, and with it a polity in which the rights of Englishmen were respected, has been considered by some commentators to be a virtue of centralization. Maitland always saw things this way. The king was "consolidating his realm," "making himself the one fountain of justice," in contrast to the feuding, feudal princes of France and Germany, where authority was decentralized to the point of chaos.[22] In England, the king had enough power to assert without challenge that his judges would determine the law and that none would interfere with them.

The theory may be true, but it makes one uneasy all the same. It embodies the paradox that the centralization of power is needed to achieve its decentralization. The truth is that allowing people to make their own decisions with respect to property, and allowing them to exchange it by consent, is the epitome of decentralization. Concentrating power in one place is not normally a prelude to such enlightenment.

We should bear in mind that Maitland (1850-1906), and the succeeding generation of scholars who relied heavily on his work, wrote at a time when centralism was admired across the board. J. E. A. Jolliffe, the author of a constitutional history of England published in 1928, saw the Norman kings as laboring under this disadvantage: "The primitive conception of a society living within the frame of an inherited law had deprived the king of the quality of lawmaker." He was reduced merely to "recognition of custom, and participation in adjustment of rights and procedure by way of assize."[23] The great merit of English law he construed as its disability. Maitland did see the danger: judges serving at the king's mercy could have become "an apt instrument of despotic rule."[24] But the common law was saved by its own complexity, he ingeniously argued. "The strongest king, the ablest minister, the rudest Lord Protector could make little of this 'ungodly jumble.'"[25]

Probably, the centralization of power was not as great as most have assumed. The Normans were invaders and outsiders who for some time did not speak the local language, and who wisely concluded that the cause of national contentment was served by tolerating local customs. We know that at the time of King John (1215), a period in England's legal history when many important changes were occurring, a weakened king was forced by the barons to accept a charter of liberties that specifically limited the royal power. The charter was retrospective in mood, demanding that former liberties be restored. It was restated and reconfirmed several times during the reign of Henry III.

Hallam ascribed England's "tendency to civil equality" to a particular cause. On the Continent, he wrote, it was not so much "for the ends of national as of private warfare that the relation of vassal and lord was contrived." Because the French barons could wage war on their rivals, they were thrown into a military relationship with their tenants, who might be transformed into a private army, either defensive or offensive, on a moment's notice. "But we read very little of private wars in England."[26]

Where such did arise, as between the earls of Gloucester and Hereford in the reign of Edward I, those responsible were punished. Soon, in England, the military service expected in exchange for tenure was replaced by payment in cash. The result was that British armies were composed of hired troops. They served for pay, and so they "preserved nothing of the feudal character." In short, you could buy your way out of the "draft," and eventually the king would have to buy you into it.

A possible explanation for England's distinctive condition, then, is that her status as an island both isolated the country from the ruinous wars and feuds that swept across Europe, and encouraged the English to see each other as allies with common enemies abroad. By the same token, they saw one another as equal in their rights. Central rule could be relaxed without running the risk that the country would break up into feuding rivalries.

RELIGION AND PROPERTY

By the seventeenth century, the richest country in the world on a per capita basis appears to have been Holland. Gregory King, sometimes called the father of national income studies, set out in 1696 to estimate the relative strength of the French, English and Dutch economies, and found the Dutch income per capita to be about 15 percent higher than England's and almost double that of France.[27] Holland also enjoyed the greatest level of religious toleration, and there was an important connection between this and its level of prosperity.

The fruitful condition of equality before the law has often been undermined by the uniting of state power and religious belief. Then the temptations of power become irresistible. Force will probably be applied to achieve moral ends appropriately left to persuasion. If so, and private actions and agreements are subjected to public scrutiny and punishment, property will be undone.

Having converted the emperor Constantine, Christians frequently relied on force rather than persuasion to win converts. Alliance with state power has been the great temptation of religious authorities ever since. It is a grave defect of the Islamic world today. The attempt to make virtue compulsory not only provoked destruction in the material realm, but had a corrupting effect in the spiritual. Great waves of anticlericalism arose in reaction. Clergymen became tax collectors, and excommunicated those not "in compliance." Church law regulated economic life. "Unjust" prices and interest-bearing loans were forbidden. Under the clerical supervision of wills, church property grew to encompass one-third of the land in Germany, one-fifth in England. Only with difficulty could such land be sold, and much of it was effectively withdrawn from commerce. The revenues of the papal see exceeded those of the secular states of Europe combined.

Karl Marx was among the first to suggest a key role for the Reformation in the emergence of capitalism. Referring to "the 'spirit' of Protestantism," he wrote: "The process of forcible expropriation of the people received in the sixteenth century a new and frightful impulse from the Reformation, and from the consequent colossal spoliation of the church property." He looked back longingly to the feudal period. Then Max Weber argued, in *The Protestant Ethic and the Spirit of Capitalism,* that Calvinism had played a crucial role. The thesis was much criticized and is no doubt wrong.[28] But Protestantism did provoke a rethinking of the relations between church and state.

Religious toleration came to Holland before any other country: John Locke took refuge there for a few years in the 1680s and, while he was there, wrote his *Letter Concerning Toleration.* It may have been as important to the security of property as his famous chapter in the *Second Treatise on Government* (which was possibly also written in Holland). In his *Letter,* Locke sensibly argued that coerced credos, "far from being any furtherance, are indeed great obstacles to our salvation." It could hardly advance moral well-being to lie about one's faith in order to retain one's possessions.

In vain, Locke wrote, "do princes compel their subjects to come into their Church communion, under pretense of saving their souls. If they believe, they will come of their own accord; if they believe not, their coming will nothing avail them." Ecclesiastical laws must be "destitute of all compulsive power." By the same token, the civil magistrate's power should be restricted. It cannot impose rites and ceremonies on any church, nor forbid the preaching of "speculative opinions"; for these do not bear on the "civil rights of the subjects." In short, the separation of church and state—distinguishing "the business of civil government from that of religion," and settling "the just bounds that lie between the one and the other"—led straight to a doctrine of limited government. In restricting compulsion, it enlarged liberty. In the *Letter,* Locke defined our civil interests as: "Life, liberty, health and indolency of body; and the possession of outward things, such as money, lands, houses, furniture and the like."[29]

The emergence of free markets was in many respects synonymous with the deregulation of the medieval world, in particular the emergence of such institutions as contract, in which the state enforced agreements to exchange property on terms that were agreeable to both parties. This was more likely to happen in countries where the secular power saw moral salvation as something that was beyond its responsibility. Just as it is possible that in Rome the multiplication of deities contributed to the "sanctity" of property, so in Europe the fragmentation of doctrine contributed to the rise of individualism and the deregulation of life. Something about the Christian teaching was essential to the emergence of the market order; in particular, belief in the underlying equality of human nature. But in permitting individuals to be the best judges of their own bargains, it was necessary also to allow them to be the best judges of their own salvation.

Under the Stuarts, property in England came under philosophical attack. Sir Robert Filmer (1590-1653) argued in *Patriarcha* that all English law, including the common law, owed its existence to the royal will, and that the king himself ruled by divine right. Subjects were therefore under an obligation to submit to his will. The royal succession had been passed down from Adam to the Stuart monarchs, and the property went with the territory. Kings had exclusive control over everything and could distribute it to whomsoever they pleased. For that reason, there was no general right to property. Omitting God from the argument, advocates of absolute power in the twentieth century would have agreed in substance.

One reply to Filmer was written by James Tyrrell in 1681, a second by Tyrrell's old friend from university days, John Locke. The publication of Locke's *Two Treatises of Government* was nonetheless delayed for a decade. In the interim, he spent five years in Holland as a political refugee. His patron, the earl of Shaftesbury, who helped found the Whig party and had organized opposition to Charles II, had already fled to Holland and died there. Locke returned to England shortly after the Glorious Revolution of 1688, and all of his major works were published there in 1689.

In the first treatise, Locke argued that since everybody is descended from Adam, no man's title to rule another could be based on such ancestry. In the second, he argued that the origin of civil society lay in a social contract, not divine right. The consent of the people was the sole basis of state authority. At the end of the work, in euphemistic phrases, he justified rebellion. For if rulers attempt to "take away and destroy the property of the people, or to reduce them to slavery under arbitrary power," the people in turn are "absolved from any further obedience, and are left to the common refuge, which God hath provided for all men, against force and violence."[30]

More famously, he justified private property. Filmer had pointed to a defect of contract theory: If God gave the goods of the world to all in common, then the movement from original communism to private property surely required that everyone in the past had consented to each act of privatization, which was absurd. Divine right encountered no such difficulty. Locke's solution was to individualize the original right to property, locating it in labor. For every man, he argued, "the labour of his body, and the work of his hands, we may say, are properly his. Whatsoever then he removes out of the State that Nature hath provided, and left it in, he hath mixed his labour with, and joyned it to something that is his own, and thereby makes it his Property." He added that "'tis labour indeed that puts the difference of value on every thing."[31] James Tyrrell had made a very similar argument.

Locke's work was published anonymously, the author denying to all comers that he had written it. "He destroyed all his workings for the book and erased from his papers every recognizable reference to its existence, its composition, its publication, printing and reprinting," Peter Laslett has written.[32] In Locke's library, the book was catalogued as anonymous, "so that even a casual browser should find nothing to compromise the secret." Even with Queen Anne on the throne, and the royal power circumscribed by a Bill of Rights, Locke kept his own relatives in the dark. "Property I have nowhere found more clearly explained than in a book entitled *Two Treatises of Government,*" he wrote to a cousin.

It is said that "the propertied classes trembled for their property under the Stuarts."[33] By the eighteenth century, however, Locke's discussion probably added little to the security of property that by then prevailed in England, although it was highly influential in prerevolutionary America. Already securely upheld by law in England, property was less in need of philosophical support then than it is today—as the numerous modern attacks on Locke suggest. But his work was a hazardous enterprise when undertaken. He must be one of the few modern philosophers to have written some of the time in invisible ink. Habeas corpus was enacted in 1679, but his dining-hall conversation at Oxford was monitored by lip readers from London.

INDUSTRIAL REVOLUTION

In *The Wealth of Nations,* Adam Smith noted a tremendous change that had taken place by the eighteenth century: "In the present state of Europe, the proprietor of a single acre of land is as perfectly secure of his possession as the proprietor of a hundred thousand." We so much take it for granted today that our rights are independent of our wealth that some effort is required to see what a great development this was. But in England there had been a further advance that had not occurred in other parts of Europe: "The security of the tenant is equal to that of the proprietor." In other countries, tenant farmers could "before the expiration of their term be legally outed of their lease."[34] In England, the tenant enjoyed legal security. He could sue, recover damages and possession, and, if dissatisfied, appeal the "uncertain decision of a single assize." A lease of 40 shillings a year was considered a freehold, giving the tenant a vote. This even applied to those with no written lease. "There is, I believe, nowhere in Europe, except England, any instance of the tenant building upon the land of which he had no lease," Smith added, "and trusting that the honour of his landlord would take no advantage of so important an improvement. Those laws and customs, so favourable to the yeomanry, have perhaps contributed more to the present grandeur of England than all their boasted regulations of commerce taken together."

So England increased in prosperity, and pulled ahead of its Continental rivals. Holland, an "enterprise zone" within highly regulated seventeenth-century Europe, lost its advantage in the eighteenth. Its prosperity was undermined by high taxation. The Dutch ruling class believed that they could not afford to reduce that burden because they had an empire to run; they failed to grasp the long-run effects of competition from ports that were more free. English travelers commented on the situation. John Ray, a pioneering botanist, wrote that in Holland "all manner of victuals both meat and drink are very dear, not for the scarcity of such commodities, but partly by reason of the Great Excise and Impost wherewith they are charged." Gregory King estimated that the average Dutchmen paid nearly three times as much in taxes as the average Englishman.[35]

The efficiency of British agriculture, and of the economy in general, was further enhanced by the large number of land enclosures in the latter half of the eighteenth century—Parliament approved some 3,000 Enclosure Acts between 1760 and 1815 alone. Enclosure was a systematic privatization in which open fields and common areas were fenced and divided among those who had enjoyed either communal or private rights to them. Problems of free riding and of "externalities" were much reduced. Animals that had been grazed on common fields often transmitted diseases to one another, for example. "The advantages of enclosed and compact farms under one man's sole control, over the dispersed and fragmented holdings in common fields were widely appreciated," the economic historian G. E. Mingay has written. The object was sometimes "to get rid of the last rump of the open fields and commons, or to confirm an enclosure carried out previously among owners, or to complete the exploitation of the waste and tidy up and inconvenient and confused accumulation of small closes. . . . [It resulted in] a rapid conversion to the conditions necessary for more efficient farming."[36]

In the more familiar view, enclosure was simple robbery—"decrees by which the landlords grant themselves the people's land as private property," as Marx put it.[37] Again, we encounter his vast influence. His interpretation, in which power wore the cynical mask of law, was accepted by J. L. and Barbara Hammond in *The Village Labourer, 1760-1832* (1911). The whole process of enclosure was rigged against the small farmer, they argued. Later research has not borne this out. Mingay in particular showed there is no real evidence that smallholders declined in the eighteenth and nineteenth centuries, as had been assumed. Nor were their rights ignored. The very fact that separate acts of Parliament were required to make these changes showed the extent to which the common law at the time respected the rights of smallholders.

In his *Rise and Fall of the Freedom of Contract,* Patrick Atiyah of Oxford adds: "What was significant about the Enclosure Acts was not that so many of them were readily passed by a property-owning Parliament, but that in general a meticulous respect for fair compensation and due process was in fact observed. The Enclosure Acts did not provide for simple confiscation of the rights of common of which the poor were generally deprived. Whatever the Enclosure Acts may demonstrate about the attitudes of the propertied classes to the rights of the poor, they certainly did not demonstrate any lack of respect for rights of property."[38]

Here, indeed, was a moment in English history when the law was changed in response to the promptings of efficiency. Communal rights are ill-defined. Enclosure therefore "economized" agriculture. Enclosure also increased the incentive to invest in new farming methods, for the returns would go to those who made the investments. Expenditures on draining and experiments in crop varieties and animal breeding greatly increased. They added up to an Agricultural Revolution that was not entirely separate from the Industrial Revolution as more generally understood.

A. V. Dicey notes that when Voltaire came to England, he felt "that he had passed out of the realm of despotism to a land where the laws might be harsh but where men were ruled by law and not by caprice."[39] The evidence would seem to be overwhelming that the Industrial Revolution came to England first because the rule of law came there first, and in "democratizing" the security of property the laws of England stimulated the creation of wealth. These laws assured entrepreneurs and inventors that their long-range plans would be allowed to come to fruition and that they would enjoy the fruits of their own labors. Laws permitting the patenting of intellectual property were valuable, but less important than the stimulus provided by the security of real and personal property more generally.

The Wealth of Nations criticized unproductive regulations of trade and commerce—corporation laws obstructed the mobility of "artificers and manufacturers," and poor laws did the same for laborers—but Smith recognized Britain's crucial advantage. In his famous discussion of mercantilism, he noted that "the improvement and prosperity of Great Britain, which has been so often ascribed to those [mercantilist] laws, may very easily be accounted for by other causes." Above all, he thought, "that security which the laws in Great Britain give to every man that he shall enjoy the fruits of his own labour, is alone sufficient to make any country flourish, notwithstanding these and twenty other absurd regulations of commerce; and this security was perfected by the revolution [of 1688] much about the same time that the bounty [on exports] was established. . . . In Great Britain industry is perfectly secure, and though it is far from being perfectly free, it is as free or freer than in any other part of Europe."[40]

Spain and Portugal were cases in point. Not only had they participated in the "mercantile system" that marred European trade policy in the seventeenth and eighteenth centuries, but Spain's mercantilism was not "counterbalanced by the general liberty and security of the people. Industry is there neither free nor secure, and the civil and ecclesiastical governments of both Spain and Portugal are such as would alone be sufficient to perpetuate their present state of poverty."[41]

Most counterproductive regulations in Britain were either repealed or allowed to wither away; the Parliament took a confined view of its role. William Pitt the Elder argued in the House of Commons in 1766 that "there are many things a parliament cannot do. It cannot make itself executive, nor dispose of offices which belong to the crown. It cannot take any man's property, even that of the meanest cottager, as in the case of enclosure, without his [case] being heard." He is not believed to have carried a single legislative measure through Parliament. David S. Landes marveled that Britain had "succeeded in effecting the Industrial Revolution without resort to the joint-stock company."[42] The creation of such companies with transferable shares required an act of Parliament, rarely approved in the case of manufacturing and trading companies.

It is fair to say that laissez faire replaced a philosophy in which it was thought to be the duty of the state to watch over the individual citizen in all his relations. The government continued to protect against force and fraud, but this was the age when competing owners in the marketplace were found to generate their own disciplinary forces. Even state finances were subject to them. The cost of government debt was much lower when interest was promptly and reliably paid. The interest rate for such debt fell from 14 percent in the 1690s to less than 4 percent in the 1750s. Arnold Toynbee, uncle of the more famous author of *A Study of History*, delivered a series of lectures on the Industrial Revolution in 1880, and was the first historian to conceive of his subject as a single great historical event. (Marx had used the phrase "industrial revolution," but not as referring to a particular development in England.) Its essence, Toynbee wrote, was "the substitution of competition for the medieval regulations which had previously controlled the production and distribution of wealth."[43]

This view became unfashionable. But it was surely more accurate than the one that came to prevail in the twentieth century, when the faith in centralization made it difficult to imagine that mere nonintervention could have played any role. Phyllis Deane wrote in 1965 that it had become "usual" to regard the Industrial Revolution as a "spontaneous event." No government could have managed "consciously to contrive" the complex industrialization that unfolded. At least in part, she agreed with Toynbee: "There is no question at all that between 1760 and 1850 a mass of government rules and restrictions on economic activity, many of them dating from medieval times, were swept out of the statute book."[44]

Meanwhile, overlooking the circularity of their arguments, economists attempted to use economic data to explain England's economic development. Effects—wages, prices, coal production, savings, capital—were tried out as causes. But nothing definitive emerged from these manipulations. One set of numbers could not very satisfactorily account for another. Mathematics could not be substituted for the neglected effect of law.

The economic historian who has most effectively drawn attention to the neglect of law in understanding the Industrial Revolution is Max Hartwell. Among modern authorities, he has pointed out, there is "skepticism that law played any significant role in the 18th century in the making of the industrial revolution." He added: "Nowhere in the vast literature of the English industrial revolution by economic historians is there a comprehensive study of the relationship between law and economy, and nowhere adequate recognition of the importance of the legal framework for economic change." The oversight that he specified (in 1971) seems remarkable:

> No historian has detailed the steps by which, for example, the market economy was achieved in terms of government action or changing law; no historian has . . . [traced] the chronology both of legal and economic change. In this neglect, surely, a major element for the understanding of the industrial revolution has been overlooked. It is my thesis that perhaps the most distinctive and unique national characteristic that distinguished England from Continental countries in the eighteenth century, in the century also of England's unique lead in industrialization, was English law.[45]

As the Industrial Revolution began to unfold, few at first realized what was happening. Adam Smith himself showed little awareness of the changes that were taking place, even though James Watt, the inventor of the steam engine, worked as an instrument maker at the University of Glasgow. Adam Smith taught moral philosophy there, and soon he began to take an interest in the "laws" of political economy.

FROM SACRED
TO PROFANE

INTRODUCTION

IT WAS PROBABLY A COINCIDENCE that the most influential treatise on economics was written at a time when private property was at the peak of its prestige. In any event, Adam Smith did not think it necessary to say much about the subject. He did refer to the "sacred rights of private property," however, and his contemporaries made similar comments. In the public prints, private property was considered to be above criticism. In a treatise on economics, therefore, it was perhaps superfluous to insist that the institutions already secured by the common law were the necessary foundations of economic analysis. No one disagreed. If there were dissenters on the merits of private property, they for the most part kept their thoughts to themselves—at least until William Godwin arrived on the scene.

All this had changed by the middle of the nineteenth century. Private property abruptly came under grave suspicion. The theory of the communists was that it should be abolished entirely. Meanwhile, Adam Smith had established an influential precedent, and by the time property was openly attacked, economists had written little in its defense. As far as the English-speaking economists were concerned, it is not too much to say that property was attacked before it was properly defended. Its transition from "sacred" to "profane" was so rapid that there was scarcely time for an intermediate stage of analysis.

By the end of the nineteenth century, there seems to have been a tacit agreement among economists to drop the subject entirely. Human nature was believed to be changing, and by the time it had undergone sufficient transformation, the institution of property wouldn't be needed anyway. It was thought to be old fashioned, destined to be swept away by the modern world. "We had learned the idea of evolution and never-ceasing change as a condition of life," wrote Richard T. Ely, the first president and cofounder of the American Economic Association.

SEVEN

THE ECONOMISTS' OVERSIGHT

IN THE GREAT BRITAIN OF ADAM SMITH'S DAY, criticism of property hardly ever found its way into print. Thomas Spence, a schoolmaster in Newcastle-upon-Tyne, was a rare exception. In a lecture to the Philosophical Society, he argued that the land of a community belongs "in an equal manner" to all those who live there. When he published it as a pamphlet, he was expelled from the society. Socialists in the nineteenth century advertised this minor event, showing how unusual such criticism was at the time. Another critic who received later recognition was William Ogilvie, a student at Glasgow when Adam Smith taught there. His *Essay on the Right of Property in Land* (1782) argued that all citizens, not just a few owners, had a right to the unimproved value of the land. But he kept his name off the title page, and his identity long remained a secret. "The sanctity of property" was not just an idle phrase at the time.[1]

Dr. Johnson argued that the danger of erroneous instruction on some issues—property in particular—was so great that people shouldn't necessarily be allowed to impart their beliefs to their own children. The community of goods is defended by "as many plausible arguments as for most erroneous doctrines," he said. "You teach them that all things at first were in common, and that no man has a right to anything but as he laid his hands upon it; and that this still is, or ought to be, the rule among mankind. Here, Sir, you sap a great principle in society—property. And you don't think the magistrate would have a right to prevent you?"[2]

Criticism of property had been published before Adam Smith, but one must hunt for it, and it made less impression than modern reprints might suggest. Sir Thomas More's *Utopia,* a harbinger of communist thought, described a supposedly ideal society in which all of life is regulated by the state, the economy is based on conscripted labor, and "there is no private property."[3] But it was thought to belong more to the realm of fancy than to political theory. The Diggers, early communists led by Gerrard Winstanley, disseminated antiproperty tracts in the seventeenth century, but by Smith's day hardly anyone knew about them. Their importance has been magnified by latter-day socialists.

Some believe that the modern attack on property was launched by Jean-Jacques Rousseau, whose *Discourse on the Origin of Inequality,* published in 1755, contained the famous passage: "The first person who, having enclosed a plot of land, took it into his head to say *this is mine* and found people simple enough to believe him, was the true founder of civil society. What crimes, wars, murders, what miseries and horrors would the human race have been spared, had someone pulled up the stakes or filled in the ditch and cried out to his fellow men: 'Do not listen to this impostor. You are lost if you forget that the fruits of the earth belong to all and the earth to no one!'"[4]

This "fed the fervor of revolutionaries and socialists for a century," Peter Gay wrote.[5] But Rousseau's political influence among his contemporaries may have been exaggerated. Cetainly it did not compare with his influence in the twentieth century academy. There is even a question whether his ideas contributed as much as has been supposed to the French Revolution. Rousseau did live in fashionable exile in England for over a year in the 1760s, but he was known mainly for his daring novels, his writings on music, and his theories on education. In his Armenian caftan and his state-of-nature fur hat, he was received in London more as celebrity than *philosophe;* perhaps an early exemplar of radical chic.[6]

Adam Smith read Rousseau's *Second Discourse,* and he discussed it in the *Edinburgh Review.* But Rousseau's views made little impression on Smith, who politely dismissed the savant of Geneva. "By the help of his style, together with a little philosophical chemistry," he had made "the profligate Mandeville seem to have all the purity and morals of Plato."* Smith agreed with David Hume that "Rousseau is as great a rascal as you and every man here [in Paris] believe him to be."[7]

---

*Bernard Mandeville argued in *The Fable of the Bees* (1723) that such "private vices" as acquisitiveness were public virtues: the demand for luxury goods spurred production and therefore increased prosperity. He disparaged saving. If frugality became widespread, employment would decline. John Maynard Keynes saw an early version of the "paradox of thrift" in Mandeville's doctrine, and much admired his "wicked sentiments." Adam Smith, on the other hand, wrote that "what is prudence in the conduct of every private family can scarce be folly in that of a great Kingdom." Bernard Mandeville, *The Fable of the Bees* (1723, 1732; reprint, 2 vols., Oxford: Clarendon Press, 1924); John Maynard Keynes, *The General Theory of Employment Interest and Money* (London: Macmillan, 1936), 359-61; Adam Smith, *The Wealth of Nations* (Oxford: Oxford Univ. Press, 1976), 457.

Although the classical economists neglected property, this did not imply indifference to it. In their general outlook, and in their more philosophical writings, Smith, Malthus, Ricardo and others were all strong advocates of the institution. In his *Lectures on Jurisprudence,* delivered in Glasgow in the 1760s, Smith began with property. The first lecture of his first series (not published until 1978) began: "The first and chief design of every system of government is to maintain justice: to prevent the members of society from incroaching on one another's property, or seizing what is not their own. The design here is to give each one the secure and peacable possession of his own property."[8]

In *The Wealth of Nations,* however, Smith gave pride of place—the first three chapters—to the division of labor. Evidently a visit to a pin-making factory had inspired him.[9] Ten men could make 48,000 pins a day, but one could hardly manufacture a single pin. This was an unsatisfactory starting point for a treatise on economics, however, for different tasks must be performed in the production of any good at all. The only alternative is work without cooperation: Robinson Crusoe conditions. But collaboration can involve very different institutional arrangements: Members of a family working at home; separate companies contracting with one another; different divisions of the same company; workers in a socialist enterprise. As a principle of organization, "division of labor" does not help us choose between them. The economist George Stigler said in 1976 that this idea, so much associated with Smith, was one of his "regrettable" failures. "There has been scarcely any systematic or regular use of this concept in economic analysis," he wrote.[10]

A treatise on economics might logically begin with observations about the creation of value and the facilitation of exchange, economics being a study of choice, primarily expressed in such exchanges. This would lead directly to the security and transferability of property as a precondition of such choices. But there is very little that is directly about property in *The Wealth of Nations.* The few paragraphs on the subject are extraneous to Smith's main argument.

In France, the physiocrat A. R. Turgot, friend and precursor of Smith, wrote an "analysis of the working of society and the distribution of wealth" for the benefit of two Chinese students visiting Paris. Published as *Reflections on the Formation and Distribution of Wealth* (1766), it began with a section explaining "the impossibility of commerce" given an "equal division of lands." Everyone would have only what was needed for his own support, and "no one would be willing to work for others." Turgot seemed to visualize economic activity as a current which could not circulate if there was no "potential difference" of energy to drive it, an image that recurs in economic thought. In any event, he added, there never has been such an equal division and if there were, it could not be sustained. That more or less exhausted his discussion of property.[11]

One early French economist did recognize the crucial role of property, however, and that was Jean-Baptiste Say. His *Treatise on Political Economy,* first published in 1803, included a short chapter on "the right of property." He reminded readers that government, although intended as the great protector of property, can also be its great despoiler. He also drew the distinction, found later in Malthus, between political economy—as economics was then still called— and politics itself.

Jean-Baptiste Say observed that devising the means to protect property lay within the province of politics, and tracing the origin of that right was a task for "speculative philosophy." Economics, or political economy, simply "recognizes the right of property solely as the most powerful of all encouragements to the multiplication of wealth, and is satisfied with its actual stability, without inquiring about its origins or its safeguards." This was perhaps the first explicit demarcation of these respective fields of inquiry, and a sophisticated one.

Say added the important point that the theoretical inviolability of property becomes a mockery when the "sovereign power," or government, "either practices robbery itself, or is impotent to repress it in others, or where possession is rendered perpetually insecure, by the intricacy of legislative enactments." In short, property must be secure in fact, not just in political theory. "Then and only then," he said, "can the sources of production, namely land, capital and industry [labor], attain their utmost degree of fecundity." He regarded the need for security of property as a truth "so completely self-evident, that demonstration is quite superfluous."[12]

Comparable warnings about the antecedent need for private property, securely held, are not to be found in the English or Scottish treatises, however. In his *Inquiry into the Principles of Political Oeconomy* (1767), Sir James Steuart discussed property only in relation to the payment of debts. He correctly noted that in recent centuries great changes in the "affairs of Europe" had altered "the plan of government," as he put it. "From feudal and military, it is become free and commercial." For this reason, he saw government as a routinely benign institution. Too optimistically, he noted in his first chapter that he had "taken for granted the fundamental maxim, that every operation of government should be calculated for the good of the people."[13]

No doubt it was the experience of the French Revolution that made all the difference for Say. In Britain, the much greater security of property disposed its economists to take that blessing for granted. It still seems remarkable, nonetheless, that the early economists did not specify the political and legal institutions that must be in place if their principles were to work in practice. They assumed a political and legal framework comparable to that found in eighteenth-century Britain, but they neither insisted on the point, nor did they spell it out in detail.

Say's distinction between the domains of political economy and "politics" was repeated by Thomas Robert Malthus in 1820. At the beginning of book 2 of his *Principles of Political Economy,* he stipulated that property belonged to the province of "politics." Its security, he said, is among "the most important causes which influence the wealth of nations." But this depends "upon the political constitution of a country, the excellence of its laws and the manner in which they are administered." It was not his intention "to enter fully into these causes." He would concentrate instead on the "more immediate and proximate causes of increasing wealth."[14]

Ever since, economists have followed Malthus's example, treating the form and security of property as "political" questions less relevant to their field than the "more immediate and proximate causes": labor, capital, "land." In 1805, Malthus was appointed professor of modern history and political economy at the East India College, and is sometimes reckoned as the first professional economist. The precedent set by Smith and Malthus was highly influential, and since then economists have been disposed to take for granted the institutional background of their subject.

Smith did elaborate on the security of property in book 5, using it as an argument for stronger government rather than a caution against it. Only under the protection of the magistrate can the owner of valuable property "sleep a single night in security," he wrote. He is surrounded by enemies, and only the "powerful arm of the civil magistrate" can protect him and his possessions. Smith's abiding tendency was to see weak government as the great danger to society.[15]

In his day, of course, government's role was modest, compared with today's behemoth state. The important lesson that we have learned over the last 200 years is that the political state of affairs that existed in the English-speaking world in the late eighteenth century, far from being the rule and therefore something that could reasonably be assumed, is more likely to be the exception. It has proved much more difficult to replicate than earlier (and more recent) thinkers imagined.

David Ricardo, who died in 1823, hardly mentioned the role of property in the entire body of his work. In his *Principles of Political Economy and Taxation* (1817), he did refer to the "security of property" as a principle "which should ever be held sacred." He encouraged the easy "conveyance and exchange of all kinds of property," so that it could "find its way into the hands of those who will best employ it in increasing the productions of the country"; an extremely important point. On the rare occasions when he mentioned property, Ricardo did not think it necessary to specify "private."[16]

THE NOBLEST TRIUMPH

The phrase "private property" barely entered the language before the nineteenth century. Adam Ferguson, a friend of Smith's, had some rather confused material on property in his *Essay on the History of Civil Society* (1767), but he does not qualify the noun. (Societies progressed from communal to private property, he thought. Therefore "property is a matter of progress." If people would only make the correct moral effort, they would succeed in "extending" property. By that he meant privatizing.)[17] William Godwin referred at different times to "the prevailing system," the "established system," the "present system," or the system of "accumulated property." The phrase "private property" does occur once or twice in *The Wealth of Nations,* and once in the first edition of Malthus's *Principles of Political Economy.* On the whole, though, it seemed unnecessary to specify more precisely an institution that was not thought to have any workable alternative.

One can make the stronger claim that when Smith wrote his treatise, property stood in higher esteem than it ever had before—or has since. The case of Jeremy Bentham (1748-1832) is worth noting. Although disposed toward sweeping criticism of existing legal and political arrangements, he was filled with an uncharacteristic deference when it came to property. On point after point he took issue with the jurist Sir William Blackstone, whose *Commentaries on the Laws of England* was published in the 1760s. But on property the two saw eye to eye. Blackstone could think of nothing "which so generally engages the affections of mankind, as the right to property," and Bentham agreed. The law that gives security to property is "the noblest triumph of humanity over itself," he wrote.[18]

Bentham was a curious fellow: he detested religion, advocated infanticide, abominated the idea of natural rights ("property and law are born together, and die together,") and had a very modern faith in the molding and curative powers of legislation. If one can engage in anachronistic speculation, it seems likely that he would have been far more suspicious of property, and perhaps its enemy, if he had been born 50 years later. His famous utilitarian maxim was so devoid of content that he could have concluded, with no fear of falsification, that the greatest happiness could be achieved for the greatest number by taking property from the few and distributing it to the many. That's exactly what later utilitarians did say.

But in his heyday, the intellectual tides still ran strongly in property's favor, and he did not try to resist them. When one of his most admired intellectual lights, a penal reformer named Cesare Beccaria ("Oh my master, first evangelist of reason,")[19] criticized property rights, Bentham took up the cudgels. Beccaria's treatise *On Crimes and Punishments* had included a reference to the right to property as "a terrible and perhaps unnecessary right."[20] Bentham retorted that although it had been abused, "it is that right which has vanquished the natural aversion to labour, which has given to man the empire of the earth; which has brought to an end the migratory life of nations; which has produced the love of country and a regard for posterity."[21]

Less than a century later, in his *Principles of Economics,* Alfred Marshall complained that, "daring analyst as he was," Bentham had "fostered in his disciples an almost superstitious reverence for the existing institution of private property."[22] But in the early part of the century it was still considered sacred—even by Bentham. Reverence would turn into irreverence soon enough.

The experience of William Paley, archdeacon of Carlisle and the author of *Evidences of Christianity,* gives us an insight into the regard for property in Adam Smith's day. His *Principles of Moral and Political Philosophy* (1785), later adopted as a textbook at Cambridge, included four short chapters on property.[23] The first is of particular interest. It asked the reader to consider a flock of pigeons in a field of corn, where 99 pigeons gathered all the grain and put it at the disposal of one—"the weakest, perhaps the worst pigeon of the flock." The privileged one devours wastefully while the rest keep mere chaff for themselves. If one of the 99, "more hardy and hungry than the rest," were to take a grain of the hoard, all the others would tear it to pieces.

By analogy, Paley added, this was the regular practice in human society. Ninety-nine workers accumulate a "heap of superfluities for one, and this one, too, oftentimes the feeblest and worst." The 99 see the fruits of their labor devoured, and if one dares to take a particle of the rich man's hoard, the others will gang up on him, "hanging him for the theft."

Here was a whisper of subversion. But with great adroitness, Paley drew a moral that supported the status quo: How great must be the advantages of an institution that has survived these "paradoxical and unnatural" features! He proceeded to list them. Without property, goods would not be preserved to maturity; corn would not ripen, lambs would not grow to be sheep; "the first person that met them would reflect that he had better take them as they are, than leave them for another." Property prevents contests, for war and tumult must be eternal where there is scarcity, and "no rules to adjust the division." And it improves the convenience of living by facilitating the exchange of what we have produced for what we need from others. For "exchange implies property."

He concluded that "even the poorest and worst provided, in countries where property and the consequences of property prevail," are better situated with respect to food, clothing, housing and the necessities of life, "than any are in places where most things remain in common." That was a deft, indeed a brilliant, recovery from his brief lapse into irreverence. But Paley was nonetheless warned by the bishop of Elphin, early in 1785: "Paley, that passage about the pigeons will not go down. It may prevent your being a bishop."

"Well," said Paley (according to his son's report), "bishop or no bishop, it shall stand." It did stand. He became known as "Pigeon" Paley, and he did not become a bishop.[24]

Perhaps the most important property-related issue of the day was entail, a restriction on the alienability of inherited estates. Heirs were not permitted to sell an entailed estate or any part of it. In turn they usually placed a like restriction in their own wills. Entail is to be distinguished from primogeniture, the feudal custom (not a legal requirement) of bequeathing the undivided estate to the oldest son. The restrictions of entail were becoming a nuisance because they impeded economic development. Entail gave assurance to the original owner that his descendants could not gamble away the estate, or exchange it for some worthless South Sea stock. But the restriction was bound in the end to have bad effects, unlikely to be felt until long after the original owner's death. Heirs were frequently reduced to custodians, and increasing areas of land became "exempted from commerce," as Lord Kames put it in his tract on property. "Landed property, naturally one of the great blessings of life, is thus converted into a curse."[25]

In his treatise, first published in 1758 and sometimes misleadingly called a "history" (it was 67 pages long), Kames devoted most of his attention to problems of succession, showing their importance at the time. He attributes the origin of entail to the desire of the owner to perpetuate his wealth and memory: "Alas! he must die and leave the enjoyment to others. To colour a dismal prospect, he makes a deed, arresting fleeting property, securing his estate to . . . those who represent him, in an endless succession: his estate and his heirs must for ever bear his name; every thing to perpetuate his name and his wealth."

In England, entails had been authorized by statute, but then they "spread everywhere with great rapidity," Kames noted, "till, becoming a public nuisance, they were checked and defeated by the authority of judges without a statute." In Kames's day, this remedy was not available in Scotland. There, in consequence, the "dead stock" of entailed property was growing daily, "and if the British legislature interpose not, the time in which the whole will be locked up is not far distant."

In Smith's England, as the concern about entail suggests, the problem if anything was the *excessive* security of property. If entailed, its use was sacrificed to its permanence. Kames's criticism was studied by Thomas Jefferson, who introduced bills to abolish entail in the Virginia legislature. In his *Autobiography,* Jefferson wrote that entails had "raised up a distinct set of families who, being privileged by law, in the perpetuation of their wealth, were thus formed into a Patrician order."[26] Adam Smith also attacked entails, as Karl Marx did later—a rare point of agreement between them.*

---

* In 1841 Marx wrote: "No, this fettering of landed property, like all entails, works directly towards a revolution. When the best part of the land is welded to individual families and made inaccessible to all other citizens, is not that a direct provocation to the people? Does not the right of primogeniture rest on a view of property which has long since ceased to correspond to our ideas? As if one generation had the right to dispose absolutely of the property of all future generations . . . as if the freedom of property were not destroyed by so disposing of it that all descendants are robbed of this freedom." The freedom of property was not a pressing concern for Marx, but his indictment of entails was on target nonetheless. Karl Marx, Frederick Engels, *Collected Works* (London, Lawrence & Wishart, 1975) 2: 147.

GODWIN VERSUS MALTHUS

It is not until we come to the curious figure of William Godwin, the father-in-law of Shelley, that we hear the first real shot fired in the war against property. His principal work, *Enquiry Concerning Political Justice* (1793), was influential in its day and attracted the attention of Coleridge and Wordsworth. Godwin's brief celebrity was such that he "blazed as a sun in the firmament of reputation," according to the writer William Hazlitt. "No work in our time gave such a blow to the philosophical mind of the country." For a while, at least, Tom Paine was considered "as a Tom Fool to him, Paley an old woman, Edmund Burke a flashy sophist."[27]

The great doctrine of his work was the perfectibility of man. By this he meant "the progressive nature of man" in his "virtuous propensities," and his social institutions. This notion was to become strongly associated with views about property in the nineteenth century. Ultimately, Godwin thought, human progress might be sufficient to prevail over death itself. A part of *Political Justice* was devoted to a fierce critique of the "existing institution of property."[28]

His work provoked a famous reply from Malthus—the *Essay on the Principle of Population*. Over the next quarter century they argued back and forth on this question: Would growing population limit the progress of mankind? Their dispute is well known to economic historians, but less attention has been paid to their disagreement about property. The irony is that Godwin came closer to the truth on population, with which Malthus's name is associated, but Malthus was correct about property, with which his name is not associated at all.

Godwin admired Rousseau, particularly *his* attack on property, and he shared his faith in education. Of the two, however, Godwin was the real harbinger of the coming revolutionary outlook. Rousseau looked back to an Eden of primal innocence; Godwin forward to a Utopia of human perfection. Like so many revolutionaries, he started out as a dissenting minister. Placidly ignoring "all inconvenient facts," he believed in "the speedy revelation of a New Jerusalem—foursquare and perfect in its plan," as the historian Leslie Stephen wrote. In the course of writing his book Godwin nonetheless became an atheist.[29]

Political Justice was published at a time of growing concern about the spread of revolutionary ideas. Days before its publication, Louis XVI was guillotined, and ten days later France declared war on England. November, 1792, saw the founding of the Association for Preserving Liberty and Property against Republicans and Levellers—the beginning of a "reign of despotism" in England, as Godwin saw it. Tom Paine had recently been charged with seditious libel and had fled to France. Handbills passed out in London accused reformers like Godwin of treason.

At just this time, William Paley published his essay, *Reasons for Contentment*. He urged "the labouring part of the public" to be satisfied with its lot. Just as theatergoers watch the play, not the spectators, so in life people should guard against "the disturbance of envy and discontent." This they would be sure to encounter if they made the mistake of comparing themselves to others of different "ranks and stations of society." "Pigeon" Paley took the opportunity to stress his continued soundness on property. The laws that put great estates in one man's possession, he reminded, are the same laws that protect the poor man. "Fixed rules of property are established for one, as well as another, without knowing beforehand whom they may affect." His argument could be seen as self-serving, but he made the crucial point, since widely forgotten, that the impartial protection of property is of special benefit to those who don't have much of it.

> It is not for the poor man to repine at the effect of laws and rules by which he himself is benefited every hour of his existence; which secure to him his earnings, his habitation, his bread, his life; without which he, no more than the rich man, could either eat his meal in quietness, or go to bed in safety. Of the two, it is rather more the concern of the poor to stand up for the laws than of the rich, for it is the law which defends the weak against the strong, the humble against the powerful, the little against the great; and weak and strong, humble and powerful, little and great there would be, even were there no law whatever.[30]

Especially were there no law whatever.

Godwin would have nothing of this argument, and the crackdown on sedition only seemed to inflame him. He revised his preface to claim that monarchy was "a species of government unavoidably corrupt." He escaped prosecution nonetheless. William Pitt is supposed to have remarked in the Privy Council that "a three-guinea book could never do much harm among those who had not three shillings to spare." But it was reprinted twice in the 1790s, then again in 1842. In the year of Godwin's death (1836), *Gentleman's Magazine* reported that *Political Justice* became so popular that "the poorest mechanics were known to club subscriptions for its purchase," enabling it to "mine and eat away contentment from a nation's roots."[31]

Godwin's philosophy is often said to be libertarian or anarchist, because minimal government, or none, was his ideal. His book nonetheless belongs to the genre of utopianism. He inveighed against marriage as "a system of fraud" and "the most odious of all monopolies"; and of course against religion. In the more perfect age to come, he guessed, "there will be no war, no crimes, no administration of justice, as it is called, and no government. . . . Every man will seek, with ineffable ardor, the good of all."[32] His condemnation of property knew no bounds. It creates "a sense of dependence," bringing with it "a servile and truckling spirit" and a "spectacle of injustice." It leads to "the ostentation of the rich," and "goads the spectator to the desire for opulence." It extinguishes genius, stifles thought, reduces mankind to "sordid cares," and promotes oppression, servility, envy, fraud, malice, revenge, ambition and "war in every horrid form."

To whom does anything justly belong? "To him who most wants it." A loaf of bread belongs to the hungry, for example. And just as we all need more than the necessities, so we can all dispense with the luxuries. Equality is the best formula of distribution. Crime would disappear, for only "the sharp sting of necessity" causes one man to rob another; envy and selfishness would die. Because we could expect an equal share of the common wealth, we would no longer need to guard our little store. Men would cease to compete, for they would have nothing to contend about. Vanity, ostentation and ambition—themselves "the produce of the prevailing system of property"—would disappear. Each of us "would lose his own individual existence in the thought of the general good."

Godwin rejected the argument that the incentive to work would be undermined by an expectation of equal shares. Admittedly, further mental and moral progress was a prerequisite. "The present age of mankind is greatly enlightened," he thought, "but not yet enlightened enough." The need for labor would be much reduced by his plan: Perhaps only half an hour's work a day for all. There would be no rich men to "fatten upon the labour of their fellows," no one would have to collect taxes, and "neither fleets nor armies, neither courtiers nor footmen" would survive. Nor would anyone have to direct "the complicated machine of government." Here we see traces of Marx's belief that under communism the state would wither away.

In a "state of equal society," Godwin believed, the love of distinction would be transmuted into fear of the "reproach of indolence"—an argument later used by Mill. There was no danger of backsliding once equality was reached. If one were to "consume uselessly" something more useful to another, he would feel that "alienation of thought" that murder now arouses in us. We would seek only "the knowledge of truth." Force would be unknown, locks and bolts would fall into disuse, no exchange of goods would take place, laws would be unnecessary, marriage would be abolished, and "the love of man" would replace "the love of individual men."[31]

Two years later, a comparable work appeared, the *Sketch for a Historical Picture of the Human Mind,* by the marquis de Condorcet; an optimist, considering that he was under sentence of death for opposing Robespierre in the French Revolution. Condorcet believed that progress was unfolding in natural stages, and that the tenth and final stage, in which he was fortunate enough to live, would see a transition to a world of abundance and peace: all distinctions of sex and inequalities of property would soon disappear. But he died in prison in 1794, shortly after his *Sketch* was written.

One who had read Godwin, and was intrigued by his hopeful views, was Malthus's father, Daniel. When the infant Robert was three weeks old, in 1766, two famous visitors came to stay at his house near Dorking—none other than Rousseau and David Hume. They "may be presumed to have assigned to the infant with a kiss diverse intellectual gifts," Maynard Keynes wrote.[34] Thomas Robert Malthus went on to study mathematics at Cambridge and became a curate. But he did not inherit his father's progressive outlook. The first edition of his most famous work was published in 1798: *An Essay on the Principle of Population as it affects The Future Improvement of Society.*

Godwin himself had earlier argued that the inequality of property kept the population down to subsistence level. "Territorial monopoly" restricted production, Godwin argued. The "established system of property may be considered as strangling a considerable portion of our children in their cradle." A single family needs only a certain amount of sustenance, after all. If it is permitted to monopolize thousands of acres, perhaps keeping them in unproductive pasture or forest, there will be no reason to produce food on them. So the food supply will be restricted, and the population with it. This in turn would subtract from the total sum of humans, and therefore the sum total of human happiness.

Malthus replied that Godwin's disdain for property undermined his dream of perfectibility. For if there were "no established administration of property, every man would be obliged to guard with force his little store." Selfishness would triumph, "the subjects of contention would be perpetual." We all would be constantly anxious about our very survival. Malthus was right about that, and his argument was sufficient to undermine Godwin's whole case for human betterment. But Malthus then went on to make his famous claim that population grows in geometrical ratio, food production in arithmetic ratio, ensuring that the former outruns the latter. Only then did he claim victory over Godwin: Whatever the property arrangement, Malthus said, the human race could not possibly become more perfect, because it was mathematically doomed to perpetual misery and vice by the problem of finding enough to eat.[35]

In his *Political Justice,* curiously enough, Godwin had already given reasons for thinking that the food-supply argument—which had been advanced by others before Malthus—was unduly pessimistic. We don't really know what the future will bring, Godwin said. To anticipate population outstripping food supply "is to foresee difficulties at a great distance." Three-fourths of the globe was still uncultivated, and the parts cultivated were capable of unknown improvement. In fact: "Myriads of centuries of still increasing population may probably pass away, and the earth still be found sufficient for the subsistence of its inhabitants. . . . Who can say what remedies shall suggest themselves for so distant an inconvenience?"

If we overlook the hyperbole of "myriads of centuries," everything Godwin said here looks reasonable 200 years later. But in his reply, as we know, Malthus brought to bear the impressive-sounding language of mathematics, awing his contemporaries (not to mention many of ours). Godwin looked befuddled, and Malthus seemed to know what he was talking about when he predicted that the "principle of population" would undo Godwin's system "in so short a time as thirty years."[36]*

Godwin's position was undermined by his ad hominem attacks and by the utopian and strident character of his opinions. Once thrillingly dangerous, his ideas began to seem merely tiresome—"the absurdity of all laws, the coming empire of reason, the vice of filial duty, and the infamy of patriotism," in Peter Marshall's modern summary. As for his views on property, not only were they extreme but they were well rebutted by Malthus. Godwin died in 1836, after repeated episodes of debt. Malthus had died two years earlier.

NO PASSING FAD

After the Napoleonic Wars, it began to dawn on people in England that property really was no longer immune from criticism. J. R. McCulloch's *Principles of Political Economy*, published in 1825, included 12 pages in its defense. The right of property, he wrote, was "the foundation on which other institutions of society mainly rest." Where it is not publicly guaranteed, men will look upon each other as enemies rather than as friends. The improvident always want to seize the wealth of the industrious; and if they are not restrained by the law, they will, "by generating a feeling of insecurity, effectually check both industry and accumulation, and sink all classes to the same level of hopeless misery as themselves."[37]

Of the earlier economists, Malthus had delved into the subject a little more than the others, probably because his dispute with Godwin had forced him

---

*The best criticism of Malthusianism came from the economist Edwin Cannan, who pointed out that census data from the years 1801 to 1831 refuted Malthus while he was still alive. The population of England in those years was increasing by a more than geometrical ratio. There should, by 1830, have been about a million people (out of only 14 million) "totally unprovided for," to use Malthus's words and reasoning. But food supply was easily keeping pace. Malthus had misleadingly equating a geometric increase with a series that doubled every 25 years. The common ratio of a geometric series can be less than two, and the time interval between the terms of the series can be longer than 25 years. It was Malthus, not Godwin, who was refuted within 30 years. But Godwin's scheme would have proved disastrous in less than 30 years if his proposal to abolish property had been carried out. Edwin Cannan, *A History of the Theories of Production and Distribution*, 3rd ed. (London: P. S. King, 1917), 140-43.

to think about it. He returned to the subject in an essay on population for the *Encyclopedia Britannica,* which includes perhaps the best argument for property made by any economist of his day. By this time he had also read Robert Owen's *New View of Society* (1813), a pamphlet calling for the abolition of private property. Owen believed that this would lead to a society both more moral and more productive than the existing one. Antagonism to property wasn't a passing fad or a personal eccentricity of Godwin's, evidently. Malthus wrote his key passage in direct response to the claims of Godwin and Owen.

It was "visionary," Malthus argued, to suppose that any stimulus short of the desire to provide for one's family and self should operate on the mass of society "with sufficient force and constancy to overcome the natural indolence of mankind." All attempts made since the beginning of recorded history "to proceed upon the principle of common property" had either been insignificant, or had failed completely. The changes wrought by modern education had not made much difference to date. We may safely conclude, therefore, "that while man retains the same physical and moral constitution which he is observed to possess at present, no other than a system of private property stands the least chance of providing for such a large and increasing population as that which is to be found in many countries at present."[38]

While man retains the same moral constitution, Malthus had stipulated. So he offered a glimmer of hope that it might indeed be changed. That was exactly what more and more thinkers were beginning to believe.

EIGHT

MILL, MARX AND MARSHALL

JOHN STUART MILL IS OF INTEREST to us because he is the first prominent economist to include in his treatise—*The Principles of Political Economy,* first published in 1848—a full discussion of property. Unfortunately, he put his two chapters in the wrong place—at the beginning of book 2, instead of (more logically) book 1. In so doing, he was guided by some economic notions that have since been discarded. To a much greater extent than today, political economy was then thought to be undergirded by "laws." But they were assumed to be scientific laws, not the laws of legislatures and courts. Economists of the nineteenth century sought to emulate Newton, not to heed Justinian or Blackstone.

They were intrigued by the following observation: The community consisted of three classes of people—landowners, capitalists and laborers—who contributed their respective "factors of production": land, capital and labor. An interesting possibility suggested itself. Perhaps the overall economy "returned" or distributed a definite, discoverable proportion of the overall output to each of these classes, in the three forms of income: rent, interest and wages.

The "principal problem of Political Economy," David Ricardo wrote in 1817, was to "determine the laws which regulate this distribution."[1] Smith, Say and Turgot had made their useful contributions, but (Ricardo added) they had provided little satisfactory information about the "natural course" of these income streams. Marx professed an interest in the same idea. In his preface to the first edition of *Capital,* he declared that his goal was to "lay bare the economic law of motion of modern society."[2]

So began the lengthy and more or less fruitless search for economic laws. Those that were subsequently proclaimed may have been more misleading than helpful. The theory of a "natural" return to the factors of production was never confirmed. The "iron law of wages," supposedly held down to subsistence levels by competition, turned out to be wrong. The related law of population, forever outpacing food supply, was a deduction from premises not discovered empirically. The Ricardian law of rent—rising endlessly given a fixed supply of land and an ever-growing population—is formally correct *if* we assume that other variables remain constant. But they never do, and the "law" has not resulted in an ever-growing income for landowners, as Ricardo feared. Imports, changes in technology and in the organization of industry upset all such predictions. The contribution of natural resources (which is what "land" means in economic discourse) to the value of economic goods has declined in the twentieth century, despite a rapidly increasing population.

The labor theory of value (the belief that economic value is proportional to the average number of work hours required to produce some good) was also wrong. A better understanding of value—as a relationship between supply and demand—did not come until later in the nineteenth century. It's of interest that the crucial error in Marx's theory of value was discovered in the 1880s by George Bernard Shaw, before the third volume of *Capital* was even published. If one capitalist can expropriate surplus value rightly belonging to the worker, Shaw wrote, a rival capitalist, "trading on the same principle," will "content himself with [a smaller] profit for the sake of attracting custom." So the unjust surplus would be competed away. Capitalists were as much subject to each other's competition as were laborers. "The criticism received no reply," George Stigler commented.[3]

The point is that Mill believed that the truth of such economic laws had been demonstrated in principle (even if their details still needed to be worked out). "The laws and conditions of the production of wealth, partake of the character of physical truths," he wrote in his *Principles*. "There is nothing optional or arbitrary in them." By way of illustration (a meager one), he pointed out that "a double quantity of labor will not raise, on the same land, a double quantity of food."[4] (This was the law of diminishing returns.) Nor can these laws be altered by mere human will, he asserted.

Mill's *Principles* was an influential book, read throughout the second half of the nineteenth century by educated people generally. Mill included property under the rubric of distribution rather than production because he thought that production was already "fixed" by the aforementioned laws. The *supply* of such goods was therefore assured, or so it seemed to Mill. The lesser positive laws, enacted by mere legislators, could make no difference to the predictable operation of those *scientific* laws. Distribution, on the other hand, was not subject to any such "iron" necessities or constraints. Here, human law could freely enter and do the right thing. In particular, it could mitigate the harsh laws of production. "The thing once there," Mill wrote, "mankind, individually or collectively, can do with them as they like. They can place them at the disposal of whomsoever they please, and on whatever terms." The distribution of wealth, therefore, "depends on the laws and customs of society. The rules by which it is determined, are what the opinions and feelings of the ruling portion of the community make them, and are very different in different ages and countries."[5] In short, we may say that Mill contrasted two kinds of law. One, scientific, ensured production. The other, human, permitted redistribution.

This may have been one of the more influential errors in the history of economic thought. It is true that legislation can bring about a redistribution of wealth. Mill's error lay in his premise: that production itself was driven by a different kind of law. This led him to suppose that the engines of production would necessarily keep on turning after lawmakers had redistributed the output away from the producers; that "the thing once there" would go on being there after "society" became the beneficiary. Like Keynes a century later, Mill believed that an economic "machine" hummed away, ensuring that production would persist more or less mechanically (depending on the maintenance of aggregate demand, in the Keynesian scheme).

In his *Autobiography,* Mill claimed (truly) that his innovation, separating production and distribution, distinguished the *Principles* from "all previous expositions of Political Economy that had any pretension to being scientific." It had been included "chiefly" through the influence of his wife and collaborator, Harriet Taylor. He gave her the credit for "making the proper distinction between the laws of the Production of Wealth, which are real laws of nature, dependent on the properties of objects; and the modes of its Distribution, which, subject to certain conditions, depend on human will. The common run of political economists confuse these together, under the designation of economic laws, which they deem incapable of being defeated or modified by human effort."[6]

It is conventional to describe Mill as a transitional figure. His teachers, among them his father, James Mill, and Jeremy Bentham, had grown up at a time when private property was not questioned. The younger Mill foresaw, but did not fully embrace, some of the great ideological changes that were to come. He noted "the very limited and temporary value of the old political economy, which assumes private property and inheritance as indefeasible facts."[7] The old guard, including his teachers, had made the mistake of attempting to construct "a permanent fabric out of transitory materials"; they had taken for granted "the immutability of arrangements of society, many of which are in their nature fluctuating or progressive." They mistook the existing conditions of society in which the writer happened to live for "universal and absolute truths."[8]

Progress, the great and dominant idea of the day, colored all of Mill's views about property. He was confident that he was witnessing a progressive change in "the character of the human race," as also in its conditions of life. Society was changing, and with it would come changes in man's mental and moral makeup.[9] In his worldview, the present was always contrasted unflatteringly with the future. On the one hand there was the "present imperfect state of moral and intellectual cultivation," "the present stage of human improvement,"[10] with its "selfish type of character," formed by the present moral standards and fostered by "existing social institutions." On the other, there was the bright prospect of progress. A "spontaneous education" was taking place in people's minds, making it difficult to take anything other than a "hopeful view of the prospects of mankind." Human beings en masse could be trained "to feel the public interest as their own."

As to the viability of communism, he admitted to some uncertainty. Whether "strenuous exertions" would be undertaken in the age to come (to win the "admiration of others"), or "the energy of labour would be diminished under Communism," was a still undecided question, he allowed. In general, however, his optimism about the future matched his disappointment in the present— "the present bad state of society"; "the present state of society with all its sufferings and injustices."

In considering a society without private property, Mill confined himself to communal versions of socialism, usually French (those of Charles Fourier or Henri de Saint-Simon). Their proposed communes "cannot be truly said to be impracticable," he thought.[11] He conceded that the familiar objection—"each person would be incessantly occupied in evading his fair share of the work"— pointed to a real difficulty.[12] But he believed that the same objection also applied to the existing system. Most laborers do not reap the full benefit of their exertions anyway, so how does private property motivate them? They work not for themselves but for day wages or fixed salaries. A worker in a private factory has less interest than a member of a communist association, he thought, since in the latter he is a partner. Even the supervision of labor in the existing system was not done by owners but by "salaried officers."[13] In a socialist farm or "manufactory," however, people would be working "under the eye, not of one master, but of the whole community."

He acknowledged that communism, in its "original principle" (of equal sharing) was "adapted to a much higher moral condition of human nature" than we know at present. So we must remain agnostic about the future.[14] In his later "Chapters on Socialism," written in 1869, he again says that "Communistic production" may "at some future time" be the form of property best adapted to mankind. It was an "open question." The present certainty was that a successful communism would require a higher moral and intellectual standard "in all the members of the community."[15]

As for its effect on civil liberties, Mill was again cautious. "It remains to be discovered" whether communism would restrict individual liberties, or perhaps allow a greater individuality.[16] There was no doubt where his hopes lay. The restraints of communism would be freedom indeed compared with the present condition of most of the human race. Any limits placed on freedom would no doubt be offset by "the probably large amount of leisure" that would result.[17] But the compulsory expropriation of property was repugnant to Mill. He consistently took the position that if the present system were to be changed it would have to be done voluntarily. By the end of his life, compulsory proposals were beginning to be heard; the more ambitious aiming to take possession of the whole land and capital of the country, "and beginning at once to administer it on the public account." Such notions were both immoral and impracticable, he thought.[18]

"The very idea of conducting the whole industry of a country by direction from a single centre is so obviously chimerical, that nobody ventures to propose any mode in which it should be done," he said.[19] If "the revolutionary Socialists attained their immediate object, and actually had the whole property of the country at their disposal," their only practicable solution would be to "divide it into portions" again. Here he correctly anticipated one of the great difficulties that would arise in the centrally directed economies of the twentieth century. Economic life is too complex and multifaceted to be controlled from a central point with even a modicum of efficiency.

In summary, he believed that life was turning out to be more fluid and mutable than the older generation had imagined. Admittedly, given the "imperfect degree of moral cultivation which mankind have yet reached," it may be expected that "the principle of individual property will be in possession of the field" for a long time to come.[20] But if people are obstinate, human institutions are malleable. Their reform could be expected to stimulate beneficial changes in human nature. Socialism was coming, its difficulties had been exaggerated, and it would probably succeed.

STRATEGY OF INEVITABILITY

Karl Marx's name is not mentioned anywhere in Mill's copious writings. They both lived in London in the 1850s and 1860s, but Marx, younger by 12 years, was little known beyond his revolutionary circle. Mill, a household name, probably never heard of him. Late in life he was sent a Marxian pamphlet by a correspondent, but it is not clear that he ever read it.[21] Nonetheless, it seems likely that, through the intermediary efforts of his wife Harriet, Mill was influenced by Marx without knowing it.

With Marx, of course, the attack on private property became open and direct: "The theory of the Communists can be summarized in the single sentence: Abolition of private property."[22] Mill's muffled hopes and doubts hardly matched this blazing new attack. One turns with interest to Marx's arguments. Had he anticipated, or said anything about, the very great difficulties that must arise when private property is abolished? No. In fact, his discussion of property includes few arguments of any description. His comments are delivered ex cathedra, his rhetorical strategy always being to suggest inevitability. Not including the fogbanks of *The Economic and Philosophic Manuscripts of 1844,* written in Paris while he was in his twenties (they were not published in English until 1960), his comments about property are occasional, spotty and generally disappointing. He always saw that the subject was important, and that the overthrow of private property would be a convulsive and revolutionary business, but that is the most that one can say.

Marx was disappointed in Pierre-Joseph Proudhon, who might have seemed a natural ally. Proudhon shared Marx's animus against property ("property is theft!"), but distrusted communism ("taking uniformity for law, and levelling for equality, [it] becomes tyrannical and unjust.")[23] Stung by this jibe, prophetic though it turned out to be, Marx fingered Proudhon's own internal contradiction: "Since theft as a forcible violation of property presupposes the existence of property, Proudhon entangled himself in all sorts of fantasies."[24]

Unlike his predecessors, Marx almost always qualified "property" with an adjective, usually disparaging: bourgeois, individual, personal, private, communal. He saw private property as an alienating force, dividing people when they should be united. And, of course, he saw property more as an effect (of the stage through which "history" was passing) than as a cause (of economic development). Property was a mere "juristic" illusion, not an indispensable legal relationship. Different property relations had prevailed in different epochs: ancient, then feudal, and now bourgeois property; but that, too, would pass away. It was a mistake to think that there was any enduring reality beneath these transient shadows. "Often the most Marx appears to be saying is that private property is doomed historically," Jeremy Waldron points out in *The Right to Private Property,* "that it is obsolescent, that it will eventually, under pressure, give way to social control."[25] In his third volume of *Capital,* published posthumously, Marx said: "From the standpoint of a higher economic form of society private ownership of the globe by single individuals will appear quite as absurd as private ownership of one man by another."[26]

He knew that *some* form of property was essential ("that there can be no such thing as production, nor, consequently, society, where property does not exist in any form is a tautology"),[27] but he says very little about the form that he believed would prevail in the classless future. He certainly believed that the immediate successor to private property would be state ownership, centrally controlled. And this would require "despotic inroads on the rights of property, and on the conditions of bourgeois production."[28] Unlike Mill or the "utopian" socialists, the Marxists encouraged this centralization. For the Fourierists and their communes, Marx had nothing but contempt: "They still dream of experimental realization of their social utopias, of founding isolated phalansteres, of establishing 'Home Colonies,' or setting up a 'Little Icaria'—pocket editions of the New Jerusalem—and to realize all these castles in the air they are compelled to appeal to the feelings and purses of the bourgeois."[29] He derided this "sentimental, utopian, mutton-headed socialism."[30] In the *Communist Manifesto,* Marx and Engels foresaw the centralization of credit, of the means of communication and transportation, and of "all instruments of production in the hands of the state."[31]

Characteristically, Marx did not bother his head worrying about the great and intractable difficulties that would arise when private property was abolished. In the *Communist Manifesto,* the caution that "universal laziness will overtake us" was raised only to be dismissed with an argument remarkably similar to the one used by John Stuart Mill in his *Principles.* If this were true, Marx and Engels wrote, "bourgeois society ought long ago to have gone to the dogs through sheer idleness; for those of its members who work acquire nothing, and those who acquire anything do not work." They added that "in your existing society, private property is already done away with for nine-tenths of the population."[32]

Mill had written: "Those who urge this [laziness] objection forget to how great an extent the same difficulty exists under the system on which nine-tenths of the business of society is now conducted." This, he estimated, was the proportion of society that was unable to "reap the benefit of their own exertions," because they were "remunerated by day wages or fixed salaries."[33]

It is remarkable that they should have illustrated their criticism of private property with the same argument and the same numerical ratio. Was this a coincidence? The two works were published within three months of one another, the *Manifesto* in January, the *Principles* in April, 1848. But Mill's comments do not appear until the third edition of his work, published in 1852. By then the *Manifesto* had been published in French (in 1848) and in English (in 1850). Mill's comments occur in the chapter "On Property," which, under Harriet Taylor's guidance, was almost completely rewritten for the third edition.

"In the first edition the difficulties of socialism were stated so strongly, that the tone was on the whole that of opposition to it," Mill later explained in his *Autobiography.* "In the year or two which followed, much time was given to the study of the best socialist writers on the Continent." Both Mill and Taylor spent time in France after the *Principles* were published, and in July, 1848, she wrote to Mill telling him about a reference to Proudhon published "in the Daily News from Paris." In the same letter she referred to David Hume as "trash" for saying that the "'attempt to establish community of property is a direct violation of the fundamental laws of society.'"[34]

As to Taylor's influence on Mill, one only has to read the letter he sent to her in February, 1849, while revising the chapter: "I dispatched yesterday to the dear one an attempt at a revision of the objectionable passages. I saw on consideration that the objection to Communism on the ground of its making life a kind of dead level might admit of being weakened. . . ." So he had rewritten the passage. He still thought that some criticism of communism was in order, but he added: "But if you do not think so, I certainly will not print it, even if there were no other reason than the certainty I feel that I should never long continue of an opinion different from yours on a subject which you have fully considered."[35] In any event, it seems highly likely that Taylor came across the *Communist Manifesto* in French while Mill's chapter was under revision and that she absorbed arguments from it.

A final point about this curious episode: As we can now see, the original version of Mill's chapter on property was far more sensible. But until the University of Toronto's 33-volume edition of Mill's *Collected Works* came out—the relevant volume only in 1965, with this original chapter included as an appendix—it would have been difficult to find. The press run of the (rare) first edition was only 1,000 copies. It is likely that all of the many editions and reprints of Mill that appeared after 1852 used the rewritten, Taylorized chapter.

In the works of Smith, Ricardo, and others, then, we see that property was for a while considered to lie outside the realm of economics. Then it was admitted into Mill's treatise, but in the wrong place—under the rubric of distribution. Some of his comments opposing its alternatives were expunged at the behest of his wife, and replaced by arguments that bore a close resemblance to those that had recently appeared in the *Communist Manifesto.* The amended version of Mill remained in print for over 50 years and influenced at least the next generation of economists, while the original version disappeared from view.

Meanwhile, the Marxists, beginning with the *Manifesto,* swept aside as unworthy of discussion the great difficulties that really are involved in eliminating one of mankind's most basic social institutions. These difficulties were neither anticipated nor discussed by the modern founders of communism—a point later made by the Cambridge economist Alfred Marshall, who noted that the socialists "did not study the doctrines which they attacked." They contented themselves with grandiloquent statements, sweeping remarks about historical inevitability, and heavy doses of scorn for those who were bold enough to disagree with them.

The idea of progress seemed to reduce all criticism and analysis to mere pedantry. In Marx this idea was to be found in his theory of historical determinism. "All history," he said, chastising Proudhon for having failed to grasp the point, "is nothing but a continuous transformation of human nature."[36] In its influence, Marx's philosophy of history may in the long run have been more important than his views on property. History itself was evolving, moving from one "epoch" to another, conditioned not by ideas or man-made institutions, but by the overall economic relations of society. The capitalist, or "bourgeois," class had overthrown the feudal. It was now scheduled for a struggle with the proletariat. The outcome was historically inevitable.

Marx seemed not to advocate the overthrow of private property or the victory of the proletariat so much as predict it. Preaching was disguised as prophecy. Superfluous, then, to discuss the difficulties that may transiently arise in attaining the more perfect state; as pointless as it would be for Christians or Moslems to argue over the details of Heaven. Marx professed himself an atheist, but in his readiness to believe in progress as a universal law, Bertrand Russell wrote, he "retained a cosmic optimism which only theism could justify."[37]

"THE GREAT EXODUS FROM THEOLOGY"

John Stuart Mill's heir in the unofficial dynasty of economists was Alfred Marshall, professor of economics at Cambridge, and the teacher of Keynes. His *Principles of Economics* was published in 1890. Here at last the subject was updated. The old-fashioned name, "political economy," was supplanted by something more technical, and when the need arose, mathematical: economics. The search for hard, scientific laws had admittedly proven to be a disappointment. Under the influence of Marshall and his "marginalist" predecessors, economics became a more self-enclosed, deductive system. It also became more academic. After Marshall, the treatises of economists would not be much read by laymen, as Mill's had been. Supply and demand curves appeared, and they were for the specialist. Marshall was a mathematician by training but disposed to preach almost as much as Marx. He was "yet another product of the well-connected clerical families which colonized English intellectual life," Robert Skidelsky wrote. He was "part of the great exodus from theology."[38]

Property was dropped—shunned as though no longer relevant to the inquiry at hand. This was surprising, because it could no longer be said that private property was so well accepted that there was no need to defend it. Marshall makes the astounding claim that the need for private property "doubtless reaches no deeper than the qualities of human nature."[39] Earlier, economists had made the great mistake of arguing as though "man's character" was to be regarded as a "fixed quantity." But no longer was that accepted as true: "This change in the point of view of economics is partly due to the fact that the changes in human nature during the last fifty years have been so rapid as to force themselves on the attention; partly to the direct influence of individual writers, socialist and others; and partly to the indirect influence of a similar change in some branches of natural science."[40]

Marshall had in mind Darwinism. After a paragraph on the "mathemat-ico-physical" sciences, he commented that the speculations and discoveries of biology were beginning to fascinate the world; and there was a marked change in the tone of the moral and historical sciences as well. Economics had participated in this general movement, he added, "and is getting to pay every year a greater attention to the pliability of human nature; and to the way in which the character of man affects and is affected by the prevalent methods of the production, distribution and consumption of wealth."

Private property, once so well accepted that there was no need to mention it, was now becoming redundant: there would be no need to retain it. Either way it could be ignored. Man's nature was changing under the influence of evolution. In his *History of Western Philosophy,* Bertrand Russell captured the mental outlook of the time: "Everything was supposed to be evolving."[41] Darwin himself had been careful not to extend biological evolution to man's mental and moral character. But he faltered right at the end of *The Descent of Man* (1871), when he wrote that man may be excused for feeling pride at having risen to the summit of the organic scale. "And the fact of his having thus risen, instead of his having been aboriginally placed there, may give him hope for a still higher destiny in the distant future."[42]

Keynes famously said that in the long run we are all dead, and later he gave Marshall credit for being the first to draw a distinction between the long run and the short in economic analysis. Now, Marshall seemed to be under the impression that time was itself accelerating. The higher destiny of man, hoped for by Darwin in the long run, was already unfolding: the past 50 years had brought great changes. Humanity was being driven forward by a beneficent force. The implication was plain. If this progress continued, the need for private property would disappear altogether.

The idea of progress, J. B. Bury wrote in his book of that name, was by the 1870s and 1880s becoming a general article of faith. Between 1880 and 1920, there appeared a large literature of social science in which indefinite progress was "generally assumed as an axiom." The doctrine brought with it the belief that future generations would enjoy "conditions of happiness denied to us, but which our labours and sufferings are to help bring about."[43]

The notion of progress was casually embedded in Marshall's *Principles,* and historians of ideas have overlooked the irony. It is normally supposed that the extension of Darwinian reasoning to the social order—Social Darwinism—was not only unjustified on biological grounds but also encouraged such evils as laissez-faire. Herbert Spencer, whose phrase "the survival of the fittest" had been adopted by Darwin in *The Origin of Species* as a "convenient" summary of natural selection, had indeed tried to use biological arguments to forestall government intervention in the economy. He failed in that endeavor. Meanwhile,

Marshall and others construed Darwinian ideas as heralding not a libertarian, but a collectivist, future:

"The struggle for existence causes in the long run those races of men to survive in which the individual is most willing to sacrifice himself for the benefit of those around him," Marshall wrote.[44] Those are the groups best adapted "collectively" to make use of their environment. As soon as deliberate, "and therefore moral," self-sacrifice makes an appearance, it is fortified by "farseeing guidance," by "prophets, priests and legislators," and inculcated "by parable and legend." The groups in which these qualities were most highly developed would, other things being equal, "be stronger than others in war and in contests with famine and disease." So they would prevail in the struggle for existence. (In the 1960s, stories of kin selection were used by theorists to make a similar case for the evolution of altruism.)

In the future, then, "men's collective instincts, their sense of duty and their public spirit," would be better developed. Note that Marshall slipped in a role for legislators, who would "fortify" these trends. Even as he wrote, new legislation was conferring privileges on trade unions and beginning to undermine property and contract. With support from Herbert Spencer, the Liberty and Property Defence League was founded at about the same time to counteract these trends. But it was incapable of checking the socialist advance.

The doctrine of progressive change was a "compensatory secular simulacrum of Providence for Victorians who were sliding into unbelief," John Offer has suggested.[45] Those who could no longer believe in the next life substituted a more glorious future in this. Beatrice Potter, among many others, struggled with, and lost, her Christian faith. For a while, Spencer's *First Principles* seemed to take its place in her mind. In his philosophy, too, almost everything imaginable was shown to be in a state of progressive change. But we should not be surprised that for those who had lost one faith and were looking for another, the collectivist dogma prevailed over the individualistic. The promise of self-sacrifice has far more spiritual appeal than the calculation of self-interest. Beatrice Potter became a socialist and married Sidney Webb. The mystical Marx won converts all over the world while Spencer's reputation hardly survived his death.[46]

Marshall's treatise was published in the midst of these developments. Contributing to what Keynes called the general chorus of praise, the reviewer for the *Pall Mall Gazette* applauded "a professor at one of our old universities devoting the work of his life to recasting the Science of Political Economy as the Science of Social Perfectibility."[47] Marshall never gave up hoping. Later he said that if he had to live his life over again he would have devoted it to psychology. "Economics has too little to do with ideals." His optimism managed to survive World War I intact. At the age of 77, he published *Industry and Trade,* in its preface observing that "the average level of human nature in the western world has risen rapidly during the last 50 years." At the end of his life he was still struggling to complete a work called "Progress: Its Economic Conditions," which ultimately was neither finished nor published.[48]

Beatrice Webb wrote in her diary in 1890 that she dimly saw "the tendency towards a socialist community in which there will be individual freedom and public property instead of class slavery and the private possession of the means of subsistence."[49] The following month she was pleased to record that the newly published *Fabian Essays,* edited by George Bernard Shaw, was doing well. The world was "most assuredly going their way." Graham Wallas contributed the essay "Property Under Socialism." In the course of a few pages, he repeatedly referred to people as though they were known to be in a transitional phase, with a more glorious future awaiting them. People "at present" still insist on having their own crockery and chairs; each family "now insists on having a separate home," and on cooking "a separate series of meals in a separate kitchen." English families "at present prefer" waste and discomfort to that "abundance which can only be bought by organization and publicity." (By "publicity" he meant "public-ness," or the opposite of privacy.) Families, mutually isolated "at present," are "more or less despotically governed."

But as the "education and moralization of society improves," he continued, everything will change. Industry will become "so thoroughly socialized that the alternative of private enterprise will be less practicable." Man will soon see "how poor a means for the production of food is his own fire when compared with the public kitchen; and he will perhaps at last not only get his clothes from the public store, but the delight of his eyes from the public galleries and theatres, and the delight of his ears from the public opera, and it may be, when our present anarchy of opinion is overpast, the refreshment of his mind from the publicly chosen teacher." But none of this would happen at the stage "of moral development at which we now find ourselves."[50]

Similar ideas prevailed in the United States. When Richard T. Ely helped found the American Economic Association in 1885, he believed that a "new world was coming into existence." If it was going to be a better world, "we knew that we must have a new economics to go along with it," he recalled. The state could no longer be mere umpire, but would have to transform itself into an agency "whose positive assistance is one of the indispensable conditions of human progress."[51]

At Harvard, Frank Taussig's opinion was similar to Marshall's. The main issue "between private property and socialism" was one "of human nature," he wrote in his *Principles of Economics* (1911). The problem was that economic reasoning had lagged behind the times. It still quaintly assumed "hedonism in its simplest form." Motives "other than self-regarding ones" were acknowledged to exist, but only outside the economic realm—in the family, for example. But in the future, a "higher moral sense" would make men more public spirited. Further change in human nature might allow for a social reorganization which now seemed utopian. In any event, we are already "much better men than our savage ancestors."[52]

When we read Taussig and the Fabians on what is true "at present," and Marshall on the rapid rise of human nature, we can see how much the intellectual climate changed in the twentieth century. It is fair to say that such sentiments are never encountered now. The faith in progress has not only been lost, but has been replaced for many by a contrary, pessimistic vision of man as planetary and environmental despoiler.

Before we dismiss the naive optimism of the Victorians, however, there is an important respect in which Mill, Marx and Marshall were clearheaded. They understood that if private property were to be dispensed with, human nature would have to change. Marx believed that it was in fact changing. So did Marshall. So their view of property was at least coherent. Today, very few people believe that human nature is changing. And we can see that such statements as Marshall's, claiming that it had already changed, were misguided.

In the twentieth century, the malleability of human nature was put to a severe test in the Soviet Union. There it was finally discredited. In retrospect, it is possible to look upon the Soviet experience as a large-scale experiment, costly in life, liberty and prosperity, that tried to confirm a theory that had preoccupied Western intellectuals since the French Revolution. As Mikhail Heller wrote in *Cogs in the Wheel: The Formation of Soviet Man:* "Everything the Communist Party has done since the Revolution, despite superficial changes and apparent departures from original ideas and replacement of leaders, has been directed at the transformation of human beings."[53]

In September, 1991, at a time when Boris Yeltsin was president of Russia but still uneasily contending with Mikhail Gorbachev, then in his last days as president of the Soviet Union, Yeltsin himself made a remarkable comment on this point. The two men were responding to questions from listeners across the United States as part of a call-in program organized by ABC News. A questioner from Los Angeles asked if, given its "dismal history," any country in the world "should continue to live under Communism."

Yeltsin replied: "I think this experiment which was conducted on our soil was a tragedy for our people, and it was too bad that it happened on our territory. It would have been better if this experiment had been conducted in some small country at least, so as to make it clear that it was a utopian idea, although a beautiful one. I think gradually this will come to be understood by other countries where supporters of the idea of Communism still exist."[54]

As it happens, different versions of the experiment were conducted on a much smaller scale. Among the first to give it a try was Robert Owen, in a community in New Harmony, Indiana. Graham Wallas explained in the *Fabian Essays* that Owen's experiment had failed because it had been "distasteful to most men as they now are." But the records from New Harmony suggest that the participants rather enjoyed it—mainly because Owen was so generously paying all the bills. He did not get his money back, but as a consolation prize he received an honorary mention in the *Communist Manifesto,* published when he was 75 years old and still going strong.

THE NEW MAN

INTRODUCTION

In a "Declaration of Mental Independence," Robert Owen proclaimed in 1826 that the most important influences that had hitherto warped the character of man, and therefore should be abolished, were private property, religion and marriage. The division of property in particular had "brought to maturity all the evils of poverty and riches existing among a people at the same time; the industrious experiencing privations and the idle being overwhelmed and injured by wealth."[1] For the remainder of his life he continued to believe that once his "rational system" was implemented, and children were trained "to acquire new habits and new feelings," there would be no more "useless private property."[2] He aspired to "merge all individualism in the social."[3] The word socialist was coined at this time, first appearing in print in the London *Co-operative Magazine* in 1827.

When everything except personal possessions was publicly owned, he wrote, "then will the incalculable superiority of a system of public property be duly appreciated over the evils arising from private property." With a well-arranged and "scientific system of public property," and with "equal education and condition," the savings of labor and capital would be incalculable. In the British

Empire alone it would probably amount to several thousand million pounds sterling annually, he wrote.[4]

His system of public property, except personal possessions, was put into place in the Soviet Union in 1917, and the experiment lasted for the average human lifespan. The Soviet regime believed, as ardently as had Owen, that human nature was malleable, and could be changed by nurture, education and indoctrination.[5] But far from bringing about savings of labor and capital, public property brought with it tyranny, injustice, stagnation and ruin. Trotsky's prediction that under collectivism the average human type would rise to the level of an Aristotle was not borne out.

NINE

ROBERT OWEN'S TRINITY OF EVILS

ROBERT OWEN MADE A FORTUNE within a society of private property, and lost it trying to establish a society without property.[1] But he remained confident throughout his life that what he called the New Moral World would soon appear. In the Communist Manifesto, he was praised for having detected the "decomposing elements" in society. Friedrich Engels thought him "among the most eminent thinkers of all times." He was a true harbinger of the twentieth century's experiments in the abolition of property. One of the earliest socialists, he was also one of the few who spent his own money on the cause in which he so firmly believed. Whatever his faults, a lack of generosity was not among them.

He was born in 1771, a child of the Industrial Revolution. He went into business with Jeremy Bentham and hobnobbed with the duke of Kent. He claimed that he had spent four days with Thomas Jefferson "in close communion upon the two systems of society," but Jefferson did not record the encounter. Harriet Martineau, the popular expositor of political economy, reported that he was capable of believing "whatever he wished," while Thomas Macaulay "fled at the first sound of his discourse."

Like Bentham, Owen believed that the happiness of the greatest number should be the goal of society, but this could be achieved only within "a system of general cooperation and community of property."[2] In one of his many pamphlets, "The Revolution in the Mind and Practice of the Human Race," published when he was 78 years old, Owen called private property "an evil of incalculable magnitude, and a never-failing cause of disunion among all classes in all countries."[3]

After a few years' schooling, he moved to Manchester, and with borrowed capital formed a partnership to manufacture cotton-spinning machinery. This was the heyday of "Manchester liberalism," with the new, and therefore unregulated, cotton industry rapidly supplanting the old, and highly regulated, wool trade. By the late eighteenth century, technological and economic changes were making the cotton trade one of the great commercial enterprises in the world, and Manchester was at its center. Between 1750 and 1830 the quantity of cotton imported into Britain increased a hundredfold.[4]

On January 1, 1800, he took over the "government" of New Lanark Mills, in Scotland, having purchased it for £60,000 with several partners. Under the previous owner, whose daughter Owen married, the work force included several hundred orphaned children who were procured from the poorhouses of various parishes.[5] Poor relief in Scotland was restricted to those who were permanently unable to provide for themselves, there was no equivalent of the dole, and the poor rates, or taxes, were lower than England's.[6] Situated on the River Clyde, New Lanark was believed to be the largest cotton-spinning establishment in Great Britain. Richard Arkwright, who had patented the spinning jenny, was initially a partner.

With Owen in charge, the labor force increased to about 1,500. "Children were employed from the age of ten, though Owen would have preferred not to take them below twelve," John F. C. Harrison wrote in *Quest for the New Moral World*. Until 1816, the hours of labor were thirteen per day; later reduced to twelve, with ten and a half hours of actual labor. Owen calculated that during his 30 years' association with New Lanark, over £300,000 in profits were divided among the partners, over and above the 5 percent paid annually on the invested capital and the cost of his various social experiments.[7]

Owen provided housing at low rent, free medical services, a retirement fund and village schools for which there was a nominal charge. These were all based on actuarial principles, and the operation could not be mistaken "for anything other than what it was: a profit-making cotton mill," Harrison added. The equally large mill of Jedediah Strutt in Derbyshire resembled New Lanark, with the same housing, schools, health care and store. But visitors did not flock to see it, as they did to New Lanark, "nor did the Strutts consider their paternalistic efforts the germ of a new system of society."

Owen did a tremendous job of publicizing his reforms. He began to spend more and more time in London, meeting with lords and bishops. All were impressed by the rich factory owner from the north who was agitating for improved working conditions. The archbishop of Canterbury gave him respectful attention, and the prime minister, Lord Liverpool, found time to see him. The duke of Kent (father of Queen Victoria) seemed to have become almost a confidant, chairing meetings on behalf of Owen's "new views." Owen loved being a lord, and his name-dropping reaches an embarrassing level in his autobiography.

He disputed with Malthus, Ricardo and James Mill, but found these "pushing, busy, and ever active political economists" to be "great talkers upon a false principle": individualism. He purchased 30,000 copies of the newspapers that reported on his meetings, and tirelessly mailed them to magistrates, bankers and bishops. The grand duke Nicholas, later czar of Russia, visited New Lanark, and hearing of the Malthusian theory of population, offered to solve it by transporting two million Englishmen to his native land. The grand duke hoped that Owen would replicate his mill in Muscovy. Owen thanked His Imperial Highness, but "being then independent in pecuniary matters," declined this "most liberal imperial offer."[8]

In 1816, Owen opened his Institute for the Formation of Character, more or less anticipating Soviet developments 100 years later. His faith in human malleability was boundless. "Children are, without exception, passive and wonderfully contrived compounds," he wrote in his "Second Essay on the Formation of Character." They "may be formed collectively to have any human character. And although these compounds, like all the other works of nature, possess endless varieties, yet they partake of that plastic quality which . . . may be ultimately moulded into the very image of rational wishes." The character of man was formed *for* him, not *by* him, he repeatedly said.

As his wealth increased, so did his independence, and he grew ever more indifferent to public opinion. He denounced "all religions," whose errors had made man "a weak, imbecile animal."[9] Machinery he regarded as mankind's greatest curse. He also believed that people should be put back to work on the land, but not in the old way. Instead, they should live together in a collectivity. Owen's son Robert Dale Owen, returning from a trip abroad at this time, found that Owen was still doing well in business but losing ground "in public estimation." Robert Dale seemed to have picked up no trace of his father's utopianism. "He had been misled by benevolent enthusiasm," Robert Dale wrote of his father, and by his sudden wealth. Having started out with $10 in his pocket, Owen was worth a quarter of a million dollars by the time he was 45. Having overseen his sons' schooling, Owen must have expected that *their* characters, at least, had been formed for them and not by them. But Robert Dale's traditional views, published in his very readable autobiography *Threading My Way* (1874), shows that Owen's faith in education did not work out as hoped even within his own family.

One day in 1815, several boatloads of Lutheran schismatics from Wurttemberg sailed down the Wabash River, in Indiana. "Eight hundred strong, clad in the garb of the Fatherland, this quaint company went ashore at a point near the site of the present village of New Harmony," George Lockwood wrote in *The New*

Harmony Movement. "They knelt on the bank about a patriarchal leader, and with a song and prayer dedicated 'Harmonie' to the uses of a Christian brotherhood. These were the Rappites—German peasants, primitive Christians, practical communists, and disciples of George Rapp. As an organized protest against the existing state of religion in Germany, they had left the shores of their Fatherland behind them ten years before."[10]

George Rapp believed that Jesus had enjoined a community of goods upon his followers, and it is interesting to see how far he was able to take his disciples in this difficult direction. When the Rappites at first established community of property, a record was made of the amount each had contributed. This was refunded to anyone who withdrew. But within three years this agreement was abrogated and burned, signifying the Rappites' desire to practice communism to the fullest extent. Initially, marriage was normal among them, but that, too, was changed. Those already married moved into houses where the sexes were strictly separated. It is a measure of the obedience that Rapp commanded that this seems to have been accepted without argument. The Rappites distilled whiskey for sale but drank none. Tobacco was also forbidden. They individually confessed their sins to George Rapp.

"From a pecuniary point of view," Robert Dale Owen wrote, the Rappites' experiment in communal living was a "marvellous success." He provides the following figures, and revealing comment: "At the time of their immigration to the United States, their property was worth no more than $25 a head." But 21 years later, a "fair estimate" was $2,000 per capita, children included. This was "probably ten times the average wealth throughout the United States; for at that time each person in Indiana averaged but a hundred and fifty dollars in property, and even in Massachusetts the average fell short of $300." Nonetheless, Robert Dale thought that "intellectually and socially" the community was a failure, for it was an "ecclesiastical autocracy," with Rapp its absolute ruler. It was said that Rapp sold the property at Harmony because life had become too easy. Some believed that the hard work of a new settlement made Rapp's disciples more submissive.

For whatever reason, Rapp's agent traveled to Scotland and offered the property to Owen. "Here was a village ready built, a territory capable of supporting tens of thousands in a country where the expression of thought was free, and where the people were unsophisticated," his son explained to Owen. "Well, Robert," the senior Owen said, "what say you—New Lanark or Harmony?" Robert Dale didn't hesitate: "Harmony."

"Does your father really think of giving up a position like his, with every comfort and luxury, and taking his family to the wild life of the far West?" Rapp's agent asked. "He did not know," Robert Dale commented, "that my father's one ruling desire was for a vast theatre on which to try his plans of social reform."[11]

In the fall of 1824, Owen crossed the Atlantic, taking his other son, William, with him and leaving Robert Dale to manage the Scottish mill. Owen purchased Harmony for $150,000—half what it was worth, according to Lockwood's account. The estate consisted of 30,000 acres, a tenth under cultivation, with 19 detached farms, 600 acres of improved land occupied by tenants, several orchards, and 18 acres of vines. The village of Harmony included a church; houses of brick, frame and log, and factories with almost all of their machinery intact.

THE HETERODOX INSTINCT

Owen believed that society should be reorganized according to a blueprint that has repeatedly recurred in the minds of reformers: private property should be abolished, the family replaced by a larger unit, and religion either revised or abolished completely. In *The Socialist Phenomenon,* Igor Shafarevitch drew attention to the repetitive way in which these ideas have been proposed, in different countries and centuries. Private property, marriage and religion constituted Owen's "trinity of evils." He was not a man who spent much time with books, and undoubtedly his thoughts on these matters arose independently of any reading. They must reflect, as Shafarevitch has suggested, a deeply embedded heterodox instinct that is relatively common in mankind.[12]

In his *Book of the New Moral World,* containing the "Rational System of Society," Owen wrote that private property "alienates mind from mind" and produces in its possessors "pride, vanity, injustice and oppression." But the time was rapidly approaching when "the progress of science, and the knowledge of the means to form a superior character for all the individuals of the human race" would render private property "not only unnecessary, but most injurious to all." The family would give way to a more "scientific" association, ranging in numbers from 500 to 2,000.[13] It is characteristic of utopian reformers that the ideal size of their communities is often given precisely. Charles Fourier's phalanx, for example, was supposed to consist of 1,620 people. Followers no doubt believed that some esoteric secret of human society had been discovered.*

Owen believed that communes should be constructed in squares, or perhaps rectangles. Education would play a major role. Once the communes

---

*The first attempt to set up a Fourierist phalanx took place in 1833. "Fourier himself had doubts almost from the beginning. He was soon chiding the disciples for taking liberties with the doctrine; and when the architect built a pigsty with stone walls 18 inches thick and no entrance, Fourier became convinced that he was in the pay of the Saint-Simonians." Jonathan Beecher and Richard Bienvenu, *The Utopian Vision of Charles Fourier* (Boston: Beacon Press, 1971), 20.

were up and running, they would reproduce themselves by "swarming." The older way of organizing life would not have to be stamped out—it simply would not survive the competition. "There will be no desire or motive for individual accumulation of wealth," Owen wrote, for all would have sufficient under his plan. Prisons and punishments would no longer be required.

The Radicals in London were scornful.[14] William Hone wrote in his *Reformist's Register:* "Robert Owen, Esq., a benevolent cotton-spinner and one of His Majesty's Justices of the Peace for the County of Lanark, having seen the world, and afterwards cast his eye over his well regulated manufactory in the said county, imagines he has taken a New View of Society, and conceives that human beings are so many plants, which have been out of the earth for a few thousand years and require to be reset. He accordingly determines to dibble them in squares after a new fashion. . . . I do not know a gentleman in England better satisfied with himself than Mr. Owen. I ask him to *let us alone,* lest he do us much mischief." Owen's leading principle, *"all things in common,* turns the whole country into a workhouse."

William Cobbett derided Owen's "parallelogram of paupers," and proclaimed it "a species of *monkery.*" The gentleman "is for establishing innumerable communities of paupers. Each is to be resident in an *inclosure,* somewhat resembling a barrack establishment, only more extensive. . . . I perceive that they are all to be under a very *regular discipline;* and that wonderful peace, happiness and national benefit are to be the result!"[15]

When he came to the United States, Owen's fame preceded him. In 1825 he addressed the Congress, the Supreme Court and the cabinet. The changes he contemplated were "greater than all the changes which have hitherto occurred in the affairs of mankind," he said. What is surprising is that he was taken so seriously. His wealth surely had much to do with it; one who had done so well in business must have known what he was talking about.

Initially, Owen considered that a few years' training would be needed to wean recruits from their old "errors and prejudices." The key would be something called the Pestalozzian system, imported from Switzerland. The "progressive and symmetrical development of all the powers and faculties of the human being" would replace rote learning. Owen was soon joined by a group of scientists and Pestalozzian educators who came down the Wabash River in a vessel known later as the Boatload of Knowledge.

More than anything, Owen was misled by his optimism and his tremendous self-confidence. He simply issued an invitation to "the industrious and well disposed of all nations" to join him at New Harmony, and within a year one thousand adventurers duly arrived. They were quite willing to occupy the Rappite housing, go to assemblies, attend meetings, or do whatever Owen wanted. Most of the time, Owen himself wasn't even on the premises. Although regarded as a practical businessman, he was far more interested in theory, even when his own fortune was at stake. He left New Harmony immediately after its founding to go on a speaking tour, and he returned to England later that summer.

The following year he returned with Robert Dale Owen, who recalled that for a time the life was very pleasant—"the common experience of intelligent and well-disposed persons who have joined the Brook Farm or other reputable community." He found the good fellowship and absence of conventionalism charming. Particularly enjoyable was the "absolute freedom from trammels," whether in dress or opinion; the evening gatherings, the weekly discussion meetings, the concerts and the weekly ball, where he found "crowds of young people, bright and genial if not specially cultivated."

The accommodations were primitive, the fare simple, but for the young Owen it was as enjoyable as a summer under canvas. He helped tear down some old cabins, and once worked in the bakery; he even went into the fields and sowed wheat by hand, but this was tiring work. Eventually he busied himself in the school and edited the weekly paper. Then disenchantment set in, as it never did for his father.[16] Robert Dale later referred to his fellow communards as "that heterogeneous collection of radicals, enthusiastic devotees to principle, honest latitudinarians, and lazy theorists, with a sprinkling of unprincipled sharpers thrown in."[17]

"No communistic experiment was ever undertaken under more favorable auspices," Morris Hillquit wrote in his *History of Socialism in the United States.* "The hardships usually attending the first years of pioneer life of every community had been successfully overcome by predecessors, and no debt was weighing on the property."[18] This may have been a part of the problem, for the spur of necessity was lacking. But the premise of New Harmony was precisely that the ownership arrangement would promote a cooperative spirit, from which would issue forth cheerful and abundant labor. This was far from being the result, however, as Charles J. Erasmus described in *In Search of the Common Good.*

> Although the one thousand Owenites at New Harmony exceeded the number of Rappites before them, they neither put the factories into operation, nor ever even got farming underway. Without any plan for the selection of members the community ended up with no skilled craftsmen and only 35 farmers. There were members from every state in the union and nearly every country of northern Europe. They shared little or nothing in religion, background, habits, opinions or interests. According to one contemporary, never before had a small community . . . consisted of one thousand strangers all oblivious to each other's feelings. . . .
>
> Freeloaders greatly outnumbered workers and little was accomplished. When the community could not even grow food to sustain itself, Owen urged

members to cultivate private, household gardens. Owen did not have the kind of charisma to command a community venture of this sort and did not stay on the premises long enough to use what he had. He left his sons in charge of the day-to-day operations, and when funds eventually gave out, the experiment ended. Living off Owen's largesse, the members developed neither social incentives to provision the collective good nor any strong commitment to the group. Most finally decided that they could do better for themselves working individually on the outside. Without previous experience working together, they had convened from all walks of life and all points of the compass, and they dispersed by the same route.[19]

Owen made his great mistake three weeks after the Boatload of Knowledge disembarked. He proposed that the Harmonites should form themselves into a Community of Equality right away, with the property—his property!—to be shared in common. This worried his son, who recalled that the plan originally called for a training period of two or three years. Until then, the community had been run something like a business. A committee estimated the value of each worker's daily contribution, and credit slips for that amount were issued that could be exchanged for goods at community stores. Communards worked for pay, in other words, with remuneration roughly proportional to output.

But Owen, like Rapp before him, was determined to put communism into practice. He couldn't wait to go on to the next stage, with all members provided for, not according to their services, but equally, receiving "as near as can be" similar food, clothing and education; "and as soon as practicable, to live in similar houses, and in all respects to be accommodated alike." The assembly of all the members duly voted that the property was to be held "in perpetual trust for the use of the community." All who signed within three days could join the Community of Equality. Most signed, becoming partners in an enterprise wholly capitalized for them by Robert Owen.

"Liberty, equality and fraternity, in downright earnest!" Robert Dale wrote in dismay. He had been counting on inheriting his father's fortune, not consuming it with a thousand strangers in a two-year spree in the wilds of Indiana. "I made no opposition to all this," he wrote. "I had too much of my father's all-believing disposition to anticipate results which any shrewd, cool-headed business man might have predicted. How rapidly they came upon us!"[20]

Within two weeks of the vote, a majority of the assembly asked Owen's help "for one year in conducting the concerns of the Community." In addition to sharing the property, Owen was now also expected to pay the bills. In return he would be able to tell his guests what to do. A general sense of relief met Owen's acceptance. The *New Harmony Gazette* reported: "Under the sole direction of Mr. Owen, the most gratifying anticipations of the future may be safely indulged."[21] There was one little problem: He could tell them what to do, but how could he get them to do it? The members were now co-owners! A contributor to the *Gazette* soon complained that "industrious members have been compelled to experience the unpleasant sensation of working for others, who are either unwilling or unable to do their share of the labor"—a plain restatement of the problem encountered at Plymouth Colony. One more attempt was made to keep track of the hours worked, but this was thought "to work injustice, as one worker might do as much in an hour as another might in four."[22]

"You have indolence, or the love of ease among you at New Harmony," a "Friendly Spectator" wrote. "It appears doubtful whether human nature can be brought to such moral perfection as to execute the social system entirely. There must be a controlling motive to urge men to physical exertion. He now has that in the possession of all that his work can give him. In the social [as opposed to the private] system, you must make his disposition so virtuous as to make him feel his responsibility. Can you do this?"[23]

In 1826, the duke of Saxe-Weimar showed up and left a good account, including a revealing glimpse of Owen. In the tavern, he wrote, he struck up a conversation with a plainly dressed man, about 50 years old, who mentioned "the disordered state in which I would find everything." When the duke asked after Mr. Owen, the man announced that he was Mr. Owen. He showed the duke over the premises and pointed out the old Rappite church, now occupied by joiners' and shoemakers' shops, and the mansion where George Rapp himself once lived. Like Lenin in the Kremlin, Owen contented himself with an austere apartment. In the evening he took the duke to an orchestral performance and a recitation of poetry, during which Owen described his plan: "He looks forward to nothing else than to remodel the world entirely; to root out all crime; to abolish punishment; to create similar views and similar wants, and in this manner to abolish all dissension and warfare," the duke recounted. He expressed some doubts to Owen, but made no impression. "He was too unalterably convinced of the result to admit the slightest room for doubt. It grieved me to see that Mr. Owen should be so infatuated by his passion for universal improvement as to believe and assert that he is about to reform the whole world, and yet that almost every member of his society with whom I talked, acknowledged that he was deceived in his expectations, and expressed their opinion that Mr. Owen had commenced on too grand a scale, and had admitted too many members without the requisite selection."[24]

Owen's money was rapidly running out, and the experiment came to an end a year later, with his farewell address in May, 1827. His intention had been to admit only the qualified, he told the Harmonites, but this was frustrated when the assembly, adopting a majority rule, had voted to admit all "preliminary" members. His optimism nonetheless remained undiminished. Returning to England, he stopped en route to deliver lectures on the New Moral World. In his autobiography, he managed to omit all reference to the New Harmony experience.

Owen generously offered land to those who wanted to set up smaller communes. Several were formed, but all failed. Some leases were obtained by "speculators who cared not a whit for co-operative principles, but sought private gain," his son wrote. "By the speculators he lost in the end a large amount of personal property, of which, under false pretences, they had obtained control."[25] Evidently a number of people said that they intended to live cooperatively, but within months privatized and sold their property. Owen had no legal recourse.

Robert Dale Owen later became a congressman from Indiana, and played a role in founding the Smithsonian Institution. By the time he wrote his autobiography, nearly 50 years after the events described, he had concluded that his father's plan was flawed in its central feature: "I do not believe that any industrial experiment can succeed which proposes equal remuneration to all men, the diligent and the dilatory, the skilled artisan and the common laborer, the genius and the drudge. I speak of the present age; what may happen in the distant future it is impossible to foresee and imprudent to predict. What may be safely predicted is that a plan which remunerates all alike will, in the present condition of society, ultimately eliminate from a cooperative associa-tion the skilled, efficient and industrious members, leaving an inefficient and sluggish residue, in whose hands the experiment will fail, both socially and pecuniarily."[26]

Owen spent on New Harmony, "and in meeting his ultimate losses the next year by swindlers, upwards of $200,000," his son wrote. "Thus, as his property did not then reach a quarter of a million, he was willing to give up more than four-fifths of what he was worth to this great experiment." He added the following touching comment: "The remainder, not exceeding $40,000, might have sufficed for a competence, had he been content to live quietly upon it. But it soon melted away in a hundred expenditures for experiments, publications and the like, connected with social and industrial reform. He seems to have felt it to be a point of honor, so long as he had means left, to avert reproach from the cause of co-operation by paying debts left standing at the close of unsuccessful experiments, whenever these had been conducted in good faith."[27]

THE FATE OF THE RAPPITES

George Lockwood believed that "ignorance and superstition" had been the most marked characteristics of the Rappite community. Yet when his book was published, in 1905, 80 years after Owen purchased Harmony, the Rappites still survived. Owen's community had lasted for just two years. All the Owenite communities in England and the United States failed within a few years. Most lasted for less than two.

It's worth taking a brief look at the fate of the Rappites. After they left Indiana, they bought land on the Ohio River. There a new village was built, called Economy. In 1832, an "intriguer" from Germany who called himself Count Maximilian joined the community. According to Charles Nordhoff's *Communistic Societies of the United States,* he advocated "a livelier life" and various other "temptations to worldliness," persuading one-third of the community to leave with him. The two-thirds who stayed on were prosperous and generous enough to pay these seceders $105,000. Those who left set up another community ten miles way "on communistic principles." They restored marriage, and quickly spent the Rappite money. "After a desperate and lawless attempt to extort more money from the Economy people, which was happily defeated, [the count] absconded with a few of his people in a boat to Alexandria, on the Red River, where he perished of cholera in 1833," Nordhoff wrote.[28]

George Rapp himself died in 1847, aged 90, at the end preaching to the community through an open window. Those elected to succeed him preserved his rules. By 1875, the community's wealth may have amounted to $30 million. A time of bad investments and declining fortunes followed. The dwindling community seems to have quietly privatized itself, and in 1903 the Liberty Land Company of Pittsburgh purchased the entire 2,500 acres of Economy for an estimated $4 million. Six members survived when Lockwood's book was published in 1905. "Before many years have passed," he wrote, "the lands once tilled by the Rappites will be grown over with factories and homes, the last of those who lived and labored in the hope of realizing the communism of the early Christians will be laid to rest under the moundless greensward of the Rappite burying ground, the last dollar of the millions heaped up through the patient labor of the stolid Harmonists will have passed to individual bank accounts."[29]

The irony was that George Rapp had shown that life without private property is possible, but only if the commune members share an overriding purpose. Probably, religion alone can achieve that, and such a community may also have to be celibate. If separate families exist, the parental self-sacrifice needed to raise children will not easily coexist with the knowledge that their efforts are subsidizing others. It may be that a religious community not only *can* live communistically, but *must* do so: can, because freed from the cares of raising children, members will be able to subordinate the material question; must, because the individual desire for property (beyond personal possessions) might otherwise subvert the religious goal of the community.

Owen strongly disagreed with such notions, needless to say. He knew about the survival of the Rappites and the Shakers, and regarded them as "perhaps the most moral societies known in consequence of their abandonment of private property." But they existed in a "very unnatural and unsatisfactory state," having excluded the "natural enjoyment by which man alone can become satisfied and happy." They had not yet discovered how to "exclude private property and to maintain the natural union of the sexes." It had been utterly beyond their powers to do so.[30] And so it had. But it had also been beyond his.

"Communities based on religious views have generally succeeded," Charles A. Dana wrote in the *New York Sun* in 1869. "The Shakers and the Oneida community are conspicuous illustrations of this fact, while the failure of the various attempts made by the disciples of Owen, Fourier and others, who have not the support of religious fanaticism, proves that without this great force the most brilliant social theories are of little avail."[31]

In a sense, Owen himself *had* tried to establish a religious community. A few days after his public denunciation of all religions, he wrote: "On this day, the most glorious the world has seen, the *religion of charity, unconnected with faith,* is established for ever."[32] He was in many ways a religious man, at times coming close to speaking of himself as a messiah. In his New Lanark address, he declared that "the minds of all men must be born again . . . All things shall pass away, and all shall become new." The path forward was clear: "The period is arrived when I may call numbers to my aid, and the call will not be in vain."

In his eighties, Owen edited the *Millennial Gazette* and took up spiritualism. According to G. D. H. Cole, "Shakespeare, Shelley, Napoleon, the Duke of Wellington and the prophet Daniel became his familiars." At the very end of his life, in November, 1858, he returned to his Welsh birthplace, visited the house where he was born, tried to see an old friend who had died 20 years earlier, arranged several public meetings, drew up a plan to reorganize the education of the town, and died a few days later.[33]

TEN

THE SOVIET
EXPERIMENT

BY THE LATE NINETEENTH CENTURY, many socialists were aware of the problem of communes. So they began to conceive of life organized in a very different way: controlled from the center. Production, indeed the work of everyone in society, would be determined by a central plan. Free riding would no longer be possible because it would be forbidden. The shortage of virtue that had disabled communes would be remedied by force. Everyone would be obliged to obey the plan and the state would assume omnipotence. Such a concentration of power might seem dangerous, but there was no need to worry, because the state would be directed by the wise and the virtuous. And the people, once liberated from their oppressors, would eventually be transformed as well. The idea that human nature would be changed once property was abolished survived the crucial transition from a voluntary to a compulsory organization of society.

The Bolshevik Revolution of October, 1917, Trotsky said, did not overthrow the Kerensky government alone, "it overthrew the whole social system that was based on private property."[1] The following steps were swiftly taken: on October 26, 1917, a land decree deprived nonpeasant owners of landed property. Urban real estate was withdrawn from commerce in December, and in August, 1918, expropriated on behalf of the state. All state debts were repudiated in January of that year. In April, the purchase, sale and lease of commercial and industrial enterprises was forbidden. "A major step in the abolition of private property was taken on May 1, 1918, with the decree outlawing inheritance," Richard Pipes noted in his history of the Russian Revolution.[2] He added that this was the most audacious and most determined effort in the entire history of mankind to reshape human nature and redesign human society. Such attempts had been made previously, but on a much smaller scale and for much shorter periods. Nor did they involve the use of force. Communism is often called a utopian experiment, but true utopianism found expression in communities of volunteers who joined freely and felt free to leave. A society brought into being by a small body of utopians through a coup d'etat and maintained by terror, with hermetically sealed borders, cannot be designated utopian. It was something new in history both in conception and implementation: an attempt to launch humanity, by compulsion, on paths it had given no prior indication of wishing to tread.[3]

One of the first economists to see the key feature of this system, and, as early as 1920, to predict its failure, was Ludwig von Mises. "*One will* alone acts," he wrote. This individual may be called a king or a dictator, but the main point was that the entire economy would be directed according to his will. With the assistance of a central planning agency, the autocrat "chooses, decides, directs, acts, gives orders." Everyone else obeys. A military model was thereby substituted for the economic. The theory was that an organized and planned order would be substituted for the "anarchy" of private production and the competing initiatives of millions of individuals.[4]

It is certain that the Bolsheviks who took this step had no conception of the immense difficulties and hardships that would arise once private property was abolished. They neither anticipated them nor "planned" for them. In fact, a remarkable feature of twentieth-century socialism has been the unwillingness of those who put so much faith in planning to plan for the onset of socialism itself. The Bolsheviks were so suffused with ideological certitude, so confident of the wisdom and justice of what they were doing, that they went right ahead with full-scale nationalization without any preparation at all.*

The policies of the early Bolshevik period, retroactively labeled War Communism, led to swift economic collapse. Some have tried to show that they

---

*After becoming prime minister in 1945, Clement Attlee agreed to fulfil the election pledge to nationalize Britain's coal mines. Emanuel Shinwell, his minister of fuel and power, later wrote: "I was optimistic enough to believe that after 25 years of talking about nationalization, at least an outline of a plan would have been available at Labour Party headquarters." But nothing existed beyond a few pamphlets for party workers and copies of resolutions passed at party conferences. In a second memoir, *Lead With the Left: My First Ninety-six Years,* he wrote: "When addressing a meeting in 1947 of the Cooperative Union at Edinburgh, I pleaded for more effective study of the problems associated with public ownership. To my surprise I was rebuked in a letter from Jim Callaghan [Labour prime minister in the 1970s], who went so far as to suggest that by my declaration I had rendered a disservice to the party." Emanuel Shinwell, *I've Lived Through It All* (London: Gollancz, 1973), 192; Shinwell, *Lead With the Left: My First Ninety-six Years* (London: Cassell, 1981), 131-132.

were foisted upon reluctant Bolsheviks by the civil war. "'War Communism' was imposed by war and ruin," Lenin himself wrote in April, 1921.[5] But this was an improvised attempt to explain its failure. It seems that Lenin all along had his reservations. In "Left-Wing Childishness and Petty Bourgeois Mentality," written in May, 1918, he complained bitterly about revolutionaries who thought that blaming saboteurs and calling for more coercion could solve all problems. "We have nationalised, confiscated, beaten down and broken more than we have been able to *keep count of*," Lenin cried out. But this was not enough. "What we lack is something quite different. We lack the proper calculation of which saboteurs to put to work, and where to place them; we lack the organization of *our own* forces for supervision."[6] But the Left Communists, led by Nikolhai Bukharin, believed that full socialism should be introduced immediately, and Lenin's proposal to retain elements of capitalism during a period of transition was resisted.

Not only was private property outlawed, but a preliminary attempt was made to eliminate money as a medium of exchange. The idea was to end private commerce entirely by abolishing all retail and wholesale trade and replacing it with government distribution. There would be compulsory labor for all able-bodied males, and for some women and children. These upheavals were consistent with the ideology of communism. A private-property economy is an exchange economy. Tens of thousands, or even millions, of producers compete with one another in producing their own goods separately, which are then exchanged using the medium of money. In order to produce automobiles, a manufacturer will have to purchase the output of numerous private suppliers of parts and raw materials, and then pay for the labor needed to assemble them into the finished product. Exchange is thus the natural concomitant of subdivided ownership, or private property.

A state-owned and centrally planned economy implies the abolition of exchange itself. Following full nationalization, everything is controlled by a single entity, armed with the power to coerce. The exchange of goods becomes unnecessary—in a sense impossible—and so does money. The planning agency simply decrees that an enterprise will manufacture a certain good for the entire country—let us say automobiles. In accordance with the plan, the various (state owned) producers of the component parts will be required to transfer to the auto factory the quantities needed to implement the plan.

At the same time, workers in the necessary numbers are ordered to report to work at the factory. Cars roll off the assembly line, and they, too, remain the property of the state. In accordance with the plan, they are assigned to the people, including (let us hope) the workers themselves. They might have to be given certificates of service, entitling them to draw goods sufficient for their needs from state distribution centers, but that is as close as the system would come to relying on money. It would depend on compulsory labor and state ownership and distribution. In attempting to include all these elements, the Bolsheviks were acting consistently in light of their theories. In fact, they never actually decreed money out of existence, although they talked about it and apologized for not doing so. "Finance should not exist in a socialistic community," said the Soviet commissar of finance, "and I must therefore apologize for speaking of the subject."[7]

Money as a store of value was destroyed, however. Savings throughout the Soviet Union were erased by the severe postrevolutionary inflation. All this precipitated economic catastrophe. By 1920, large-scale industrial production had fallen to 18 percent of its 1913 level, coal production to 27 percent, iron to 2.4 percent. The number of employed industrial workers fell by half from 1918 to 1921. Lenin was puzzled. "What kind of a proletariat is it? Where is your industry? Why is it idle?" he wanted to know.[8]

We catch a glimpse of a frustrated Lenin in a *Pravda* account. He had already pronounced his famous adage that "communism is the Soviet power plus the electrification of the whole country," and he came to believe that a plan for the electrification of the Soviet Union was synonymous with the "Single Economic Plan." Such a plan, published in 1920, had been drawn up "by the best scientists in our Republic." By 1921, however, not much was happening, and Lenin concluded that "the conceit of the bigwigs," and "Communist journalists" were to blame. They had opposed putting "bourgeois experts" on the planning board and did not understand that while the experts might be bourgeois, they were also scientific, and so should be accorded a little respect.[9]

Lenin's remarks on the stalled plan are of interest. The plan contained "a detailed program of work," and it enumerated "the responsible persons, scientists, engineers, agronomists and statisticians." Their tasks had been "precisely defined." Specific jobs filled "ten printed pages of the first number of the Bulletin"; over 180 "experts" had contributed. Two hundred books had been consulted. The fuel budget for the entire Soviet Union covering the next decade had been worked out; the future of "agriculture," "transport" and "industry" had also been included. The number of workers required over the next decade had been minutely calculated. "We have the precise calculations of the experts on all the principal questions," Lenin reassured his readers. Everyone would be needing two pairs of shoes, for example, which by multiplication meant that 300 million pairs of shoes would soon be needed. So, that amount of leather would be needed. (Lenin didn't say anything about sizes or styles, and one wonders if the plan ever delved into such details; almost certainly not.)

Nobody seemed to be doing anything, however. The plan was just sitting there. "Of course, by their very nature, plans are things that can be talked and argued about endlessly," Lenin said. It was high time for implementation: "to begin to build this and that, to collect and transport such and such material, and so forth." It was also time for the Communists to do less bossing, "or rather, not to boss at all, but to observe an extremely cautious and tactful attitude to experts in science and technology."

One of the great problems with planning is that the information on which the plan is based will always be out of date. Lenin's planners were beginning to realize this, and so they were updating the plan. Lenin saw correctly that this could go on forever. He also realized that he was no longer running a school for revolutionaries. To be sure, the old order had been destroyed, but a new society had yet to be "built." Actual power plants had to be constructed if "the whole country" was to be electrified. "In the end," according to the authors of *Utopia in Power*, the electrification plan "remained on paper."[10]

AUSTRIAN OBJECTIONS

Of planning's many difficulties, Lenin had encountered only one: the difficulty of piecing together the information needed to formulate the plan. Planners must know a lot if they are to have any chance of directing the lives of an entire population. It was pure fantasy to imagine that it would be easy to accumulate so much knowledge, and use it to control so vast a country. The dean of Canterbury, the Reverend Hewlett Johnson (the "Red Dean"), visited the Soviet Union in the 1930s and was reassured that planning was working as intended. His description of planning headquarters in Moscow, which he may really have visited, is of particular interest because it inadvertently draws attention to the central difficulty.

> There is centered in a series of buildings in Moscow an organization unsurpassed in the world for the extent and importance of its operations. Its ramifications stretch on and on until they penetrate every corner of a sixth of the world's surface. No factory, no farm, no school, no theatre, no court of law, no hospital, no regiment escapes its scrutiny. By statutory law every public institution in every branch of activity throughout a union which embraces a twelfth of the human race must supply to that central office in Moscow complete data of their present and prospective needs and operations.
>
> The mass of information that pours daily and hourly into those central offices is seized upon, sifted, sorted, and utilized by what is undoubtedly the largest staff of trained statisticians and technical experts in the world, served by thousands of clerks and assistants. (Of the competence of those statisticians even several years back Mr. Friedman, the American expert, says, "In general Russian statistics seem correct, and they check with each other during successive years and with related figures.")

That office is no dead, cold, scientific, and heartless place of red tape and officialism; it is primarily concerned with the fate of men and women, boys and girls. Every individual throughout the whole Soviet Union has his or her place among the figures that enter those doors. If he is able bodied his name enters one series of figures, if sick or too old or too young to work . . . his name or hers enters other appropriate series. In this way the experts learn the total number of active workers upon whom the country can depend for making things and rendering services. Another set of essential data is the estimation of the needs of all those same multitudes for food, clothing, housing, education, health, or leisure, and of the people as a whole for defence and for capital production in the form of mines, railways, or machines. These figures and others continually pour in.[11]

It did not occur to the dean to question whether "accurate data" really was pouring in. If provided at all, such information would be out-of-date when tabulated. Compiling it would itself require the labor of millions of people. It is no easier to move a lot of information to a central point than to roll thousands of ball bearings into a small hole. Almost all will have to wait their turn. In a country with tens of millions of people, it is impossible to transfer knowledge of their whereabouts, activities, health, dispositions and abilities to a central bureau.

This objection to planning seems to have been first made by Friedrich Hayek, in *Collectivist Economic Planning,* in 1935. The central authority cannot give wise commands to the managers of factories if it doesn't know what is going on in them. This constraint is not just created by the technical problem of transferring reliable data to a single point. In a dictatorship, people will only provide information about themselves under duress, because they understand that there is safety in anonymity. Adding to the problem, totalitarian governments always monopolize the press. The leaders are rationally afraid that the people will communicate their dissatisfactions to one another, and perhaps rebel. But this only adds to the difficulty of finding out what is happening.

The problem can be appreciated by thinking about getting a message into the Oval Office. Speechwriters in the White House itself cannot easily do it. They can pass on their brilliant ideas to the chief of staff—who might not think them so brilliant. He has other messages to deliver, and the president is busy. Most messages must be excluded. A whole White House bureaucracy has already been established to decide which things are urgent, which things can wait.

But in a planned economy, the planners were supposed to control minute details of faraway events. If a deputy commissar in Omsk needed Moscow's permission to switch a consignment of harvesters from one destination to another, he could wait—and ruin the harvest by abiding by the law. Moscow is in the dark, recall. Or he could break the law (ignore Moscow) and save the harvest. But if he gets into the law-breaking business, he might well see the wisdom of teaming up with a particular state-farm manager who needs the harvesters, and who offers a reward in exchange for switching them his way. If the favor is accepted, economic decision making has been decentralized: Moscow is no longer "in the loop." The economy is functioning again, but private property is on its way to being restored. In the Soviet Union, of course, any such restoration of efficiency was identified as "corruption."

Introducing terror into the equation did not encourage producers to "adopt the economy-wide viewpoint," as Thomas Sowell has pointed out.[12] On the contrary, when imprisonment was added to the penalties for failing to obey the plan, managers stuck even more closely to the letter of the law, "without regard to larger economic considerations." In one case, mining equipment was badly needed but never delivered, because the plan specified red paint; the manufacturer had only green. Unpainted equipment then piled up in the factory because, the manager said, "I don't want to get eight years."

Here, the plan had been overarticulated; the final product had been specified in too much detail. But if such details are omitted, other problems will arise. David Shipler of the *New York Times* described a case in which the quotas of Soviet nail factories were given in weight only. Managers then favored the production of large, heavy nails. Most of them remained unused on the shelf even as the country was "crying for small nails."[13]

In both examples, the manufacturer's incentive is to put obedience first. Profit making is illegal anyway. So the plan will be undermined by adherence to it. The planners are unable to give commands that take into account local conditions—like the local availability of paint—because they don't know what those conditions are. How about a phone call to Moscow? ("Can we use green paint?") It would have been as difficult to get through as it would for a plant manager in Peoria with a similar difficulty to reach the secretary of commerce (let alone the president of the United States). Underlings might have been reachable, but lots of others would have been phoning them, too. Even then, underlings would not have the authority to change the plan. They would be afraid to make exceptions without permission from on high.

The problem can be solved by decentralizing decision making across the entire economy, but that is the antithesis of central planning. It's a solution that takes us back to private property. Could not the makers of harvesters, nails and mining equipment somehow be permitted to think and act independently without making owners of them? The problem is that "thinking and acting independently" is a good part of what we mean by ownership. If those in charge of such enterprises are deprived of the full incentives of ownership, including profit making, they will be induced to make choices quite different from those of real owners.

The tremendous difficulty for planners created by the problem of knowledge was not considered by the socialists until the 1930s. Their conviction that central planning would replace an antiquated and chaotic system with a modern and rational one disposed them to dismiss all such criticism as the expression of class interest. "The outstanding fact in the history of socialism between 1848 and 1920 was that the essential problems concerning its workings were hardly ever touched upon," as Mises wrote in *Human Action*. "The Marxian taboo branded all attempts to examine the economic problems of a socialist commonwealth as 'unscientific.'"[14]

It is a great irony of communism that those who did not believe in God believed that godlike knowledge could be concentrated at a central point. It was believed that government could be omnipotent and omniscient. And in order to justify the idea that all lives should be determined by a single plan, the concomitant tendency of communist regimes was to deify the leader—whether Lenin, Stalin, Mao or Kim Il-sung.

Mises had earlier made a more detailed criticism of planning, but it was really a variant of the problem of information. In abolishing private property, the planners were also abolishing legal markets, and therefore market-determined prices. But in a capitalist system, producers and consumers are continually guided by prices in their choices; guided in what they want to manufacture, in how to do so, and in what they want to purchase. There are thousands of ways of making an automobile, for example, and knowing the prices of its parts enables a producer to decide which materials, and how much of each, to use. Auto bodies made of silver might look nice, for example, and they would be durable. They would also be very expensive.

In a market economy, producers know the approximate prices that their finished products will fetch. They therefore have a way of knowing whether the thing produced will end up having more value than the sum of its parts. If they don't achieve this outcome—sometimes called profit making—they will soon go out of business. But the abolition of markets and market prices in the Soviet system made all such calculations difficult, and production equally so. Primitive planning and stop-start production without prices was possible, but often resulted in goods that no one wanted. Ironically, the problem was not as severe as it might have been because markets continued to exist in other countries. Soviet planners were able to consult commodity prices in such capitalist organs as the *Wall Street Journal*.

Even this gave them only moderate help, however. Market prices fluctuate from one region to another, and from one day to the next, depending on local supply and demand conditions. If Lenin's dream of worldwide communism had been implemented, all market price information would have been lost, and the revolution would have collapsed in short order. Stalin's policy of "socialism in one country" was wiser than he knew.

In the 1930s, the economists Oskar Lange and Fred M. Taylor responded to Mises with the argument that state planners could rationalize production with notional "bookkeeping" prices. They would be able to arrive at the "correct" price by trial and error. If inventories piled up in warehouses, prices were set too high; if there were shortages, prices were too low. But capitalism works because managers bid for resources using money whose loss has real consequences. The overriding incentive of state factory managers was to implement their quota, and in pursuit of this goal, with notional prices, their bidding would be unconstrained. It would resemble a game of poker played with Monopoly money. Bidders have nothing real at stake in such a game. All can go on bidding as high as they like, because at the end of the evening they will only lose chips. The game of "economy" likewise must be played with real money.

For years, nonetheless, Lange's reply was cited in economics textbooks as though he had won the debate. But after the collapse of Eastern Europe, Robert Heilbroner generously set the record straight. "Fifty years ago," he wrote in the *New Yorker,* "it was felt that Lange had decisively won the argument for socialist planning. . . . It turns out, of course, that Mises was right."[15]

A SLAVE ECONOMY

All these objections about knowledge and calculation were true enough, and sufficient to disable the dream of planners, but there was a more fundamental problem. The workers were reduced to a state of servitude, and had no particular reason to work hard. In being compelled to carry out someone else's plan, they were prevented from carrying out their own.

The arguments about transferring information and the problem of pricing conjure up a misleading picture of Soviet life: frustrated factory managers wait at their desks for the phone call that never comes, giving them permission to modify the plan. Workers stand at their lathes eager to press ahead with the task, but are unable to do so because wrong prices have misallocated goods. They are visualized as though frustrated by a combination lock (in Robert Hessen's image). They try different combinations, always in vain. With the right combination the lock will spring open; with the right price combination, the workers will spring into action. In the more realistic picture, the worker is not on the job at all, or may be drunk; the manager is privatizing the parts as they arrive at the loading dock, and so on.

A glimpse of real life on the job was provided by the Soviet dissident Vladimir Bukovsky in *To Build A Castle.* In the 1950s, the Communist Party decided that students needed some experience of life in the factory. It "did indeed widen our horizons," Bukovsky reports, though not in the manner intended:

[M]y classmates and I saw for the first time what a Soviet enterprise is like—with all its deceptions, its hollow facade, and its coercion. Nobody in the bus factory was in a hurry to work; the workers preferred to sit in the smoking room until the foreman appeared, when they all dashed to their places. "Why should we hurry for the money they pay us?" said the workmen. "Work's not a wolf, it won't run into the forest!" In the mornings they were almost all drunk or hung over, and throughout the working day people would be regularly detailed to slip over the fence for some vodka. Only one man put in a full day's work. The rest hated him, and when pointing him out would rotate one finger meaningfully by the temple. They were always looking for chances to do him dirt, either by surreptitiously damaging his machine or by stealing his tools. "Want to be a champion and raise the targets?" they said spitefully. It turned out that if one man exceeded the target, the target would be raised for all of them the following month, and they would have to work twice as hard for exactly the same money.[16]

The coercive and tyrannical nature of planning, with or without reliable information, had been definitively described by Walter Lippmann in 1937. His argument, published in *The Good Society*, was never rebutted, though it was later restated by Friedrich Hayek. "A plan of production is a plan of consumption," Lippmann wrote. "If the authority is to decide what shall be produced, it has already decided what shall be consumed." It followed that a plan of production is incompatible with voluntary labor, and with the freedom of workers to choose their occupations. The plan must also dictate how long and where people shall work, and what they shall do. For with consumption rationed and standardized, the unpleasant jobs would otherwise be avoided. Therefore the conscription of labor must accompany the rationing of consumption. This conscription would have to be achieved either by edict or by force, or (as Trotsky saw) by offering workers starvation as the alternative. All this meant that the thoroughly planned state was the equivalent of the militarized state. The conscription of labor and the rationing of consumption are not just accidental features of a planned economy, they are the very substance of it. Lippmann went on to point out that drawing up a plan and then sticking to it entailed the abolition of democracy:

Who, in a civilian society, is to decide what is to be the specific content of the abundant life? It cannot be the people deciding by referendum or through a majority of their elected representatives. For if the sovereign power to pick the plan is in the people, the power to amend it is also there at all times. A plan subject to change from month to month or even from year to year is not a plan; if the decision has been taken to make ten million cars at $500 and one million suburban houses at $3,000, the people cannot change their minds a year later . . . and decide to produce instead skyscraper apartment houses and underground railroads.

There is, in short, no way by which the objectives of a planned economy can be made to depend upon popular decision. They must be imposed by an oligarchy of some sort, and that oligarchy must, if the plan is to be carried through, be without responsibility in matter of policy. . . . Not only is it impossible for the people to control the plan, but, what is more, the planners must control the people. They must be despots who tolerate no effective challenge to their authority. Therefore civilian planning is compelled to presuppose that somehow the despots who climb to power will be benevolent.[17]

Lippmann's argument was restated by Hayek in his *Road to Serfdom* (1944). He was a strong defender of private property, and saw that without it liberty would be swept away. But the phrase "private property" then still had strongly pejorative overtones, and in *The Constitution of Liberty* (1960) he said that he preferred the more obscure "several property," sometimes used in the nineteenth century.[18] In noting the refusal of planners to recognize "autonomous spheres in which the ends of the individual are supreme," he of course had private property in mind.

Commenting on the thesis of *The Road to Serfdom,* John Maynard Keynes wrote to Hayek: "Dangerous acts can be done safely in a community which thinks and feels rightly, which would be the way to hell if they were executed by those who think and feel wrongly."[19] Nonetheless, everything that Lippmann and Hayek said proved to be true. Central planning led to despotism in practice. And this had a devastating effect on the willingness to work. The workers understood that they had become the pawns of tyrants and so made minimal efforts. If we can rank the interrelated defects of so disastrous a system, this was probably the principal reason for the failure of the Soviet and all other centrally planned economies.

The Soviets were able to turn out some economic goods, but they were always shoddy and never in sufficient supply. The state was unable to build apartments in anything like the required numbers, for example. Units intended for a single family were occupied by four or five. Why weren't more built? The cost of the raw materials were not great. The blueprint of one building could be used for others. The authorities had unlimited land to build on. No building codes or environmental laws or zoning regulations impeded the planners. The problem was that the Soviet economy was like an automobile that had run out of gas: it had to be pushed every inch of the way. The most serious problem was the shortage of human energy.

The system had reduced the proletariat to serfdom, and the proles knew it. They could see that, contrary to propaganda, their efforts benefited a Party elite, with special stores and privileges. Workers realized that hard work benefited specific people, not "everyone." The meager product that did become available was diverted first and foremost to the military, and there wasn't much left over for civilian use. A few months before the Berlin Wall fell, Mikhail Gorbachev all but threw in the towel, saying that Soviet workers "forgot how to work because they got used to being paid, often for just coming to work."[20] The problem inherent in a command economy was perhaps best expressed in a saying that became widespread in the years leading up to the Soviet Union's demise: "We pretend to work and they pretend to pay us."

NEW SOVIET MAN

It is difficult to find in Lenin's writings much evidence that he believed in the New Man. Nor is it safe to say that he was free of the illusion. In *The State and Revolution* (1917), he does say that communism presupposes "a person unlike the present man in the street."[21] No published study in English traces the development of this key idea in the Soviet Union itself. Lenin, of course, was perfectly reconciled to the use of force where necessary. Trotsky, on the other hand, was a true believer. In his *Literature and Revolution,* he argued that under collectivism, "Man will become immeasurably stronger, wiser and subtler. His body will become more harmonized, his movements more rhythmic, his voice more musical. The forms of life will become dynamically dramatic. The average human type will rise to the heights of an Aristotle, a Goethe, or a Marx. And above these heights new peaks will rise."[22]

A year later, in the course of a speech entitled "A Few Words On How to Raise a Human Being," Trotsky asked if it were not possible to "improve man." Yes, he answered, it could be done. But first a more mundane task lay ahead (reality was already breaking through). Labor productivity would have to be increased. The complete and invincible victory of socialism would only arrive when "the unit of human power gives us more products than under the rule of private property." But before that could be achieved, Trotsky had gone into hiding in Mexico City.

The idea of the New Man, Western in origin, is much more in evidence in the writings of those who lived at a safe distance from the Soviet Union and occasionally paid a carefully orchestrated visit: Lincoln Steffens and Sidney and Beatrice Webb come to mind. In a section of *Soviet Communism: A New Civilization* (1944), the Webbs even explained "How The New Man Is Made." Their fantastic comment on a Stalingrad tractor factory is worth comparing with Bukovsky's Moscow bus factory: "To the statesman of the Soviet Union, what is produced in the factory or the mine, or the farm or the oil-field, is not merely wealth but the workers themselves, as they are moulded by their work.

The 40,000 male and female operatives of the Stalingrad Tractor Works, whom the factory itself has created out of the raw peasants who began to build it, are as much part of its product as the tractors that it constructs out of steel. This Remaking of Man by the factory in which he works is not taken into account by the balance sheet and profit and loss account insisted on by the Western economist."[23]

In the course of a visit to the Soviet Union in 1931, Julian Huxley found that the people's thoughts and feelings were different from his own, partly due to a different "racial temperament," but mainly because the new conditions were "modifying the human type."[24] In the same year, George Bernard Shaw reported that the Soviet government had shown human nature to be as easily molded as putty. Reflecting on Russia, Lincoln Steffens wrote in 1935 that "everything is in the course of evolution," and that "whatever you see will be changed to something better next year." He wondered (with private property in mind) "what will happen to institutions founded by the cave-men." A couple of years later, he believed that "Russia proved you can change human nature sufficiently in one generation."[25]

With a group of American teachers, A. P. Shatter visited the "Defectology Institute" in the summer of 1936, and there found the Soviets were "remaking human beings." The environment was "carefully controlled" and principles of "persuasion and compulsion" were applied to refractory children. They "belong to the 'collective' and in every way are led to become part of it. . . . I and Me gives way to We and Us."[26] Another educator who went to see for himself was Thomas Woody. In *New Minds, New Men,* published in 1932, he reflected on the "mental traits of the 'new men,' for whose cultivation all are charged to strive, and who already exist in substantial numbers."[27] As if to confirm all this, it was reported in 1935 that a coal miner named Aleksei Grigorevich Stakhanov had set a record by extracting 102 tons of coal in one shift—14 times the quota. Then, three weeks later, he really outdid himself and produced 227 tons of coal in one shift--30 times the quota. He soon became a member of the Communist Party, founder of the Stakhanovite movement, and a Hero of Socialist Labor. Later it was disclosed that all the statistics had been fabricated.

The myth of New Soviet Man really blossomed in the Khrushchev era. The Communist Party Program adopted in 1961 ("Communism—the Bright Future of All Mankind") foresaw a time when "labor and discipline will not be a burden to people," and predicted that "the material and technical basis of communism will be built up by the end of the second decade (1971-1980)." The "molding of the new man" was to be achieved by "his own active participation in communist construction," thereby recasting "the minds of people in a spirit of collectivism."[28]

By the 1980s, however, there was a tremendous change. Gorbachev expressed at one point "indignation about all sorts of shortcomings and those responsible for them—people who neglect their duties and are indifferent to society's interest: hack worker and idler, grabber and writer of anonymous letters, petty bureaucrat and bribe-collector."[29] Three years later, as the Soviets retreated from Afghanistan, Deputy Foreign Minister Anatoli Adamishin said: "To alter the world is difficult. To alter human beings is almost impossible."[30]

These illusions about human putty were for a long time sustained by the acceptance of false statistics of economic growth. The launch of *Sputnik* reinforced these impressions. For perhaps ten years thereafter, Western faith in Soviet performance remained extraordinarily high. "When I really feel gloomy I think that five years from now [the Soviets] will be obviously superior to us in every area," said Jerome Wiesner of MIT in 1957. "But when I am optimistic I feel it will take ten years for them to achieve this position."[31] In 1961, the *Saturday Review*'s Norman Cousins found that the Iron Curtain had become "the Red Magnet." He encountered there a "mammoth exuberance." What was being celebrated, along with Sputnik and "modern apartment houses and chromium-plated new cars and television sets and wristwatches and cameras and savings banks and vacation resorts and modern universities—was the culminating proof that the Russians had finally and indisputably arrived as a great nation."[32]

Westerners were much impressed that the Soviets had apparently been able to solve problems by force. The great defect of central planning was seen as its strength, giving rise to soul-searching about the conflict between liberty and prosperity. After visiting the Soviet Union in 1955, a Republican senator, William Benton, noted in *This is the Challenge* that "a dictatorship can order that more steel mills or machinery plants be built. In the free world, the consumer and his wants must largely provide the impetus for increased production." So we faced a quandary: our system was perhaps more moral (because based on consent), but theirs was more efficient (as the statistics showed). They could *command* the construction of steel mills. Benton concluded that war, revolution, tyranny and disaster had created "progress through catastrophe" in the Soviet Union.[33]

Meanwhile, it was not for the economists to agonize. "When men do not know what to do," Heilbroner wrote in *The Future as History,* "men must be told what to do. . . . Peasants, money lenders, petty bureaucrats can be told—ordered—to do what must be done." New nations emerging in the Third World would also have to centralize their economies, as they no doubt would do anyway because of their "bitter past experience with laissez-faire."[34]

Khrushchev promised in 1961 that communism would be "built" by 1980. By then, "public wealth" would "gush forth abundantly." GNP would have multiplied by five, production would be double that of the United States. Every Soviet family would have a free apartment and utilities, and "all that a man could reasonably want." Public transportation and lunches would be free. For those who wanted "rest in an out-of-town environment," there would be holiday homes and country hotels "at a discount or gratis." As for the United States, monopoly capital had "doomed bourgeois society to low rates of production and growth."[35] He could cite a good source for his optimism. CIA director Allen Dulles said in 1958 that the Soviet economy had been growing, and was expected to continue growing "at a rate roughly twice that of the United States."[36]

These figures were widely repeated and believed. Paul Samuelson's *Economics* sold over three million copies and has been the most influential economics textbook since World War II. In successive editions, it included a graph showing the growth paths of Soviet and American GNP, the Soviet output starting from a lower level, but rising more steeply. Theirs was shown as overtaking ours approximately twenty years in the future. With each new edition the paths remained unchanged, but the date of intersection was advanced. But in 1980 the long-promised crossover was no nearer at hand, and in the 1985 edition the graph was at last eliminated. In the 1989 edition, however, it was reported that "measured Soviet GNP has grown more rapidly over the long run than have most of the major market economies."[37]

Glasnost was tried, then *perestroika*. Then, in September, 1989, the Soviet Parliament debated what *New York Times* reporter Bill Keller called "the ultimate issue": the ownership of property. It touched upon "the most sensitive articles of Communist faith," he wrote, and had already stimulated "new flights of euphemism." Market-oriented reformers in the Kremlin were trying to go as far as they could, "while avoiding the p-word: private property." Two days later, a *Washington Post* reporter described the same debate as promising to disturb "some of the most sacred ground of traditional Marxist-Leninist ideology." Private property was "once one of the greatest taboos of Soviet Communist orthodoxy."[38]

"This word still frightens some people," said Aleksei N. Boiko, a professor of economics and a member of the Parliament's Committee on Economic Reform. But he favored at least its partial restoration. He was trying to think of a more tactful way to put it. Among his euphemisms were "household means of production," "individual property," and "property for citizen's labor activity." Two years later, Boris Yeltsin made his remarkable comment about Russia's unhappy role in the "experiment" that had been conducted. By the early 1990s, a consensus had emerged that private ownership should be restored. Many obstacles remained, some political, some practical. But the details were trivial compared to the recognition that the experiment in life without private property was over. Two hundred years had elapsed since William Godwin inveighed against "the existing institution" of property; one hundred since Alfred Marshall observed that the need for private property goes no deeper than human nature.

The failure of the experiment gives rise to the question: What was the aspect of human nature that proved to be so intractable—that refused to bend even in the gulag? Robert Owen had spoken of creating a new "rational world," and it is sometimes said that the failure of communism showed the impossibility of establishing a "rational society," or of "rationalizing" all aspects of life. But there is something quite misleading about this. The key feature of the communist plan was precisely its irrationality, and the intractable feature of human nature was precisely the faculty of reasoning.

Normally, in countries like the United States, society works reasonably well because individuals, looking out at the world from their respective vantage points, with their varying and unequal talents and interests, are permitted to use their reason—the most basic aspect of what is called "human nature." They can decide what it is that they want to do and then try to do it. In conjunction with their liberty, and their property rights, they can strive to attain some goal.

Humans come equipped with brains, and perhaps in our computer age it helps to substitute the word "computer." Society functions best when most of these "computers" are working and interacting in a network. Private property builds a domain of autonomy around individuals, permitting them to aspire to something more than obedience. Because they can secure the fruits of their efforts, they can make long-range plans. At the economic level, the price mechanism—which cannot function without private property—will permit thousands or millions of people to interdigitate and arrive at agreements.

Communist society tried to operate in an entirely different way. It tried to shut down all the "computers," except for a few at the center. Everyone else was expected to follow orders—to switch their brains to the "slave" position. This was tyrannically enforced precisely by depriving people of property. Liberty and autonomy was thereby destroyed, and people became dependent on the state whether they liked it or not. But the brains in their heads were still quietly and unobtrusively working; people could work out for themselves that their work helped their masters a great deal more than it helped themselves.

For a number of years, Communist propaganda seems to have been at least partially effective. The people may have been briefly persuaded that it was in their long-run interest to become willing slaves. But before too long, the continued exercise of the faculty of reason—put another way, the inability of Communist officials to rewire the human brain—told the people that it made no sense to continue working in anything other than minimal fashion. The "rational system of society" that Robert Owen and others had conceived was made unworkable by the faculty of reason itself.

RIGHT AND JUST

INTRODUCTION

After the Soviet experience, many people will admit that on economic grounds, a private property system is a necessity. But what about justice, what about our rights? Is it not possible to devise something more morally uplifting than a system that is efficient only because it encourages people to consult their own interest?

"The problem of property, as it occurs in contemporary political theory, is a problem of justification," Kenneth R. Minogue wrote in 1980.[1] For those philosophers who have taken an interest in the subject in recent years, the relationship between property and justice has overshadowed all other considerations. In these inquiries, it has always been private property that has been in the dock. Its defenders had to be ready for this challenge from the academy: What is your justification? The intellectual climate was such that the supporters of state property were for many years waved through all such checkpoints. It is a remarkable fact that only in 1995, four years after the demise of the Soviet Union, did the British Labour Party finally drop "clause four"—its platform statement calling for state ownership of the means of production.

Does private property satisfy the requirements of social justice? By way of illustration, I examine the great transformation that takes place when a master-metered condominium building is converted to a system of individual utility meters; the change is the equivalent of changing from a system of communal to private property. In addition to a gain in efficiency, there turns out to be a hitherto unrecognized connection between the very operation of a private property system and the classical definition of justice.

What about the relationship between property rights and civil rights? In the eighteenth and nineteenth centuries, it was understood that the "superior" rights of life and liberty would not be secure without property rights. More recently, primarily as a result of the Soviet experience, we have come to appreciate the related point, that the "subordinate" rights—free speech, religious liberty, the right to bear arms and other rights—also cannot be held securely if property rights are not respected. Therefore, property is the great mediator in the hierarchy of rights. Because we are corporeal beings, the physical space we occupy must be secure against invasion if we are to be free to enjoy our civil rights.

ELEVEN

TO EACH HIS DUE

CONDO

WE LEAD LIVES THAT ARE SO IMMERSED IN PRIVATE PROPERTY that we easily take its benefits for granted. Some everyday situations give us the opportunity to examine aspects of life without it, however. They permit us to see the great transformation that takes place when a communal arrangement is privatized: efficiency is enhanced, and, far more important, justice itself is routinized. The argument can be illustrated by an apartment building in Washington, D.C., in which the author lived. In one significant respect, the living arrangement resembles Plymouth Colony. It is a condominium building of approximately 300 privately owned apartments, bought and sold on the free market. Its total population is perhaps twice as large as that of Plymouth in the 1620s. Owners are assessed a condo fee, arrived at by adding up all expenses jointly incurred, and dividing them by a formula that takes into account the size of the apartments. But for the sake of simplicity, it is here assumed that all units are the same size and that all owners are charged the same condo fee.

The key point is that there are no individual utility meters. The entire building is "master metered" as an undivided whole. The utilities bill is then divided up (equally, I shall assume) among all unit owners. The utilities—gas, water, fuel oil and electricity—make up about one third of the building's million-dollar annual budget. In the consumption of energy, then, great opportunities for free riding occur.

How are property rights to utilities allocated in the building? All apartment owners (or their tenants, for many units are rented) may use as much water, electricity and heating oil as they like, without limit. Each owner is then assessed approximately one three-hundredth of the building's total utility bill. In short, it would be a miraculous coincidence if consumption and billing were proportional. In the absence of separate meters, it is very difficult or impossible to achieve such proportionality. This leads directly to the following scenarios. Both are hypothetical, but plausible.

Consider first Mary, a resident who conscientiously turns off her lights and turns down her thermostat. By the end of the year, she will have reduced the building's overall energy consumption by a small amount, and will personally "recapture" only one three-hundredth of her own saving. She will export to everyone else in the building the benefit of her frugality, but will herself experience the full cost of that frugality (in terms of dimmer lights, hotter summers and chillier winters). And she will receive a bill only fractionally lower than it would have been if she had been an "energy hog." Let us assume that by her frugality, she saves $150 in utility consumption in the course of a year. That saving is then spread over the entire building. As a result, her condo fee—and that of everyone else—will be reduced by 50 cents per annum.

Now we come to Tom, her neighbor (whose resemblance to the author is entirely coincidental). At the supermarket, he buys high-wattage light bulbs, and when he goes out in the evening he carelessly leaves lights on; he turns up the heat in the winter and lets the air conditioner run in the summer. But he will bear only one three-hundredth of the cost. Master-metering and equal division of the bill permits him to saddle everyone else with the consequence of his extravagance, and yet to enjoy the benefits himself. He lives comfortably and makes others pay for it.

Consider what happens when he goes away for a week in August. He briefly considers, in a moment of public-spiritedness, turning his air conditioner off. Then he thinks again: He will have to return to a hot apartment, which will take hours to cool down. So he leaves the unit running. Let us say that the additional cost of this extravagance is $15. Consciously or subconsciously, he may have performed the following calculation: *He* will pay only one three-hundredth of this increment, which is to say five cents. But so will everyone else. His cost of enjoying a cool apartment during the few hours that it would otherwise be hot is a nickel; but everyone else in the building will be unjustly burdened with an additional nickel as well.

Such an arrangement obviously encourages wasteful consumption. Historically, the building's utilities bills have slowly risen, as a percentage of overall expenditures, despite the gradual replacement of inefficient electrical equipment by more modern hardware. When you drive past the building at night, it is a Christmas tree of blazing lights. A spokesman for the Potomac Electric Power Company reports that when individual meters are installed in such buildings, energy consumption usually drops by about 25 percent.

The corrective mechanism is readily at hand—separate meters for each apartment. The condo equivalent of separate checks, meters would effectively privatize utilities within the building. Thanks to the walls separating one unit from another, energy *consumption* within the building is already privatized. The role of meters is to permit billing in proportion to consumption. The utilities in the building would then be converted from communal to private property.

But the internal politics of the building make such a remodeling change difficult to carry out. The rewiring is expensive. Admittedly, the energy saving is large enough to permit the cost to be recaptured, perhaps within ten years; but the condo board is reluctant to consider such an expenditure, mainly because the owners of the units (which is to say, the people who elect the board) generally do not consider their investment in the building to be a long-term one. The building's future may not be in their future. Most are planning to sell and move out within a few years, and do not want to finance improvements that may benefit the next generation of occupants more than it will benefit them.

Admittedly, separate meters would increase the value of the building, and the sale price of apartment units would rise commensurately. A persuasive board could possibly prevail on the membership to approve such an expense. In reality, however, the problem of free riding in utilities is virtually invisible. When the great scope for free riding was brought up at a board meeting, one member responded that *less* energy would surely be used in a situation where everybody "took in" everybody else's consumption. He was persuaded otherwise, but this showed that the free-rider problem is not intuitively clear, even to those elected to an office in which they are expected to hold down costs. The inconspicuous nature of the problem, and the visible upfront cost of correcting it, ensures that the issue is perennially postponed. (The problem may eventually be solved by the development of less-expensive metering technology.)

Let us take the logic of communal utilities one stage further. Suppose that board members do conclude that the single-meter system is intolerable. But they resist installing separate meters, let us assume, not just because of the expense, but also because the board members share a philosophical aversion to privatization. They recognize that free riding in utilities results in winners and losers—good people subsidizing bad people—and they decide that this must be corrected. So they declare a goal of "eliminating energy selfishness," and "achieving energy justice" within the building, but without privatizing. How can they do this?

First, they try exhortation. Slogans are posted in elevators and along corridors, circulars are slid under doors. THINK OF OTHERS! TURN OFF LIGHTS WHEN NOT IN USE! A big sign is placed along the roof (as in Soviet Moscow): "Another Building Dedicated to Energy Fairness and Justice!" But within a few months, it is clear that this is not having the desired effect. Tom ignores the signs, Mary is more frugal than ever.

Now the condo board adopts a sterner measure. "Energy monitors" are hired, and they spend their evenings patrolling the corridors and knocking on doors. "Is anyone at home? The weather just turned cooler. Did you turn down your air conditioning?" But after a few months the occupants learn to ignore the knock. Mary has already been doing the right thing. Tom remains unregenerate. Energy consumption remains at its old level.

Then a more drastic step is taken. The energy monitors are provided with apartment keys. It is explained to all occupants that the invasion of privacy will be minimal, because the monitors may enter only after knocking and receiving no reply. That way, they will only enter apartments when people are not at home, "and when people are away, they shouldn't have their lights and air conditioners on anyway." After a while, however, it is discovered that some apartment owners, who are in fact absent, learn to reply to the knock with prerecorded "decoy" messages. Others bribe monitors to stay away.

Meanwhile, the board has saddled the building with a considerable new expense: wages for the energy monitors. And so it goes. Nothing seems to work. Eventually the monitors are given full police powers and may enter any apartment at any time. How does the board justify this final, draconian step? They cite a twentieth-century authority on the subject. It was Lenin who said, in 1918: "We recognize nothing private."

The scenario is fanciful, of course, because the membership would have elected a new board long before the conflict escalated to such a level; or the members would have sold their apartments and left the building. Nonetheless, it is useful in suggesting that if private property is banished, and exhortation (or "education") is put in its place, both economic efficiency and justice will prove elusive. If coercive measures are introduced, privacy must be swept aside.

THE MORALITY OF PRIVATE PROPERTY

According to Gresham's Law, bad money drives out good. According to the logic of the commons, bad people drive out good. Consider an example that may appear unrelated to energy consumption: the federal budget. The budget can be thought of as a common pool of money replenished every year with approximately 1.7 trillion dollars from taxpayers. Gathered around the pool are 435 congressmen and 100 senators. What gives them power and influence is that they have exclusive "siphoning rights." They are subject to the constraint that siphoning operations can proceed only if a majority participates simultaneously.

When this constraint is satisfied, money can be siphoned out and channeled back to constituents within the congressional districts. The necessary majorities may be achieved by "logrolling": one congressman votes for a project in a colleague's district, in return for a reciprocal favor for his own, and so on.

Federal spending keeps on rising for the same reason that utility consumption keeps on increasing in master-metered buildings. Congress itself is "master metered," because the taxpayers, like the residents of our apartment building, are all "billed" at the same rate, whether or not federal projects are financed in their districts. The point is that the federal tax code is the same in all states. This encourages all legislators to behave like energy hogs—to siphon from the common pool as fast as they can (that is, to vote for most spending bills).

Suppose that a candidate campaigns on the promise that, unlike his opponents, he will be cautious with the taxpayers' money. He will dare to vote "no" on spending bills when he gets to Washington. The problem is that his restraint, meritorious though it may be, will not encourage a like restraint in others. On the contrary, it will leave more money for them to siphon back to *their* districts. It is unlikely, then, that such a candidate will be elected. But let us assume that he is.

Having arrived in Washington, he figures out something that he hadn't quite visualized on the campaign trail: If he votes "no" on spending bills, he will frequently deprive his constituents of an opportunity to get back from Washington what they put into the common pot (in taxes). So, instead of voting to hold down spending, he joins in the general logrolling, teaming up with other big spenders to form majorities (some of the money being earmarked for his district). Some voters back home, recalling his campaign promise, may think that he "sold out." In reality, it was the institutional arrangement of Congress that encouraged his change of heart, not weakness.

The analysis of the budget as a "commons" helps to explain why voters tend to elect both big-spending legislators and fiscally conservative presidents. Armed with the veto power, and with influence over tax proposals, the president (unlike the separate legislators) is in a position to hold down the size of the overall "pool." It also helps to explain why voters will tend to support limits on congressional terms. They give voters an opportunity, not available in regular congressional elections, to effectively vote against all the other legislators—the ones who are siphoning dollars away to remote and unknown places.

The budgetary equivalent of individual meters would be to change the tax code so that the income-tax rate would be adjusted up or down in each congressional district, depending on how much the Congressman from each district voted to spend in the previous year. Big spenders would then impose high tax burdens on their own constituents. It is a safe prediction that this reform would bring about a rapid decline in federal spending, and all talk of the budget deficit would be a thing of the past. Needless to say, no such reform of the tax system is contemplated.

It can hardly be denied that the outcome in the master-metered building is unjust, or that Tom's behavior is selfish. Injustice arises because the institutional arrangement (of collective billing) permits him to impose on his neighbors costs that rightfully should fall on him; and in taking advantage of this arrangement he acts selfishly. The billing system actually "pays" him to do the wrong thing, both morally and economically. That is, it pays him to be both wasteful and selfish. What this suggests is that selfishness, so often said to be the great moral flaw of capitalism (the economic system that is based on private property), is far more likely to arise in situations where private property either does not exist, or where the definition and enforcement of property rights are difficult to achieve.

Suppose that the building's electricity has now been privatized. Meters have been installed, and Tom once again is preparing to go away for a week in the summer. This time he definitely turns his air conditioner off. He knows that if he leaves it running, his bill at the end of the month will be $15 higher. In switching the air conditioner off, did he act selfishly? It hardly makes sense to accuse someone of selfishness for adopting a prudent course. Do we judge a worker of moderate means to be selfish because he buys chopped steak rather than steak?

Suppose, this time, that Tom decides to leave his air conditioner on. Again, his electricity use is metered, but he dislikes the thought of a hot apartment more than he worries about a $15 addition to his bill. Does he act selfishly? The accusation makes no sense, once again, because he will bear the cost himself. His action may be thought wasteful, but he is the one who will pay for the waste. His penalty is proportional to his extravagance. If at the same time his bank balance is low and he is trying to save money, we may say that his leaving on the air conditioner is a foolhardy, but not a selfish, act.

Consider the case of a man who goes to the grocery store and buys food for six people, invites five others to share dinner with him and then eats the lion's share of the food himself. The others go home, still hungry, at the end of the evening. Did he act selfishly? Certainly he did. (Rudely, might be a better description.) Consider now that the six go out to a restaurant and agree that they will pay with separate checks. One orders expensive items from the menu—and pays for them himself. Has he acted selfishly? Now assume that they agree to a single check, paid by equal division. Five of the diners order considerately from the menu, but one blithely orders expensive items. Has he acted selfishly? Certainly. Consider a communal meal eaten from a common pot. One man arrives early and eats as fast as he can. Does he act selfishly? Yes.

I said earlier that in the single-metered apartment building, Tom considered in a moment of public-spiritedness turning his air conditioning off before going away. What all of these examples suggest is that, where the situation admits of public-spiritedness as a guide to action, selfishness is by the same token possible; but when private property is introduced, supplanting communal property, it no longer makes sense to talk either of public-spiritedness or of selfishness. It is precisely in situations where property rights are imprecisely defined or not defined at all that selfish acts are possible, because it is in those situations that the individual, in considering his own interest, has the opportunity to inflict his own costs on others.

A selfish person is one who takes an unfairly large share of some common good, thereby leaving unfairly small shares for everyone else. But where all shares have been defined and allocated and agreed upon, this is no longer possible. We may therefore turn the tables on those who say that if private property "works," it does so only because it gives free rein to selfishness. We may respond that, where private property does not exist, selfishness will be given free rein.

The opponent of private property may nonetheless insist that people ideally should act selflessly, without the inducements of these economic sticks and carrots and meters. By their very existence, such mechanisms must inevitably subvert the hope of pure moral betterment—thought of ideally as something to be attained without benefit of carrot. (The abbot of a monastery, after all, does not try to advance the cause of spirituality within the community by offering material rewards to the pious.) Even if we agree that selflessness is a social ideal, however, it might be better not to try advancing it within a system in which the most selfless people are placed at the mercy of the most selfish. An arrangement that *systematically* tends to reward the worst among us will not bring out the best in anyone. As Garrett Hardin wrote, an unmanaged commons will breed "harsh egoism, inequality and injustice."[1]

Readers will no doubt agree that the installation of individual meters in an apartment building will reduce energy consumption: that is, that it will be economically efficient. But the more important point is that such a change will also introduce the missing ingredient of justice. When Tom leaves his air conditioner running in the summer, knowing full well that it will cost "the building" dollars but him only pennies, the waste may be bad but the injustice is worse. Systematic injustice within a society will introduce a far greater sense of discord than systematic waste.

In his *Summa Theologica,* Saint Thomas Aquinas argued that "the act of justice is to render what is due,"[2] and Thomas Hobbes thought this "the ordinary definition of justice in the schooles."[3] On another page, Aquinas said that "justice, properly so-called, is one special virtue, whose object is the perfect due, which can be paid according to an exact equivalence. But the name of justice is extended to all cases in which something due is rendered." By seeing to it that something due is rendered (high utility bills to the squanderers of electricity, low bills to careful users), private property helps to establish justice in the economic realm. We see that when private property is instituted in a communal setting for the first time, it has the effect of concentrating on individual agents the economic consequences of their actions, rewarding them or penalizing them as the case may be.

In the condo, then, the effect of privatizing the utilities corresponds exactly to the traditional definition of justice. The great blessing of private property, then, is that people can benefit from their own industry and insulate themselves from the negative effects of others' actions. It is like a set of invisible mirrors that surround individuals, households or firms, reflecting back on them the consequences of their acts. The industrious will reap the benefits of their industry, the frugal the consequences of their frugality; the improvident and the profligate likewise. They receive their due, which is to say they experience justice as a matter of routine. *Private property institutionalizes justice.* This is its great virtue, perhaps dwarfing all others. We may say with the economists that private property "internalizes the externalities," or with the philosophers that it gives rise to "social justice."

JUSTICE AND DISTRIBUTION

Of course, there's an important difference between the condo and life in the broader society. In the condo, there is a starting point of equality. We have equal owners who each have one unit, and therefore equal access to the building's utilities. This is not the case in the outside world, where people have unequal holdings as a starting point. What the condo case does show is that given the initial allocation, the working of a communal system of utilities will encourage injustice, and separate meters will correct that. For the analogy to hold in the outside world, therefore, we must be prepared to overlook initial holdings that may be very unequal.

There's no denying that any private-property system that we know of starts from a position of inequality; it's also true that an approximate equality of wealth is morally preferable to great inequalities. Human beings are "created equal," and justice does have *some* connection to equality. Thomas Aquinas allows that it is "a kind of equality." If a parent treats two children differently, or if a judge is severe to one prisoner and lenient to another for the same offense, this may at first seem unjust. In both cases we will attribute the injustice to the unequal treatment. On closer examination, of course, it may be justified. One child may be handicapped, one prisoner a repeat offender.[4]

In society at large, however, it is not possible to "start over" in a new position of equality of property. Its present division has been arrived at over a long time by voluntary transfer and bequest, thereby allowing the fruits of labor and foregone consumption to accrue, both over a lifetime and across many generations. Precisely for this reason, of course, its critics have succeeded in raising doubts about its legitimacy: How do we know that the original acquisition was peaceable and noncoercive? How can we be sure that the first owners were not "those who seized them, hung onto them, and finally got everyone to accept the legitimacy of 'first possession,'" as the political philosopher Alan Ryan has put it.[5] If this is what happened, the entire subsequent pattern of ownership is surely tainted. In the eighteenth century, Tom Paine alleged that this really did happen at the time of the Norman Conquest. In England, he wrote,

> the great landed estates now held in descent were plundered from the quiet inhabitants at the conquest. The possibility did not exist of acquiring such estates honestly. If it be asked how they could have been acquired, no answer but that of robbery can be given. That they were not acquired by trade, by commerce, by manufactures, by agriculture, or by any reputable employment, is certain. How, then, were they acquired? Blush, aristocracy, to hear your origin, for your progenitors were thieves. They were the Robespierres and the Jacobins of that day. When they had committed the robbery, they endeavored to lose the disgrace of it by sinking their real names under fictitious ones, which they called titles.[6]

In his *Treatise of Human Nature,* written 50 years before Paine's diatribe, David Hume argued that the "stability of possession" was so important to the life of any society that it was unwise even to think about dispossessing those who had held property for a long time. "It often happens that the title of first possession becomes obscure through time," he said, and it was impossible to resolve such controversies. In such cases "long possession or prescription naturally takes place, and gives a person a sufficient property in any thing he enjoys. The nature of human society admits not of any great accuracy; nor can we always remount to the first origin of things. . . . "[7]

Because this riposte was merely pragmatic, it did not lay to rest the moral concern. He might have added that where we do not *know* that the property was acquired by force, but can only say that it might have been, the injustice involved in seizing it from its owners would be far greater than tolerating the possibility that their remote ancestors were thieves. A distant and possible injustice would be "corrected" by a present and certain one. Raising the possibility of felonious ancestry merely insinuates a mood of grievance and discord into society. It cannot in justice be grounds for redistributing property generations later. If an organized political movement were to call for the redress of so theoretical a complaint, it could hardly pretend to be anything other than revolutionary.

Inheritance itself may also give rise to a sense of injustice. It cannot easily be justified on desert-based grounds. Here, however, we should look to the original owner's rights, among them the right to bequeath to preferred recipients. The designated heir may not be deserving, but still less do others have the right to prevent the voluntary transfer of honestly earned wealth. It's worth bearing in mind, too, that competition in a free-market economy is so unrelenting that good habits, or their corresponding vices, will before too long overpower the lotteries of inheritance. George Orwell's comment that a man has the face he deserves by the time he is 50 suggests its free-market analogue. In a market economy, a dynasty may well have the wealth it deserves after the third or fourth generation.

The moral defense of a free-market system must rest ultimately on the legitimacy of voluntary transactions and the illegitimacy of force. The present division of property is arrived at by the accumulation of wages that are offered and accepted, in exchange for labor that is voluntarily supplied. Earnings are exchanged for real and personal property, at mutually acceptable prices. Any alternative runs up against the difficulty, from the point of view of justice, that force must be used to implement it. Someone must hand over property, or perform work, under duress. It is difficult to see how that can ever be morally preferable to consent.

But the faint blemishes of first acquisition and inheritance were repeatedly brought up, and in the twentieth century "social justice" was more and more construed in terms of the distribution of wealth and income. The statistician replaced the theologian as our moral tutor. This immediately gave rise to a more radical transformation, one that we live with politically today. If justice is to be construed as egalitarian distribution, then the individual differences of character and talent that will undermine any new arrangement based on equality will have to be opposed by a ceaseless redistribution. Desert, virtue, moral delinquency, industry and idleness must be entirely withdrawn from the calculus of justice, and their consequences steadily offset.

In his influential book *A Theory of Justice,* John Rawls of Harvard proposed to do just that. Imputing injustice to human diversity itself, he favored nullifying "the accidents of natural endowment and the contingencies of social circumstance as counters in quest for political and economic advantage."[8] Such inequalities were "undeserved," he wrote, and called for "redress."[9] In fact, he believed, talent should be treated as a "collective asset." It is striking that he turned to the out-of-fashion notion of desert in order to delegitimize the older understanding of justice.

Because we live with it today, it is easy to overlook how revolutionary it was to make welfare entitlement a function of income and wealth rather than of character. The system was deliberately de-moralized. But if the unequal material outcomes that flow from differences in moral character must be evened out by redistribution, we have certainly become unmoored from justice. The goal of equality has been silently substituted for it. In fact, theories of justice that put distribution ahead of all other criteria permit injustice to be called its opposite. For the taking of property for the purposes of redistribution, without any regard to its method of acquisition, or to the virtue and industry of those who acquired it or are to obtain it, is itself surely unjust.

It is also a materialistic philosophy. Often, people have less because they are indifferent to material goods: the murmurings of philosophers may not have come to their ears or aroused their discontent. Invidious comparison lies at the heart of such a system. Each person is supposedly preoccupied with how all others "fare in the quest for benefits," as M. W. Jackson noted in his *Matters of Justice.*[10] People compare their position with others', and are entitled to feel aggrieved even if their portion in life is greater than that enjoyed by 99 percent of the human race throughout history. Rawls took note of envy "as something to be avoided and feared," and he did worry about it. But "for reasons both of simplicity and moral theory," he "assumed [its] absence."[11]

In *The Mirage of Social Justice,* Friedrich Hayek gave an additional reason why the "distribution" of wealth is an unsatisfactory measure of justice. A "free-market distribution" is what the Oxford philosopher Gilbert Ryle called a systematically misleading expression: it implies the existence of a nonexistent distributor. Acquisition by voluntary exchange is quite unlike distribution. A real distribution might indeed be unjust, of course. If state officials are charged with seeing that everyone receives a fair parcel of land, but distribute it to some and not to others, or give the best land to their friends, there has been an unjust distribution.[12] This is the situation that Aristotle described in his account of "distributive justice" in the *Nicomachean Ethics:* "One kind of justice concerns itself with the distributions of honor or property or the other things which are to be shared by the members of the state (for it is these who may be so related that some possess a fair share and others an unfair share)."[13]

Notice that distributions really do occur in command economies and in communal societies. Injustice is then a live possibility. When it was privatized, the land at Plymouth Colony was distributed, no doubt by William Bradford himself. Obviously, it could have been distributed unjustly; almost certainly, it was distributed unequally. It would have been difficult to allow for differences in the quality of land. But it is certain, from Bradford's report, that such inequalities as arose were thought insignificant compared to the great moral gain that was experienced by all. We should also bear in mind that there is no inequality so great as that between command givers and receivers—a point made by Antony Flew. And we must be so divided if goods are to be redistributed by force. To most people, this inequality is far more objectionable than a mere difference of income.

PRUDENCE AND SOCIAL JUSTICE

Since Rawls's *Theory of Justice* played an important role in legitimizing our present interpretation of "social justice," it is worth looking briefly at an important criticism of that work, raised by the Oxford philosopher J. R. Lucas. The "theory" of Rawls's title posited a group of constitutional framers placed in the "original position" of choosing the basic design of a society. They would themselves be obliged to live in this society, but in deciding on the rules they would remain behind a "veil of ignorance." That is, they could not know what their future position in the society would be. They might be talented, handicapped or something in between. What was the best set of rules to formulate in this situation? That was the problem of justice as Rawls conceived it.

He concluded that the framers would draw up two broad principles. First, each person would enjoy the greatest amount of liberty that was compatible with an equal liberty for all. Second, the material goods of society—income and wealth—were to be "distributed equally unless an unequal distribution of any or all of these goods is to the advantage of the least favored."[14] He was essentially advocating the (classical) liberal doctrine of an equal right to liberty, combined with the greatest degree of equality compatible with the continued functioning of society.

In 1980, Lucas raised the interesting question of whether Rawls's account was really about justice at all. "It seems to be a rational reconstruction not of justice but of prudence," he wrote. If one were a constitutional framer in the "original position," burdened with a veil of ignorance and trying to decide what rules to establish, it might indeed be sensible to devise a safety net in case one turned out to be poorly situated. "But this counsel, thus presented, has little to do with justice. It is prospective, not retrospective; it is based on ignorance, not knowledge; and it is concerned with my own advantage, not others' rights."

Justice is "more exact" than Rawls allows, Lucas added. "It is concerned with particular individuals and their particular wrongs, and seeks to remedy these." Anyone may be wronged—even the rich. A theory of justice should concern itself with all the members of society, not just the poor, and it should seek to ensure that nobody is done down, and that everyone can dwell at peace with society.[15]

Driven by egalitarian sentiment, then, justice was de-moralized and envisioned as a safety net. But equality is no more than a first approximation of justice—a starting point. Equality is on the surface, but inequality is in the details of justice, which requires something that is distinctively tailored to each individual.

It was suggested earlier that a free-market system will tend to make justice routine. This is because in our normal civil dealings, the terms under which trading occurs are usually so nondiscretionary that injustice cannot easily enter. If I go to the grocery store and select $50 worth of goods, I am not acting "justly" when I hand over a $50 bill to pay for them. No virtue or wise judgment is involved. And when there is competition, it cannot easily be claimed that the grocer has priced his goods unjustly (if those prices are higher than his neighbors') or justly (if they are the same, or lower). He could, of course, be guilty of injustice if he sold misleadingly labeled goods. But his life-long avoidance of such deceptions would make him an honest, rather than a "just," merchant. Property and competition have already institutionalized the ingredient of justice in his dealings with customers.

We can easily overlook the virtue of such a system. It enables us to disregard considerations of character in making exchanges. This may be contrasted with societies in which the customer is unsure of the value of goods, in which caution is advised and haggling expected. Such a society places a burden on those with less information and power, and puts the humble at the mercy of the cunning. Westerners who have taken their own system for granted might profitably spend a few days shopping in the bazaars of the Third World. A huge benefit of the private-property system is that it simplifies life by largely freeing us from the concern that we are the victims of injustice in most of our daily transactions.

In some situations, we really do have the opportunity to act with injustice. As we might expect, these particularly arise when the property and contractual relations are indeterminate. Power may then become dominant. It may not be easy for the grocer to treat his customers unjustly, but that is not true of his dealings with employees. The workplace often provides scope for unjust behavior, because relations between managers and subordinates are, inevitably, ill defined. The elaboration of job descriptions can be seen as attempts, usually within large organizations, to narrow the zone of discretion by drawing up quasi contracts, thereby limiting the scope for arbitrary power.

In private life, the family probably gives the greatest scope for injustice. It is the equivalent of a commons in which there is room for free riding, and in which there are no contracts. "Who owns what" is undefined. This is not as disabling to parents as it is within a commune, however, because they have "bargained for" just such a result—by having children in the first place. Nonetheless, the undefined tasks, duties and ownership within a family, its intimacy and privacy, and the sheer physical strength of parents compared to children, leave plenty of scope for the exercise of power, and therefore for outcomes that are appropriately characterized as unjust. Giving children their due can become a full-time job.

Injustice and its remedy will, by the same token, become important considerations in societies without well-defined, and well-enforced private-property rights. The weak will be at the mercy of the strong, and there will be many disputes that must be arbitrated by the sovereign. If not at the mercy of their neighbors, most people will be at the mercy of the magistrate. At best, justice will be an occasional and haphazard thing. The people might sometimes be lucky and find themselves with a "just" ruler, or judges who diligently try to be fair. Mostly, however, the complexity and onerousness of administering justice in a society where free riding is not discouraged by private property will defeat the good intentions of the most benign authority.

In short, a private-property system is the guarantor of social justice because it establishes individual responsibility and accountability, and acts as a bulwark against power. Prof. Alan Ryan has commented that the borderlines of property are insufficient to hold back storm troopers.[16] That is true, but it is an argument against storm troopers rather than property lines. Power will be even less restrained when the property lines are down, and justice, under those circumstances, is something that the people will be lucky to encounter at all.

TWELVE

RIGHTS—AND
PROPERTY RIGHTS

INDIVIDUAL RIGHTS WERE IMPLICIT in the British common law, but an explicit doctrine of rights, delineating the proper relationship between citizen and state is recent in human history, not appearing plainly until the seventeenth century. By the twentieth century, rights had been redefined, much as liberalism itself had been. The rise of rights corresponds to the decline of "rank" in Western society. Rank implies privilege, or inequality before the law; whereas rights bring in their wake the important, but much misunderstood, idea of equality: We all have the same rights. The doctrine of rights recognizes what John Locke called "the Equality of men by Nature."[1]

Rights may be defined as "just claims," but in relation to the state, they refer to aspects of the human person that belong to us in consequence of our nature. If we are deprived of them without due process, injustice is done. The rise of the doctrine of rights is a facet of the slow democratization of life in the West, and may owe its origin to the influence of Christianity. "All equal are within the Church's gate," George Herbert wrote.[2] The privileges of rank will not carry weight on Judgment Day—they may turn out to be a disadvantage, in fact. This theological insight was by degrees transported into the secular realm: All men were created equal, and although individual men might differ greatly in the "content of their character," in their talents and in their aptitudes, they should be presumed equal in their rights, and should be treated equally by the law.

The argument here is that it is self-defeating to talk of protecting individual rights if the right to own property is not prominently among them. At the most general level, the phrase "life, liberty and property" does outline our most fundamental rights. As an eighteenth-century Virginian (Arthur Lee) said: "The right of property is the guardian of every other right, and to deprive a people of this is in fact to deprive them of their liberty."[3] This truth became obscured in the twentieth century, especially in the period of false hopes for collectivism. It is imperative that it be revived today.

Individual, natural, and human rights are different ways of referring to the same idea. They naturally belong to individuals in virtue of their humanity, whether the state exists or not. When the state comes into being, its duty is to respect and defend these rights, which at that point can be thought of as civil rights. Rights cannot be exhaustively listed, because they can be stated at different levels of generality: the right to travel, for example, is an instance of the right to liberty. The Fourth Amendment, protecting "the right of the people to be secure in their persons, houses, papers and effects," is an aspect of the more general right to property. The same is true of the Third Amendment: "No soldier shall, in time of peace be quartered in any house, without the consent of the owner. . . ." (This is a dead letter today because nothing prevents the government from building military bases with housing.)

The rise of the doctrine of individual rights in the seventeenth and eighteenth centuries coincided with the rise of capitalism, and can be regarded as its proximate cause. Government, for perhaps the first time in history, was confined to the role of umpire—the impartial defender and adjudicator of our rights—and enterprise was thereby greatly stimulated. The plunder of wealth, always tempting to those vested with official power, was constrained. The whole idea of constitutional government was that the state cannot legitimately infringe upon our rights, even if democratic majorities vote to do so. Justice Robert H. Jackson of the U.S. Supreme Court made a lucid statement about rights in 1943, just when intellectuals were beginning to lose sight of the point: "The very purpose of a Bill of Rights was to withdraw certain subjects from the vicissitudes of political controversy, to place them beyond the reach of majorities and officials and to establish them as legal principles to be applied by the courts. One's right to life, liberty and property, to free speech, a free press, freedom of worship and assembly, and other fundamental rights may not be submitted to vote; they depend on the outcome of no elections."[4]

This correct understanding of rights took a long time to emerge. Thomas Hobbes (1588-1679) thought that rights were what subjects (not citizens) agreed to transfer to the state for their own good. Failing this, "every man has a right to every thing; and consequently no action can be unjust."[5] His vision was in some respects modern. As he saw it, all government edicts were legitimate. We had better obey them for our own good. The alternative was worse—a war of all against all. Freedom was a residual. Subjects were permitted to do what the government did not forbid them to do. As for the ancient liberties praised by historians, it was not "the liberty of particular men, but the liberty of the commonwealth" that they had had in mind.[6]

John Locke, born 44 years after Hobbes (his *Two Treatises* was begun in the year of Hobbes's death), advanced the doctrine of natural rights to establish a presumption against state power. In Locke's philosophy, adopted in its essentials by the framers of the U.S. Constitution, the zones of sovereignty were reversed. People were free to do those things that did not infringe upon the similar rights of others, while governments could do only what they were constitutionally authorized to do. Specific powers were delegated to the federal government, and those not delegated were retained by the people.

Properly understood, rights are held "against" the whole world—against both private individuals and the state. But because private violations (fraud, theft and murder, for example) were already against the law, the effect of the doctrine of rights was to limit state power. Nonetheless, Locke wrote, we need governments, "for the mutual preservation of [our] Lives, Liberties and Estates, which I call by the general name, Property." In fact, the great and chief end "of mens' uniting into Commonwealths, and putting themselves under Government is the preservation of their Property."[7]

A hundred years later, the doctrine of rights was more boldly stated in the Declaration of the Rights of Man, adopted by the French National Assembly in 1789. The marquise de Lafayette, its principal author, had fought in the American Revolutionary War, and he took a copy of the Declaration of Independence with him back to France. In its preamble, the French Declaration noted that "ignorance, forgetfulness or contempt of the rights of man are the sole cause of public misfortune and governmental depravity." In their rights, the document added, "men are born and remain free and equal," and the purpose of political institutions is "the preservation of the natural and imprescriptible rights of man. These rights are those of liberty, property, security and resistance to oppression."[8]

Thomas Jefferson famously substituted "the pursuit of happiness" for property in the classical trinity of rights. There is no certain explanation for this. The famous phrase does not appear in Locke's *Second Treatise* either, nor anywhere else in his writings. But it was well known in Jefferson's day, and the first Continental Congress, in 1774, approved a Bill of Rights invoking the protection of "life, liberty and property." Jefferson's admiration for private property is not in doubt, however, and we have no reason to think of him as a protocollectivist, or as subordinating individualism to "the social nature of man," as Gary Wills has suggested.[9]

Writing to Pierre Samuel DuPont in 1816, Jefferson briefly stated the most important reason for accepting a natural right to property. It is founded "in our natural wants, in the means with which we are endowed to satisfy these wants, and in the right to what we acquire by these means. . . . " We must perish from starvation or exposure unless we provide for ourselves, but we also have the ability to perform the necessary labor. Therefore we have the right to retain its fruits. The obvious limitation, Jefferson added, is that we must proceed "without violating the similar rights of other sensible beings."[10]

The same argument was restated a generation later by the French writer Frederic Bastiat, whom Joseph Schumpeter called "the most brilliant economic journalist who ever lived." His "Property and Law" was published in the *Journal des Economistes* in 1848, within weeks of the *Communist Manifesto*'s appearance. Bastiat's object was to show that property is a right that we possess even if the law doesn't agree. The law must protect it, but it does not follow that the underlying right to property is a mere creature of law. Bastiat restated Jefferson's argument with great clarity: "Property is a necessary consequence of the nature of man. In the full sense of the word, man is born a proprietor, because he is born with wants whose satisfaction is necessary to life, and with organs and faculties whose exercise is indispensable to the satisfaction of these wants. Faculties are only an extension of the person; and property is nothing but an extension of the faculties. To separate a man from his faculties is to cause him to die; to separate a man from the product of his faculties is likewise to cause him to die."[11]

Just because property is insecure in the absence of law, it does not follow that it is a mere legal contrivance, as Bentham thought. Among primitive people lacking written laws, Bastiat wrote, one who has labored to build a hut may indeed be chased out of it by a stronger neighbor. But "not without angering and alarming the whole tribe. It is this very abuse of force which gives rise to association, to common agreement, to law, and which puts the public police force at the service of property." Hence, law is born of property, not the reverse.*

Inconveniently for many existing states, the idea of rights legitimized the overthrow of the government. Conservatives were its early opponents for that reason: ancient regimes might topple. In centuries past, few had paid attention

---

* Bastiat's writings were revived by the Foundation for Economic Education. By coincidence, Ayn Rand's essay "Man's Rights" appeared in 1964, just as Bastiat's most important essays were reprinted. In part she repeated Bastiat's argument, and never has the doctrine of rights been more forcefully stated:

> The right to life is the source of all rights—and the right to property is their only implementation. Without property rights, no other rights are possible. Since man has to sustain his life by his own effort, the man who has no right to the product of his effort has no means to sustain his life. The man who produces while others dispose of his product, is a slave. Bear in mind that the right to property is a right to an action, like all others: it is not the right to an object, but to the action and the consequences of producing or earning that object. It is not a guarantee that a man will earn any property, but only a guarantee that he will own it if he earns it.

Ayn Rand, "Man's Rights," in *Capitalism: the Unknown Ideal* (New York: New American Library, 1967), app. 1.

to such niceties as their subjects' rights. Edmund Burke allowed that natural rights were real enough, and existed "in total independence" of government. But tearing down the old and fabricating a new government filled him with "disgust and horror." Hitherto, reform had proceeded on the principle of "reference to antiquity," not "abstract principles." To acknowledge the rights of Englishmen was fine: those rights were specific, harked back to the Magna Carta, derived from our forefathers, and would be transmitted to future generations. But these "speculatists" with their abstractions would do nothing but harm. They had "wrought underground a mine that will blow up at one grand explosion all examples of antiquity, all precedents, charters and acts of parliament." He wrote before the revolutionary Terror in France, and when it ensued his distrust of abstract rights seemed farsighted.[12]

Jeremy Bentham was even more hostile. Natural rights were "simple nonsense," imprescriptible rights, "nonsense upon stilts." As an adjective, "right" was "innocent as a dove," breathing "morality and peace," he wrote. But in its incarnation as a noun, it "sets up the banner of insurrection, anarchy and lawlessness." He would have taken exception to Bastiat's claim that property was prior to law. On the contrary, Bentham said, "property and law are born together, and die together. Before laws were made, there was no property; take away laws, and property ceases."[13]

But the Lockean conception of rights proved just as unappealing to the slowly emerging "new class" on the Left as it was to the defenders of the old order. In Marx's writings, we see in undisguised form the attack on individual rights that has been camouflaged in our own day. Marx didn't try to co-opt and redefine the idea, in the modern fashion. Rights were wrongs, because they were claimed by "egoistic man, separated from other men and the community." The right to liberty treated man as "an isolated monad."[14] Unlike Bentham, who feared that rights would provoke revolutions, Marx saw the grim possibility that they might lead to bourgeois bliss. As for calling property a right, "independently from society" and "without regard for other men," this was nothing but an enshrined "right of selfishness."

The classical-liberal conception of rights is likely to be discomforting to any ruling class, no matter how constituted, because it reliably subtracts power from those who rule, or hope to, and distributes it among the people. Decentralized private property has had precisely that effect. Not surprisingly, therefore, individual rights found their fullest expression in the United States, a country that lacked an entrenched ruling class at the time of its founding.

The nineteenth century turned out to be the heyday of individual rights. Property in particular was more secure than at any time in history, both in England and the United States. The Congress rarely took property by regulation. The law of property and contract was primarily left to judges' interpretation. Their job was not striking down legislative interference with property on constitutional grounds (few such laws were passed), but, Morton Horwitz has written, using the common law to construe property rights in ways that encouraged competition and economic development.[15] Judges accepted that contracts were justified by the fact of agreement between parties, not by independent measures of fairness. Contracting parties were assumed to be the best judges of what was in their own interest. All that began to change in the twentieth century.

RIGHTS WITHOUT PROPERTY

It began to seem that property did not so much contribute to our liberties as detract from them. Andrew Carnegie could say that "upon the sacredness of property civilization itself depends—the right of the laborer to his hundred dollars in the savings bank, and equally the legal right of the millionaire to his millions."[16] Others, especially the well educated, were no longer so sure. The great wealth in some bank accounts seemed to explain its shortage in others. State legislatures were disposed to regulate property, but for a long time the Supreme Court, ignoring the election returns, struck down such laws as a denial of "substantive due process." An income tax adopted by Congress in 1894 (the rate was 2 percent on income over $4,000), was declared unconstitutional in the same year.[17] The Constitution had to be amended before such a tax could be imposed.

In the 1905 *Lochner* case, a law restricting working hours in bakeries was overturned; the Court ruled that the law interfered with the "right of an individual to be free in his person and in his power to contract in relation to his own labor."[18] But Justice Rufus Peckham's majority opinion is less well known than Oliver Wendell Holmes's dissent. The case had been decided on a theory "which a large part of the country does not entertain," he wrote. That theory was laissez faire—a "shibboleth." Holmes added that "a constitution is not intended to embody a particular economic theory, whether of paternalism and the organic relation of the citizen to the State, or of laissez faire."[19]

The defense of property, once seen as indispensable to individual liberty, was now reduced to the status of an "economic theory." Peckham's majority had appealed not to economics but to "the rights of the individual." Holmes's argument tacitly viewed property as something that merely provided economic goods. And if that was all it did, well, there were other theories about the production of goods; perhaps rather more sensible ones, for all we knew. They might be less respectful of property rights, but more respectful of human rights. One such theory was waiting in the wings, of course, and it would have no truck with private property at all. Theodore Roosevelt spoke for many when he said, in 1910:

We are face to face with new conceptions of the relations of property to human welfare, chiefly because certain advocates of the rights of property as against the rights of men have been pushing their claims too far. The man who wrongly holds that every human right is secondary to his profit must now give way to the advocate of human welfare, who rightly maintains that every man holds his property subject to the general right of the community to regulate its use to whatever degree the public welfare may require.[20]

Thinkers of the day expressed their doubts about classical liberalism in pragmatic terms. Herbert Croly thought that individual rights might yet be justified, but only if they could meet the test of "functional adequacy." If something better came along, they would have to give way to a more collectivist approach. Walter Lippmann agreed. Whether or not Jeffersonian rights were still viable depended simply on whether they worked. "It's a question of good use and bad use, wise use and foolish use."[21]

So rights were reordered, and property soon acquired second-class status. Discussing a case with Felix Frankfurter, Louis Brandeis argued that the Fourteenth Amendment should be used to protect "things that are fundamental," among them: "Right to Speech. Right to Education. Right to Choice of Profession. Right to Locomotion." There may be "some aspects of property that are fundamental," but not to the extent of freeing it from legislative restriction. In 1921, he expressed the view, then still in the minority on the Supreme Court, that "all rights are derived from the purposes of the society in which they exist; above all rights rises duty to the community."[22] Here, then, individual rights were subordinated to duty—to the community.

Nonetheless, the "old Court" doggedly kept much regulation off the books for a generation after *Lochner.* Finally, the Depression precipitated what Robert Bork has called "a collision between an emergent Zeitgeist, reflected in the political branches, and the old ideas, entrenched in the courts."[23] Justices were replaced, the judiciary fell into line with the other branches, the Zeitgeist was enacted. In *West Coast Hotel Co. v. Parrish* (1937), a state minimum wage law was upheld, Chief Justice Charles Evans Hughes declaring that "the Constitution does not speak of freedom of contract." The Court rejected "the point that has been strongly stressed, that adult employees should be deemed competent to make their own contracts."[24]*

---

*Feminists today would accept the ruling but deplore the reasoning, which was literally paternalistic. The parties to the contract were women, "in whose protection the State has a special interest," Hughes wrote. Their "physical structure and the performance of maternal functions" put them at a disadvantage compared with men. Even though they had accepted employment and signed on the dotted line, in other words, they weren't really responsible for their actions. Contract had here yielded to physique.

The following year saw the case *(United States v. Carolene Products)* in which the Court explicitly separated economic from other rights. "Regulatory legislation affecting ordinary commercial transactions is not to be pronounced unconstitutional," wrote Justice Harlan Fiske Stone, unless it cannot be shown to rest upon "some rational basis within the knowledge and experience of the legislators." In the famous, confusingly worded "footnote 4," around which a whole legal literature has blossomed, Stone observed that some legislation may henceforth call for a "more searching judicial inquiry," for example, legislation that restricts "political processes," or involves "prejudice against discrete and insular minorities." Legislation on economic matters would have to pass only the "rational basis" test—a low level of scrutiny. (Legislators who had voted for it would certainly think it rational.)[25]

From the Progressive Era to the New Deal, then, property was by degrees ostracized from the company of rights. The law was changing, and no doubt was doing so in response to changes in the "economic relations" of society. The law of contract was weakened, unions were protected from antitrust prosecution, the National Labor Relations Act became law. "On the whole I would say that, especially since World War I, the bulk of the legislation did not further the interest of the dominant economic class," said the philosopher Sidney Hook, contradicting Marx.[26]

A new class was coming to power, replacing the old business elite, and adjusting the law to its convenience. Not the proletariat, of course. Workers would provide the rationale, and sometimes were the beneficiaries of change, but it was a new intellectual class that was advancing. Under the new dispensation, property was weakened and other rights elevated, as the Brandeis list noted: "Right to Speech"; "Right to education." (Locke would not have considered the latter a right at all.) It was most important to the new class that they be able to get their message out. And given that, it was necessary only to tame property, not to abolish it.

Something quite new, called "economic rights," began to supplant the old property rights. Their novelty was that they imposed obligations, not limits, on the state. The original meaning of "rights" was effectively destroyed at that point. In 1936, Franklin D. Roosevelt observed that an organization called the Liberty League put "too much stress on property rights, too little on human rights." Once in harmony, these two would henceforth often be viewed as adversaries. In his Four Freedoms speech (1941), rights old and new were conflated. Two genuine rights (freedom of speech and of worship) were mixed in with two that wrote a blank check to the cause of government expansion (freedom from want and freedom from fear).

These Roosevelt aspired to implement not just in the United States, but "everywhere in the world." His pronouncements began to move the topic closer to what, in 1948, became the UN's Universal Declaration of Human Rights. In his 1944 state of the union address, Roosevelt propounded a "second Bill of Rights," including some that would have puzzled the framers. His premise was that "true individual freedom can't exist without economic security. . . . " And security included "the right to a useful and remunerative job," to a "decent home," to "good health" and to "a good education."[27] This new understanding of rights transferred vast, ill-defined powers to Washington.

At the signing of the United Nations charter in San Francisco in 1945, Secretary of State Stettinius referred to the forthcoming "international bill of rights" as "an enumeration of individual and collective human rights." In most of the signatory nations, the latter would trump the former. The Universal Declaration of Human Rights even included the right to "periodic holidays with pay." The new list ended in what the philosopher Antony Flew called a "crescendo of absurdity," with the claim that education should be free, "at least in the elementary stages," and "shall be compulsory."[28] Thus did the UN Declaration go the *Communist Manifesto* one better. In the final provision of its decalogue, the *Manifesto* had called for free education, but Marx and Engels had been content to leave it voluntary.

The old idea had been that government power was a cause for concern. The new belief was that it was on the whole benign, just as long as the press was free to tell us what was going on and the people, especially minorities, were allowed to vote; voting rights are collective, of course, in that the individual achieves little unless 50 percent of the population votes the same way. In the decades that followed, the struggle for rights became largely a struggle for political rights. The big change was this: The old rights imposed restrictions on government; voting rights permitted people to participate in government. Politicization was considered a good just so long as everyone could become involved. The advocates of individual rights were skeptical of official capacity for virtue. Advocates of political rights believed that as long as no one was prevented from participating, government would be virtuous—because it would express the will of the people.

Thomas Paine had been perhaps the first to construe the "rights of man" in such terms. His hobbyhorse was the removal of property qualifications for voting. An expanded franchise made property more secure, for when property "is made a pretense for unequal or exclusive rights," (used as a qualification to vote) it provokes only "indignation and tumult."[29] Against those who claimed that extending the franchise would make property more insecure, David Ricardo argued that poor voters would hardly be so foolish as to vote themselves money from the pockets of the rich. They would understand as well as anyone else that this would render all property unsafe.[30]

John Stuart Mill disagreed. Although he was the great progressive of his day for championing votes for women, he thought it was "required by first principles that the receipt of parish relief should be a peremptory disqualification for the franchise."[31] Welfare recipients should not be allowed to vote, in other words. By becoming dependent on others, they abdicated their claim to equal rights in other respects. Today, in contrast, our concept of political rights has become so enlarged that the law was changed in 1993 to permit welfare clients to register to vote while visiting the welfare office.

Showing how much intellectual opinion changed in the century after Mill's comment (1861), Charles A. Reich argued in the *Yale Law Journal* (1964) that welfare recipients should have a property right in their welfare checks. This, and other government "largess," should not be taken away at will, he argued, because they are a part of the "property" that the Fourteenth Amendment shields from taking without due process. Entitled "The New Property," it is thought to have been the most-cited article in the history of the *Yale Law Journal*.[32] So property rights did make a comeback after all—embedded in an argument to make government transfers as permanent as property of the old-fashioned variety.*

Abroad, a human-rights policy was adopted, but once again property rights were overlooked (at least at first). In its 1980 "Country Reports on Human Rights Practices," the State Department listed the "internationally recognized" categories of rights. A first category restricted government action (the right to be "free from governmental violations of the integrity of the person," such as torture); a second category demanded such action (the right to the "fulfillment of vital needs such as food, shelter, health care and education"); while a third included "the right to participate in government,"[33] by voting, for example. In the second category, the Human Rights Bureau gave high marks to the Soviet Union, which had placed "considerable emphasis on economic and social rights." In its housing, there was a "rapid growth of large suburban apartment complexes around cities and towns." The bureau credulously noted that "free universal health care" was "guaranteed by the Soviet Constitution." These comments showed how much the Western understanding of rights had been weakened by the substitution of "economic rights" for property rights.

---

* Thanks to Justice William Brennan, Reich's sentiments were in part incorporated into the law. In *Goldberg v. Kelly* (1970), the Supreme Court held that welfare recipients are constitutionally entitled to a hearing before their benefits can be ended. At the twentieth anniversary celebration of the ruling, Reich noted that the Constitution was written at a time when "it was sufficient to be left alone." But today, "the world is like an expensive hotel where even the smallest needs cost money." And this puts many at risk. "The negative constitutional guarantee of one era becomes the affirmative obligation of another era, not because the words of the Constitution have changed, but because the Constitution cannot be given its true meaning without affirmative action." By 1990, New York State alone was holding 75,000 hearings a year as a result of the Court ruling. Welfare recipients prevail in 80 percent of these hearings, preserving their benefits against the recommendation of their own caseworkers, according to New York's social services commissioner. (See Linda Greenhouse, "New Look at an 'Obscure' Ruling, 20 Years Later," *New York Times*, May 11, 1990.)

SIGNS OF RECOVERY

The intellectual tide has nonetheless begun to turn slowly back in favor of property. Some of those who most persuasively made the case were refugees from Communist states. It's worth mentioning one who, much earlier, had inadvertently made the case for property: Leon Trotsky. He put his finger on something that the pragmatists of the Progressive Era had completely overlooked. "In a country where the sole employer is the state, opposition means death by slow starvation," he said. And he was candid enough to add: "The old principle, 'Who does not work shall not eat,' has been replaced by a new one: 'Who does not obey shall not eat.'"[34]

If the state monopolizes the property, it also controls the jobs, and the means of livelihood. Trotsky saw state ownership as something that could be used to compel obedience to the state. He indirectly drew attention to the key point that most rights are dependent on property rights. Without that grounding, other rights will always be more theoretical than real. Angels and spirits perhaps can enjoy freedom of speech and religion without worrying about their property rights. But our too-solid flesh requires some material to stand on and work with.

Alex Kozinski, a federal judge on the Ninth Circuit U.S. Court of Appeals, born in Romania, recalled that the absence of private property in his native country had made it physically impossible for individuals to publish their views, however much their "rights" were extolled by officials. "Private citizens did not have access to printing presses and could not obtain sufficient paper or ink," he recalled. "The government even outlawed private ownership of photocopiers and required registration of typewriters."[35]

Editors and reporters rightly object if their First Amendment rights are threatened. Their occasional willingness to overlook property rights only shows that they have been lucky enough to take them for granted. Privately financed exposes of government corruption, something relatively new in history, are a measure not just of the freedom of the press but of the security of property. If publishers' First Amendment rights were safe, but they could no longer rely on office space and printing presses, they would not feel any security. Suppose that the owners of the *Washington Post* were told that they could continue to occupy their building, but it was no longer theirs. Long-term occupancy would be contingent upon "improved" coverage of the news. Property rights, anyone?

"No other civil right ever need be subjected to a direct attack when its protection can be nullified by the simple expedient of regulating an offending or unpopular party's property," wrote Mark Pollot, formerly a lawyer with the Justice Department's Land and Natural Resources Division. Owners who must appear before administrative agencies to exercise their rights "are acutely aware of these problems," he added. "They know the power of the agencies to affect their property and their economic well being, and they know they must exercise caution to avoid offending any member of that body."[36]

Property demarcates "zones" within which government is normally expected to keep out, although exceptions obviously arise when the superior rights of life and liberty are at stake. We can hardly expect immunity from prosecution if we enslave or imprison people on our property. But civil rights other than life and liberty must normally rank below property. When conflicts arise, these other rights are subordinate to the owner's will. If not, chaos must ensue. Freedom of the press is not infringed when editors refuse to publish articles they dislike. Nor are rights abridged when booksellers refuse to sell works they disapprove of. Employees cannot claim that their freedom of movement has been curtailed when they are obliged to come to work on time. They undertake contractual obligations in exchange for pay, and so voluntarily accept such restrictions. Freedom of religion is not undermined by rules against prayer meetings on the job, and if churches were obliged on First Amendment grounds to host the services of alien religions they would rapidly acquire a healthy (and overdue) respect for property rights.

Private universities that chose in the 1990s to impose speech codes on students, restricting the expression of "politically incorrect" opinions, are surely "within their rights." Students who regard such codes as incompatible with the idea of a university are, of course, free to go elsewhere; and for that reason, such speech restrictions are likely to be minimal or short-lived. By the same token, the administrators of such fundamentalist establishments as Bob Jones University should also be free to impose restrictions on their students. But government funding complicates this issue, and most "private" universities nowadays receive a lot of such funding.

Another (early) refugee from Communism, Ayn Rand, illuminated this issue in her analysis of the 1960s student rebellion. The appeal to "free speech" easily stymied state-university administrators, she pointed out. "There was no way for the Berkeley administration to answer the rebels except by invoking property rights. It is obvious why neither modern 'liberals' nor 'conservatives' would care to do so. It is not the contradictions of a free society that the rebels were exposing and cashing in on, but the contradictions of a mixed economy." Taxpayer-funded universities could hardly oppose the dissemination of any ideas—"one of the reasons why the rebels would choose a state university as their first battleground." In fact, the controversy illuminated a point that was far from the students' minds: The orderly exercise of all civil rights depends on a prior acknowledgment of property rights. "It is only on the basis of property rights that the sphere and application of individual rights can be defined in any given social situation," Ayn Rand concluded. "Without property rights, there is no way to solve or to avoid a hopeless chaos of clashing views, interests, demands and whims."[37]

Perhaps we may summarize the developing understanding of rights as follows. The old arguments of Jefferson and others emphasized that the superior rights of life and liberty could not be sustained without private property. (This is now widely accepted with respect to liberty; and the famine reported in North Korea in 1996-97, contrasted with the simultaneous prosperity of South Korea, suggests that it was no exaggeration with regard to life, either.) The more recent point that has emerged, particularly in light of the Communist experience, is that the subordinate rights of free press, freedom of speech, freedom of worship and so on—the rights particularly admired by modern-day liberals—must inevitably be insecure if property rights are insecure.

By the late 1980s, as the Soviet Union declined and fell, the whole question of economic and property rights received new scrutiny. The 1985 publication of Richard Epstein's book *Takings* played an important role. A professor of law at the University of Chicago, Epstein argued that the takings clause of the Fifth Amendment ("private property shall not be taken for public use without just compensation") was a neglected tool and could be used to strike down redistributionist and welfare legislation—even to outlaw the National Labor Relations Act.[38]

Robert Bork replied that Epstein's conclusions were "not plausibly related to the original understanding of the takings clause."[39] That was no doubt true, but it was no less true that the vast income redistributions of the preceding 50 years were not plausibly related to the restricted powers delegated to the federal government in 1787. It's a question of which was the greater sin: striking down unanticipated laws with weapons not designed for that purpose, or letting stand constitutionally unforeseen legislation. Bork's view, that major corrections in constitutional course could be made only by Congress, was certainly prudent. But Epstein's book had its impact.

In 1991, when Clarence Thomas appeared before the Judiciary Committee as a Supreme Court nominee, the proceedings began with Senator Joseph Biden waving a copy of Epstein's *Takings* before the cameras, and asking Thomas if the book had been on his reading list: "[There is] a new, fervent area of scholarship that basically says: Hey, look, we, the modern-day court, have not taken enough time to protect people's property, the property rights of corporations, the property rights of individuals, the property rights of businesses," Biden said. "And so what we have to do is we have to elevate the way we've treated protecting property, we have to elevate that to make it harder for governments to interfere. . . ."

Biden wondered what would happen "were Mr. Epstein's views to take hold." If the property rights of businesses were to be respected, making it "harder for the government to regulate them without paying them," then that would be a "multi-million-dollar change in the law," he worried (correctly). Biden may also have had it in mind that increasing the security of property would make it more difficult for politicians to redistribute it, and then take credit for having done so.[40] Clarence Thomas contrived to say little, beyond reminding Biden that the takings clause was still a part of the Constitution.[41]

In 1987, for the first time in 50 years, the Supreme Court used the takings clause to strike down a land-use regulation. The California Coastal Commission had told the owners of a beach house that their permit to rebuild was contingent upon their granting a right of way through their property. The Court held, 5 to 4, that this was a taking, because the condition imposed was unrelated to rebuilding the house. It was a historic turn for the judiciary. Earlier courts had ruled that the property right was restricted to ownership of the land in its "natural state."[42] In a 1972 case, the Wisconsin Supreme Court even held that there was no taking of a couple's property when they were prevented from building on it, because everyone else—the public—had "rights" in the land remaining in its natural state. Following these "fundamental changes in the takings law," the Reagan administration issued an executive order in 1988, directing federal agencies to evaluate the effect of their actions "on constitutionally protected property rights."

A more significant victory occurred in a 1994 Oregon case. The Supreme Court limited the ability of local governments to require owners to set aside land for environmental or other public uses. Requiring a public "easement" as a condition of getting a permit was a taking, and unconstitutional, unless the government could show a proportionality between the requirement and the harm posed by the development, the Court ruled. The city of Tigard was prevented from requiring an owner to make 10 percent of her land available as a bike path as a condition of being allowed to enlarge her store. The Court was again divided ideologically. Harking back to the post–New Deal Court, Justice Stevens declared that the ruling broke "considerable and unpropitious new ground." Such business regulations had hitherto warranted a "strong presumption of constitutional validity," he said. But Chief Justice Rehnquist said for the majority that he saw "no reason why the Takings Clause of the Fifth Amendment should be relegated to the status of a poor relation." Justice Stevens worried that "property owners have surely found a new friend today,"[43] and John Echeverria of the Audubon Society was dismayed that the ruling "elevates the interests of property owners over the interests of the community as a whole."

One more development, although not a legal one, is worth noting. The federal government had been making ever-increasing use of asset-forfeiture provisions of the law, enabling prosecutors to seize the property of those accused (but not necessarily convicted) of violations of drug laws. Often, the goods seized were put at the disposal of local law enforcement agencies. This, in turn, finally alerted the American Civil Liberties Union to the importance of property rights. Formerly, that organization had been either indifferent or hostile to property, and its litigation had sidesteped questions of economic rights. But in 1993, the president of the libertarian Cato Institute in Washington introduced the ACLU's Nadine Strossen to a large crowd as "the first president of the ACLU who understood the importance of private property to the protection of civil liberties."[44] Milton Friedman was sitting beside her on the dais.

A law professor at New York University, Strossen told the crowd she thought the phrase "property rights" was a misnomer, and alluded to Justice Potter Stewart's famous comment that people, not property, have rights.* But with the abuse of asset forfeiture, Stewart's statement had "undergone an Orwellian reversal," she said. The rationale for taking property without due process was that "only" the property was affected. This flimsy pretext was now being used to justify "flagrant violations of classic personal liberties." In light of the recent high-handed expropriation of assets by law-enforcement agencies, Potter Stewart's statement should be amended, Strossen said: "Property doesn't have rights, and people don't either."[45] At the Supreme Court level, meanwhile, attempts to declare asset forfeiture unconstitutional found support from the liberals on the Court. The conservatives, especially Chief Justice Rehnquist, were not yet ready to join them, but the ACLU, at least, was beginning to appreciate that when property is insecure, so are all our other rights.[46]

---

*This is often quoted to imply that Stewart disparaged property rights. What he actually said was: "The dichotomy between personal liberties and property rights is a false one. Property does not have rights. People have rights. . . . A fundamental interdependence exists between the personal right to liberty and the right to property. Neither could have meaning with the other." *Lynch v. Household Finance Corp.,* 405 US 538, 552 (1972).

AMERICA'S DOUBLE STANDARD

INTRODUCTION

Since the end of World War II, thousands of Western experts have traveled abroad, and hundreds of billions of foreign aid dollars accompanied them. The "underdeveloped" world became known as the "lesser developed" world, then the Third World. The theories and equations of the economists became more and more abstruse. Poverty endured, nonetheless, and in parts of Africa it perhaps worsened. The gap between the rich countries and the poor grew wider. It turned out that Western emissaries had neglected the principal source of their own prosperity. In attempting to impose planning, they had perpetuated colonialism in the realm of ideas. Almost without recognizing that that was what they were doing, they undermined the very institutions that had yielded Western prosperity.

Freedom House's *World Survey of Economic Freedom, 1995-96* found that only 27 nations enjoyed economic freedom. With just 17 percent of the world's population, they nonetheless produced 81 percent of total world output. There can now be no longer any doubt that if new countries are added to the list they will be those that ensure that property rights are widespread and protected by law. The great difference between the developed and the undeveloped economies is not that the former have markets and the latter do not. The difference is one of scale, and of legal protection. "In Britain the legal system has created property rights that can be exchanged in an expanded market, whereas in Peru it has not," Hernando De Soto said. "Britain is a property economy, Peru is not."[1] It was this great difference in the range and elaboration of the law that the economists for a long time overlooked.

Observing the maldistribution of property and income in the Third World, experts from the West could see that something needed to be changed. But their diagnosis was usually in error. The underdeveloped countries were somehow "feudal," it was believed. Addressing the General Assembly of the United Nations in September 1950, Secretary of State Dean Acheson discussed "the problem of the use and ownership of land" in the underdeveloped world. As he saw it, the problem was one of "distribution." Where redistribution had been carried out, the result had been "to give the individual farmer an opportunity to work for himself and to improve his status."[2]

Thereafter, land reform was doggedly pursued by American officials for 35 years. But it did not go to the root of the problem. In fact, it created new ones. It is exceedingly difficult to create property rights that are legitimate, and respected by all, by expropriating the property of some purely on the grounds that they are the wealthiest owners. Frequently, the effect was more to delegitimize property than to redistribute it. In a number of countries, including Chile, Vietnam, Iran and El Salvador, the efforts of land reformers undermined the local economy and contributed to the political turmoil that for a number of years made news on the front pages of our newspapers.

THIRTEEN

WHY ISN'T THE WHOLE WORLD DEVELOPED?

IN HIS 1980 PRESIDENTIAL ADDRESS to the Economic History Association, Richard Easterlin of the University of Pennsylvania asked: "Why isn't the whole world developed?" A generation had elapsed since the success of the Marshall Plan. The Industrial Revolution was more than two hundred years old. Economic production had grown at rates never before seen, prompting the economist Simon Kuznets to call it a new epoch in world history. "Yet," Professor Easterlin added, "after two centuries, the great majority of the world's population continues to live in conditions not much different from those at the start of the epoch." He added a further question, and an unaccustomed note of doubt: Will the whole world eventually become developed?[1]

A few years later, at a conference held at Williams College, the old optimism that had prevailed since World War II had all but disappeared. Something had gone wrong. In 1989, the Harvard historian David Landes asked Easterlin's question once again, this time all but conceding defeat. For a century and a half following Adam Smith, he noted, "confidence in the inevitability of material progress prevailed." In fact, this had been "one of the unspoken assumptions of a world caught in the wonder of science."[2] Even the socialists of the nineteenth century had shared in the general optimism. *Especially* they had.

For a while, it was assumed that the residue of imperialism had delayed the expected triumph. If a colonized world remained stubbornly unimproved, that was not thought surprising. Universal development would no doubt have to await independence, and the resulting liberation of indigenous energies. Hopes were thereby sustained until the 1970s. "We have been disappointed since,"

Landes added. True, there had been some successes. But also failure—failure "to the point of despair."

Initially, natural resources were thought to be the key to wealth. To the extent that countries such as Saudi Arabia or the United Arab Emirates are regarded as wealthy today, when really they are the beneficiaries of transient natural-resource windfalls, that view still lingers in some quarters. In the 1960s, the preeminent success of the United States was sometimes attributed to its "abundant natural resources." But with the rise of Japan, poor in resources, followed by Taiwan, South Korea and Hong Kong, the materialist argument became untenable.

A rapidly expanding population has, since Malthus's day, been suspected by some of being an impediment to economic growth. GNP divided by population gives income per capita, and a smaller denominator yields a larger quotient. The United Nations and other organizations have been counting heads for decades and trying to control population. But people come with brains as well as stomachs, and the poorest countries are often the most sparsely populated. Since World War II, concern about population growth has stemmed primarily from the view of people as consumers and the state as their provider

Another false scent was pursued after World War II, when there was a tremendous vogue for planning—supposedly proving itself in the Soviet Union. Underdeveloped countries were urged to establish planning agencies, with the power to invest the capital accumulated from domestic sources. If domestic savings were in short supply, foreign aid would make up the difference. If home-grown planners were unavailable, foreign advisers and experts could be sent abroad, along with the aid.

Planning was a twentieth-century idea. No reference to it is to be found in the works of Marx or the Fabians, or in the histories of English socialism up to the end of the First World War. The English economist John Jewkes concluded that it originated, "as many evil ideas originated," as a method of war administration in the Germany of 1914-18. When Lenin tried to apply it to a real economy in 1920, he could find no guidance from existing socialist literature. After World War II, the gospel of planning was preached mostly by British policymakers, even as the Attlee government tried, half-heartedly, to put it into practice at home. When its totalitarian implications became plain, they wisely declined to pursue it.[3]

Early proponents of a planned economy, including William Beveridge and Sir Oliver Franks, believed their schemes to be compatible either with socialism or with private enterprise. Henry Simons of the University of Chicago thought this "disingenuous," however. Beveridge's planning was collectivist in all but name; he was only willing to tolerate private enterprise if it survived "anomalously or vestigially, in spite of policy," Simons wrote. If a company could be told what to manufacture, whom to employ, and what prices to charge, it ceased to be private. The principal failing of the early advocates of planning was that they did not understand the very different incentive structures that impinge upon public and private enterprise.

It is remarkable that so many economists were enthusiastic about planning, for there was no reliable evidence that it had worked anywhere at the time when they were most enthusiastic about it. It played "no part in the development of any one of the now highly developed countries," P. T. Bauer wrote in his *Dissent on Development.** The planning vogue arose because it was thought to be scientific, and science seemed to be the answer to everything. Mathematics was so much more rational than faith and ideology, and so much more respectable, too. Ideologues need not apply. It was just a matter of scientists with their slide rules, working on their "models" and getting their equations right. As India's prime minister Nehru told a journalist in 1960: "Planning and development have become a sort of mathematical problem which may be worked out scientifically. . . . It is extraordinary how both Soviet and American experts agree on this. If a Russian planner comes here, studies our projects and advises us, it is really extraordinary how his conclusions are in agreement with those of, say, an American expert. . . . . The moment the scientist or technologist comes to the scene, be he Russian or American, the conclusions are the same for the simple reason that planning and development today are almost a matter of mathematics."[5]

Gunnar Myrdal, one of the leading missionaries of planning, who received the Nobel Prize in 1974, exaggerated only slightly when he said in 1956 that "grand-scale national planning" was "unanimously endorsed by governments and experts in the advanced countries."[6] Nehru exaggerated not at all when he said that planning was thought to be "almost a matter of mathematics." There were models aplenty to prove it. As the years passed and not much in the way of housing and consumer durables appeared, the equations became more complicated. The Harrod-Domar model was replaced by the Solow model, and then it, too, had to be made more elaborate. Confounding variables were hunted down. By the time Albert O. Hirschman of Princeton's Institute for Advanced Study was reduced to pondering the chain of disequilibria, backward and forward linkage, and polarization effects, the planning game was up.[7]

---

*A rare holdout against the post-war consensus, Professor Bauer of the London School of Economics was the leading critic of foreign aid and of economic-development policy in the postwar period. Lord Bauer, made a life peer by Mrs. Thatcher in 1982, emigrated from Hungary to Britain before World War II. *Dissent on Development* (Cambridge, Mass.: Harvard Univ. Press, 1976), 72.

The faith in economic planning illustrated Keynes's dictum that the ideas of economists, "both when they are right and when they are wrong, are more powerful than is commonly understood."[8] The Third World was ruled by little else for 40 years. Free markets and the regime of private property were thought no longer necessary in the modern world. New countries couldn't afford to wait for their benefits to appear. By then we would all be dead, indeed! Charles Kindleberger of MIT plainly stated the erroneous conceptions of the planners: Government ownership was embraced because private enterprise "performs, or is expected to perform, so badly"; government enjoys a clear advantage over private enterprise in the areas of risk taking, innovation and decision making; but its "real edge" in underdeveloped lands came from "its advantage in recruiting men of ability and energy needed to get growth underway."[9] Today, all these ideas are generally rejected by economists.

The apparent success of the Marshall Plan had greatly encouraged the development experts. In the four years following its announcement, the United States spent $13 billion on the economies of Western Europe (perhaps $90 billion in 1997 dollars), and Europe duly recovered. The neglected point was that the recipient nations had already possessed, and in 1947 had not lost, the political and legal infrastructure indispensable for development. But the plan's success was often attributed to cash transfers—to American generosity rather than European institutions. As Sen. J. William Fulbright said years later, the Marshall Plan created "the false impression that we could solve any problem by throwing money at it."[10] Fulbright himself had helped formulate the plan.

Forty years later, with much soul-searching about subsequent failures, the misdiagnosis persisted. Some who had worked on the Marshall Plan at its inception were, by the late 1980s, still thinking in materialistic terms. "Infrastructure" was considered important, but it could hardly have been construed in more earthy fashion. Rotterdam was restored without difficulty, for example, because there was "already a layout of streets and water mains," Professor Kindleberger said.[11]

The misleading precedent of Marshall aid stimulated great transfusions of aid to non-European countries. In his 1949 inaugural address, President Truman announced "a bold new program for making the benefits of our scientific advances and industrial progress available for the improvement and growth of underdeveloped areas. More than half the people of the world are living in conditions approaching misery. Their food is inadequate. They are victims of disease. Their economic life is primitive and stagnant."[12] By the end of the cold war, at least $2 trillion in foreign aid, adjusted for inflation, had been sent to what was by then called the Third World.[13] Overall, this may have retarded economic development, for without its emollient effect, helping to conceal from heads of state the ill effects of their policies, errors would not have been so persistently pursued. Economic difficulties would have forced them in a more productive direction. It's worth noting that in countries where nondemocratic rule aroused U.S. disapproval, and as a result an aid cutoff was either threatened or implemented—South Korea, Taiwan and Chile are the leading examples—market-oriented reforms were implemented and economic fortunes improved.*

Material backwardness, without regard to the political circumstances that created it, was usually sufficient to trigger aid, however. "In committing itself to a worldwide campaign against physical poverty," Nicholas Eberstadt wrote, the United States was willing to allow the condition of man to be separated from the nature and quality of his government. As a result, we attempted to "purchase improvements in the physical circumstances of individual men and women" without reference to "the character and practices of the political authority" under which they lived.[14]

Because the difference between rich and poor countries was a material one, it was believed to be amenable to a material solution. The underdeveloped nations could be developed by cash transfers—politely called "capital." Consequences were mistaken for causes. It is difficult to find references to property in the early foreign assistance literature, other than as an implicit obstacle to be circumvented. The shocking truth was that by 1949, one of the central institutions responsible for two centuries of American achievement and progress was no longer understood either by American elites or by most of those professionally engaged in economic development.

INPUTS WITHOUT INSTITUTIONS

"Labor" and "capital" are thought of as "inputs" in the economic worldview. Economists believed that they would retain their essence in an institutional vacuum. In the black box of theory, these "factors of production" worked their

---

* In 1963, A.M. Rosenthal reported in the *New York Times* that the U.S. was about to cut economic aid to South Korea. Their officials were reported to be in a "dither" about the news. Ours were said to believe that Korea had engaged in "totally inadequate planning." In addition, Rosenthal reported, "there is no particular admiration for the decision of Korean businessmen to squirrel away their funds while the country is on the brink of a new economic disaster." Too much hoarding and not enough planning, in other words.

Economic aid to Taiwan was terminated in 1965. Thereupon, a Taiwanese minister recalled, "serious efforts" were made "to improve our investment climate." In the 1960s, the United States also poured economic aid into Chile and used its leverage to support collectivist policies there. The Marxist Salvador Allende won the 1970 election, and when he was deposed by the Chilean military and General Pinochet came to power, aid was cut off and the country had little choice but to move in a market direction. (A. M. Rosenthal, "U.S. Will Cut Aid to South Koreans," *New York Times,* April 4, 1963; and see *Promoting Democracy and Free Markets in Eastern Europe,* ed. Charles Wolf, Jr. [Santa Monica, Cal.: Rand, 1991], 53.)

usual magic. One who marveled in his way, not quite sure whether to believe in this miracle of abstraction, was Albert O. Hirschman of the Institute for Advanced Studies at Princeton. "One of the astounding feats of modern economics," he wrote, was the way the analysis of growth in advanced countries had yielded an "apparatus" that seemingly applied "to the most primitive economies."[15] Could it really be? Mix the naked inputs in the right proportions and then count the outputs as they came rolling off the assembly line?

Economists have often thought of labor as something that is simply "supplied"—a reliable function of man's "wealth-maximizing" nature. The truth is that labor is always ready to hide. Capital is even more shy; it will take flight at the first sign of trouble. The problem is that foreign aid, dignified with the title of capital, was thought of as comparable to private investment. Recipient governments merely had to agree that it would be "invested." But once a sum of money has been sent to Ghana, Gaza or Guyana, and is available for disbursement by a local official, it has already ceased to be capital. Capital is expected to yield a return, but no one in the local government experiences the lost opportunity of failing to realize the return on a gift from the U.S. Treasury.

There is even less interest in preventing it from being used politically. Politicians empowered to spend it will derive immediate benefits from treating it as spending money. As a result, life in aid-receiving countries became increasingly politicized. International development agencies have to some extent recognized the problem, but have been unable to do much about it because the necessary remedies would infringe upon jealously guarded national sovereignty.

Believing that countries can be enriched by the delivery of foreign money, without the existence of appropriate "receptacles"—private enterprise subject to the discipline of profit and loss—is like believing that an arid land can be made fertile by the dispatch of water tankers. Without proper receptacles (reservoirs), merely hosing the water onto the ground will be an expensive failure. The water will evaporate, clouds will form and the rain will fall back in distant continents. Eventually, it will be recaptured by the reservoirs of the West. In the same way, it has not been unknown for Western aid to the Third World to return to reservoirs known as Swiss bank accounts.

Planning depends upon force, and this was assumed to be efficacious. Governments had all along used force to protect private property, its proponents liked to observe. John Prior Lewis, who held posts with the Council of Economic Advisers, the Agency for International Development and the UN Reconstruction Agency, noted that if Communist China's economy was growing more rapidly than India's in the 1950s, the explanation lay in the greater "ruthlessness" of Chinese planners. The laissez-faire system had worked well enough for Britain, and for the "uniquely circumstanced" United

States, he allowed. But now there was a new world. Those who denied the legitimacy of "centrally conceived and directed development," he wrote in *Quiet Crisis in India* (1962), were likely to be "cast inescapably" as "crackpots."[16] Big increases in foreign aid would be needed to support the latest of India's series of five-year plans.

Private property was rarely attacked directly, except by those on the Left who were bold enough to disdain the algebraical disguises that were increasingly coming into fashion. Joan Robinson of Cambridge allowed that private property and "great inequalities of wealth" may have been necessary in the eighteenth century, when "egalitarian ideals" would have stifled the Industrial Revolution. "But now private property has become otiose," she added.[17] In 1962, Paul Baran of Stanford University thought "the dominant fact of our time is that the institution of private property in the means of production—once a powerful engine of progress—has now come into unreconcileable contradiction with the economic and social advancement of the people in the underdeveloped countries." No planning worth the name was possible if "the means of production remain under the control of private interests."[18]

Jawaharlal Nehru considered private property to be "immoral, far more so than drink," because it gave "dangerous power to individuals over society as a whole." There was no way to end India's poverty, unemployment and degradation, he remained convinced, "except through socialism [and] the ending of private property." Private profit would have to be replaced "by a higher ideal of cooperative service." If the "building up of a socialized society" was to proceed, it could not be left to chance.[19]

The faith that economic growth was a matter of applied science was still flourishing when W. W. Rostow published his *Stages of Economic Growth* (1960).[20] The book now looks quite dated, and one idly wonders if his "stages" were not subconsciously abstracted from the novelties of jet travel. First comes the traditional society, which develops the "preconditions for take-off." The take off itself is next. It is followed by a "drive to maturity," engines of production roaring. Finally, when the seat belt signs are turned off, and the drink trays emerge, there comes the "age of high mass-consumption." The book was billed as a "non-Communist manifesto."

The all-important "preconditions for take-off" had been developed in Western Europe 250 years earlier, Rostow wrote. The "insights of modern science began to be translated into new production functions in both agriculture and industry." But when insights are translated into functions, all concreteness is lost. Rostow did note that Britain was the first to develop the preconditions for take-off. How did that come about? The country was favored by geography and natural resources, and by "social and political structure. . . ."[21] Here he was getting warm, but he failed to come to grips with the "political structure." Britain had "more nonconformists," he noted at one point.[22] At key points, his argument was circular. "The pre-take-off decades are, generally, dominated by changes in the economy and in the society as a whole which are essential for later growth."[23]

In *Politics and the Stages of Growth,* he made one more pass at the problem. Now he asked the good question: "What happens if one makes politics rather than growth the focus of analysis?" But his analysis remained apolitical in its essentials. The upheaval of the Bolshevik Revolution, with its collectivizations, he viewed as a mere hiatus in the rapid economic growth begun under the czars and now being restored under the commissars. The rate of growth of industrial output was given as 9.9 percent a year from 1928-40, and 9.6 percent a year in the 1950s. Here was a take off that just wouldn't quit. Later on, the Soviet plane was found to have remained all along on the runway.[24]

The planning disaster that unfolded in many countries was partly the result of an unlucky coincidence. Decolonization came just at the time when socialism was fashionable in Western capitals. As they packed their bags, departing colonial officials not only gave bad advice to new rulers, but meant it, and sometimes took it themselves. Given the reports of Soviet success, the enthusiasm for planning can hardly have seemed utopian to the new rulers. It also comported with their own ambitions, especially in Africa. The centralization of power is easy enough for authoritarian leaders to rationalize. Sometimes it was dressed up in native tongue, as in Julius Nyerere's *Ujamaa* (translated as "familyhood" by Nyerere[25]). Like many other African leaders, he was only too happy to adopt a philosophy with this threefold advantage: it brought economic aid in its wake, it seemed to encourage rapid economic growth—and it was sure to discourage political opposition.

There was, of course, another way of looking at Professor Easterlin's question. In the Second, or Communist, world, property had been undermined deliberately. In the Third World, people had usually been subjected to tyranny. The constant was that economic liberties were disdained in both. Only in the First World was the rule of law, private property rights and freedom of contract protected. Even there, in many countries, nationalization and high taxes were taking their toll. Development experts from countries where economic liberties survived had failed to recognize their own good fortune. Meanwhile, their support for planning and disregard of property only increased the oppression that was routine all over the underdeveloped world.

In Africa, natural change was beginning to bring about improvement just as the socialist enthusiasm appeared. Most tribal land in sub-Saharan African was communally owned, therefore subject to the tragedy of the commons. But there was so much of it that tribes could move on to new areas, allowing the eroded ground to recuperate. But as population expanded, this became more difficult, and the pressure to privatize increased. Such changes, including the buying and selling of land by individual tribesman, were occurring at the end of the colonial period. Colonial officials balked, however, because such trade was not "customary" in Africa.

S. Rowton Simpson, a critic of this reaction, observed that "where a tenure has arisen which has all the characteristics of 'freehold' it appears that the central government and civil courts will not recognize it because it is inconsistent with 'native custom.'" It was perfectly true that when the land had been "as free as air and water" it had not been sold, "just as there was no sale of land among the early Britons." Now, however, the natural inclination of the tribes to change, just as Britain had centuries earlier, was being stymied by modern Britons. After independence, of course, the new leaders were encouraged neither to go back to the old communal ways, nor to privatize, but to move forward into the bright future of planning.[26]

As time passed, it became apparent to Western officials that political safeguards were also needed; capital, planning and expertise were not enough. It was thought that democracy would provide the missing element. Did not the United States and the European countries hold elections every few years? But voting inadequately describes any constitutional system, and has subsequently proved insufficient, as many countries have shown. The idea that the security of property was itself "the missing ingredient" in economic development did not begin to sink in with Western leaders until the Berlin Wall was on the verge of collapse. President Reagan mentioned it in a few speeches in his second term, but it wasn't until Hernando de Soto's book *The Other Path* was published, in 1989, that we began to see something new.[27] Like his sixteenth-century namesake, de Soto explored North America, but it was American institutions rather than geography that he was interested in.

THE MISSING INGREDIENT

De Soto, too, had wondered: Why had real economic development occurred in only a handful of countries? At the International School in Geneva in the 1950s, he had noticed that his classmates, from 64 countries, showed unpredictable abilities. National stereotypes were unreliable. "It wasn't that the Latin Americans danced better and the Germans were better at mathematics," he said. He would study his friends' snapshots, and it was clear that his own Peru was poorer than almost all the other countries. A lot poorer. At first he thought it was merely more romantic. The Peruvians had lots of sunshine, horses to ride, more gold in their teeth. They were not so much poorer as culturally different.

Later he discarded this explanation of poverty. He could see no real reason why Peruvians shouldn't be as prosperous as the Swiss.[28]

Meanwhile, international aid officials and foreign observers would show up in Lima and allow that, yes, the North Americans were richer. They had this thing called capitalism, but the Latins . . . well, they had a different culture. Not an inferior one, mind you, not a deprived one at all. A different culture, and a noble one. Was there not something stirring about the authentic descendants of the Inca greatness, blanket-draped outside their honest hovels, with the Andean peaks rising magnificently in the background? It enraged de Soto to be told that Peruvians were not suited to the market system. He went to the University of Geneva, and between the lines of books about development he always found this argument about culture. But there had to be something more precise, above all something that could be changed. What was the missing ingredient?

Eventually he returned to the Peruvian maelstrom: a world of 23 million people, mostly impoverished; coca growers who within a few years would be furnishing two-thirds of the raw material for the world's cocaine; drug traffickers working with Colombian cartels; an unstable government accustomed to acting as the private instrument of Peruvian elites, yet impoverished by its own disregard of individual rights. It was a world of power cuts, curfews and cholera (caused by a polluted water supply). The judges were corrupt, and the great majority of the people lived and worked outside the law.

The system was one that had long endured all over Latin America. A web of laws protected a privileged class from the competition of newcomers and outsiders—the great majority of the population. Inequality before the law was entrenched. By exclusion, the system preserved the monopolies of a business elite, which in turn controlled both laws and lawmakers. It resembled the system that Adam Smith had called mercantilism.[29] That, too, had been defined by close ties between a dominant state and a clique of merchants.

Like other Latin countries, Peru had misleadingly named institutions that were mere facades; Latinate separation of powers, political parties, Treasury Departments and Reserve Banks that mimicked their North American counterparts. Mechanisms such as news media scrutiny and public rule making, encouraging accountability in the United States, barely existed at all. A vast corruption enabled a privileged few to dismember and privatize foreign investment. De Soto told a hearing of the U.S. Joint Economic Committee that "some governments are suspected of paying as much as double the true dollar value of the capital investment projects for which they contract." "Budget committees" free from scrutiny devised projects tied to particular suppliers without competitive bids or publication in any government register.[30]

In Peru, de Soto did what World Bank country teams, busy with their office-jobs, tinkering by computer with the paper economy, rarely do. He set forth into the streets of Lima. On the two sides of the Rimac River, he found two very different communities, each covering about three acres and containing the homes of about 500 people. On one side were crude huts of mud-brick or cardboard; on the other, brick homes with shops, neat gardens, sidewalks, and merchants living above their businesses. Both were founded by Indians who had come from the same part of Peru. Neither "culture" nor "exploitation" could explain the difference. "Are the Yanqui imperialists exploiting the residents on the river's left bank and not those on the right?" he asked.

He found a retired official from the Housing Ministry who knew the history. In both communities, rural migrants had settled on vacant lands as squatters. But there was no simple legal procedure to obtain title to land. Titling and registration was the preserve of the ruling class, a literal "privilege" in its original meaning of "private law." Over the decades, the ruling class had made access to these registers so expensive that most people did without. The difference between the two settlements arose because the leader of the more prosperous one had persevered with Lima's officials for six full years until his residents finally received legal titles; across the river, such protection had not been extended. Owners on one side felt secure that the fruits of their labor would be protected; squatters on the other had no such reassurance.

"It's all perfectly logical," de Soto told the journalist Eugene Methvin. "The legal protection of the fruits of a man's labor and creativity, what we call property rights, turns out to be a crucial liberator of enterprise."[31]

In Peru, if you want to go into business for yourself, de Soto concluded, you are almost obliged to do so illegally. It was the same in other Latin American countries. *The Other Path* was a bestseller in Mexico, and there the writer Octavio Paz told him: "All you have to do is change the names and you are describing Mexico."[32] De Soto's Institute for Liberty and Democracy has carried out pilot programs in Ecuador and El Salvador, and has been invited to Guatemala, Honduras and Indonesia. All over the Third World, de Soto has found, the problem of titling and registering property has not yet been solved.

His institute has more recently been supported by the U.S. Agency for International Development. A key discovery has been that the great majority of Peruvians—60 percent of the people in the cities, 90 percent of those in the country—do not have secure property rights. They have property of a sort, but it is not legally secure. All over the Third World, most people are in a position like the squatters of Lima: permanently at risk of eviction, seizure, or inundation by a new wave of squatters. In such a world, long-range enterprise cannot be undertaken.

The figures were not easy to come by. Ask officials in the ministries what the figures are, de Soto said, and you will be told that 80 percent of homes are titled. Is the title uncontroversial? "Oh no, there are conflicting claims on 40 percent of property." Are squatter areas included? "Oh no, we don't count them. They are invaders." How long ago did they invade? "Twenty, fifty years ago."

Put all the exceptions back in, de Soto said, and you get back to the 90 percent figure. People living in the woods, in the Andes, in the Amazon basin, on the city outskirts, have been excluded from the count. Since the inception of foreign aid, no research comparable to this has been undertaken in the Third World. American aid officials would have lacked both the boldness and the knowledge of local conditions necessary to question official statistics and to come up their own. De Soto's people could do it because they were Peruvians working in Peru.

"As far as titles go, most Latin Americans probably have them," de Soto added. "There have always been dictators or political candidates willing to shove paper around. But it's worthless paper—title that cannot be registered. There is no place where you can go and find someone with a map who is willing to testify that there are not four other people with the same piece of paper giving them title to the same piece of land."[33] That is why property registers are important. In Europe, too, they were a late development. "In the fifteenth and sixteenth centuries, the lords complained that you can't have that kind of information in the public domain," de Soto said. Like Swiss bankers, they preferred that such information be kept private.

In his research in other countries, notably El Salvador (where 40,000 informal owners were given property titles in less than a year), de Soto found that officials often wanted to give land titles to informals. But it was expensive. How could they be sure that others did not have a better title than the squatters? In order to reassure themselves, they often found themselves resorting to the old Spanish system of registration that had caused so much trouble in the first place. With funding from international institutions, for example, officials spent about $12 million titling and registering 7,200 parcels in northeast Brazil.[34]

But shortcuts can be found.[35] In Peru, with government cooperation, de Soto's institute was able to register and title 155,000 families, at a cost of about $13 per parcel—a fraction of the cost in Brazil. The key to that success was allowing informal owners to use their own papers and forms of agreement, so they could prove their ownership to one another. Essentially, what de Soto did was to persuade the Peruvian government to accept and legalize the existing insecure arrangements. "When you have a system of weak property rights, as we do, people don't have homes like yours, where one lawn rolls into another," de Soto said.[36] "In the informal sector, you have to make the property rights physically manifest. All over Latin America, first you build a wall around your land, then you build your house inside the wall."

In order to register the property, de Soto's staff needed only to ask local leaders who lived where; in most cases, the occupying family was regarded by the community as the legitimate claimant. Parcels contested as a result of feuds or divorce were put to one side and dealt with later. De Soto persuaded President Fujimori to incorporate these informal arrangements into the law of the land by establishing a parallel system of registration. Once done, hitherto insecure property doubles in value overnight. After ten years, it multiplies nine times. By 1995, 340,000 informal businesses had been formalized, increasing the future value of their economic contribution by an amount that the most generous foreign aid could not hope to match.

De Soto's study of informal communities led him to great insights about the role that legal property rights play in the ordering of economic activity. In acquiring these rights informally, he pointed out, the newcomer has to do everything in reverse. First he has to occupy the space physically, so that he can acquire "squatters' rights"; then he has to bring in some furniture, because he has to be prepared to sleep there; then he has to put a roof over his head; then put up some walls; then tear them down again if plumbing is to be installed; then, if he is lucky, and the relevant bureaucrats are merciful, he may be able to acquire legal title years later.

When property rights are formalized, everything is done in the order familiar in developed countries. First the owner acquires title, then installs plumbing hookups, then walls and roof are built, furniture is brought in, and only then does the owner move in. Property in informal communities can be bought and sold, de Soto said, "but your transaction costs are those of the anthropologist." You have to find out all about your prospective neighbors and the surrounding community to learn what is customary and what is expected— to find out what your actual property rights are. The person with legal property rights "can defend himself on paper," he said. "In the informal sector, the squatter must be prepared to defend himself on the land itself."[37]

De Soto also used a property analysis to explain the behavior of the country's 200,000-odd coca growers. Like their urban counterparts, they have unregistered property. They turn to "suitcase farming" as a result. Coca bushes are planted furtively, and the harvest is sold quickly to Colombian buyers. It is not very profitable—the farmers make little more than $500 a year from coca. The big money is made by traffickers. But the coca leaf is easily grown, with little preparation of soil. Alternative crops such as coffee, cocoa (chocolate) or palm oil would be more profitable, but they also require far more investment and, above all, longer time horizons. Oil palm yields an economic benefit six times greater than coca, but obliges the farmer to wait five years. Without clear property rights, it's difficult to get the credit needed for such crops and risky to wait for their maturation.[38]

Coca growers who are attacked by army units move to new terrain without much loss. Such attacks are bound to be indiscriminate, for without legal property there are no addresses, and without addresses, police operations become army operations. Enforcing a law that criminalizes tens of thousands of people in effect means making war on a large segment of the population. An attack on one is construed as an attack upon all. "That's how all the Vietnams got started," de Soto said. For that reason, coca growers have sometimes welcomed the protection of Shining Path guerrillas.[39]

In 1991, U.S. authorities signed an agreement with Peru accepting that growers were not to be treated as criminals. In return for titled and registered property, they agreed to switch to alternative crops. Legalizing the property would alter their incentives.[40] The underground newspaper of the Shining Path complained in 1990 that de Soto's organization was "distancing young people from participating in the popular war." The ILD's building in Lima was bombed twice, in 1991 and 1992.

De Soto spoke to street vendors and minibus drivers and the workers of the "informal" economy. All were working illegally, he found. There were so many rules on the books that it was as difficult for them to become legal tradesmen as it was for them to join the country club—and for the same reason. The regulations functioned like admission fees, protecting the business activities of a ruling class. The ILD set up a small garment factory to document the costs of entering the system legally. After paying essential bribes and filling out myriads of forms, they found that one person would have to spend 289 days, working six hours a day, to become certified. In Tampa, Florida, complete legal certification of the same business took less than four hours.[41]

When it works as it is supposed to, the law may be almost invisible. De Soto studied many books on the poor but could not find one saying that they usually worked illegally. Above all, their inability to enjoy secure property rights was ignored. No one seemed to appreciate the connection between poverty and the law. "Maybe the law has been the missing link that has prevented us from seeing what has been happening," he said.

"The institutions underlying the success of the American market system and the genuine participation of Americans in their own governance were constructed over 200 years," De Soto later wrote.[42] "So unnoticed has this process been that Americans have taken it for granted, losing their ability to recognize and teach the importance of these institutions and failing to incorporate them into their foreign policies." In fact, the West "never preserved a blueprint of its own evolution."[43]

THE LESSON BROUGHT HOME

Alan Woods, who was appointed administrator of the Agency for International Development in 1987, was one who had given De Soto assistance. In Woods's short but fruitful tenure, the agency for the first time questioned its own approach to development in the Third World. In February, 1989, the agency published a report, "Development and the National Interest: U.S. Economic Assistance into the Twenty-First Century," bringing some of these problems into the open. No country in the last 20 years had "graduated" from less-developed to developed status, Woods told reporters.[44] Paul Craig Roberts, a former assistant secretary of the treasury, observed that the underlying error was that the aid givers had lacked faith in American institutions and had "assumed that private enterprise was exploitative and would allow greed to hold sway."[45]

The Western failure to understood the real basis of economic development has meant that for decades aid was misspent; Americans are still far from understanding the point. They think the government spends far more on foreign aid than it really does—the figure is believed to be 10 to 15 percent of the budget, but it is actually about 1 percent—but they may also imagine that the money helps when it gets there. The real problem is actually worse than imagined. Everywhere the money went, it undermined the impulse to make the systemic legal reforms that were needed.

The result of Alan Woods's apostasy (he was within a few months of his death when his report came out, and perhaps he was not worrying about politics) was that an organization called the Center for Institutional Reform and the Informal Sector was funded by AID, and established at the University of Maryland. A draft paper in 1990 immediately acknowledged that economic "institutions and legal infrastructures" had long been overlooked by AID.

Even pointing this out was "contrary to the traditional approach to economic development," the paper added. The traditional approach had concentrated on "the analysis of developing country problems with minimal regard to the successful institutions and legal infrastructures in place in developed countries."[46] The "principal investigator" of the new organization was the economist Mancur Olson. In 1993, he noted that all the rich countries of the world had secure and well defined property and contract rights, all the unsuccessful ones lacked them.[47] Earlier he had written that proper economic development

> requires institutions that most people in the economically developed democracies take for granted, but that the emerging democracies of Central and Eastern Europe and the societies of Africa, Asia and Latin America usually do not have. A thriving market economy requires, among other things, institutions that provide secure individual rights—rights that insure that individuals, and the firms that they create, can best advance their interests by being as productive as possible and engaging in mutually beneficial trade. The incentives to save, to invest, and to produce depend particularly upon individual rights to marketable assets—on property rights."[48]

Critics have predicted that de Soto's reforms will fail, that he underestimates the ability of the ruling class to fight off his changes.[49] That may be. But the important point is that he made the correct diagnosis. Those who preceded him knew that Latin American elites were privileged, knew that the system was unjust. But their remedies were almost always redistributive. Because the ruling class in those countries had benefited from unfair rules, the goal should have been to change the rules. De Soto discovered anew the widely overlooked point that if property laws are applied equally, they will work above all to the advantage of the poor. But because property had for so long been regarded as the manifestation of privilege, it was difficult to see that it could also be its antidote; that it could be, as G. K. Chesterton said, "the art of the democracy."[50]

FOURTEEN

LAND REFORM: TAKING LIBERTIES ABROAD

AN EARLY SUCCESS

IN THE POSTWAR YEARS, land reform became the great cause for the champions of the underdeveloped world. Often, it was as close as they came to thinking about the role of property. Foreign aid provided the leverage for American idealists to rearrange the ownership of land in a number of countries. The exercise began with a great success, in Japan in 1945, and ended 40 years later, with a bitter failure in El Salvador. The great difference between Hernando de Soto's vision and that of the land reformers' was this: de Soto realized that the slender property base in the Third World needed to be expanded. Land reformers thought in zero-sum terms. Their goal was to redistribute the property that already existed.

A euphemism for the expropriation of landowners, land reform has been widely practiced in the twentieth century. Its supporters have generally believed that beneficiaries should enjoy a form of tenure that resembles ownership, but they usually forgot that expropriation undermines one of property's key features—its security. Well intentioned people felt that they could be entrusted with Leninist means in order to achieve Jeffersonian ends. And to them, the distribution of property was more important than its security. As for the real institutional defects that did exist, and continue to exist in many of the countries in which they worked, land reformers were not really interested in them. The single word "feudal" sufficed to cover a multitude of sins, which did not need to be examined in detail. Foreign laws and customs were too difficult to unravel anyway, and the peasants were in no mood to await the remaking of laws and legislatures. The sword of expropriation could be used to slice through the local problem, whatever it was. Property could simply be taken from the feudal overlords, and redistributed. Justice would then prevail, and everyone would become more productive.

The land reform literature is often technical and always tedious—Karl Marx was a witty writer by comparison with the authors of agrarian-reform treatises. It is also very much a literature of approval, often punctuated with calls for bolder action. It is rare to find any criticism of land reform, but a cogent comment did come from an unexpected quarter early on. John Kenneth Galbraith wrote in 1951:

> Some of our current discussion of land reform in the undeveloped countries proceeds as though this reform were something that a government proclaims on any fine morning—that it gives land to the tenants as it might give pensions to old soldiers or as it might reform the administration of justice. In fact, a land reform is a revolutionary step; it passes power, property, and status from one group in the community to another. If the government of the country is strongly influenced by the landholding group—the one that is losing its prerogatives—no one should expect effective land legislation as an act of grace. . . . The world is composed of many different kinds of people, but those who own land are not so different—whether they live in China, Persia, Mississippi or Quebec—that they will meet and happily vote themselves out of its possession.[1]

That's why American pressure was needed. Land reforms that have taken place without such pressure have usually been empty decrees, or adjuncts to military coups in which the existing regime was overthrown. Egypt in 1952 and Peru in 1968 are examples. An oft-cited and much admired land reform accompanied the Mexican revolution of 1910-20. It is often said that land was "given" to the peasants in that reform, but in fact state-controlled collectives called *ejidos* were created, and by the late 1990s privatization still had not gone beyond the talking stage. From the U.S. perspective, however, the instructive agrarian changes were those that accompanied the Communist revolutions of the twentieth century.

U.S. support for land reform cannot be understood without appreciating the supposed appeal of communism for the agrarian poor. Many Americans were convinced that this appeal was genuine, and that it accounted for the expansion of communism after World War II. The conviction therefore arose that the only way to combat it was to offer the peasants something similar to, but ultimately less deceptive than, communism. The argument went like this: The Communists promised land to the peasants, but after seizing power betrayed that promise and collectivized the land. What the democracies should do, then, is undertake democratic reform before the Communists do it their way. Galbraith said that land reform was revolutionary? Then make benign revolutions. Landowners will not expropriate themselves? "With dollars, all things are possible," the Americans replied.

It shows the power of communist ideas in mid-century that expropriation seemed the best avenue to ownership. If the Communists only seemed to promise property, why copy them at all? Yet we find Barbara Ward arguing that the Communists succeeded in China because they had "played on" the peasants' "fundamental hunger—the hunger for land."[2] In Russia in 1917, "the peasants' instinct for private property—for private ownership of the land—[had] consolidated in power a government committed to the destruction of private property." She might well have derived the lesson that expropriation as a prelude to establishing a more equitable society is a risky proposition. It not only could lead to the worst kind of tyranny, but had done so in Russia and was doing so in China even as she wrote.

From 1945 until about 1965, the most influential advocate of land reform was Wolf I. Ladejinsky, an official at the U.S. Department of Agriculture, later a consultant to the World Bank. Born in Ukraine in 1899, he left the Soviet Union on foot after his family's own property was expropriated by the Bolsheviks. After graduating from Columbia University, his former professor, Rexford Tugwell, offered him a job at the Department of Agriculture. He wrote academic articles about collectivization in the Soviet Union and "agrarian unrest" in Japan. After the war, he was given the rare opportunity to put theory into practice. Invited to Japan by Douglas MacArthur, he became the architect of that country's influential land reform. It was important because its success— and there were related successes at the same time in South Korea and Taiwan— inspired many subsequent efforts. But these were undertaken in crucially different circumstances, and met with no success.[3]

In December, 1945, MacArthur instructed the Japanese government to submit a program of land reform. The goal was to remove obstacles to the "strengthening of democratic tendencies, establish respect for the dignity of man, and destroy the economic bondage which has enslaved the Japanese farmer to centuries of feudal oppression," and to "exterminate those pernicious ills which have long blighted the agrarian structure" of a country where half the population farmed. The "more malevolent" of these included overcrowding, excessive rents and indebtedness, fiscal policies "which discriminate against agriculture," and government controls such as crop quotas. The solution— plainly not relevant to most of these "ills"—was the "transfer of land ownership from absentee land owners to land operators."[4]

Under the reform, three million farm families did acquire land, and by 1950 about 70 percent of Japan's farmers owned their land. The virtue of the reform was that real property rights were created. It did not undermine the security of property in Japan generally, as later happened in other countries. MacArthur's directive had hobbled the new owners with resale restrictions, but these were sensibly relaxed and then abolished by the Japanese themselves as they took control of their own affairs.

The key feature of the reform is that it came at a historically unusual moment of military defeat. Within a few years, similar reforms were also carried out in South Korea and Taiwan, and they were successful for the same reason. Both had been under Japanese rule, which came to an abrupt and final end in 1945. The decisive break in the continuity of government made a rearrangement of land ownership an acceptable part of the new order. In South Korea, the U.S. Army itself distributed a large percentage of the land, both before and during the Korean War.[5] In *Land Reform in Japan,* R. P. Dore identified the ingredients of success:

> For all the posters proclaiming the "liberation" of two million cho [4.8 million acres], for all the writings of left-wing and right-wing authors in the newspapers and magazines, and for all the activities of peasant unions and landlord unions, it was rare for the land reform to be carried out in an atmosphere of naked class antagonism. It remained, for most of the people whom it affected, the "Occupation Army's reform," imposed, as the Japanese phrase has it, "from the heavens above." Left-wing writers at the time of the reform and since have deplored this. Had the tenants won the land themselves "on the barricades," the argument runs, it would have been many times more effective as a means of destroying the traditional feudal structure.

Dore saw that, on the contrary, external imposition helped to make the reform peaceful:

> Tenants could take over the land, not with the light of revolution in their eyes, but half-apologetically, as if it hurt them more than it hurt their landlords, for the cause was not in themselves but in a law for which they bore no responsibility either personally or collectively. And the overwhelming power and prestige of the Occupation Army which lay behind the law, symbolized in the imposing and somewhat imperial figure of its Commander, helped to induce in the landlords a feeling of overawed resignation. [As a result], only 110 incidents between landlords and tenants involving physical violence were reported in the two years 1947-8.[6]

As a member of the Joint (United States and China) Commission on Rural Reconstruction, Ladejinsky next traveled to Szechwan Province, China, in October,

1949, and attempted to bring about reforms there. He was only a week or two ahead of the Communist forces; even if his ideas were correct, he was plainly too late. He reported back to the commission that most of the "land hungry, or just hungry" tenants of Asia "would sell their souls to their governments for a piece of land in fee simple or for reasonable tenure conditions." There followed some advice, which came to be known as the Ladejinsky thesis:

> If for no other reason than enlightened self-interest, in the contest with the Communists in Asia, the United States cannot be friendly to agrarian feudalism simply because we are against Communist totalitarianism. Our attitude should be one of positive support of agrarian democracy. We should lend our influence and prestige in whatever form possible to the agrarian reforms already in being and those yet to come. We shall thereby help cut the political ground from under the feet of the Communists.[7]

This was especially urgent in Asia, where Western "traditions, institutions, [and] habits of thought" were absent. Such institutions amounted to "natural defenses against Communism"; without them, communism would meet with little resistance. A cultivator who was also an owner "would guard that society against extremism. Private property would be strengthened where it has been weakest, at the huge base of the social pyramid. The common man of Asia would become a staunch opponent of Communist economics and politics."[8]

There was a good deal of truth in this. Unlike most of his contemporaries, Ladejinsky understood the importance of legal institutions. He was certainly right to argue that "technological improvements alone" would not transform poor countries. His mistake was to think in terms of redistributing property rather than creating more of it. He also exaggerated the "populist" character of Communist revolutions, which he saw as spontaneous uprisings. In fact, they more closely resembled coups.

One might also ask: If the peasants could not acquire property by buying it in the normal fashion, either because the present owners enjoyed legal privileges, or because titles could not be transferred, or because the land was controlled by a state apparatus that preferred not to allow the people to become independent, then didn't the real problem lie in these restrictions? But such political barriers to peaceable reform were rarely discussed by land reformers. Were whole classes not permitted by law to acquire property? Were there obstacles to registration? Was the government so tyrannical that even existing landlords owned property insecurely? Could property not be alienated under any circumstances? Land reformers rarely bothered with such questions. Their hearts were set on expropriation as the bold remedy for injustice.

Chester Bowles, ambassador to India and congressman from Connecticut, was a great land-reform enthusiast. At his request, Ladejinsky next went to
India, in 1952. But the complacent peasants there frustrated him. Their passivity
ensured that land reform never rose high on the political agenda, and it was never
seriously undertaken. It was a source of wonder to Ladejinsky that the poor so
meekly labored "without resorting to violence." He told a World Bank seminar
toward the end of his career: "If we are to wait until the peasantry of India—or
for that matter a number of other Asian countries—decide to take the law into
their own hands and fight for an out-and-out radical agrarian revolution, I think
we would have to wait a long, long time."[9] The Japanese, of course, had precisely
not taken the law into their own hands. It was handed to them.

Ladejinsky had his great success, in Japan, but it seems that he never
quite understood it. The country had been destroyed in war, creating a clean
break with the past; its people were then ready to accept externally imposed
reforms. Their own sensible amendments to those reforms ensured that real
property rights were created in Japan, as they were also in South Korea and
Taiwan. But the Americans tended to think that all a government had to do was
take land from its existing owners and give it to deserving others, and everything
would work out for the best. As a result, land reform was tried again, and then
again, with quite different consequences.

THINGS GO WRONG

Articles on land reform appeared in popular magazines, including the *Saturday
Evening Post*. The U.S. representative to the UN General Assembly explained it
with a homeopathic metaphor. "If he is to be immunized against the promise of
Communist propaganda," Isador Lubin wrote, the free governments of the world
must initiate programs "in which the individual farmer can see that his lot is
improving."[10] When Fidel Castro seized power and implemented a land reform
program, the U.S. government said it was "sympathetic to the objectives which
the government of Cuba is presumed to be seeking." Programs for "rural
betterment" could contribute to "political stability and social progress."[11] Castro's
government was free of Communist infiltration, assured Cuba's short-lived
president, Manuel Urrutia, who pointed to Fidel's land reform as proof. For land
reform "works against Communism."[12] When Castro handed out land titles in the
Sierra Maestra, he "spoke of the joy of the Cuban peasant in receiving title," the
New York Times reported. "In today's celebration, 1,912 titles were delivered. The
Premier declared that the peasant in Cuba would no longer be exploited."[13]

Latin American leaders saw billions of foreign aid dollars heading their way
if they obliged Washington. But they could no longer "be bought off with trinkets,"

one warned.[14] At the conference setting up the Alliance for Progress, Treasury Secretary C. Douglas Dillon said that perhaps $20 billion would be forthcoming by the end of the 1960s. Che Guevera challenged Dillon to put it in writing. The Americans, led by Richard Goodwin and Arthur Schlesinger, made sure that progressive policies—land reform, higher taxes on the rich—were implemented in return. There would be "programs of comprehensive agrarian reform leading to the effective transformation, where required, of unjust structures and systems of land tenure and use, with a view to replacing latifundia and dwarf holdings by an equitable system of land tenure." In the committee's final vote on that statement, C. Douglas Dillon and Che Guevera raised their approving hands simultaneously.[15]

Chile became the testing ground for the new policy. The United States vowed that Chile would not become another Cuba, and believed that dollars would make the difference. In the 1964 presidential election, the CIA spent $3 million to support the Christian Democrat, Eduardo Frei, who duly defeated the Marxist Salvador Allende.[16] The new U.S. ambassador to Chile, Ralph Dungan, told an interviewer that the United States believed in land reform "as an act of humanity." He caused a stir by adding that "from a social viewpoint, private property is not an unlimited right." Enacted in July, 1967, land reform subjected to expropriation all privately owned farms in Chile of more than 192 acres, and any farmland judged to be "poorly cultivated" or "neglected." Owners were paid 10 percent in cash, with the remainder promised over 25 years. The architect of the reform was Jacques Chonchol, who had been an adviser to Cuba's Agrarian Reform Institute in 1960-61. He remained an ally of Castro, and later became minister of agriculture in Salvador Allende's government.[17]

A clause in the Chilean Constitution protecting property rights was swept away, and Frei issued the familiar warning: Those who oppose democratic reform now "will have to suffer it tomorrow with violence and disorder."[18] Castro cleverly attacked the reforms, legitimizing the claim that something more violent had been prevented.[19] Here, then, was the middle way between Communist revolution and rightist reaction. Taxes were increased and the copper industry "Chileanized." The United States was by then providing "decisive financial assistance" to Chile, Frei said.[20] Chile's ambassador to the United States boasted, in a 1967 speech at Notre Dame, that Chile had extracted from the United States "at least three times more than was promised" when the Alliance for Progress was created. [21] But contrary to homeopathic theory, the reforms helped bring Salvador Allende closer to power.

Land invasions and strikes only increased once the state itself began to expropriate land. Chonchol "unleashed a veritable tumult in the countryside," one author wrote.[22] Eventually, 1,400 farms were taken in the Frei years, covering over eight million acres. A much larger number were taken in the three Allende years. Between 1965 and 1973, almost half of Chile's arable land was expropriated. Scenes all too familiar to the student of land reform were ritually reenacted:

The president himself appears in the countryside, and is met by cheering peasants; 12,000 strong near Santiago in July, 1967. Farm output will at last increase, he says; credit and seed will be made available—the government will see to that. For once, the president does not try to curry favor by distributing phony title deeds. Banners are waved and solidarity is proclaimed. A small detail emerges: peasants living on the "reformed" lands will not be getting private plots, not for a few years, at any rate. In the interim they will be required to form collective farms. That was the price of doing business with Chonchol and his Communist allies. As the curtain falls on the first act of the drama, the *New York Times* applauds, saying that "an ambitious and badly needed agrarian reform law, which President Frei has just signed, took two and a half years of hard driving to get through the reluctant Congress. President Frei is a true Christian and a true Democrat." His government is "often considered the Latin-American answer to Cuba's Marxism-Leninism."[23]

The familiar second act follows within a year: Inflation becomes "runaway,"[24] and landowners are in effect expropriated, for their bonds are not adjusted for inflation. Farm output declines, the need for food imports increases. The incentives of the owners have been destroyed. "Since the United States created this economic disaster with its support for the Christian Democrats, the United States is morally obliged to pay the nation's food bills," a Chilean senator says.[25] The United States is once more happy to oblige. By 1968, U.S. food gifts are helping to feed a quarter of the Chilean population.[26]

We read of rising tensions between "angry landlords" and "increasingly militant" agrarian reformers. Gunplay is reported, and reformers from the Agrarian Development Institute are at hazard from "right-wing extremists." Bad weather descends—"Chile's Drought Worsens Strife Over Reforms."[27] Political observers foresee that in the 1970 election the Right and the Left will gain at the expense of the center. The only solution is "to accelerate the agrarian reform," Jacques Chonchol declares, to head off the "rural violence."[28] That too is done, but somehow it only makes things worse. The reviews, initially so favorable, have turned negative: in 1969, *U.S. News & World Report* finds Chile "A Latin American 'Showcase' Where Reforms Went Sour."[29]

In 1970, Salvador Allende was narrowly elected president in a three-way race; the Christian Democrats' share declined from 56 percent in 1964 to half that figure. The Jesuit Centro Belarmino, a source of liberation theology, saw the "New Man" coming over the horizon at last, along with Allende's Government of Popular Unity.[30] Farm seizures steadily increased, as witnessed by Suzanne Labin, a French writer: "A band armed with clubs and rifles forces its way onto a farm, orders the whole of the owner's family to pack their bags;

pushes them out onto the road, gathers together all those who work upon the farm, tells them that it is their property from now on, and sets up a banner with the words: 'This property has been seized by the people.'"[31] If such armed bands met with armed resistance, the resisters, not the invaders, were prosecuted. And so it went for two or three more years, until Augusto Pinochet and the Chilean military seized power in October, 1973.

In their disillusioned work *The Peasant Betrayed,* John Powelson and Richard Stock wrote that "Countries where peasants are 'given the land and left alone' are so rare that analysts must cherish each one."[32] This was demonstrated in the extraordinarily sweeping and high-handed land reform that was imposed on South Vietnam in the critical years 1970-72. The evidence suggests that it seriously undermined such support as President Thieu still enjoyed, and it may explain the sudden collapse of his regime. Here a key figure was Roy L. Prosterman, who today is a law professor at the University of Washington Law School.

Like Ladejinsky, Prosterman had written articles about land reform, and then graduated to a policy role (he was also to become involved in El Salvador, as we shall see). Arriving in South Vietnam in 1967, little more than 30 years old, he achieved the remarkable feat of writing the legislation and bringing it to President Thieu's attention without going through official channels.[33] The State Department by this time had become wary of pressing too hard for land reform, sensing its destabilizing potential.

The bill was submitted to the National Assembly in 1969, and was enacted "in virtually its original form," Prosterman wrote, "after an eight-month fight against landlord interests."[34] (But the *New York Times* reported that "surprisingly, the overwhelming opposition from the wealthy landed interests did not materialize as some predicted."[35]) Saigon was now "immunized." It had "stolen a major plank from the Communists' platform, which is as good a way as any to compete with them," Iver Peterson wrote in the *Times.*[36] Landowners were reimbursed with a 20 percent down payment, with the rest payable in bonds. But once again inflation greatly exceeded the interest rate, and after landlords received their down payment, they had little reason to stay. The political analyst Jude Wanniski wrote: "The landowners packed their worthless bonds and valuable capital and moved to Saigon or Paris. Each community lost the human capital of the departed landowner, his political and organizational skills. The invisible fabric of the community having been destroyed, it became easy prey for the Viet Cong as productivity slumped and bills came due. The program was pushed even harder, right up to the end of the war in 1974; the last pockets to fall to the VC were those that had resisted land reform."[37]

The reform effectively destroyed property rights in about three-fifths of the cultivated land of South Vietnam. As a part of what was called Vietnamization, the landlords who were the backbone of Thieu's support were driven off with a down payment. Prosterman described the program as calling for "the free distribution of substantially all privately owned land that is not owner cultivated." It was to be "given" to those who tilled it. But the tillers never enjoyed anything resembling property rights, and in fact were put in a hopeless position.

The *New York Times* called the reform, with reason, "probably the most ambitious and progressive non-Communist land reform" of the twentieth century: "The new land-to-the-tiller law, which pledges the country's one million tenant farmers ownership of practically all the land they rent, promises more than social justice. It has become an important element in the efforts of the Saigon Government to gain political support. By reducing the Vietcong's appeal in the countryside, it could add inducement to Hanoi to negotiate peace. . . ."[38]

Lyndon Johnson said in 1967 that the tillers would be given aerial photographs as a form of title.[39] By 1970, however, we learn that a "giant IBM 360 computer" in the U.S. AID building in Saigon would "soon begin churning out titles for about 2.5 million acres of land."[40] Thieu himself handed out the first batch of AID-printed titles to several hundred tenant farmers. Later, the law was "simplified" to achieve its true purpose: abolition of tenancy. All rentals were "terminated."[41] Anyone working the land of another simply became its owner, "without any prior need for formalities such as western-style titles," Prosterman said. Furthermore, the new "owners" were not allowed to sell their land for 15 years. This destroyed the market for land. If a new "owner" himself decided to leave the land and find another to till it, he became an "absentee" himself, and was subject to expropriation in turn.[42]

In 1972, the *New York Times* sent a reporter into the field, and he did what land reformers so rarely do. He interviewed a landlord: "A 52-year-old peasant landowner with 20 acres said, 'I have never been a rich man, just enough to eat, but now the government has taken away most of my land and they have given me nothing in return.'"[43] Another farmer in Longan Province told the reporter, Thomas Fox: "I do not know a single landowner who has received money for land taken from him." By that time, apparently, 30,000 former owners, covering a tenth of the redistributed land, had received a down payment. Perhaps as many as 200,000 South Vietnamese landowners in all were expropriated.[44]

Tillers were treated as absentees if they were drafted, Fox found. The land was then transferred (as the law required) to those who were doing the tilling—"draft dodgers and those too weak or too old to fight." So the tillers never became owners at all. There was no way they could sell their land. They were anchored to the paddy fields in the worst kind of feudal way. As for the original owners, many are believed to have bought air fares with their down payments, and some of them are surely running restaurants and convenience stores in the United States today.

"Landlessness" is the theme of Prosterman's book *Land Reform and Democratic Development*. Those who rent land lack a "secure and remunerative relationship" with it. His ideal seemed to be a world of self-employed smallholders with no tenants. But his belief that collective-farm workers in Marxist countries do enjoy "ownership or ownership-like rights" seems peculiar. In his eccentric Land Productivity Index, published in 1987,[45] East Germany ranked ahead of the United States in agricultural productivity, Bulgaria ahead of Norway, and collective farming was said to provide an "engine for development" in the Soviet Union.[46] His chapter on Vietnam reads like the account of a successful operation—at the end of which the patient died. (It came too late.) He cites U.S. Department of Agriculture claims that rice productivity increased 30 percent after the reform.[47] But this is not believable in light of the following facts.

The price of rice jumped by 40 percent in 1973, and "the United States now plans to bring in 400,000 tons of its own rice in 1974," Robert Shaplen reported in the *New Yorker*.[48] In March, 1974, President Thieu was "ordering" an increase in agricultural production, and vowing to "force war refugees in the cities to move back to farm areas." By April, the *Far Eastern Economic Review* reported, rice in South Vietnam was in "extremely short supply."[49] William Shawcross reported from the field in 1974 that "in 1971 rice cost $150 a ton in Saigon. Now it is $500," and "priced out of the reach of millions."[50] In the coast area near Hue, "people are eating roots of trees and bushes," and in Quang Ngai, Shawcross wrote, "whole families are attempting to survive on one meal of three sweet potatoes and a few land crabs a day. Government officials admit that the only short-term solution to the food shortage is for people to eat less." In April, 1975, another 100,000-ton emergency shipment of U.S. rice was reported. In October, 1975, with the Communists in charge and Saigon about to be renamed Ho Chi Minh City, it was announced that 1.5 million people were being sent "back to the land," for a "return to farming."[51]

In July, 1975, Roy Prosterman testified before Congress that Vietnam's land reform had "worked very well in productivity terms."[52] It had been "highly effective," he thought in 1976.[53] In light of the general turmoil and war, it is difficult to assess the consequences of this land reform, but it is possible that South Vietnam was crucially destabilized by it. The subject has received almost no attention from historians of the Vietnam War and should be examined in greater detail.

THE GREAT SATAN

It was Iran, perhaps more than any other country, that demonstrated to well intentioned Americans the hazards of using dollars to change life for the better, without first understanding the legal and cultural environment they were operating in. The background belief was that if we did *not* persuade the shah of Iran to implement reforms, land reform prominently among them, the Iranians would be seduced by the fatal attractions of communism. So, once again, land was duly "reformed," "given" to peasants, then taken back again and this time given to international "agribusiness" corporations. Their optimistic investments were turned into jobs programs by Iranian officials, and finally into multimillion-dollar losses. The journals of David E. Lilienthal give us unguarded glimpses of these dealings. The former chairman of the Tennessee Valley Authority and the Atomic Energy Commission, Lilienthal went into the economic development business himself in the 1950s, and the Iranian government became his principal client. Impressed by Lilienthal's reputation, the shah of Iran usually took his advice.[54]

By the late 1950s, officials with the Economic Cooperation Administration (predecessor to the U.S. Agency for International Development) were thick on the ground in Iran. Their role was to tell the Iranians what to do, while pretending they were doing no such thing. They established themselves in all the major towns, and, together with the Ford Foundation, made detailed policy recommendations. Even though Iran was three times the size of France and then had a population of only 22 million, they concluded that ownership would have to be rearranged, whole populations moved, and the country "put through the industrial reform wringer," to quote a Ford Foundation participant.[55]

A preliminary land reform law was passed in 1960, having been drafted by U.S. officials.[56] News reports always implied that these Iranian reforms, known as the White Revolution, were home grown. But even the prime minister was appointed by the shah at President Kennedy's request. The United States wanted "its own man in as Prime Minister," the shah later wrote. "This man was Ali Amini, and in time the pressure became too strong for me to resist."[57] Land reform was soon thereafter decreed, at a time when the *majlis* (parliament) was dissolved. While giving lip service to democracy, the United States sometimes preferred to use dictatorial powers to impose its own policy without debate. Amini's land reform plan was almost certainly written for him by American officials. Afsaneh Najmabadi's detailed investigations never quite proved the point, but she notes:

> The archival material at the John F. Kennedy Library, for instance, is heavily sanitized wherever there seems to have been a reference to the nature of Amini-U.S. relations. Nevertheless, the same documents indicate total U.S. backing of Amini's program, as if Amini was, indeed, "their man." A National Security Council document dated May 15, 1961, that is, nine days into Amini's term of office, speaks of American policy being "directed towards the support of the Iranian Government rather than support of the Shah personally. . . . The

goals which we envisage and which we believe to be in the long-term interests of Iran and the Iranian people are wholly consistent and almost identical with those which the new Prime Minister has publicly declared as his program."[58]

David Lilienthal's journals confirm that Iranian policy was made by Americans, even within ministries. In one entry he noted that the "policy of integration of the Point Four [foreign aid] work was a mistake."[59] American foreign-assistance people had been placed in Iranian ministries, where they were meant "to pretend that they are only 'advisors,' that the real work is being done by Iranians. The Iranians know better, and the net effect is not only hypocrisy but less effective than to do a straightforward job of getting the work done. . . ." The U.S. ambassador agreed. When higher ranking Americans arrived and tried to find out what was going on, "the Iranian in the Ministry would start to explain it, but since it was clear he didn't know, the American Point Four man, who started by saying he was only an advisor . . . would take over the discussion."

The land reform took effect by decree in January, 1962. The Communist Tudeh Party's agrarian program of the 1940s "was quite similar to that proclaimed by the shah in 1962," Najmabadi wrote.[60] It was, in any event, "far more radical than anything produced on paper by the National Front or implemented during the brief term of Mossadeq's government." The Tudeh Party applauded the reform. In January, 1963, the government announced that the reform would be extended to *waqf* land, held in trust for mosques and Islamic clerics. This and earlier land reform decrees "set off large demonstrations by Muslim clerics, including Ruhollah Khomeini," Barry Rubin wrote in *Paved With Good Intentions*. In June, 1963, "three days of anti-government riots in Tehran were crushed with as many as 3,000 dissidents killed."[61] Khomeini was deported in 1964.

Surveying and registration of title were unknown in Iran. The new rule was adopted that no "owner" could retain more than one village. Ann Lambton wrote that about 200 families "owned" more than a hundred villages each. The 290 largest owners affected by the new law included merchants, state officials, doctors, engineers and lawyers. Of these, she wrote, "206 were absentees living in Tabriz, Tehran and elsewhere." Many of them responded by selling "all their landholdings to the government."[62] In her *Landlord and Peasant in Persia,* Lambton made the crucial and little-noted point that the Iranian landlord himself "owned" the land only nominally, for he was insecure "against the caprice of the government."[63]

It is therefore misleading to think of such "owners" as property owners in the Western sense. They had not obtained rights to the land by buying it. There was no market for the buying and selling of land. More accurately, they were permitted to collect rents from villagers in return for their support of the regime.

In effect, they were authorized predators upon the peasantry. The effect of the reform was to further centralize an already centralized system and to transfer more power to the shah.[64] "Instead of paying a landlord when the crops were in," George Baldwin wrote in *Planning and Development in Iran*, "peasants would pay the government according to a 15-year schedule of amortization."[65] Eric Hooglund noted in *Land and Revolution in Iran* that the shah's power was increased. With the landowners bought out, "the central government could extend its power into the villages."[66] The peasants were now more than ever at the mercy of the state.

The U.S. press represented the shah as a progressive. One day he was giving away his Caspian estates "to 4,300 peasant families"; another he was handing out land titles to subjects who kissed his feet.[67] State farms were started, and top Iranians were sent to Moscow to learn the latest methods.[68] By October, 1967, nationalization of forests, profit sharing for workers and votes for women had transformed the shah from playboy into "reformist, benevolent dictator," according to the *New York Times*.[69] A literacy drive had changed the villages, and now the "feudal landholdings" were no more. Oil revenues were working wonders, having been "pumped into dams and industrialization projects."[70] One of these dams, on the Dez River in Khuzestan, had been built by Lilienthal's company, the Development and Resources Corporation (D & R).

Until then, the "tillers of the land" had been nothing—thought to be "hopelessly defeated by centuries of half-animal existence," Lilienthal wrote. But now the great dam was ready to serve, and the peasants were "taking over the land from landowners." The uplifted tillers would "rebuild the agricultural sinews of a region that was green and fertile in the ancient days when it was the center of power of the great Persian Empire. When I first saw it only seven years ago it seemed a hopeless desert."[71]

But with the dam built, and the land redistributed, Lilienthal's company had little to do. Then he hit on an idea. American-style agribusiness could increase food production. In November, 1966, he lunched with "Jack" Heinz, the president of the H. J. Heinz Co., at the Fifth Avenue Club in New York. In his journal, he noted that he was looking for "a workable way" to put agribusiness to work "on the stubborn problem of increasing food supply in the underdeveloped world."[72] Within days, the new plan took shape: D & R would put together a business consortium that could "take" a slice of Khuzistan and "make it really produce, on a commercial basis." This would "improve our standing with the higher authorities in Iran," and "give us an exciting new action program for Khuzistan."[73]

There was one problem. How to "take" the land? A letter was soon on its way to the shah, praising the "great agricultural potential" of Khuzistan. The progress to date showed what small farmers could do. How much more productive large-scale agriculture would be! Lilienthal cautiously added that among the "specifics" would be the "conditions under which the use of land in the Dez area might be made available to private enterprises. . . ."[74] Three weeks later he received a letter from a minister, "expressing real excitement" about the new idea. So now they would be taking the land back from the peasants.

The anthropologist Grace Goodell happened to be doing her field research in the Dez region at the time. Every so often she would be summoned to chat with Lilienthal, who had dropped in to visit the shah. She described her experiences in *The Elementary Structures of Political Life*. More recently she has been head of development studies at the Johns Hopkins School for Advanced and International Studies. "Lilienthal's Development and Resources Corporation persuaded His Imperial Majesty that foreign agribusinesses could best realize the potentials of the Dez Irrigation Scheme," she wrote. "Having demurred momentarily—Ladejinsky weeping for the small farmers of the Dez (in a visit some of them recall, although they did not know its purpose at the time)—the World Bank agreed to finance the Empire's yearnings to uplift Khuzestan once again, according to centralized Plan."[75]

Peasants had received 30-year leases, not titles as promised, but even this "spelled unimaginable permanence," Goodell reported. At first, the land reform had seemed to work—peasants more than doubled crop yields and increased livestock production. Then came the agribusiness scheme. "Even as the Dez peasants . . . embraced their new management challenges, even at that moment their exit from the stage had already been written," she wrote. "Their newly acquired land would be taken away from them ('repurchased') and leased to foreign agribusinesses, which would hire those of them who were needed on a day-wage basis."

Some peasants evidently suspected something like this. Since they had not gained the land through any initiative of their own, they looked upon the state's announcement that they were now its owners as a gimmick of the shah's. Goodell reported: "'If the Shah is powerful enough to wrest the land from the rich and give it to us,' Abbas accurately reflected, 'how much easier it will be when he wants to take it back from us at his pleasure.'"[76] There is more wisdom in that comment than in all the treatises of land reformers.

One of the outside businessmen was Hashem Naraghi, an Iranian who had left for California in 1944. There he became the world's largest independent almond grower and a multimillionaire. By the 1960s, he was back in Khuzistan, planning to invest $10 million in 45,000 acres he had obtained from the shah. "Labor cost is a tenth of what it is in California, and almost everything does well," he told *Fortune*. Asparagus grew faster, irrigation water was purer, the alfalfa protein was higher. He was planning to airlift asparagus to Europe, pelletize alfalfa for Japan, plant 5,000 acres of lemons and oranges. "Anyone who cannot make it in Khuzestan has no business being a farmer," he added rashly.[77] Another was George Wilson, former head of the California Farm Bureau Federation. He had seen Khuzestan from the air in 1949. The land looked good to him. He thought he would "like to have a piece of it someday." Now he had 25,000 acres, and he too was planning a $10 million investment.

By coincidence, both men were reinterviewed five years later. Naraghi had already pulled out by 1975, citing "creeping nationalization." Wilson was still hanging on, but "bureaucrats in Tehran were beginning to obstruct [his] project for reasons he did not understand."[78] Naraghi told an American visitor that the Khuzestan Water and Power Authority (a "child conceived by us," Lilienthal had boasted in 1960[79]) had about 500 vehicles working on the irrigation project alone. By contrast, California's Imperial Valley had employed 60 people using 15 vehicles to irrigate a much larger area.

The investors had miscalculated badly. They had failed to recognize the huge difference between the entity called government in Iran and its Western counterpart. Their "investment" had simply been construed by Iranian officials as an employment opportunity for Iranians. Investors had mistakenly assumed that the system of law that protected their rights in the United States could be taken for granted abroad on the mere say-so of top officials.

One day, an assistant to the shah and "guardian of the development funds" spoke to Lilienthal about his "concern" about the agribusinesses. "This has the seeds of great trouble for this country," he said. "There are places where if we moved the farmers off the land they own and put it into an agricultural corporation to be managed as a consolidated operation, there would be great social unrest." Lilienthal was unconcerned: "What we now propose in Persia is to provide consolidated or large-scale agriculture in lieu of small and inadequate tracts that resulted largely from the mistaken (I think) and fervid slogans of the 'land reform' legislation of only a few years ago."

By 1974, he felt that the shah was "the most influential man in the world," and that "what is going on in Iran is a transformation—physical, mental, economic—on an epic scale."[80] But elsewhere we catch glimpses of the chaos of disordered development in a command economy with oil money to spend: Luxury hotels going up in Teheran—a city without a sewage system; donkeys and Cadillacs jostling for space on unpaved highways; camels tethered to Dior boutiques; expensively built irrigation canals, from which women fetch water with earthenware pots; brand-new tractors for state farms immobilized by stolen parts; Herefordshire herds helicoptered in because the shah has been told there is a milk shortage.

By 1976, all the major agribusinesses in Iran had declared bankruptcy, having lost hundreds of millions of dollars. And by 1978—even before the revolution—the government began asking the peasants who had already been given the land once, and then had seen it taken away, to buy it back again. "The [Dez] Project was not two decades old," wrote Goodell. "Hundreds of millions of dollars of debt had been incurred. The Dez dam's original life expectancy of eighty years had been revised to thirty."[81] In October, 1976, Lilienthal brought the bad news to the shah. "The entire program of agricultural production has not succeeded," he said. "The country is importing more and more food and becoming less and less self sufficient."[82] The Shah conceded there was unrest. The lives of peasants were still untouched by the "general prosperity" that he believed oil revenues had created. The Khomeini revolution came in 1979.

NEAR DISASTER, AND RECOVERY

At first, the Iranian disaster did little to warn officials of the need for a different approach to development: one that emphasized the security of property in the Third World. American-backed land-reform schemes proceeded undisturbed in a number of countries, notably El Salvador. Here was the latest laboratory, with communism once again nearby. In March, 1980, 469 leading farmers in El Salvador were unceremoniously run off their own property with no warning, at gunpoint, and told not to come back. They were "compensated" with bonds redeemable in the year 2000, once again unadjusted for inflation. Once more, collective farms were created, not private property.

In the words of Roy Prosterman, who had helped devise the "land-to-the-tiller" phase of the reform in El Salvador: "A team of agronomists and other technicians, accompanied by an army truck with military personnel, went to each farm to notify the farm's administrative office that the property was being intervened by the government and turned over to the peasants working there and other landless families." In his account of this reform, Prosterman (like other agrarian reformers) treats owners not as individuals whose particular circumstances are worth examining, but as an undifferentiated class enemy.[83] In fact, one of the "intervened" (expropriated) farmers was Roberto Aguilar, who in the 1930s had attended Stanford University. Interviewed in 1988, at the age of 75, he gave this account:

> On March 10, 1980, two truckfuls of armed soldiers went to the farm and told everybody to leave immediately. We had a big farm—1,300 head of cattle, cotton, baby corn, sugar cane. The man who was fumigating the cotton fields changed clothes in a special room. But they wouldn't even let him go back and change his clothes. They wanted to take over his plane as well. Just ran everybody off right then and there. We weren't told, "Today we're going to take over your land," no. They came into the different haciendas and took them over by force without warning.

So they took over the farm and they established a cooperative, with 60 members. And they got financed to plant corn. But they had a very poor crop because nobody worked. They thought of themselves as owners and they thought: "Owners do not work." So they had all this idle membership. They were being paid anyway—paid by the government. None of these cooperatives have worked, you know. The cooperative that was once my farm now owes the government $4.5 million to date. Nobody has worked on it for the last two years because they were not given any more money—they do such a poor job of producing. I think the 60 are still on the farm but they don't get anything from the government anymore. I had seven tractors, a big workshop. That's empty of all the tools I had there. And the tractors are not around.

At first the government told them to spend all the money they needed. They just threw it at them. On payday four different paymasters came to the same farm. All the cooperative members were saying they were going to get paid for two years and that would be enough to get fixed for life. The man who ran the show was the Ambassador of the United States, Robert White. About a week after the agrarian reform was put into effect, they asked him how it was going. And he said on TV, "Divinamente!" He said it in Spanish, and he said it perfectly. And we were all being driven off the land.[84]

Officials were able to show up on payday because the money was coming from the U. S. Agency for International Development. Over $200 million had been sent to pay for this latter-day experiment in collectivization.[85] But that was only a fraction of the total amount. In the 1980s, the U.S. government spent about $6 billion overall in El Salvador. The land reform policy, launched in the Carter years, was continued by President Reagan. "With regard to the reforms the Duarte government has been trying to implement," Reagan said on March 6, 1981, "the land reform, the creating of farms for the former tenants and all—we support all of that."[86]

The co-op members had not been given the land at all. They were merely told that they now owned it collectively. Individual shares were not apportioned, nor were titles given. This was meant to ensure that the members did not sell the land back to its original owners. The result was that the new "owners" were reduced to the status of serfs; they had squatters' rights and a stipend from the state. Their ownership in common gave rise to the by now familiar problem. The system "separated monetary reward from work accomplished," wrote William Thiesenhusen of the Land Tenure Center in Madison, Wisconsin, and "diluted the incentive to work at capacity. Members were tempted to 'free ride.' Why work hard when the same monetary reward could be obtained by slacking off?"[87]

To make matters worse, they could not (even collectively) sell the land to anyone, so they had no incentive to maintain its value—especially since they were being paid anyway. If anything, the U.S.-supported collectivization in El

Salvador was more extreme than the simultaneous efforts of the Sandinista government in Nicaragua. Banks and the coffee industry were also nationalized in El Salvador, and the overall result was catastrophic: the country's GNP declined by 23 percent from 1979 to 1983.

Asked why this continued under Reagan, former assistant secretary of state Elliott Abrams replied: "Because Duarte believed in it. He was a brave, admirable democrat when it came to politics; and essentially a socialist when it came to economics." But Abrams added that "the idea of breaking the back of the old economic oligarchy was something that we did support. The country had been run for decades by the army and the oligarchy."[88]

The 469 expropriated owners, among them Roberto Aguilar, received no due process, as would be required in the United States. They were not convicted, or even accused, of any wrongdoing. Abroad, American officials evidently believed, revolutionary methods are justified to advance noble-seeming goals. A few of these owners, having been treated with such contempt, are thought to have responded by taking the law into their own hands. In January, 1981, the head of the Salvadoran land reform agency and two American advisers, one of them Roy Prosterman's law student, were shot to death by soldiers in the coffee shop of the San Salvador Sheraton Hotel.[89]

By the 1990s, the land reform scheme had ended and the political climate was much improved. The 30-year resale waiting period in the land-to-the-tiller phase of the reform was abolished, and as for the co-ops such as Aguilar's former farm, a 1991 decree of the Alfredo Christiani government permitted members to vote on whether their collectives should be privatized. And a more general lesson had been learned. According to John Bruce of the Land Tenure Center in Wisconsin, the U.S. Agency for International Development was by the 1990s no longer involved in land reform programs involving "compulsory acquisition" anywhere in the world.[90]

The United States had also insisted on one reform that in the end did benefit El Salvador: elections. Under Christiani's leadership, more-sensible policies were pursued and the country largely recovered. It is unfashionable to say so, but Chile also dramatically recovered under Pinochet. Land reform was partly reversed there, and by 1976, U.S. aid was completely cut off. By 1987, the *New York Times* reported, Chile had developed a "stockholders' culture."[91] It even privatized its social security system—something that has barely reached the talking stage in the United States. At last, the U.S. Agency for International Development pulled out of Chile. Vietnam is still Communist in name, but moving toward a free-market system in fact. It is only a matter of time before the pretense of communism is abandoned there. Only in Iran has property not reasserted itself. But as we shall see, property has not been secure in the Islamic world for a long time.

HISTORICAL PUZZLES

INTRODUCTION

The incentives of private property are potent and can be used to examine many social and historical puzzles. When those incentives are imperfect or absent, there will be telltale signs. We have so often tried to explain history by reference to military victory, natural resources, population pressure, or to otherwise unexplained economic strength or weakness, that we have forgotten how to look at the institutional structures of law and government. Especially after a period of disuse, the half-hidden role of property turns out to have considerable explanatory power. Anomalies may deliver up their secrets once the property-rights structure is examined.

One of the great unresolved questions of history is why the Muslim world suddenly began to fall behind the Western world in the late seventeenth century. In the three centuries since, despite huge oil discoveries and payments from the West, the gap if anything seems to be widening. In earlier centuries, Islamic civilization was thought to be on a par with the West economically, and perhaps ahead of it in other respects. Something changed, but historians have not been able to agree on what it was.

The explanation offered here is that the great change in some parts of western Europe—adoption of the institutional infrastructure of the free-market system—did not occur in the Middle East.

Property could not be held securely against the ruling power in the Arab world for a long time, and broadly speaking this has remained true. Oil has solved nothing. Indeed, it may have exacerbated the problem by placing great wealth at the disposal of the central authorities. It also encouraged the belief that wealth is more like manna from heaven than the consequence of hard work. The problem was only made worse in the twentieth century by the adoption of "Arab socialism" in several countries.

The green and fertile land of Ireland could hardly provide a greater contrast. The question of why it was afflicted with a catastrophic famine in the mid-nineteenth century, in which a million Irish people died, is a subject of continuing debate that has never been satisfactorily resolved. The country was as fertile then as now, and by no means overpopulated by comparison with other parts of Europe. Thomas Malthus observed ten years before the famine that something other than the "principle of population" was causing grave difficulties in Ireland: the insecurity of property. He didn't elaborate, and the issue has not subsequently received the attention it deserves.

The debate has suffered from the reluctance of historians to examine the issue from the point of view of the Anglo-Irish landlords—the traditional villains of the story. A central insight of a property-rights analysis is that it is not in the interest of owners to behave in self-destructive ways. Property that is held securely allows us to predict that its owners will not, over time, act in opposition to their own interest—by impoverishing their own tenants, for example. But in Ireland it seems that they often did just that. This suggests that the land was held less securely than has been recognized.

FIFTEEN

PROPERTY IN ARABY

ARABIAN RIGHTS

WHEN WEALTHY ARABS bought property in the West after the oil boom, it came with secure title attached. By contrast, property is held insecurely all over the Arab world. The brutal punishments meted out to thieves may suggest that property is highly prized and well protected there. The problem is that there is no security against the depredations of the state itself. Police states are the rule everywhere, and rights as understood in the West scarcely exist. Ruthless autocrats, guarded by their own military, have been able to prevail for decades against impoverished masses. Economic decline has been just one consequence. Excluding the emirates of the Persian Gulf, we find stagnation almost everywhere we look, from Algiers to Cairo to Baghdad.*

"There is no disputing the fact that today the overwhelming majority of Muslims live in police states that deny them their basic human rights," wrote Ismail al Faruqi, a Palestinian who taught at McGill University. "In Iraq, Syria, Jordan, Egypt, Sudan, Libya, Algeria, Morocco and the Peninsula, no one is free to engage in political activity critical of the government and its policies."[1]

---

* This chapter deals principally with the Arab world, meaning those countries whose primary language is Arabic. Also included are references to the Muslim world—a far more extensive entity. I primarily have in mind countries that are both Arabic-speaking and Muslim. Persia, today Iran, is the principal exception. Although non-Arabic, it acquired Islam and its corresponding codes from the Arabs. There are also references to "Turks," and to the Ottoman Empire. "Turks" was once used indiscriminately to describe both Arabs and inhabitants of modern Turkey; at its peak, the Ottoman Empire was the preeminent Muslim power and the entire Arab world was subject to it. In modern Sudan and Mauritania, Arabic is the official language, although those who speak it are a minority.

Edward Said, a professor of English at Columbia University, commented in 1991: "So overbearing have Arab rulers become that the most grotesque situations are tolerated with scarcely a smile. Most national newspapers today solemnly report the comings and goings of the ruler as if they were central events of mankind. No Arab president or king is accountable to his people. . . . The bureaucracies and the secret police rule more or less unchallenged."[2]

Professor Bernard Lewis of Princeton has written that the Arab caliphs and Turkish sultans of the past could hardly have achieved the "arbitrary and pervasive power wielded by even the pettiest of present-day dictators."[3] Slavery itself endures in parts of the Arab or Muslim world, notably in the Sudan and Mauritania. Estimates of the number of slaves held in North Africa range from 90,000 to 300,000.[4]

Oil payments for decades helped to disguise the economic consequence of this repression. A few countries have even been able to finance welfare states. But the oil wealth is dwindling and it will continue to do so. The region has a (rapidly growing) population of 260 million, but its non-oil exports are less than those of Finland (population 5 million).[5] In Saudi Arabia, per capita income declined from $17,000 in 1981 to $7,000 in 1993.[6] It is unlikely that the Arab rulers themselves fully grasp the underlying cause of the problem, and it is still not properly understood by Western elites.

The embrace of "Arab Socialism" in the 1950s by a number of countries—Iraq, Syria, Algeria, Libya, Egypt—only compounded the underlying problem. It gave Western legitimacy to the expropriation of property and to a presumption in favor of central control by the state. The small progress toward constitutional government that was made in the nineteenth and early twentieth centuries was thereby undermined. When the French were driven out of Algeria, their land registration system was swept aside by Ben Bella, and the land was nationalized. In several countries, contracts were abrogated, ownership was "reformed," production nationalized. Arab rulers were encouraged by progressive elites in the West to intensify what they had traditionally been inclined to do anyway: centralize power.

For a while, it even seemed to work. In Egypt, Arnold Toynbee heaped praise on the Nasser regime. The provision of housing "for the ordinary poor people of the world" was something that could be done "only by public enterprise financed by tax money," Toynbee asserted. When Nasser asked the famous historian what had changed since his earlier visit, in 1961, Toynbee mentioned the "new housing on this grand scale." He even compared Cairo's housing favorably to London's.[7] The state meanwhile continued to confiscate land and real estate holdings; by the 1980s, American aid was needed to rebuild Cairo's infrastructure and to pay for Hosni Mubarak's palace guard. As for the housing, Milad Hanna has more recently written: "The huge area in the northeast of Cairo, which was allocated for centuries as the cemetery, known as the 'City of the Dead,' is no longer occupied only by the dead."[8]

Arab regimes live in constant fear of their own subjects. Fully respected private property creates zones of independence from which challenges to power holders can be launched. The result is that "nowhere in the Arab world is there security guaranteed under the law for persons and property," as David Pryce-Jones has written.[9] There is no principle of succession other than overthrow of the existing power holder. "My family took this country by the sword," a brother of King Fahd would remind Saudi subjects.[10] An Egyptian diplomat has called modern Arab countries "tribes with flags," and the wealth of such nations is regarded as the legitimate spoils of seizing power. Western recognition, seats at the United Nations, and government-to-government aid confer further strength and legitimacy. But the principal concern of the rulers is the ever-present danger of overthrow by secretly plotting rivals.

This situation is potentially serious for the rest of the world. Young men growing up in large numbers with no material prospects have in the past posed a serious threat to civilization. As Daniel Doron of the Israel Center for Social and Economic Progress has written: "Arab politics is shaped excessively by volatile mobs, because Arab societies abound with desperate, unemployable youths who have nothing but time on their hands. A small middle class is too fragile to advance human rights against autocratic habits. This is particularly true in the Gaza Strip and the West Bank, as well as in the Lebanese refugee camps. In those areas, decades of dependence on United Nations refugee relief have created a disintegrating society, similar to that found in American and European inner cities, but with a far more lawless and violent framework."[11]

The problem is acute in the emerging nation of Palestine. Since the Rabin-Arafat handshake at the White House, it has been well understood that a thriving Palestinian economy is vital to peace. But neither the Palestinians nor the aid-giving "international community" seems to know how to attain it. When the Palestinian Authority was created, in 1993, a Ministry of Planning was created, and thanks to foreign aid, the planners began to receive salaries before any wealth was created. Yasser Arafat's bureaucracy laid its heavy hand of economic controls onto Gaza. Forty percent of the land was confiscated by the Palestinian Authority. In the two years following the White House agreement, more than 2,000 small production facilities were closed down, and more than 40,000 laborers were laid off.[12] Unmistakably, the old planning model was alive and well in the minds of Western elites. Meanwhile, the increasingly prosperous Israel is a tempting target for surrounding Arab potentates who do not know how to create wealth, and who receive no useful guidance in such matters from Western leaders.

A recent World Bank study of Middle Eastern economies pointed out that in 1960 the seven leading Arab economies had a per capita income higher than that of seven East Asian "tigers" (including Hong Kong, Taiwan, Singapore and South Korea); today, the Arab world has fallen far behind, to less than one-third of the East Asian level. "Since 1986 real per capita incomes have fallen by 2 percent a year—the largest decline in any developing region," the report noted. The underlying problem is never precisely identified by the World Bank, but here and there one finds reference to the "postponement of reform," the resistance to privatization, and the "huge investment in state-owned enterprises."[13]

Subsistence economies endure, and portable property exchanged for cash in the bazaar may often be secure in practice—even free from state regulation. The state's toleration of family-level enterprise has preserved the region from total impoverishment. Essential needs of food and clothing are met; hand-made jewelry, providing both personal adornment and portable capital, may even permit a small increment of luxury. But even that is not always secure. Reporting from post-Khomeini Iran, a *Wall Street Journal* reporter described a bookkeeper who preferred his Byzantine trade to any more open business, which was "subject to the state's fickle attitude toward profit and private property. 'If your capital is on your body, they can take it away,' Mr. Amirkhas said. 'If it's your brain, how can they take it?'"[14]

In the absence of legal recourse, business cannot develop much beyond the family circle. The head of a family may be able to trust other family members and cousins who work for him. But transactions outside that group will be hazardous. In practice, business on a larger scale in the Arab world will arise only with official blessing and control. And at that point it will be operated as a state-owned enterprise, in fact if not in name.

Political power is maintained by military force, which may also be backed up by Islam-based appeals to obedience. Compliant clerics stand ready to admonish the community that acceptance of the state's purpose is the path to salvation. According to one Sunni religious leader: "If any danger threatens the State, he who willfully refrains from making a sacrifice of his life and property to ward off that danger has been called a hypocrite in the Qur'an."[15]

Classical liberalism never remotely took hold in the Arab world. Bernard Lewis notes that in Islamic countries, freedom as a political notion (as opposed to a description of legal status) does not appear until the late eighteenth century, and then "patently due to European influence."[16] Scholars did not know how to translate the word into Arabic. Good government was regarded as a duty of the ruler, "not a right of the subject, whose only recourse against bad government was patience, counsel and prayer." All power emanated from a single ruler, and private corporate entities were never in practice protected by the law.

More generally, the whole notion of individual rights, upon which our understanding of property rights is based, never emerged. Western feminists who have drawn attention to the lack of women's rights in the Muslim world are correct, but they have overlooked the more general problem: neither gender enjoys civil rights. Men may indeed be free to oppress women, but they may in turn be oppressed by other men with more power. In a polity based on power, women are sure to be at the mercy of men.

In her recent study of Islam and human rights, Ann Elizabeth Mayer of the Wharton School amply documents the point that Muslim leaders have rejected Western notions of rights generally—not just women's rights. The law lacks "institutional mechanisms to deal with actual situations where governments disregarded Islamic law and oppressed and exploited their subjects," she notes.[17] In the writings of A. K. Brohi, the keynote speaker at a major international conference on human rights in Islam in 1980, sponsored by the Union of Arab Lawyers, "the idea that individuals enjoy inalienable rights [was] dismissed with scorn." The Western concept of human rights presupposes individualism, which is "not an established feature of Muslim societies or Islamic culture, nor can one find a historical example of an Islamic school of thought that celebrates individualism as a virtue."

Abul Ala Mawdudi, the author of *Human Rights in Islam,* joined many other Islamic authorities in substituting the concept of duty for rights. In *The Islamic Law and Constitution,* he pronounced it "obligatory on the citizens of the Islamic State to cooperate wholeheartedly with the government and to make sacrifices of life and property for it." Mayer finds reference to an exception in the area of property rights, "where the *shari'a* did provide remedies for the individual wrongfully deprived of property by official action."[18] It is important to maintain skepticism with respect to tenets of the *shari'a,* or Islamic law, however. As with the Soviet Constitution, the gap between theory and practice is likely to be considerable. And as in the Soviet Union, courtroom verdicts often depend less on the law than on what the higher authorities demand.

Joseph Schacht, an expert on the *shari'a,* candidly acknowledged that Islamic law has been "to some extent content with mere theoretical acknowledgment," and "was never supported by an organized power." Court decisions might reflect the consensus of the *ulema* (legal scholars), but then again they might not. "As long as the Sacred Law received formal recognition as a religious ideal, it did not insist on being fully applied in practice," he wrote.[19] In the same vein, two-thirds of the way through his *Law Reform in the Muslim World,* the British scholar Norman Anderson entered the "major caveat" that there is "a yawning gulf between the law that lawyers learn and expound and the way in which this law is—or is not—applied in real life." There could be "no doubt," he allowed, that the Muslim reforms he had been discussing, some of which had been on the books for over a hundred years, remain "of little more than academic—and also one hopes, of educative—relevance."[20]

As to legal remedies with respect to official violations of property, Bernard Lewis was close to the mark when he wrote: "Islamic law unequivocally recognizes the sanctity of private property, but Islamic history reveals a somewhat different picture, in which even a rich man's enjoyment of his property has never been safe from seizure or sequestration by the state."[21] He observed that the insecurity of property in the Arab world is "symbolized in the architecture of the traditional Muslim city, in which neighborhoods, and even the houses of the wealthy, are turned inward, surrounded by high blank walls."

Clifford Hallam, a professor of literature who taught in Riyadh in the early 1980s, made a similar observation about the local architecture, perhaps at the same time misinterpreting it. "The horror of rape, literal or metaphorical, is unmistakably reflected in the unique character of Saudi architecture," he wrote. "There is no public building or private villa without its forbidding wall topped with shards of glass, no windows without bars; one is confronted with a convict's bad dream of locks, bolts, chains, barbed wire and spiked fences at every point of entry. The present city of Riyadh was begun in essence fewer than 20 years ago, yet it resembles nothing so much as a cluster of fortresses."[22]

We find the same story centuries earlier. A Frenchman who visited Cairo in the late eighteenth century described the houses as having "the appearance of prisons, for they have no light from the street; as it is extremely dangerous to have many windows in such a country; they even take the precaution to make the entering door very low."[23] This was to ensure that predatory officials could not ride on horseback directly into the house.

The historical record generally confirms Bernard Lewis's claim that property in Araby has long been insecure. This same evidence also suggests the answer to an important question about history that has never been satisfactorily addressed. Why did the Muslim world suddenly decline in relation to the West? One reason why historians have found it difficult to provide an answer to this fundamental question is that they have themselves insufficiently considered the institutions that gave rise to Western prosperity.

PROPERTY IN HISTORY

The high-water mark of the Ottoman Empire was reached in 1683, when the sultan's army laid siege to Vienna. The defending garrison launched a surprise counterattack, and the sultan's troops fled in disorder. The following year Athens was recaptured, and in 1685 the capital of Hungary was wrested back from the Turks. At its peak, the Ottoman Empire had extended from Austria to Persia, south to Arabia and west along the African coast to Morocco. But by the eighteenth century the Islamic world was in conspicuous and inexplicable decline. The vast area under Ottoman rule remained premedieval in character, little affected by the great changes that were taking place in the West, particularly as a result of the Industrial Revolution. The shift in the balance of power continued in the nineteenth century, and has endured throughout the twentieth.

Historians today are uncomfortable with such judgmental notions as rise and fall. "Rather than speaking of decline," Albert Hourani writes in *A History of the Arab Peoples,* "it might be more correct to say that what had occurred was an adjustment of Ottoman methods of rule and the balance of power within the empire to changing circumstances."[24] He is at a loss to explain the great shift of power. "Technical skills" in Europe improved; "quarantine systems" limited the plague's ravages. Marshall Hodgson devoted a heavy chapter of his magnum opus, *The Venture of Islam,* to "the great Western Transmutation." He saw that a "general cultural transformation" took place in the West between the late sixteenth and late eighteenth centuries, culminating in the French Revolution. And he was among the few to note that the Industrial Revolution was a consequence, not a cause, of this change. But he was unable to account for it. A "great increase in productivity" took place. Such neologisms as "technicalistic process" or "technicalization" were of no more help in understanding what had happened than was W. W. Rostow's notion of "take-off." At one point he allowed: "It is not yet established what determined that the Transmutation should occur just there and then."[25]

It was said that the Ottoman Empire grew too large for effective administration. Finances were "mismanaged." Corruption increased. The sultan "dissipated in the harem the energy needed to discipline the army."[26] According to Arnold Toynbee, the Ottomans were unable to "respond to the tremendous challenge from the West, to which the failure of their own indigenous institutions has exposed them." He referred to the Ottoman tyranny, nonetheless, as "this wonderful system of human cultivation." It had brought the empire to "a dizzy height of military and political greatness."[27] He so much admired the centralization of power that he was unable to account for its failure. The Ottomans themselves attributed the great reversal to the superior military equipment of the West. It was true that the West by then had better ships and arms, but why was this technical advance confined to the West?

We may recall the great institutional change that took place in the West. Individual rights were not only formulated in political theory, but incorporated into law and practice. Constitutional government emerged. Western governments more and more accepted that they did not have the right to interfere with the law-abiding activities of their own citizens. Property became more secure and contracts were enforced. In the period when the great shift in the balance of power occurred, the notion of rights generally, and property rights in particular, emerged in the Western world. The result was a tremendous increase in material prosperity.

Writers and eastbound travelers in earlier times sometimes regarded the security or insecurity of property as a topic worthy of comment, remarkably enough. The classical economists read some of these books, and so they grasped the nature of the problem that prevailed even then. Adam Smith, like Marx a believer in the "stadial" theory of history, saw the Arab world as still in the primitive, "shepherd" stage. "Simple nations" such as the Tatars and Arabs, he pointed out, "frequently do without any regulations of law." The "consumable nature of their property necessarily renders all such regulations impossible."[28]

In the second edition of his *Essay on the Principle of Population,* Thomas Malthus attributed "the low state of population in Turkey," by which he meant the Ottoman Empire more generally, to "the nature of the government," in particular its tyranny, its bad laws and the "consequent insecurity of property."[29] His main source was the French writer Constantin-Francois Volney, whose description of the peculiar architectural features of Cairo we have already encountered. His account of life in general under the Mameluke tyranny provides just one more confirmation of the oppression that Muslims have for centuries endured at the hands of their own rulers.

Volney was astonished to see the ruined condition of Alexandria, with its decayed remains of buildings, its harbor (into which only "Mussulman" ships were admitted) clogged with sand. As he proceeded to Cairo, he reflected that "the Arabs knew how to conquer, but by no means how to govern: wherefore, the misshapen edifice of their power soon mouldered into ruins." In a mild aside, he truly observed that "the political situation of this country is very unlike that of Europe." In Egypt, everything the visitor sees or hears "reminds him that he is in the country of slavery and tyranny." He concluded that there was "no security for life or property. . . . Such is the condition of Egypt. The greater part of the lands are in the hands of the beys, the Mamelukes and the professors of the law; the number of the other proprietors is extremely small, and their property liable to a thousand impositions. Every moment some contribution is to be paid, or some damage repaired; there is no right of succession or inheritance for real property; everything returns to government, from which everything must be repurchased."[30]

In the early nineteenth century, Muhammad Ali managed to overthrow the mamelukes and set himself up as pasha of Egypt. But the tyranny only intensified. He "became literally the owner of Egypt," Elie Kedourie wrote. "When he exterminated the mamelukes, he also confiscated their lands to his own benefit." On various pretexts, he confiscated lands held in trust for the upkeep of mosques and charitable purposes. "The title to all private property whatsoever became highly uncertain." Owners were obliged to provide documents and title deeds, which proved unsatisfactory to the pasha's officials unless accompanied by bribes. Fraudulent land surveys used measuring rods smaller than the standard; land areas appeared to increase, and taxes were accordingly inflated.[31]

In his *Narrative of a Journey into Khorashan,* published in 1825, James B. Fraser vividly described the tyranny and poverty that he found. Hearing the names Baghdad, Bussora and Ispahan, he wrote, the naive European is apt to imagine "columns, minarets and cupolas." He is quite unprepared for "the mass of misery, filth and ruins which the best of these cities present to his gaze." He concluded that "the principal direct check to improvement and prosperity in Persia is the insecurity of life, limb and property, arising from the nature of the government. . . . This must always repress the efforts of industry; for no man will work to produce what he may be deprived of the next hour." Even the "greatest noble in Persia," he wrote, is not "for one moment secure in his person or property."[32]

J. R. McCulloch's *Principles of Political Economy* was published in the same year. He pointed out that the finest brains cannot create wealth if the government "does not respect and maintain the right of property." And this was the "principal cause of the present wretched state of the Ottoman dominions." Proprietors had been reduced to the status of occupiers who, as a result, were "comparatively careless of futurity." Ottoman subjects constructed impermanent dwellings because "it would be a gratification to them to be assured that they would fall to pieces the moment after they have breathed their last. Under this miserable government the palaces have been changed into cottages and the cities into villages. The long continued want of security has extinguished the very spirit of industry."

McCulloch made the important distinction between official claims and actual practice. "The *stated* public burdens to which the Turks are subject are light compared with those imposed on the English, the Hollanders or the French," he wrote. "But the latter know that when they have paid the taxes due to government, they will be permitted peaceably to enjoy or accumulate the residue of their wealth; whereas the subjects of Eastern despotisms have, generally speaking, no security that the moment after they have paid the stated contributions, the pasha, or one of his satellites, may not strip them of every remaining farthing!"[33]

Nassau W. Senior, professor of political economy at Oxford, traveled to Cairo and Constantinople in the mid-nineteenth century and vividly described the Ottoman tyranny and poverty. Turkey, he found, was a society without books, roads or the rule of law; without a middle class, public opinion, newspapers or post office. It was a society of polygamy, wanton divorce and the seclusion of women; a society in which there seemed to be more dogs than people, yet with vast tracts of unoccupied land; and in which all official transactions were mediated by bribery. Property was perennially insecure, and any wealth not concealed from the authorities would soon be confiscated by them. "Everyone, however rich, knows that in a generation or two his grandchildren or great grandchildren will be porters or hewers of wood." All power was vested in the sultan, who had stolen "from the treasury more than a third of the public revenue," and who was building on the shores of the Bosporus endless pasteboard palaces. Yet he could remedy nothing for he knew nothing. In describing the sultan, an Armenian friend of Senior's pinpointed a key defect of despotism: "He can know nothing of anything that his ministers do not choose to tell him. He does not read, and if he did, there is no press; he sees nobody, he never has seen anybody, except his brothers-in-law and sons-in-law, his women and his servants, and occasionally a minister or an ambassador who comes to bully him or to deceive him."[34] He might have been describing the shah of Iran in the 1970s.

A few years before Senior traveled to Constantinople, Marx and Engels had corresponded on the subject of Eastern despotism. Marx was much impressed by a work entitled *Travels in the Mogul Empire, 1656-1668,* written by a French doctor, Francois Bernier. Included in the book was a letter forwarded to Jean Baptiste Colbert, Louis XIV's finance minister. Bernier there summarized the impoverishment he had seen in the East:

> We may judge of the effects of despotic power unrelentingly exercised by the present condition of Mesopotamia, Anatolia, Palestine, the once wonderful plains of Antioch, and so many other regions anciently well cultivated, fertile and populous, but now desolate, and in many parts marshy, pestiferous, and unfit for human habitation. Egypt also presents a sad picture of an enslaved country. More than one tenth part of that incomparable territory has been lost within the last eighty years, because no one will be at the expense of repairing the irrigation channels, and confining the Nile within its banks. The low lands are thus violently inundated, and covered with sand, which cannot be removed without much labor and expense. . . .

After several pages along these lines, Bernier observed that "Turkey, Persia and Hindoustan have no idea of the principle of *meum* and *tuum,* relative to land or other real possessions; and having lost that respect for the right of property, which is the basis of all that is good and useful in the world, necessarily resemble each other in essential points: they fall into the same pernicious errors, and must, sooner or later, experience the natural consequences of those errors— tyranny, ruin and misery."[35]

Writing to Engels in 1853, Marx enthusiastically quoted Bernier and added: "Bernier rightly sees all the manifestations of the East—he mentions Turkey, Persia and Hindustan—as having a common basis, namely the *absence of private landed property.* This is the real *clef,* even to the eastern heaven." He somewhat misrepresented Bernier, who had specified that property rights in land and in "other real possessions" had been lost in the East. Still, it is interesting to see Marx putting his finger on this passage and calling it "the real key."[36] Although totally wrong about property, he always recognized its importance.

"The absence of landed property is indeed the key to the whole of the East," Engels replied. "Therein lies its political and religious history. But how to explain the fact that orientals never reached the stage of landed property, not even the feudal kind?" He believed that this was largely "due to the climate, combined with the nature of the land, more especially the great stretches of desert extending from the Sahara right across Arabia. . . ."

Such conditions made irrigation essential—and thus the responsibility either of communes or of the central government. And here was the problem: in the East, governments consisted of three departments: Finance ("pillage at home"), War ("pillage at home and abroad") and Public Works. The British had neglected the third, allowing irrigation conduits to fall into disrepair, and this explained "the otherwise curious circumstance" that vast expanses of the East "are now arid wastes which once were magnificently cultivated." (He cited the famous ruins of Palmyra, in Syria, and other ruins in Yemen, Egypt and Persia.)[37]

This exchange between Marx and Engels launched the study of "oriental despotism," with particular reference to what Karl Wittfogel would, a century later, call "hydraulic societies." Wittfogel's *Oriental Despotism* advanced the thesis that in such "hydraulic" societies, the state tends to be "inordinately strong," which in turn tends to make private property "inordinately weak." The claim that the need for large-scale irrigation puts much power in the hands of the state and therefore weakens property rights is of interest but ultimately is not convincing, however. Large-scale projects can be privately financed, and some irrigated societies are not tyrannical.[38]

By the 1830s, traveling Ottoman officials were beginning to notice the great differences between their stagnant system and that of Western countries. When an Egyptian who had lived in Paris published (in Arabic) an account of European constitutional procedures, he regarded the idea that the subject had a right to be treated justly as something new and alien to Muslim thought.[39] Discussing the critical difference between Turkey and Europe at about the same time, the Ottoman ambassador in Vienna concluded that European progress and prosperity depended on "complete security for the life, property, honor and reputation of each nation and people, that is to say, on the proper application of the necessary rights of freedom."[40] In contrast, the British consul-general in Turkey wrote in 1876 that "the Turks laugh at Europeans who talk of their 'rights,' for, to their understanding, anyone who does not avail himself of his might is a fool."[41]

ISLAM AND PROPERTY

This centuries-long oppression would be conveniently explained if the founding documents of Islam—the Koran and the sayings of the Prophet and his companions—were found to contain teachings inimical to private property and to free markets. But they do not. The Koran teaches that all goods are ultimately owned by God and that man is their "viceregent." But Islamic scholars have not construed this as detrimental to private ownership. A good reason for thinking that the Prophet himself accepted private property is that the Koran lays down detailed rules for its inheritance. Those rules—briefly, that property should be divided among family members—are not sufficient to preclude free-market economies.

Furthermore, the Koran is not concerned about inequalities of wealth, and does not encourage schemes for its redistribution. It specifically enjoins disciples not to "covet what Allah hath bestowed in bounty upon one more than another." It also stresses the ultimate equality of all in the sight of God. This might be construed as a particularly hopeful sign by those looking for the emergence of a capitalist Islam, because equality before the law is perhaps the most important prerequisite of free markets. In his *Islam and Capitalism,* Maxime Rodinson is surely correct when he argues that the failure of capitalism to emerge in the Islamic world cannot easily be attributed to the Koran:

> There are religions whose sacred texts discourage economic activity in general, counseling their followers to rely on God to provide them with their daily bread, or, more particularly, looking askance at any striving for profit. This is certainly not the case with the Koran, which looks with favor upon commercial activity, confining itself to condemning fraudulent practices and requiring abstention from trade during certain religious festivals. The Koran, as a present-day Muslim honestly sums up the position, does not merely say that one must not forget one's portion in this world, it also says that it is proper to combine the practice of religion and material life, carrying on trade even during pilgrimages, and goes so far as to mention commercial profit under the name of "God's bounty."[42]

For centuries, Islam was friendly to the accumulation of wealth. Most international trade either originated in or passed through the Islamic world. Those parts of the Middle East subjected to early Islamic conquests seem to have experienced those events as liberating, perhaps because debts were abrogated. It is only in more recent centuries that the tyranny became severe. By the nineteenth century, some Ottoman rulers sought to adopt Western ways, including the security of property. Reform did not last, but some headway was made in Turkey and Egypt. Daniel Pipes, the author of *In the Path of God*, believes that "the predicament is transitory, not inherent in the Islamic religion." If it were, he argues, Islam would not have been dominant in the world for several centuries after its founding.[43]

There are nonetheless trouble spots in the Koran. For one thing, it countenances polygamy and divorce. If intact, monogamous families are essential to capitalism, as seems likely, the Koranic provisions are difficult to circumvent. Today, however, polygamy is confined to an elite, and it is possible that the family in the Muslim world is now more stable than in the West. The Islamic prohibition of interest is often cited as a problem, but here the difficulty arises not within the Koran itself, but with the subsequent interpretation of the word "riba," which most scholars interpret as usury. This suggests, unexpectedly, that a more "fundamentalist" approach, in which lawyers can go back to the Koran itself, might even be economically liberating.

Construed as zeal, however, fundamentalism is counterproductive. Religious police with a mission to save souls do not respect property rights. In Saudi Arabia, a Reagan-appointed commercial counsel noted: "A man's home is no longer his castle." The informal police called the Mutawa feel free to burst into private houses and jail occupants if they find violations of the *shari'a*— liquor, unmarried women, fornication. Neither embassy officials nor wealthy Saudis are immune. A Saudi businessman influential enough to have been visited by the Saudi king at his home was invaded by the Mutawa only a few months later. Because he was having a party with liquor and airline stewardesses, he spent 18 months in jail.[44]

Pipes believes the decline of Islam began in the fifteenth century; others say it was even earlier than that. A striking development did occur in the medieval period. Gradually, Islamic law was "frozen," so that the law's interpreters could no longer apply their independent reasoning to it. They were obliged to live with the interpretation that had been reached when the "freeze" took place. This event is known to *shari'a* scholars as "the closing of the gate of *ijtihad*"—*ijtihad* meaning "the struggle for understanding,"[45] or more simply the use of reason. It was replaced by *taqlid*—the submissive acceptance of earlier interpretation. Continued interpretation ceased because it was said to show disrespect for earlier jurists.

This brought with it serious problems. In U.S. terms, a comparable event would be a prohibition of all further interpretation of the law in 1900. The Supreme Court's "separate but equal" doctrine would still stand, because to amend it would show disrespect for the Court of 1896. Notice, again, that the "closing of the gate" was not a "fundamentalist" doctrine. It precisely did *not* permit scholars to examine problems in light of the Koran. It insisted on preserving the worldview of the fifteenth century (or earlier). Perhaps this shutting down of the law accounts for a curious feature of the Arab world, since noted by many travelers to Cairo, Damascus, and the Arab quarter of Jerusalem alike: the sense that these places exist as though frozen at some earlier period—perhaps when the law itself was "frozen."

Some Islamic scholars in the United States now are arguing for a restoration of *ijtihad.* At the International Institute for Islamic Studies, for example, they believe that the closing of the gate was a major cause of the decline of Islam. Taha al Alwani, chairman of the Fiqh Council of North America, believes that "the Muslim *ummah* [community] only entered its current crisis after *ijtihad* fell into disuse." With independent thought no longer desired, law in the Muslim world became dominated by people who were attracted to the service of power. Al Awani notes that Al Ghazzali, writing in the twelfth century, had already noticed that scholars of the Koran had gone "from being sought after to being seekers after, from being respected for their spurning the offers of rulers to their being scorned for their opportunism."[46]

Taha al Alwani denounces the fallen state of the Muslim world in language that few non-Muslims would dare use today. "Muslims and non-Muslims alike are amazed that one of history's most advanced civilizations could fall into such a state of overwhelming wretchedness, ignorance, backwardness and overall decline," he wrote in 1991. "A civilization which has placed such emphasis on literacy and knowledge remains largely illiterate [and] mired in a mass of misunderstanding. . . . Why does the *ummah,* blessed with all of the means and resources for economic prosperity, continue to suffer from abject poverty?" He believes that the engrained deference to authority and the discouragement of reason that began with the "closing of the gate" is an important part of the explanation.[47] "Basically we're trying to get Muslims to use their heads again," his assistant, Yusif de Lorenzo, said.[48]

Although it was later interpretation rather than the Koran itself that prohibited the payment of interest, the Book does frown on hoarding ("That which they hoard will be their collar on the Day of Resurrection"), and this has been used to justify immense power in the hands of rulers. Interpreters of the law have consistently agreed that the injunction against hoarding also applies to land. This in turn has led to a highly destructive "use it or lose it" interpretation of land tenure.

In "Property Rights in Contemporary Islamic Thought," Sohrab Behdad reports little disagreement among scholars that "plain or unworked land may not be privately owned by individuals. But one may claim priority in the use of such land by improving it with one's labor and capital." Continued "priority," however, will depend on its continued use. Someone with control over a patch of land who fails to use it can be construed as hoarding it. Because unworked land cannot be owned, it also cannot be rented. A *hadith,* or saying of the

Prophet, is explicit on this point: "He who has land should cultivate it. If he will not or cannot, he should give it free to a Muslim brother and not rent it to him."[49] The rental of cultivated land is acceptable, however.

This has created serious obstacles to the improvement of land in the Arab world. If you can't own land until you have irrigated, drained, built upon or planted it, these costly activities must be undertaken in an atmosphere of insecurity. Only a foolish homesteader will mix his labor and capital with a patch of desert that he knows is not his to begin with and that only with luck may become his in the end. Such an arduous undertaking must be backed by the full assurance of law. Given pervasive corruption, it will not be undertaken at all. Rather than contribute to the gains of their oppressors, the Arab *fellaheen* will sensibly remain inactive.

In Syria, in the 1780s, Volney found that private property had been swept away, but by despotic rule rather than Koranic interpretation. Either way, the result was catastrophic. "The Sultans, having arrogated to themselves, by right of conquest, the property of all the lands of Syria, the inhabitants can no longer pretend to any real, or personal property; they have nothing but a temporary possession. . . . Hence arises an indifference to landed estates, which proves fatal to agriculture. In the towns, the possession of houses is in some measure less uncertain and less ruinous; but everywhere the preference is given to property in money, more easy to hide from the rapine of the despot."[50]

We may conclude, then, that subsequent interpretation rather than original intent created the material problem in the Muslim world. The interpretation also helped to create a serious environmental problem.

THE DESERT ENVIRONMENT

A contributor to the eleventh edition of the *Encyclopedia Britannica* (1911) noted that "the true Arab despises agriculture." More recently, in *The Arab Mind,* Raphael Patai refers to the Arab's "unwillingness to persevere for the purpose of deferred achievement," and to his "aversion to physical labor." Above all, Patai said, the Arab dislikes "tilling the soil, fighting its thorns and thistles, toiling and sweating to make it yield."[51] Understanding the difficulty of obtaining property rights to land in the Arab world helps to neutralize this conventional majority stereotype. This was cruelly applied by C. S. Jarvis, a British army officer who was governor of the Sinai in the 1930s. "The Arab is sometimes called the Son of the Desert, but this is a misnomer as in most cases he is the Father of the Desert, having created it himself," he wrote in *Three Deserts.* "The arid waste in which he lives and on which practically nothing will grow is the direct result of his appalling indolence. . . . In his campaign of destruction, the Arab has been most loyally supported by his animals, the camel and the goat."[52]

Jarvis failed to grasp the underlying disincentive, and so misconstrued as idleness a rational response to despotism. The intriguing question arises: Is it pure coincidence that deserts flourish where such disincentives have persisted for centuries? Engels commented on the "curious circumstance" that vast expanses, once cultivated, had since become "arid wastes." It seems likely that the discouragement to ownership, produced by despotism or scriptural interpretation or both, has contributed to desertification in the Islamic world. Over a long enough time, such disincentives will result in the loss of soil and the permanent degradation of the land.

The historian Ibn Khaldun, who lived in Tunis in the fourteenth century, wrote in his *Introduction to History* that "civilization always collapsed in places the Arabs took over and conquered." It was noteworthy, he added, that "such settlements were depopulated and the very earth there turned into something that was no longer earth. The Yemen where the Arabs live is in ruins, except for a few cities. Persian civilization in the Arab Iraq is likewise completely ruined. The same applies to contemporary Syria." Formerly, Khaldun records, "the whole region between the Sudan and the Mediterranean had been settled." On the previous page he wrote of the Arabs: "They recognize no limit in taking the possessions of other people. Whenever their eyes fall upon some property, furnishings or utensils, they take it. When they acquire superiority and royal authority, they have complete power to plunder as they please. There no longer exists any political power to protect property, and civilization is ruined."[53]

A part of the region that Khaldun described is now Libya, over 90 percent of which is desert today. In Roman times, western Libya—Tripolitania—was well wooded and productively grazed. "Under the [Roman] empire the farmlands of Tripolitania reached a level of prosperity equalled neither before nor since," wrote John L. Wright in his book on Libya.[54] The British economist John Burton noted that in the Roman era, cultivated farmland was far more extensive than it would later become, and huge areas that have become desert were once green and productive. In eastern Libya, the desert was held far more extensively in check in Roman times than in the later times of Vandal, Berber and Arab rule. Historical research suggests that there was no significant change in climate to account for the subsequent trend to desertification. Burton continued:

> Systems of common land ownership now account for the bulk of Libyan acreage, and have done so for over 1,500 years, since the Vandals expelled the Romans from Libya, circa A.D. 455. But under Roman rule the land was extensively farmed under a system of private property rights. During the early empire it was

farmed primarily by Berber peasants and other small-holders such as retired soldiers who had been granted private property rights in plots of land. . . . With land held privately, there was an incentive to conserve vegetation, rather than to treat it as a free good. . . . Following the decline of Roman rule, the system of private property in land reverted to that of tribal ownership, [and the consequences] are written in the encroaching sands of the Libyan desert today.[55]

Nomadic herding is itself an indicator both of tyranny and of insecure property. An inefficient and arduous way of life, it is likely to be replaced by farming when private property is secure. In *The Arab World,* William R. Polk wrote, the nineteenth-century Ottomans did periodically induce tribesmen to settle: "Purchase of land was made extremely easy, bedouin and peasants were assisted with government loans." But then, with a "return to government exploitative practices," the peasants would again "abandon their newly acquired lands." Polk revealingly adds: "It was only as the bedouin could be induced to settle and invest in immovable objects that they could be controlled."[56] For "controlled" read "taxed," which is to say: expropriated.

Nomadic tribesmen are sometimes praised as "independent." As we might put it today, they preferred to evade their rulers by remaining in the "underground economy," that is, in the desert, where they were difficult to track down. There they would set up their own rules, establishing who grazed where and when. With their animals, they would add to the expansion of the desert, and then move on in timely fashion to other areas not yet reduced to dust.

C. S. Jarvis was not entirely wrong about the goat, as has been shown more recently in Israel. By 1967, the West Bank border was plainly visible from the air as a "green line," with farmland on one side and barren ground on the other. This border is known in Israel as the Green Line. In biblical times, the hills of Judea and Samaria were cultivated and terraced, which protected the top soil when heavy rains came. But with the arrival of the Arabs, everything began to deteriorate. Their goats would uproot young trees and vegetation, thereby damming the terraced hills. Rainwater would build up and then burst through, washing away soil and stones and patiently accumulated labor. After the creation of Israel, in 1948, the old terraces were restored, and by the Six Day War the Green Line was visible.

Goats have flourished in the Arab world precisely as a result of insecure property. The goat is a portable scavenger that can be sent out to forage on communal land, where it finds sustenance in the rockiest soil. It will return to its specific owner when called, and if necessary it can be kept indoors at night, where it will be safe from rival herdsmen and assorted enemies and thieves. The goat thereby enables its owner to "privatize" whatever meager resources may be available on the most inhospitable terrain. It will also contribute to its further destruction. But no one minds that when no one owns the land anyway. On the other hand, where fencing is inexpensive, and the policing of property is regarded as an important function of the state, sheep and cows will usually be preferred to goats for the provision of wool, meat and milk. But in an unpoliced, beggar-thy-neighbor commons sheep and cows will be either very expensive or downright impossible to keep in private possession. So a healthy demand for goats has arisen in the Arab world.[57]

A pentagon in the desert provides an appropriate conclusion to the story of property in Araby. A satellite photograph taken in the 1970s and published in NASA's *LANDSAT Views of the World* unexpectedly showed a green pentagon, 400 square miles in area, in the North African Sahel. For some reason, not explained in the NASA volume, the area had a private owner, who divided the pentagon into five parts, each consisting of a fenced triangle with its apex at the center. Animals were allowed to graze only in one triangle at a time, while the grass was growing back in the others. There is some rainfall in the region (just south of the Sahara), but not much. Vast areas around the pentagon had been turned into desert by common (tribal) ownership.[58] That land belonged to everybody, and therefore to nobody. Along with everything else that we have learned, the satellite image leaves us with the suspicion that the considerably "deserted" character of the Arab world may indeed not be a coincidence.

SIXTEEN

WHY DID IRELAND STARVE?

WITHIN A FEW YEARS in the middle of the nineteenth century, about a million people died of starvation in Ireland—the last large-scale natural demographic disaster to strike Europe. With the help of massive emigration, the Irish population declined from perhaps 8 million in 1840 to 4.5 million in 1900—one of the greatest declines ever recorded in modern times. The population has never returned to its old level. Meanwhile, the famine and its causes have been once again in the news. Shortly after his election, in 1997, British prime minister Tony Blair apologized to the Irish for what happened. Those who governed in London at the time had allowed a crop failure to "turn into a massive human tragedy," he said.[1] In America, the New York state legislature passed a law requiring schools to include discussion of the famine in the curriculum, and several other states have mandated that the famine be taught as an example of "genocide."[2]

Ireland's green countryside could hardly have been more unlike the sunbaked sands of Araby. And economic historians have never been able to provide a satisfactory explanation for why so fertile a country should have been the scene of so great a tragedy. In his book *Why Ireland Starved,* the economic historian Joel Mokyr sees that the problem must be restated in the more general form: "Why was Ireland poor?" The proximate cause of the famine was the fungus *Phylophthora infestans,* which spread disastrously throughout the country beginning in 1845. It reduced the potato crop, on which much of the population depended, to a fraction of its normal yield. But the famine is not easily explained by the blight, which also struck Belgium, the Netherlands and Scotland with little demographic effect. The underlying problem, whatever it was, had already driven Ireland to an extremity of poverty, and in that condition the fungus was sufficient to create widespread starvation. Therefore: Why was Ireland so poor? Historians have never been able to agree on an answer.[3]

Mokyr himself does not answer the question implicit in his book's title, but along the way he undermines some of the more frequently heard explanations: that Ireland was overpopulated, for example; or that it lacked the natural resources (coal and iron) needed to fire up the Industrial Revolution— which still had not appeared in Ireland by the mid-nineteenth century; or that the Irish character was inconsistent with the requirements of economic growth; or that emigration (starting before the famine) reduced Ireland to a residual population; or that the system of land tenure undermined the farmers' incentives. (But the last point cannot be quite so easily dismissed.)

Another frequently heard argument—used to justify the modern claim of "genocide"—is that ample food was exported from Ireland to England at the time of the famine. But "the amounts exported were small," Timothy W. Guinnane has written, "and by 1847 Ireland was a large net *importer* of food." An associate professor of economics at Yale University, Guinnane is the author of a recent book on the rural economy in postfamine Ireland.[4]

Irish poverty is of importance to the issues raised in this book, for as Mokyr comments on his final page: "Ireland was a principal reason why the young science of economics abandoned its steadfast adherence to the sanctity of private property and free enterprise and realized that under certain circumstances, Adam Smith's invisible hand transformed itself into a claw capable of holding the economy in a deadly grip of poverty."[5] Irish poverty may indeed have been a "principal reason" for this conclusion. But the argument here is that the young science was misguided in arriving at it. For the real problem was not that property in Ireland was regarded with sanctity, but that it was held insecurely. Mokyr himself suggests as much, noting in his next sentence that the Irish experience was characterized by conflicts and "poorly defined property rights." It would be a pity indeed if property should take the blame for its negation.

Even before the famine, the "Irish Question" was widely debated in England. Few understood it. In a speech to the House of Commons in 1844, Disraeli drew attention to the general confusion: "I want to see a public man come forward and say what the Irish Question is. One says it is a physical question; another a spiritual. Now it is the absence of the aristocracy, then the absence of railroads. It is the Pope one day, potatoes the next." He believed that "teeming population" was the key, in a country lacking "those sources of wealth which develop with civilization." That population "inhabits an island where there is an Established

Church which is not their church, and a territorial aristocracy the richest of whom live in distant capitals. Thus you have a starving population, an absentee aristocracy and an alien church. . . . That is the Irish Question."[6] The potato blight struck in the following year.

Visiting Ireland before the famine, Thackeray wrote that the traveler "is haunted by the face of popular starvation. It is not the exception, it is the condition of the people. In this fairest and richest of countries, men are suffering and starving by millions."[7] De Tocqueville's friend, Gustave de Beaumont, in Ireland shortly before the famine, was appalled by what he saw. "I have seen the Indian in his forests and the negro in his irons," he wrote, "and I believed, in pitying their plight, that I saw the lowest ebb of human misery; but I did not then know the degree of poverty to be found in Ireland."[8] Oddly, he blamed it on the weather—the misty rain blowing in from the Atlantic.

A frequent accusation, popular in England, was that Ireland suffered from the idleness of its inhabitants. The charge was made by Anthony Trollope, who visited Ireland before and after the famine, and was astonished to find so many idle Irishmen. The *Times* thought the cause was genetic. "By the inscrutable but invariable laws of nature," the paper editorialized in 1847, "the Celt is less energetic, less independent, less industrious than the Saxon."[9] The economist Nassau Senior concluded that the Irish needed overseers. The Irishman "works hard in Great Britain or in the United States of America," he wrote. But in his own country "he is indolent." This was obvious "even to the passing traveller."[10] But it might have aroused his suspicion. Why did Irishmen behave one way at home, another abroad? Senior's observation undermined the claim that the Irish were naturally idle. An institutional defect at home was the more logical explanation.

Marx and Engels, toiling away in England, followed the controversy with interest. After visiting Ireland in 1856, Engels wrote to Marx about the great estates he had seen, surrounded by enormous parks, "but all around is waste land, and where the money is supposed to come from it is impossible to see. These fellows ought to be shot. . . . If one makes an inquiry, they haven't a penny, are laden with debts, and live in dread of the Encumbered Estates Court."[11] Here was an important but widely overlooked clue from Engels: the landlords lived on vast estates but were often impoverished. Why was that?

Thomas Malthus looked into the Irish question. Having returned from a tour of the country, he wrote to Ricardo in 1817, claiming that the "predominant evil of Ireland" was a population "greatly in excess of the demand for labor." The land was "infinitely more peopled" than England; and to give full effect to the country's natural resources, a great part of this population "should be swept from the soil into large manufacturing and commercial towns."[12] At that point, then, he saw Ireland as illustrating his own principle of population. Who should do the sweeping he did not say.

By the second edition of his *Principles of Political Economy* (1836), he had changed his mind. He saw that Ireland's capital shortage, and the failure to industrialize, was more an effect than a cause. Then, briefly, he hit on something far more important: "There is indeed a fatal deficiency in one of the greatest sources of prosperity, the perfect security of property; and till this defect is remedied, it is not easy to pronounce upon the degree in which the redundant capital of England would flow into Ireland with the best effect."[13] Malthus did not elaborate upon what he meant by the insecurity of property in the context of Ireland, but we pick up the same theme elsewhere.

Overpopulation was not the problem. In the mid-nineteenth century, Ireland had more cultivated acres per capita than Holland, Belgium, England, Scotland, and Sweden.[14] More people per square mile lived in England and Wales (272) than in Ireland (251).[15] In the eighteenth century, the Irish population was only half its 1840s total, yet there had been famine and misery then. Oliver Goldsmith had described the scene in his "Deserted Village," set in his native Ireland. In short, as Joel Mokyr said, "the [overpopulation] hypothesis is not confirmed by the evidence."[16]

An alternative explanation has been much discussed. It is said that the real problem lay in the system of land tenure. The idea is of interest, but it should be regarded more as a clue than a solution. A parliamentary commission known as the Devon Commission, set up in 1844, collected a mass of evidence on the subject. "Uncertainty of tenure is constantly referred to as a pressing grievance by all classes of tenants," the commission concluded. "It is said to paralyze all exertion and to place fatal impediments in the way of improvement. We have no doubt that this is the case in many instances."[17]

John Stuart Mill, for one, believed that land tenure—he called it the "cottier system"—was the true problem. He wrote editorials on Ireland for the *Morning Chronicle,* debated the subject as a member of Parliament, published a pamphlet, *England and Ireland,* and devoted two chapters of his *Principles of Political Economy* to the subject. Abundant labor allowed owners to raise rents, and the effect was "to bring the principle of population to act directly on the land." The land was fixed, the population had "an unlimited power of increase"; so tenant farmers, by their rivalry, reduced each other to a bare subsistence. This was all deduced from the economists' "laws" of population and rent. Landlords pocketed their rents and cottier farmers were impoverished.[18]

Mill was fond of quoting the comment of the writer Arthur Young on the merits of property: "Give a man the secure possession of a bleak rock, and he will turn it into a garden; give him nine years lease of a garden and he will convert it into a desert. The magic property turns sand into gold."[19] It is curious that Mill would quote this, because it undermined his whole argument. Why were owners in Ireland different? Mill's answer was most unsatisfactory, yet in retrospect seems to have colored the entire debate: Landlords in England were enlightened; those in Ireland were shortsighted. It is unsatisfactory, obviously, to impute folly to a whole class of people. Something else was going on. Perhaps the landlords in Ireland were shortsighted for a reason.

If tenure was the problem, long-term leases were the solution. They would allow farmers to benefit from their own improvements. Men could not be expected to exert themselves to improve the land if they believed that the fruits of their labor would be reaped by others. Indeed, in the province of Ulster (today Northern Ireland), there was a "custom" whereby the new tenant paid a sum of money to the departing tenant, compensating him for his improvements. Many observers noted that conditions were indeed better in Ulster. The famine was also much less severe there.

How much land in Ireland was held under lease, and how much "at will," is an enormously complicated question, presenting the kind of sampling and statistical problems that warm the hearts of modern-day economists. Mokyr looked into the question, and concluded that leases were definitely shortening before the famine.[20] Some experts say that over half the land was held at will. Predatory behavior by landlords was certainly a possibility. But before we assume what has been widely assumed—that the landlords in Ireland were merely avaricious—we must consider the obvious objection. Landlords have an interest in the prosperity of their tenants. Capturing improvements by raising tenants' rents would only discourage such improvements in the future. Why would owners engage in self-destructive behavior? As Mokyr put it: "The 'neoclassical' landlord sees his rent increase steadily as the tenant accumulates capital. The predatory landlord earns a once-and-for-all windfall, but at the cost of a future flow of rents. . . . Predatory landlordship was not likely to persist among large number of rational landlords, as it amounted to the willful sacrifice of future income on their part."[21]

Predatory behavior is nonetheless rational when the owners' time horizons are short. Landlords may try to grab what they can today if next year's prospects are worse. We have seen that many Irish landlords did become impoverished; Engels did not misrepresent that point. It begins to seem likely that horizon-shrinking conditions in Ireland encouraged the uneconomic behavior that in the end impoverished both tenants and landlords. What were these conditions, more precisely? This is the approach to the Irish question that has not received the attention it has deserved.

The terrible situation meanwhile dragged on and brought discredit upon the private property system. Marx saw the long-awaited revolution coming at last. In 1870, he told friends in the United States that the decisive blow against the English ruling class would be delivered in Ireland.[22] The phrases "absentee landlord" and "middlemen" became well known in connection with the troubles in Ireland. Reform was time and again defeated in the House of Lords—for decades dominated by Anglo-Irish landlords—with the argument that the "sanctity of private property" was at stake. Ireland caused Mill to renounce his faith in "absolute property in land." Henry George, the author of *Progress and Poverty*, believed that Ireland vindicated his theory that the private ownership of land lay at the root of poverty. He met Charles Stewart Parnell, the president of the Irish Land League, and later wrote a book entitled *The Irish Land Question*.[23] But like Mill, George failed to identify the critical issue. In order to see it more clearly, we must look further back into the past.

A TITLE OF CONFISCATION

Other countries have been overrun by foreigners and have seen their lands confiscated. The case of Ireland was anomalous, however. The British left the majority of the Irish where they found them and, instead of settling among them and attempting to govern them, took possession of much of the property while preferring to live in England as absentees. Jonathan Swift asserted that at least one-third of the rent collected from the Irish was spent in England.

Before the Reformation, British attempts to conquer Ireland had been sporadic and ineffectual. British rule was mostly confined to the Pale, within about 20 miles of Dublin. (Outside it, the Irish were "beyond the Pale.") After the Reformation, however, the British responded to the survival of Catholicism with great ferocity. Ireland was conquered, yet was neither assimilated nor subdued. Lord Clare suggested in 1800 that this outcome was worse than defeat: "If the wars of England, carried on here [in Ireland] from the reign of Elizabeth, had been waged against a foreign country, the inhabitants would have retained their possessions under the established law of civilized nations, and their country have been annexed as a province to the British Empire. But the continuing and persevering resistance of Ireland to the British crown during the whole of the last century was mere rebellion, and the municipal law of England attached upon the crime."[24]

Ireland's Catholic allegiance threatened Britain's "national security," as we would now say. Limitless brutality was thereby rationalized. For their part, many Irishmen felt that the survival of Catholicism depended on the downfall of England, and so they supported the enemies of their oppressors. "In the defeat of the Armada, Ireland's hopes of independence went down," Cecil Woodham-Smith wrote. "With the name of William III and the glorious revolution of 1688, the very foundation of British liberties, the Catholic Irishman associates only the final subjugation of his country. . . . [Ireland] for centuries provided a refuge for enemy agents, a hatching ground for enemy plots; her motto was 'England's difficulty is Ireland's opportunity,' and in every crisis of England's history she seized the moment of weakness to stab her enemy in the back. It is the explanation, if not the excuse, for the ferocity with which the English have treated the Irish."[25]

In 1796, French warships were prevented only by bad weather from landing in the southwest of Ireland. At that moment, Mill wrote, "it was on the cards whether Ireland should not belong to France, or at least be organized as an independent country under French protection." If the ships had landed, the great landowners would have fled to England, Mill believed, and "every farm on their estates would have become the property of the occupant. . . . Ireland would then have been in the condition in which small farming, and tenancy by manual labourers, are consistent with good agriculture and prosperity. The small holder would have laboured for himself."[26]

Fearing an Irish alliance with their enemies, the British had already imposed harsh penal laws: Outrage Acts, Test Acts, Coercion Acts, Public Peace Acts, Suppression of Disturbance Acts. Habeas corpus was routinely suspended. Above all, property was expropriated. Englishmen acquired title to a vast amount of confiscated land in Ireland. No Catholic was allowed to buy land, inherit it or receive it as a gift from Protestants. If a Catholic secretly purchased land owned by a Protestant, the first to inform on him became the new owner. William Lecky wrote:

> The whole country was soon filled with spies, endeavoring to appropriate the property of Catholics; and Popish discoveries became a main business of the law courts. The few Catholic landlords who remained after the confiscations were deprived of the liberty of testament, which was possessed by all other subjects of the crown. Their estates, upon their death, were divided equally among their sons, unless the eldest became a Protestant; in which case the whole was settled upon him. In this manner, Catholic landlords were gradually but surely impoverished. Their land passed almost universally into the hands of Protestants. . . . [The penal code] was inspired less by fanaticism than by rapacity, and was directed less against the Catholic religion than against the property and industry of its professors. It was intended to make them poor and keep them poor, to crush in them every germ of enterprise, to degrade them into a servile caste.[27]

Catholics were burdened with tithes to support the Anglican Church; denied the vote; excluded from the magistracy, the bar, and the bench; could not be sheriffs or constables; and could not possess arms. In his own country, Lecky wrote, the Catholic was recognized by the law only for repression and punishment. The lord chancellor and the chief justice both laid down from the bench "that the law does not suppose any such person to exist as an Irish Roman Catholic." A system that induced Catholics to abandon their faith, and an army of spies to prey upon their property, had an extremely demoralizing effect. The people "gradually acquired the vices of slaves."

England and Ireland were united under British rule in 1800, and the Irish parliament abolished. Although the law in Ulster was no different from that in other provinces, the Ulster tenants enjoyed a customary right that improved their position. The Devon (parliamentary) Commission concluded that "the present tenant-right of Ulster is an embryo copyhold,"[28] referring to an important development of the common law in England. A copyhold was a secure lease on the land, with the holder's name "copied" into a ledger kept by the local court. This ensured legal protection for the tenant in case of dispute. "The disorganized state of Tipperary, and the agrarian combinations throughout Ireland, are but the methodized war to obtain the Ulster tenant-right," the commission added.

The great difference between Ulster and the rest of the country was that in earlier centuries the native Irish there had been more thoroughly vanquished in battle. The land was then settled by predominantly Scottish and English tenants. In the seventeenth century, a particular attempt had been made by Sir John Davis, James I's attorney general,* to ensure that the land in northern Ireland was "divided amongst many," and not "granted away in gross, or by whole counties to any one man."[29] By the eighteenth century, then, landlords and tenants in Ulster did not regard each other as hereditary enemies and, as another commission of inquiry noted, "the Ulster tenant felt (and feels) he had a property in his farm—something on earth he could call his own; and the fruits of his industry would be allowed to accumulate into a small capital."[30]

In Ulster, then, the custom arose that new tenants paid for improvements that the departing tenants had made. Lord Lurgan's agent testified before the Devon Commission: "Tenant-right I consider to be the claim of the tenant and his heirs to continue in undisputed possession of the farm so long as the rent is paid; and . . . in the event of a change of occupancy at the wish of either landlord

---

*In a dispatch to Robert Cecil, Davis observed that insecure tenure had promoted civil strife in England. It had permitted lords at the time of the barons' wars to raise their own armies. By the seventeenth century, however, if any of the great lords of England had tried to raise an army, they might be able to muster "some of their household servants, or some few light-brained factious gentlemen to follow them." But tenants who had enjoyed good leases for years would not lay down their farm tools to take up arms. Some of them—copyholders—could even "bring an action for trespass against their lords if they dispossess them without cause of forfeiture." Such people would on no account give up their livelihoods "for the best landlord that is in England." In short, copyhold tenure, recognized by the courts, was slowly making tenants independent of their lords; in fact, making de facto property owners of them. And so it became much harder to roust them from their homes and press them into military service. R. B. O'Brien, *The Parliamentary History of the Irish Land Question* (London: Sampson Low, 1880), 134.

or tenant, it is the sum of money which the new occupier pays to the old one for the peaceable enjoyment of his holdings." If landowners in Ulster try "to invade tenant right, I do not believe there is a force at the disposal of the Horse Guards sufficient to keep the peace of the province."[31]

In the rest of Ireland, overwhelmingly Catholic, no such custom existed. "The antipathy between him and his landlord forbade any arrangement based on mutual goodwill," James O'Connor wrote in his *History of Ireland*.[32] "In Ulster, the Presbyterian Scot was of sturdier mould, for he had not been under the heel of class, religious or race oppression. There was this bond between him and his landlord, that each was an intruder and knew he was looked on as such."

The same point was made by Isaac Butt, professor of political economy at the University of Dublin, brilliant pamphleteer and leading nineteenth-century analyst of the Irish land question. He was one of the few to see the problem in its political, legal and economic aspects. In his *Land Tenure in Ireland: A Plea for the Celtic Race* (1866), he said of Ulster tenant right: "The fulfillment of that obligation has been forced upon the landlords in Ulster, because they had to deal with a tenantry belonging to the dominant class. It was neglected in other parts of Ireland, because the old population was crushed down by civil war and penal laws. Even in Ulster the prevalence of tenant right and of Protestantism will be found to be nearly identical in the several districts."[33]

A notorious rack-renting case (the term denotes a torturously high rental) in County Clare illustrates the problem elsewhere. The marquis of Coyningham had imposed a rent increase equal to the full value of the tenants' improvements, and then foreclosed on those unable to pay. This drove out half the population, leaving them "to wander about Ireland, or to England or America, and swell the ranks of the bitter enemies of Great Britain," as Mill put it.[34] Many such cases were reported. The Irish attempted to redress such grievances by "agrarian combination"—by "unionizing" tenants. Whiteboys, Ribbonmen and Fenians used terrorist tactics to prevent new tenants from moving in. The reprisals against those who did were horrifying. The newcomers were themselves often on the verge of starvation, and willing to promise the landlord any rent to gain a brief access to the land before being evicted in turn. Lawlessness was endemic. Ireland was in a state of degradation, Isaac Butt wrote, because

> the great mass of the people have been treated as belonging to a conquered race. All legislative and administrative efforts have been directed to secure the position of the landowners, to protect them against the people, and to enable them to raise as much as they can from the serfs that were located on their estates. . . . In a country of which the dominant caste consist of those who hold their properties by a title of confiscation it is not, perhaps, surprising that the rights of property have been religiously, or rather irreligiously, upheld; the rights

of industry and labour slighted, and no account taken of the first and most sacred of all rights—the right of the Irish people to live in their native land.[35]

The penal codes had been lifted in the 1780s and 1790s, but the law in Ireland was by no means the same as that in England. Mill and others were under the impression that it was, and their misconception is significant. It led Mill to suppose that the law itself was not the place to look, in trying to account for the great economic differences between England and Ireland.[36] How could it be? It seemed to him that the same law had produced two starkly different outcomes; the world's leading economy on the one hand, and, right next door, the most impoverished part of Europe on the other. Mill believed that in England, too, landlords were free to rack-rent tenants, but were restrained from doing so by their own good character and by a "powerful public opinion"—by the media, as we might now say.

Isaac Butt became queen's counsel in London and so was well versed in these legal matters. In fact, English law did not fully apply in Ireland, he noted. The common law in England discouraged eviction of tenants, even for nonpayment of rent, and a landlord who tried to proceed against a tenant "was held strictly to every requisite of the law. Forfeitures were odious in all English courts." But special legislation had reversed these principles in Ireland. An Ejectment Code, enacted at the time of the anti-Catholic laws, eased the eviction of Irish tenants. "Statute after statute was passed for those purposes," Butt wrote. "If defects were discovered in the old penal law, they were met by a new one. As some latent principle of common-law protection was discovered unde-stroyed, a new and more stringent enactment mowed it down—until, as I said, the whole principle of the common law was reversed."[37]

The underlying problem in Ireland, then, was the chronic guerrilla war between tenants and landlords, and between Irish subjects and British rule generally. The British had tried to crush the Irish into submission; when they gave up trying, the Irish were in no mood to coexist peacefully with their oppressors. It was this guerrilla conflict that Malthus referred to as producing the insecurity of property in Ireland. The religious disagreement that lay at the heart of the conflict only made it that much more intense.

Under the rule of law with secure property rights, the self-impoverishing behavior that Anglo-Irish landlords engaged in will not occur. What all this suggests is that the long-neglected actor on the Irish stage has all along been the landlord. He has long been such a stock villain that we thought we knew all we needed to know. Mill said that he was shortsighted, Thomas Carlyle added that he was foolish. It is his incentives that have been overlooked. When we look at the situation a little more closely, we see that his condition must often have seemed even more precarious than the "land war" would suggest.

NOMINAL PROPRIETORS, GARRISONED ESTATES

Ownership in Ireland was often a trophy of politics, not the result of free exchange. Such titles had in the past been subject to confiscation when the political regime changed. It was said by Lord Clare, at the time of the Act of Union between England and Ireland, that the whole of Ireland had been expropriated three times within little more than a hundred years. That is, the expropriators had been expropriated at least twice. For a long period, then, politics in England, in addition to the guerrilla war in Ireland, rendered the landlord insecure in his property. An 1840 parliamentary commission recounted the history: "In the south of Ireland [before Cromwell], the title to property was unsettled. For more than a century, confiscation and re-confiscation followed each other, until the Acts of Settlement and Explanation [in 1660] secured the followers of Cromwell in their estates." When James II was driven from England, he retreated first to France and then to Ireland. Before his defeat at the Battle of the Boyne (1690), Protestant landowners were driven out and all lands confiscated since 1641 were restored to their original owners. "The repeal of the Irish Act of Settlement by the Parliament of James II gave the Protestant proprietors a fright from which they have not perfectly recovered even to this day," the report added. "Since that time they have been persuaded that every change of policy, or isolated disturbance, threatens their titles. They deem that they only garrison their estates, and therefore they look upon the native occupants (I cannot call them tenants) as persons ready to eject them upon a favourable opportunity. Hence, the Munster landlord was afraid to give the persons who occupied his ground a permanent hold upon the land, or a beneficial interest in its occupancy. The old struggle of title, in natural course, produced the new contest of tenure."[38]

After 1690, William III obtained control of more than a million acres of forfeited estates in Ireland. These he disposed of in large swaths to his English and Dutch friends: to William Bentinck, eldest son of the duke of Portland, 135,000 acres; to a former mistress, the countess of Orkney, 95,000 acres; to the earl of Albemarle, 108,000 acres, and so on. But then they were seized again, this time by Parliament. "These immense grants were within eight years resumed by the English Parliament in spite of the king," J. A. Fox reports in *A Key to the Irish Question,* "and the whole offered by auction to the highest bidder, regardless of right or justice."[39] Parliament was now dominant, and henceforth it would dispense the Irish patronage, not the monarch.

Landlords were again reminded of the precarious nature of their titles when the Act of Union between the two countries was debated in 1800. Lord Clare, the lord chancellor and colleague of Lord Castlereagh, encouraged landlords who were opposed to the Act of Union to vote for it anyway, because the retention of their Irish acres depended wholly on the survival of British military rule:

> The whole power and property of the country has been conferred by successive monarchs of England upon an English colony, composed of three sets of English adventurers who poured into this country at the termination of three successive rebellions. Confiscation is their common title; and from their first settlement they have been hemmed in on every side by the old inhabitants of the island, brooding over their discontents in sullen indignation. . . . What, then, was the security of the English settlers for their physical existence at the Revolution [of 1688], and what is the security of their descendants at this day? The powerful and commanding protection of Great Britain. If by any fatality it fails, you are at the mercy of the old inhabitants of the island.[40]

This timely reminder to landlords of their insecurity encouraged a sufficient number of them to vote for the Act of Union in the House of Lords, even though they knew how unpopular it was among the Irish. Title to property seemed as insecure as everything else in Ireland. Arthur Young's description of the country, published in his *Tour of Ireland in 1780,* indirectly illustrates the point. Valuable forests had been cut down in haste, he noted. The short time horizons of landlords in Ireland could not have been better illustrated:

> In conversation with gentlemen, I found they very generally laid the destruction of timber to the common people, who, they say, have an aversion to a tree. At the earliest stage they steal it for a walking stick, afterwards for a spade handle; later for a car [buggy] shaft; and later still for a cabin rafter. That the poor do steal it is certain, but I am clear the gentlemen of the country may thank themselves. Is it the consumption of sticks and handles that has destroyed millions of acres? Absurdity! The profligate, prodigal, worthless landowner cuts down his acres, and leaves them unfenced against cattle, and then he has the impudence to charge the scarcity of trees to the walking sticks of the poor, goes into the House of Commons and votes for an Act, which lays a penalty of forty shillings on any poor man having a twig in his possession which he cannot account for.[41]

Arthur Young brilliantly described the situation, but failed to explain why landowners were "profligate" and "prodigal." They feared, with good reason, that the lands they owned today would no longer be theirs tomorrow. So they took every opportunity to convert their insecure real property into secure bank balances. As we have seen elsewhere, patiently awaiting the slow maturation of plans or plants is not something that insecure owners rationally do. We know that at the time of

William and Mary, confiscated estates were immediately pillaged by those who received them. The commissioners of confiscated estates reported that new owners, far from being grateful, "have been so greedy to seize upon the most trifling profits that large trees have been cut down and sold for sixpence each."[42]

With the end of the Napoleonic Wars, title to property in Ireland did become more secure. By the 1840s, however, many owners were so impoverished that they were unable to pay their creditors. They had borrowed heavily against their estates, but had been unable to collect the "fictitious rentals" that "pauper tenants had covenanted to pay," as Isaac Butt wrote.[43] The landlords suffered severe reverses during the famine. At least one-third were ruined and many others were in financial difficulties. By 1849, it was said, "the tenants looked as though they had just come out of their graves, while the landlords looked as though they were just entering theirs." The economist C. P. Scrope noted that "the land is in the hands of nominal and embarrassed proprietors, who either cannot or will not themselves improve their estates."[44]

Parliament established the Encumbered Estates Court in 1849, forcing all Irish landowners to sell their property on petition of any creditor. Engels had noted that landlords lived "in dread of the Encumbered Estates Court." Compulsory sales led to a general auction of property in the 1850s. Hundreds of thousands of acres were sold—often for one-half to one-third of the purchase price—usually not enough to cover debts. An example was "Martin's Estate," described by a French traveler, Leonce de Lavergne, in the 1850s. "This domain is of such extent that the porter's lodge stands twenty-five miles from the house. The inheritor of this vast property died in poverty, upon the ocean, while flying from the soil that no longer belonged to him."[45] By 1857, over 3,000 estates had been sold and divided between 8,000 new owners, mostly Irish.

There was an additional reason why owners had miscalculated. In 1797, the Bank of England suspended the convertibility of sterling into gold, thereby permitting inflation. Commodity prices increased by 44 percent in the next three years. With the introduction of the sovereign (a gold coin worth one pound) in 1817, convertibility was resumed, but at the prewar parity. To prevent the loss of its gold reserve, the Bank of England tightened money until prices fell back to their prewar level. Commodity prices in England fell by half, from an index level of 182.5 in 1813, to 90 in 1845. "This price deflation was by far the most severe England had ever experienced, both in depth and duration," Roy W. Jastram wrote in *The Golden Constant*.[46] Hardly anyone understood what was going on, and many attributed the general hardship to laissez-faire economics rather than monetary deflation. "Hard times" were also felt in England, of course, and described by Charles Dickens, and should be understood in light of this deflation.

Landlords who had acquired property in Ireland at a time of inflated prices found with the restored gold standard that their estates were worth far less than they had paid for them. To the insecurity of property, then, was added the unpredictability of money. Economists have usually overlooked this point in connection with Ireland; and indeed England. The landlords themselves didn't understand what was happening—deflation wasn't understood at all at the time. Nonetheless, they attempted to recoup their losses by any means, including rack-renting their tenants and expropriating their labor; in doing so, they were barely constrained by law, and were encouraged by a climate of opinion holding that the Irish were lazy or subversive, or both.

After the forced sales, the Irish situation slowly improved. Estates were broken up, helping to create what had long been lacking—a middle class. According to the French observer, new owners received a title that was "legal and indisputable, conferring an absolute right to the property, called in English fee simple"[47]—an acknowledgment that earlier titles had been dubious. Most of the new owners were Irish. "It was hoped that English or Scotch purchasers would have been induced to buy land in Ireland, and farm it; but neither, it seems, have come forward," Lavergne added. "There exists an old distrust of Ireland, not soon to be eradicated. They fear the revival of jacqueries, and detest popery and the papists. Ask an Englishman to invest his capital in Ireland, promising him at the same time a return of eight or ten percent: it is much the same as proposing to a Frenchman to send his to Africa among the Arabs."[48]

With the Irish Land Act of 1870, the tenants' right to be recompensed for improvements was acknowledged, and landlords were given incentives to grant long leases.[49] With the restoration of full civil rights to the Irish, economic conditions finally became tolerable, and the Irish question at last receded. Numerous estate records have yet to be examined, and the subject continues to be investigated by scholars. Further inquiry should pay particular attention to the condition and incentives of the landlords. If property owners in Ireland really thought that they "only garrison their estates," they were not true owners at all. Their shortsighted behavior suggests that C. P. Scrope's label—"nominal proprietors"—was closer to the truth.

If so, everything falls into place. The insecurity of property in Ireland explains the pillaging of estates, the scarcity of capital, the rack-renting of tenants and the "contest of tenure." It more generally explains why, in 1845, in a green and fertile and by no means overpopulated land, the country was already destitute and on the brink of starvation, needing only the potato blight to trigger the catastrophe.

ISSUES OF THE DAY

INTRODUCTION

Different facets of property have seemed important at different periods of history. In our own day, two issues have cropped up time and again. One has received a great deal of attention— intellectual property. The other has been stressed by a small but growing group of environmentalists—the relationship between property and the environment. They stand in sharp contrast. The environment is earthy: the earth itself, its natural products. Intellectual goods are nonmaterial, incorporeal, made by humans. They fall within the modern category of information.

Perhaps the most important reason why we must have property rules in the physical world is that we don't have enough free goods for everyone. Air is the exception, but scarcity is the rule. Without property rules, goods will be used up, chopped down, worn out, degraded, denuded. Not so with informational goods. They are subject to quite different rules. Our usual understanding of scarcity does not apply to them. One more copy can be made without taking anything from those who already own copies. The public domain of information is quite unlike the material commons.

In fact, the public domain may be as constructive in the realm of information as the unfenced commons is destructive in the realm of physical goods. It is not immediately clear, then, that intellectual goods need property rules. But perhaps they do, too. Information can be scarce. It is certainly "scarce" when it doesn't yet exist. In any event, intellectual property emerged suddenly within the last 15 years as an important category of law. Why did this rather arcane aspect of property rise up so quickly from obscurity? The answer helps to shed light on the subject of property more generally.

What is the proper relationship between ownership and the very broad field that is called "the environment"? Intellectuals are satisfied with the argument for intellectual property because they understand the toil that goes into creative endeavor. Such work deserves to be rewarded, and they see property rights as a system of rewards. They also see that this line of reasoning does not apply to the physical environment. Human beings did not create nature, after all. So perhaps they do not deserve the rewards of owning it.

In the eyes of patent and copyright owners, the ease with which informational goods can be copied makes an intellectual-property regime essential. And for many, the impossibility of reproducing the natural world undermines the case for property rights in the environment. Precisely because it is unique, private owners should not be given free rein to despoil it. Nonetheless, the argument here is that the environment will be better protected when it is privately owned than when it is controlled by the state. Property is a system of punishments, in addition to rewards. A despoiled environment is likely to be less valuable than a carefully tended one. As to the widely accepted alternative to private property, state ownership, government managers have their own incentives, which can be counterintuitive.

SEVENTEEN

INTELLECTUAL PROPERTY

A GOLDEN AGE

THE LIBERTARIAN WRITER LYSANDER SPOONER used the phrase "intellectual property" in the 1850s, and may have been the first to do so.[1] Its widespread use is recent, however. It first appeared as a heading in the *Reader's Guide to Periodical Literature* in 1985, and only in 1993 did the relevant subcommittee of Congress change its name to Intellectual Property and Judicial Administration. It is also the most active field of property in our day. *Industry Week* noted with amazement in 1994 that we are living in the "golden age" of intellectual property. "Never before have the owners of patents, copyrights, trademarks, trade secrets and other products of the mind enjoyed so much government protection and financial reward."[2] In 1988, the *New York Times* referred to the "intellectual property mania."[3] The question arises: Why did this rather arcane aspect of our subject—hitherto an outpost in the empire of property—become so important? Perhaps the answer will illuminate the topic of property more generally.

Physical property confers upon specific people a monopoly in the use of some good. The owner can (physically) exclude the rest of the world. Patents and copyrights also confer monopolies. It is somewhat paradoxical that the first English patent law was part of a statute intended to outlaw monopolies; a special exemption from the ban on monopoly was given, for a period of 14 years, to "the true and first inventor of new manufactures." Copyright also emerged from an unexpected background: censorship rather than concern for authors' rights. When the Stationers Company was chartered in the 1550s, new books had to be licensed, and only specified presses were permitted. Members of the Stationers Company became the immediate beneficiaries of this new regulation of commerce. And like regulated industries almost everywhere, they vigorously opposed deregulation.[4]

Before the printing press, authorship was less celebrated than it is now. Copyists were thought to do the useful work. "The real task of the scholar was not the vain excogitation of novelties but a discovery of great old books, their multiplication and the placing of copies where they would be accessible to future generations," Ernst Goldschmidt said.[5] "Paradoxically," Elizabeth Eisenstein wrote in *The Printing Press as an Agent of Change,* "we must wait for impersonal type to replace handwriting . . . before singular experiences can be preserved for posterity, and distinctive personalities can be permanently separated from the group or collective type."[6] The technofuturist John Perry Barlow has made a similar point: "From the Neolithic to Gutenberg (monks aside), information was passed on, mouth to ear, changing with every retelling (or resinging). The stories which once shaped our sense of the world didn't have authoritative versions. They adapted to each culture in which they found themselves being told. Because there was never a moment when the story was frozen in print, the so-called 'moral' right of storytellers to own the tale was neither protected nor recognized."[7]

Authors' names began to appear less to acknowledge their rights than to identify the sources of sedition. Milton's *Areopagitica* (1644) argued not for the author's interest but for the "Liberty of Unlicensed Printing." His agreement with the printer Samuel Simmons is one of the first known contracts calling for payment proportioned to copies sold. The work was *Paradise Lost,* the initial printing 1,300 copies, the "advance" £5. From Shakespeare's time to Samuel Johnson's, authors often gave away their rights in a spirit of noblesse oblige. Members of the nobility, and gentry eager to distinguish themselves from the hacks of Grub Street, preferred to share their manuscripts with their friends, and a copy might find its way to a printer. *Shakespeare's Sonnets* were so circulated, and printed without the author's approval. Thomas Gray wanted no payment for his *Elegy,* and his publisher was happy to oblige.

In the Statute of Anne (1710), the author is for the first time mentioned as worthy of protection. Printers had "of late frequently taken the liberty of printing, reprinting and publishing books" without the authors' consent, and "to their very great detriment," the preamble noted. It established a 14-year time limit for copyright. This was later reaffirmed in the important case of *Donaldson v. Beckett* (1774).[8] Among the first to sell cheap reprints, Donaldson came into conflict with the main London publishers, one of whom claimed a perpetual right in an author's work, and sued. But Lord Camden reaffirmed the statutory time limit. "Otherwise," he said, "all our learning will be locked up in the hands of the Tonsons and the Lintons of the age [early publishers], who will set what price upon it their avarice choose to demand."

Ever since, it has been accepted that the right to intellectual property has a time limit—a distinction between intellectual and physical property that hints at an underlying fissure between the two. The recent tendency has been for the protected period to increase. Current copyright law, enacted in 1976, extends protection to 50 years beyond the life of the author (75 years in the case of a corporation). For patents, the protected period has been 17 years from issuance, but in international trade the General Agreement on Tariffs and Trade changed it to 20 years from the filing of the patent application.

In general, copyright is the more restrictive grant. Neither facts nor ideas can be copyrighted, only their expression. With patents, the distinction between idea and expression is not so clear cut, and some patents do seem to grant a monopoly in the idea itself. To be patented an invention must be original and "nonobvious," and it must also be useful—defined as having economic value. A defect of patents is that mechanical inventions utilize laws of nature, which are put to use but not really "invented." For that reason, independent discoveries are sometimes made, but the one who arrives first at the Patent Office wins the monopoly. The winner may have done little more than add the final touch to earlier discoveries. Literary creations are unique products of the mind, on the other hand, and it is almost impossible for them to be independently created.

Trademarks and trade secrets are counted as intellectual property, and the critics of intellectual property generally find little fault with them. Trademarks usefully differentiate products, and are infinite in their possible variety. The invention of one does not prevent a competitor from thinking up another. As for trade secrets, secrecy is surely preferable to legal monopoly as a protective device, because it can be maintained without benefit of the state's enforcement apparatus. It can be preserved by the ordinary rules of physical property. It doesn't rely on the Patent Office's peculiar combination of public temptation and legal prohibition ("Here is what we have invented. If you copy it without permission, we'll sue you.")

The Coca-Cola formula was never patented, and the company has refused court orders to disclose it. In 1977, it left India rather than hand over the formula to the government. A product protected by secrecy can be made available to the world without limiting others' right to *try* to copy it. But Coca-Cola has received a far more important protection from its trademark. While researching his book, *For God, Country and Coca-Cola,* Mark Pendergrast stumbled across the original formula in company archives. He asked a spokesman what the effect of publication would be. Obviously, another company would be able to produce the same drink. "They couldn't call it Coca-Cola, because you'd sue them," Pendergrast said. "Let's say they call it Yum-Yum." "Fine," said the Coca-Cola man. "Now what? What are they going to charge for it? How are they going to distribute it? How are they going to advertise? See what I'm driving at? We've spent over a hundred years and untold amounts of money building the equity of that brand name. Without our economies of scale and our incredible marketing system, whoever tried to duplicate our product would get nowhere, and they'd have to charge too much. Why would anyone go out of their way to buy Yum-Yum, which is really just like Coca-Cola but costs more, when they can buy the Real Thing anywhere in the world?"[9]

Pendergrast "couldn't think of a thing to say," but he might have said that the name and the price are as important as the taste, and that the trade secret is really not so valuable after all. In the emerging digital world, however, secrecy (codewords) has emerged as the most important and efficient method of controlling access to intellectual goods, thereby permitting the development of market mechanisms for its transfer.

FORCED SCARCITY

The most important argument for treating intellectual goods as property is that without ownership, artists and inventors would not create their works. "With respect to a great number of inventions in the arts," Jeremy Bentham wrote in 1785, "an exclusive privilege is absolutely necessary in order that what is sown may be reaped." Such a monopoly "produces an infinite effect and costs nothing."[10] The argument became prominent at the time of the French Revolution, and may be construed as a declaration of independence from aristocratic patronage. In presenting a patent bill to the French Assembly, Stanislas de Bouffler said that invention, the source of the arts, was also the source of property. It was "primary property," while all other was "merely conventional." In 1791, the Assembly proclaimed the inventor's property right to be one of the "rights of man."

The economist Fritz Machlup, a critic of patents, has claimed that de Bouffler's language was deceptive, and that substituting property (good) for monopoly (bad) persuaded the public to regard patents "not as a government intervention designed for a purpose but, rather, as an integral part of the institution of private property; not as an enforcement of a monopoly granted by the state but, rather, as a prevention of theft."[11] The same idea nonetheless found its way into the U.S. Constitution without any help from the word property. Article 1, section 8 defined the powers of Congress, one being "to promote the progress of Science and the useful Arts, by securing for limited times to Authors and Inventors the exclusive Right to their respective Writings and Discoveries."[12]

Mark Twain, among others, inveighed against the time limit. When he wrote his autobiography, in 1906, copyright lasted for 42 years. It was his opinion that in the past century, England and America had not produced more than 20 authors whose books had outlived that time limit. Of 220,000 published volumes, "not a bathtub-full" was "still alive and marketable." Therefore it would have been all the same "if the copyright limit had been a thousand years."[13]

Intellectual property is said to be not just a stimulus to intellectuals, but a blessing to society. When financially rewarded, invention will increase, and we all benefit from that. But it has never been conclusively shown that invention really does depend on patents. The printing press itself had no legal protection. Some of the key inventions of the Industrial Revolution were so protected, others not. James Watt believed that "an engineer's life without patent was not worthwhile."[14] But Samuel Crompton's "mule" and James Hargreaves' spinning jenny were not patented.[15] Crompton was remunerated by Parliament. A statistical study of the effect of patent protection on the development of pharmaceutical drugs from 1950 to 1989 found that patents were "not a prerequisite for inventions."[16] There was a significant correlation between economic development and invention, however. But another study estimated that without patents, 65 percent of new pharmaceutical drugs in the United States would not have reached the market.[17]

Some patents may have stood athwart the road to further improvement for a decade longer than was needed to encourage the original invention. An early steam-engine patent held up James Watt for a number of years, and Alexander Graham Bell's telephone patent stymied Thomas Edison.[18] Then again, Watt's business partner, Matthew Boulton, is believed to have invested in Watt's steam engine only after patent protection for it was assured.[19]

A strong antipatent movement arose in Europe in the 1850s, suggesting that the defects of the system may at times outweigh its advantages. The movement lasted for 25 years, then petered out. In Britain, a bill reducing protection to 7 years passed the House of Lords, and patents were repealed outright in the Netherlands. Switzerland did not accept patents at all until the 1880s.[20] The pro-patent counterattack of the late nineteenth century has been linked to the rise of protectionism. In the ensuing economic contraction, support for patents increased.

Among the criticisms of intellectual property, the most important was originally made by Thomas Jefferson. Even before the Constitution was ratified, he wrote to James Madison suggesting that the patents and copyrights clause be nullified. He thought that the argument that monopolies were an "incitement to ingenuity" was "too doubtful, to be opposed to that of their general suppression."[21] By 1789 he proposed that "monopolies" be allowed for literature and the arts, but for "no other purpose." Later, as secretary of state, he supervised the Patent Office, and was "oppressed beyond measure" by the task of examining claims. Among those he granted was the patent to Eli Whitney, in 1793.[22] By the time he had retired Jefferson had thought about the subject in depth, and in a letter to Isaac McPherson he put his finger on the missing ingredient in the case for intellectual property: scarcity.

If nature has made any one thing less susceptible than all others of exclusive property, it is the action of the thinking power called an idea, which an individual may exclusively possess as long as he keeps it to himself; but the moment it is divulged, it forces itself into the possession of everyone, and the receiver cannot dispossess himself of it. Its peculiar character, too, is that no one possesses the less, because others possess the whole of it. He who receives an idea from me, receives instruction himself without lessening mine; as he who lights his taper at mine, receives light without darkening me.

That ideas should freely spread from one to another over the globe, for the moral and mutual instruction of man . . . seems to have been peculiarly and benevolently designed by nature, when she made them, like fire, expansible over all space, without lessening their density at any point; and like the air in which we breathe, move and have our physical being, incapable of confinement or exclusive appropriation. Inventions, then, cannot in nature be a subject of property.[23]

We need to establish property rights in physical goods because they are naturally scarce. Two people cannot both occupy the same patch of ground. The property system works by allowing particular people to control particular patches. Intellectual goods, on the other hand, lacks this quality of scarcity. They are not "in" a particular place; they can, in fact, be in lots of places at once. Many people jointly can know the plot and details of a novel, and one's knowledge does not detract from others' enjoyment; it may even add to it. There is no "tragedy of the commons" in the public domain. It seems, then, that material and nonmaterial goods are subject to quite different laws. The nonmaterial cannot wear out. It requires no maintenance. It can "be" in more than one place at once. "The information at the heart of the intellectual property can be 'consumed' without the supply being exhausted," as the Office of Technology Assessment noted. "In contrast to markets for housing or antiques, consumers don't have to bid to exclude each other in order to use information."[24]

Private property protects the value of scarce goods. Intellectual property creates the scarcity of products that are appropriated. It protects value by making goods scarce. By nature, the intellectual "content" can be replicated indefinitely. This is the most important reason why the proprietary status of intellectual goods must be regarded with a preliminary suspicion. There are good reasons for building fences around land; around ideas and inventions, such reasons are not so easy to see. Arnold Plant of the London School of Economics, Ronald Coase's teacher, pointed out in the 1930s that markets seem to function adequately without the protection of intellectual property. Books are offered for sale even when they are not copyrighted.[25] Friedrich Hayek also thought it "not obvious" that "forced scarcity is the most effective way to stimulate the human creative process."[26]

Artists and inventors could simply be paid a fee to create a work that becomes the property of the publisher (as happened in Beethoven's case); or be employed by a court, with a job description that includes composition (as in Bach's); or be paid by a corporation to think up new products (as with many inventors today). But this does not solve the underlying problem. It merely shifts it, from author or inventor to publisher or business. If publishers are to be able to pay the author or composer an adequate sum, they presumably must feel confident that others cannot buy one copy and then go into business producing more of the same on their own account.

The best reply to Jefferson's objection is that information really is scarce—in the dimension of time. It is "scarce" before it exists at all; before it has been organized in the human mind. The question is how to treat these valuable goods once they are brought into existence. Intellectual property law gives the owner control over the copying of the good. Historically, however, a different form of protection has in practice served the same purpose.

The information content, whether the story in the book or the idea in the machine, has to be put in physical form before it can acquire value. As long as the invention or creation remains in someone's head, it obviously can't be stolen. After it is put down on paper, it can be protected by the ordinary rules of property—the rules against trespass and theft. Manuscripts are kept under lock and key. Employees sign agreements not to divulge valuable information. After publication, the work may be protected by copyright, but there may also be an extralegal support. The advantage of priority, combined with the cost of "embodying" the idea in physical form, has often in the past been sufficient to deter other producers from making and selling their own copies.

Everything depends on the cost of making these additional copies. If it is high enough, the discouragement to creativity will not arise, and the arguments in favor of intellectual property are weakened. This economic approach to the subject—analyzing the cost of making additional copies—is the key to understanding the recent high level of interest in the subject. As a result of recent technological change, in particular the computer and digital revolutions, the cost of copying intellectual goods has plummeted.

THE COST OF COPYING

Before the invention of the printing press, scribes took so long—perhaps a whole year—to copy a book-length manuscript that the new copy was inherently more valuable than the old, just as a new suit of clothes is more valuable than the one it replaces. The value was mostly in the labor that created the new book. The book was owned by the monastery or scriptorium where it was made, and no thought was given to evaluating the information content separately from the physical book.

Post-Gutenberg, additional copies became cheaper and cheaper relative to the original. But right up to the 1990s, it seems, that cost usually remained high enough to protect the interests of authors and their business partners. U.S. copyright law, which did not extend to foreign works for most of the nineteenth century, illustrates the point. The market for books in the public domain survived without legal protection. Prominent authors such as Thackeray and Dickens had no intellectual property in the United States until 1891. Even in the absence of enforceable rights, however, U.S. publishers paid British authors to send them early galleys. T. H. Huxley testified before a royal commission in the 1870s that his American publisher "remits me a certain percentage upon the selling price of the books there, and that without any copyright which can protect him."[27] (In Dickens's case, serial publication made this method impossible.)

In gaining access to the galleys, the American publisher had the advantage of priority, and this was sufficient to deter competition in most cases. The cost of assembling the book remained high enough to deter most competitors. If a rival publisher did put out its own edition, "the practice of all the great houses of America," Huxley said, was to publish "a cheaper edition at any cost." In such a price-cutting environment, the reading public was the beneficiary. Books were much cheaper in the United States than in England in the nineteenth century. So even without copyright, most of the time, the advantage of priority matched or exceeded the cost of obtaining that head start. It was unlikely that narrowly profitable books would be pirated even when it was legal to do so.

That markets are possible in the absence of intellectual property is further shown by classics that remain in print, their copyrights long expired. In the absence of copyright, publishing would survive, but as a "cutthroat" rather than a "gentlemanly" business. We know that the costs of making and distributing a book are high, relative to the value of the content, from the lamentable fact that authors are usually paid a mere 10 percent of the retail price and still their publishers often lose money!

The Xerox machine never quite upset these calculations, although it made the unauthorized copying of text difficult to prevent. Who can afford to police a machine that steals pennies a day? But copying a book two pages at a time is likely to seem less worthwhile than buying the book itself. Copying takes time, and the unwieldy pile of pages delivered by the machine does not compare with the compact convenience of a book. At a nickel a page, there is no contest.

The digital revolution, on the other hand, may have changed everything. Once information is digitized, its physical embodiment drops away. It then becomes much more difficult to protect, and therefore to own. Information wants to be free, as Stewart Brand was supposedly the first to say, and in cyberspace it is free at last. It can multiply as easily as the flame on Jefferson's candle. What took the scribe a year, and the Xerox machine an hour, can now be copied in seconds. And when copies multiply, value collapses. Information can be multiplied almost without cost and transmitted to any number of distant terminals. Furthermore, it can be copied exactly, not in a form that becomes increasingly inexact with each succeeding "generation."

"Digital technology is detaching information from the physical plane, where property law of all sorts has always found definition," John Perry Barlow wrote. We can now get the wine (the content) without the bottle (the physical book). As information enters cyberspace, it is possible "to replace all information storage forms with one metabottle."[28]

To economists, the replication of high-value goods at almost no cost is close to a contradiction in terms. Most things throughout history have been so difficult to "copy" that this alone has preserved their value. Patented or not, a Cadillac is difficult to reproduce. One could be assembled from junkyards. A hundred would require capital equipment and highly paid workers. Cheaper to buy authentic "copies" from the nearest showroom! They would run better, too. Assembly lines were devised to lower the cost of "copying" things, but are themselves very expensive productions. The too-solid flesh of most goods in the marketplace has therefore prevented the price deflation that one can foresee coming on the Internet.

High-value articles that can be inexpensively replicated will become low-value articles—unless something prevents that fall. This is the great paradox of the Information Age. An information economy is one in which the value added by intellectual goods, such as songs and films and software, is higher at the margin than that added by steel and oil. But thanks to the possibility of almost costless replication, that "value added" is threatened with collapse. Such goods are like pillars of sand—perhaps one should say silicon. They will tumble down unless shored up. If a borrowed car could be "copied" as easily as borrowed software, the automobile industry would collapse immediately. This may be the predicament of Microsoft, a creation of intellectual property and human capital.* Free or very inexpensive copying of its goods could cause its capitalized value to fall as swiftly as it rose.

---

*As we enter the information age, the elusive thing called capital has been expanded to include human capital. Like intellectual property it is an intangible: in mind rather than matter. Education and good habits are regarded as the human capital that can yield a future income stream. Human capital is a store that we acquire and carry in our heads rather than our bank accounts. This is an appropriate expansion of capital because the Latin root of the word, *capitalis,* means "of the head." By implication, the old idea of capital was incomplete and only now has come into its own. The former capital was tainted by its association with a particular class: capitalists. But with human capital we can all become capitalists, even without bank accounts. Human capital democratizes capital, as befits a democratic age.

Bill Gates has likened the physical matrix in which information is embodied to friction. The information highway will be "largely friction free," he wrote, and this will allow information on any subject to be distributed quickly and cheaply.[29] Friction is an incommodious force, and the digital world rids us of most of it. Another metaphor is the bodyguard—a useful protector. Throughout the Industrial and Gutenberg eras, physical embodiment has acted as the protector of the information content, making it expensive to copy. What this suggests is that for a long time we didn't have to worry too much about theft of the information because it inevitably had a physical corpus attached to it: iron and steel, paper and ink.

In moving out of the Industrial and into the Information Age, then, we find that the sudden rise of intellectual property is the legal expression of this transition. What the current "mania" reflects is the information content's loss of its old bodyguard and its need for a new protector, especially in the friction-free world of cyberspace. Software—"all design and no manufacture," in one description—illustrates these developments.[30] The design is arduous, the copying child's play. Free riding in software has costs in time and energy, but the money cost of software was for a while high enough to make it worthwhile for users to search out friends who would lend their programs. Producers, in turn, built in anti copying devices and displayed legal warnings.

The information content has continued to find its unexpected physical protector. Paper-and-ink manuals were needed to figure out how the thing worked. Upgrades, made available to those who showed they had bought a genuine copy, also came to the rescue. In addition, computers more and more came with the software preinstalled, which made it unnecessary for software producers to police copying at the retail level. So markets flourished, despite the ease of private copying. Meanwhile the price of software programs fell by a factor of ten. The price of software is tending toward that of "free" television programs, which come "bundled" with advertising.

Comparable developments have occurred in the world of manufacturing more generally. Robots are making not just computer hardware, but all replicable physical goods, much cheaper. The physical matrix of the computer chip is worth only a minute fraction of the mental labor inscribed upon it. But there, too, the copying has become very inexpensive. With the old physical bodyguard increasingly being stripped away by robotized manufacturing, a lot of economic value became precarious. The law was suddenly needed to shore it up. Intellectual property lawyers found themselves much in demand.

BODYGUARD OF LAWYERS

In the early years of Silicon Valley, high-tech companies often just forged ahead as fast as they could without bothering about intellectual property. Lawyers were hired to keep companies out of court, not get them into one. Most patents were not upheld in litigation, and many companies hadn't even filed for protection. Some of today's most litigious companies were themselves founded by entrepreneurs who, when they left their previous employment, took with them not just their human capital, but a lot of intellectual property in their heads. The technology was moving so rapidly that it was difficult to catch up with something that had already reached the marketplace.

Eventually, however, the bodyguard of lawyers entered the picture in Silicon Valley and elsewhere. But all this would not have happened without a change in the legal climate.[31] Here we do come to a case in which the law was plainly adapted in response to economic forces. The "play" changed the rules, with the new technology acting as the underlying force that was bringing about the crucial shift in relative economic value. Software was brought under the purview of the Copyright Act, and in 1984 the legal protection of semiconductors was strengthened. Jimmy Carter's attorney general argued that the United States was lagging behind the rest of the world because weak patent protection was discouraging our inventors. The U.S. Court of Appeals for the Federal Circuit was created in 1982 to streamline patent appeals; judges were handpicked for their pro-patent views. By the early 1990s, the Patent Office was handing out patents to about half of those who filled out the forms (about 100,000 were issued in 1994), some of them plainly invalid. This development in turn threatened to restrict rather than encourage new invention. The high cost of lawsuits, and the presumption by juries and courts that patents are almost always valid, could "spell the death of the industry's small players, locking up the computer industry in the hands of giants like Microsoft, Novell and Lotus," Simson Garfinkel wrote.[32]

Far from lagging in innovation, meanwhile, it turned out that the United States was well ahead of the world. The International Trade Commission claimed that foreign piracy of U.S. intellectual property was costing $40 billion to $60 billion per year.[33] (But the figures were based on the "static" assumption that the number of copies made would be unaffected by the payment of license fees.) The General Agreement on Tariffs and Trade permits trade reprisals if piracy abroad goes unpunished, and unauthorized producers are from time to time shut down. In the long run, however, it seemed likely that people all over the world will eventually be getting a lot of useful intellectual property free, courtesy of American inventors and American industry. For good or bad, digitization is proving to be an instrument of cultural imperialism: it is transmitting our cultural artifacts around the world with unimaginable ease.

At home, the ease with which information can be copied on computer networks is creating pressure for further changes in the law. Assistant Commerce Secretary Bruce Lehman's 1995 "White Paper" on intellectual property on the "information highway" would in effect make it a copyright violation to read a document on the screen without authorization. "Whenever a work is placed into a computer, whether on a storage device (such as a disk, diskette, ROM), or in RAM for more than a very brief period, a copy is made," Lehman said.[34] Copyright owners want to change the law so that making such temporary copies would be a violation. On-line providers would be held liable for the copyright violations of their own subscribers.

Copyright owners do have a reason to worry. With the information now able to slip around the Internet almost without friction, only one copy has to "escape" for it to become a thousand copies in as many computers at very little extra cost. Software may have been protected by its hardware, but now the hardware is disappearing, too. The problem is that every user can become a publisher. This puts the first publisher in the position of an engraver who goes to the trouble of making metal plates that are then given to someone else who is free to sell the prints.

But legal changes of the type proposed by Bruce Lehman are problematical, nonetheless. They represent the interests of current market leaders. Intellectual property law is supposed to encourage creativity, and as the intellectual property expert Jessica Litman has written, copyright exemptions or lacunae have historically been the great stimulus to rapid investment and growth in new media:

> Player pianos took a large bite out of the markets for conventional pianos and sheet music after courts ruled that making and selling piano rolls infringed no copyrights; phonograph records supplanted both piano rolls and sheet music with the aid of the compulsory license for mechanical reproductions; the jukebox industry was created to exploit the copyright exemption accorded to "the reproduction or rendition of a musical composition by or upon coin-operated machines." Radio broadcasting invaded everyone's living rooms before it was clear whether unauthorized broadcasts were copyright infringement; television took over our lives while it still seemed unlikely that most television programs could be protected by copyright. Videotape rental stores sprung up across the country shielded from copyright liability by the first sale doctrine. Cable television gained its initial protection with the aid of a copyright exemption.[35]

In *Universal v. Sony,* Sony was held not liable for contributing to copyright infringement by selling its videotape recorders. The movie producers "lost," but they didn't foresee the new market that was about to open up for their products in the form of videotape sales. Still less was the outcome anticipated by Sony. By the time the Supreme Court decided the case, in 1984, their Betamax system was being overtaken by Matsushita's VHS. Sony had made the mistake of holding its intellectual property too closely, choosing not to license Betamax to competitors. Matsushita had freely licensed its technology, and several other companies were producing the VHS system. It became so much more widespread that when a choice had to be made between the two, VHS prevailed.[36]

Apple Computer also kept its intellectual property on too tight a rein. The company reaped "monopoly profits" from its Macintosh computers, but it also lost market share. While Apple kept its proprietary goods to itself, IBM allowed others to make compatible versions of its PCs. By the time Apple began licensing its goods, nine out of ten computers conformed to the IBM standard. In the realm of intellectual goods, the lesson seems to be the one taught by Ecclesiastes: "Cast thy bread upon the waters, for thou shalt find it after many days."

Cyberspace will pose a great challenge to intellectual property's supposed indispensability. If we really are moving into a world in which the economic significance of the material realm is reduced, and ever more transactions take place in the virtual realm of cyberspace, we will enter a world in which the logic of the commons is no longer one of tragedy, and in which the old property rules no longer apply. In the nineteenth century, Karl Marx imagined that a transformation of human nature would be the price of admission to such a world. At the end of the twentieth century more and more people believe that a transformation of technology may have the same effect. Shakespeare, Dante, and the printing press attest that creation and invention can and did occur without the protection of intellectual property. But some way will still have to be found to reward creative endeavor—to kindle the first flame that lights all the others.

EIGHTEEN

PROPERTY AND THE ENVIRONMENT

A JOURNALIST AT THE 1992 EARTH SUMMIT in Rio de Janeiro expressed the "enlightened view" of the respective environmental merits of public and private ownership when he said that man does not own nature, and that "common ecological or even aesthetic values" must supersede such "feudal notions."[1] The successful inculcation of this view, he added, had been "one of the accomplishments that the twentieth century conservation movement can justly claim to its credit." It may indeed be the "enlightened" view. But the environment has been the worse for it. The (unowned) Brazilian rain forest is a case in point. The (state-owned) mess created in the Soviet Union is another.

The truth is that private ownership is conducive to a more careful stewardship than public ownership. The claim may seem counterintuitive, and some rebel against it. Private owners are at liberty to despoil their property, after all, and private property encourages the "exploitation" of resources. Public property, on the other hand, can be managed in the public interest. Environmentalists can be put in charge. With good people in control, they believe, bad things will not be allowed to happen. Furthermore, public servants are not allowed to make a profit. As long as they are paid good salaries and pensions, and cannot easily be fired, they will be insulated from all such temptations and worries. They won't feel obliged to make a profit.

Environmental ruin in the former Soviet Union admittedly undermined the enlightened view. No private property there, and what was the result? "No other great industrial civilization so systematically and so long poisoned its air, land, water and people," Murray Feshbach and Alfred Friendly, Jr., wrote in *Ecocide in the USSR*.[2] The same problems arose in Eastern Europe. State managers had no incentive to economize in the use of unowned resources. Meanwhile, the care and feeding of the military and the production of basic consumer goods were always more urgent considerations than environmental quality. Because wealth creation was so difficult under state ownership, protecting the environment (to the extent that officials thought about it at all) was an unaffordable luxury.

Environmentalists are sometimes inclined to think that the Communist experience is not relevant to democratic countries. The party bosses in the Soviet Union, not subject to elections, resembled old-fashioned labor leaders in their indifference to such niceties as air quality. Voters in democracies, on the other hand, can insist that those promoted to key government jobs "support" the environment. The problem is that it is incentives, not intentions, that are dispositive. Incentives work to much the same effect on good people, bad people or in-between people. Incentives will survive changes in administration, from Democratic to Republican and back again.

Richard Stroup of the Political Economy Research Center in Bozeman, Montana, found this out on the job. From 1982 to 1984, he directed the Office of Policy Analysis at the Department of the Interior. The secretary, James Watt, was considered to be "against" the environment; he had replaced Cecil Andrus, who had been considered to be "for" the environment. The national news media were, of course, very hostile to Watt. What amazed Stroup was the nonchalant attitude of the seasoned bureaucrats he dealt with every day. They assumed that policy would not change much under Watt, and in this they were proved correct. Interior secretaries succeed one another, and "even though they have their different visions of where they want to go," Stroup said, "most of their decisions are the same because they face the same political pressures."[3] Those pressures are not necessarily good for the environment.

A serious defect of government ownership is that it tends to universalize one approach to the task at hand—managing the environment, in this case. The approach may ultimately be shown to be wrong, but central control will meanwhile impose it everywhere. In a faddish field, each fad (as long as it lasts) is likely to be imposed nationwide under government sponsorship. Private property, on the other hand, ensures a diversity of approaches, because it decentralizes decision-making. As to the cycle of fads, the environmentalist Alston Chase has written:

> At the turn of the century, saving big game animals was the rage. Officials fed elk, bred bison and bashed wolves. Today they do the opposite— batter bison, breed wolves and encourage hunters to shoot elk. A generation ago, old-growth forests were called "biological deserts." Now they are revered for "biodiversity." Over the years, the field known as "restoration ecology" went

into, then out of, then back into popularity, without once having been tried. Wildfires were first thought good, then bad, then good and seem to be on their way out again. Ditto the mysterious doctrine called "sustainable development."[4]

The more sensible approach is to let myriad independent owners make their own decisions. Their different experiments and outcomes will point to the wisest course.

The crucial defect of public ownership, however, is that it puts land and natural resources at the mercy of politics. Those in charge will assuredly not be philosopher-kings weighing an abstract public interest, but politicians worrying about the next election. Their goal is satisfying constituents, and to that end they will make logrolling alliances with other politicians. They will usually act shortsightedly. So will the managers they appoint. The next election, the loss of office, the loss of one's job, and the effect of budget cuts on the department will be more pressing concerns than the fate of forests or the ravages of soil erosion. It's not that these environmental goods will be forgotten or viewed cynically. It's just that they will seem less urgent than concerns that affect political survival itself.

The incentives generated by secure private ownership are quite different. From the point of view of conservation, one of property's greatest advantages is that it has no time limit. It gives owners permanent control. Their decisions cannot be reversed by the next election, or altered by bureaucratic pressure. An environmental organization that itself owns valued terrain can control its property in perpetuity. Such long horizons of ownership are exactly what the environment must have. Environmentalists are the first to agree that those who make decisions about natural resources—whether private owners or government managers—must plan for a distant future. Hardwood trees and old-growth forest need more than a human life span to mature, after all.

Again we encounter a paradox. If long horizons are important, then it is government agencies that last forever. Private businesses go under every day. But the saleability of private assets gives owners and managers the incentive to consider carefully all decisions that affect their future value. Government-owned property, on the other hand, is not usually for sale; even when it is, its managers have no incentive to sell it profitably, for the proceeds will disappear into the common pool of the treasury. Furthermore, managers cannot benefit from any sales or sacrifices that they may make. They have no way of "capitalizing" into present value the stream of future benefits derived from the wise use of state property.

In the United States, environmental problems are more common in the west than in the east, and by the same token a much higher percentage of land west of the Mississippi River is owned by the Federal government. (Not counting Alaska and Hawaii, 25.6 percent of the land west of the Mississippi is federally owned, compared with 3.8 percent of the east.[5]) Meanwhile, environmentalists are beginning to discover the benefits of private ownership. In Chile, an American millionaire bought 670,000 acres of pristine forest for $12 million, and by one estimate owns 78 percent of the remaining old-growth forest in that country. He wanted to put into practice his belief in "deep ecology," holding that the life of a tree is as valuable as that of a human being.[6] Chile's status as one of the few Latin American countries where property receives something close to constitutional protection enabled him to carry out his plan.

In the United States, the National Audubon Society discovered that the development of mineral resources on private land is consistent with good conservation. The society owns a 26,000-acre haven for migrating birds in the Rainey Wildlife Sanctuary, Louisiana, where natural gas was discovered. Audubon permitted drilling, and since the early 1980s has earned over $25 million in royalties. Elsewhere in Rainey, cattle graze for a per-head fee. The society notes that "there are oil wells in Rainey which are a potential source of pollution, yet Audubon's experience in the past few decades indicates that oil can be extracted without measurable damage to the marsh."[7] Because Audubon owns the land, it can control the way the oil companies operate, and require that strict precautions be written into contracts.*

Ownership meant that Audubon directly experienced the "opportunity cost," or lost opportunity, of not allowing drilling. On public land, no one notices this loss—certainly not "the public." Their interest is too attenuated to have reason to know what is going on. Elsewhere, Audubon has opposed oil drilling on publicly owned land, but this does not imply hypocrisy. "Decisions about public lands are entangled in a never-ending political process," Jane Shaw and Pamela Snyder have pointed out. "Control is always up for grabs in a 'winner takes all' setting. If energy companies win the right to explore [on public land], environmental groups will have little ability to control exploration or production. If environmental groups win, they prevent energy development."[8] Private organizations such as Audubon can act with much greater freedom on their own land because they are accountable only to their own dedicated supporters, who are much more disposed to learn the facts of the case.

---

* In this respect the United States appears to be unique. It may now be the only country in the world where the subsurface mineral rights are retained by private owners. Elsewhere, even in countries where property is private, "land owners" are just that—surface owners. Mineral rights are almost everywhere owned by the state. This makes it difficult for the surface owners to control contracts with oil companies. When oil is found, or suspected, the state may soon show up with drilling equipment in tow, and may tear up the land without regard to the environment. For this reason, there have been reports of landowners in Latin American and Third World countries dreading rather than praying for the discovery of oil on their land. Problems created by the "split estate" help to explain why about 90 percent of the oil wells ever drilled in the non-Communist world have been drilled in the United States. (Robert Bradley, speech at Institute for Energy Research, Houston, April, 1994; and personal communication.)

The property-rights analysis of environmental issues can easily be confused with an older, very different view: the belief that private industry should be the beneficiary of resources on public lands. For decades, the dominant philosophy of public-land management was that animal, mineral and vegetable resources were there to be exploited. If mining, railroad and logging companies needed subsidies to extract them, subsidies were often granted: the companies had the know-how, and the consumers, it was thought, would benefit in the long run. Why let these resources go to waste, especially if there was an "energy crisis" or a national emergency? James Watt was perhaps the last public exponent of this philosophy. Not only was he far from supporting the very different property-rights approach, but he subverted what was by 1980 a promising movement to privatize public lands. In supporting subsidies for mining and energy companies, he became in the public eye the supporter of big business against the very environment that he was supposed to be protecting.

The great sea change in favor of environmentalism began in the 1960s. The environment was there to be appreciated, not exploited. Our very health and the air we breathed seemed to demand that we adopt a different philosophy. Within a decade, the environmentalists were highly influential, and have remained so. But they have found it hard to believe that the public ownership they have so often espoused might yield unintended consequences. They dominated politics so successfully that they have been inclined to believe that they could win whatever they wanted in that arena without compromise. So politics seemed to hold no dangers for them.

The new movement was a child of prosperity. With the necessities taken care of, Americans began to demand luxuries, such as more wilderness and more wildlife. As the economy grew and technology changed, natural resources were making a less important contribution to the national wealth; digging up land in search of raw materials was no longer worth the price of a Caterpillar. It became uneconomic to cut down what had once been too valuable to pass up. Between 1850 and 1920, the forest economist Randal O'Toole wrote, the United States lost about 13 square miles of forest a day, mostly to agriculture.[9] At the beginning of the twentieth century, 10 of the 12 largest companies in the United States were natural-resource companies.[10] But farmers learned to grow more food on less land. The automobile eliminated the need for horses and their pasture. Oil and natural gas reduced the demand for wood as fuel. As a result, many millions of acres reverted to forest. Since we no longer needed to wring these resources out of the land, perhaps we should stand back and enjoy them.

"The West is moving from an economy based on extractive industries to an economy based on 'attractive' industries," as former Senator Tim Wirth of Colorado put it.[11] If only every American could spend a few days in such places as the Raggeds Wilderness of Colorado, he believed, there would be little debate over protecting them. Most of us probably would agree that such wild places should be protected. But how? Turning them over to private owners may seem particularly inappropriate for this reason: we don't need to own land in order to enjoy it. Appreciation is immediate and can be "fulfilling" in days or hours. It is therefore tempting to think that the long horizons of private ownership are irrelevant to the problem at hand. Conservation nonetheless remains a long-term project, however brief one's communion with nature. Wirth and many others think that the best way to achieve long-term conservation is to set the land aside: turn it over to the government, then keep close tabs on what the officials do.

But as Tim Wirth noted in passing (and this might have prompted second thoughts): "Every year, virtually every national forest in the Rocky Mountains and the Intermountain West loses money while building more logging roads and cutting down more trees. In the bargain, we lose precious wildlife habitat; sedimentation increases dramatically, clogging streams and killing fish, and recreational potential is lost." How could this be? For an answer, let us take a brief look at the Forest Service—a division of the U.S. Department of Agriculture.

WORLD'S LARGEST ROAD-BUILDING COMPANY

The Forest Service was founded in 1905, with Gifford Pinchot in charge. He believed that the country's "unexampled wealth" was directly the result of its "superb natural resources."[12] And so the Forest Service's mandate was to "improve and protect the forests." Today, its forests cover 191 million acres, or nearly 10 percent of the land in the "lower 48" states. By the 1980s, nonetheless, an amazing thing had happened. As John Baden of the Foundation for Research on Economics and the Environment put it, the Forest Service was by then "perhaps best understood as the world's largest road-building company."[13] By 1991, the service had constructed 360,000 miles of roads—eight times the length of the U.S. Interstate Highway System.

Until World War II, plenty of timber was available from private lands, but the postwar housing boom increased the demand on the national forests. To reach this timber, the Forest Service embarked on large-scale road construction. Budget rules allowed them to increase their own expenditures as they did so. The cost of road-building was paid out of the U.S. treasury, but some receipts from the timber sales could be retained in the service's own budget.[14] So it didn't matter to the Forest Service if it lost money on every sale. According to one study, below-cost timber sales cost taxpayers $5.6 billion in the 1980s alone.[15] In effect, the treasury subsidizes the Forest Service to cut down trees, and Congress permits the service to retain part of the proceeds.

A 1930 law allowed the service to pay for reforestation out of timber-sale receipts. And an inconspicuous 1976 amendment permitted "discretionary use" of receipts to cover "overhead."[16] Distributed to all district offices, these funds generate pressure throughout the service to keep on logging. With employees in 46 states, the service keeps many private logging companies in business. Those so employed are happy to lobby Congress at the first sign of any change in the law. Since 1976, then, the service has logged a lot of timber, and soon the damage became visible. But it was usually attributed to the "greed" of sawmill operators. Few saw the underlying problem, although O'Toole has repeatedly commented on it, and Perri Knize wrote a revealing article on the subject for the *Atlantic Monthly*.

Knize joined the Forest Service as a volunteer in 1983. Like most Americans, he thought of it as a conservation organization. He was vaguely aware that it sold trees, but was unprepared for what he found in the Beaverhead and Bitterroot National Forests, in Montana. "Entire mountainsides were shorn of cover, and rough roads crisscrossed their faces, creating terraces that bled topsoil into the rivers when the snows melted in spring." All over the United States, he found the same or worse. Mountain ranges were shaved in swaths of 40 to 100 acres. Charred and smoking from slash-and-burn logging, forests looked like battlefields. "The Forest Service is deforesting our national timberlands at a rate that rivals Brazil's," he concluded.[17]

Topsy-turvy incentives encouraged managers of one national forest to raise funds in odd ways. In order to protect grizzly bear habitat in one area, they built more roads into other grizzly habitat, cut down more trees and sold them. Wanting to reforest shorn acres caused by an earlier timber sale, managers of another national forest paid for it by clear-cutting another patch and selling that, too. The *Washington Post* reported that in just four national forests in North Carolina in 1989, the Forest Service spent $4.8 million selling trees worth $2.9 million.[18]

A private company would have to take into account the costs of its own logging. That is why profit—an excess of receipts over costs—turns out to be the unexpected safeguard of nature. Most Forest Service road building would be uneconomic for a private owner. The logging of mountainside timber, sparse and slow growing, would be too expensive. But when these expenses are met by taxpayers, and proceeds can be retained to buy office furniture and hire more workers, a government agency will slash and burn to reach marginal trees. Liberated from the account book, the public manager is free to act with the carelessness of a wastrel heir. Resources so captured may be marginal—they are usually sold for a low price by the Forest Service—but they may have a high ecological value: better for the environment for them to have remained undisturbed. Profit and loss statements encourage that outcome on private land.

By the time of the Earth Summit in 1992, satellite photographs showed that forests in the northwest United States were damaged.[19] At its peak, the Forest Service was cutting and selling almost 12 billion board feet of timber a year. A dissident movement within the service generated adverse publicity, but little public understanding of what was wrong.[20] The temptation was to blame bad people. President Bush wanted to be the "environment president," but no one explained the budgetary incentives of the Forest Service to him. There were calls for the resignation of F. Dale Robertson, chief of the service since 1987. "We intend to be more environmentally responsible," he reassured.[21] But his good intentions were never in doubt.

Private property is a system of penalties in addition to rewards. High costs without offsetting receipts are discouraging. They are to be expected in the remote areas that conservationists want to preserve. These are just the places where, sans subsidies, costs will exceed returns. Wilderness trees won't be logged if access roads must first be paid for, and unsubsidized mining companies cannot afford to shovel for shale.

Forest Service logging was reduced in the 1990s by opposing politics with politics. The Endangered Species Act was construed in such a way as to give "property rights" to the spotted owl. Logging was thereby reduced to half its peak level. But politics lay in wait around every corner. In 1995, a "salvage plan" permitting increased logging passed a House committee within weeks of the Republicans' recapture of Congress, and ultimately became law.[22] Allies of the timber industry argued that thousands of acres of federal timber damaged by insects and fires would be wasted if not logged soon. At such times, environmentalists must have second thoughts about entrusting their treasures to politicians. They believe the politicians can be controlled, of course. But when people lose their jobs and call their congressmen, environmentalists are apt to find their position much weaker than they thought. Old victories, supposedly irreversible, have to be refought.

The Forest Service may seem anomalous because of the curious way in which it can expand its own budget; it is as though the Defense Department could enlarge itself by starting wars on its own initiative. But all government agencies worry about losing out in budgetary infighting, and their perpetual anxiety is the Achilles' heel of environmental stewardship. To allay it, agencies will think up ever new ways of increasing demand for their services. Environmentalists who want land turned over to the government so that it will be left alone are likely to be disappointed for this reason.

Consider the National Park Service, created in 1916 "to conserve the scenery and the natural and historic objects and the wildlife therein, and to provide for the enjoyment of the same in such a manner and by such means as will leave them unimpaired for future generations."[23] By the 1990s, there were many reports of overcrowding in the parks, of hard-packed ground, dead and diseased trees, a lack of species diversity. As a way of letting Congress know about the high demand for its services, the Park Service boasts of high visitation figures. According to the service, 270 million Americans visited the parks in 1995—more than the population of the United States. (The figure includes all those who drive on highways managed by the Park Service.)[24]

When parks are owned privately, large numbers can be accommodated with entrance- and user-fees. This both reduces demand and gives owners the wherewithal to do their job. But because national parks are publicly owned, they cannot easily be managed by this method. The Park Service cannot by law retain the (low) fees that it does collect. Except for 15 percent for collection costs, these fees go to the common pool of the U.S. treasury. It is the same with other agencies such as the Fish and Wildlife Service, the Bureau of Land Management and the Forest Service. They cannot use "market" mechanisms, and as a result they remain forever dependent on politics to pay their bills. High visitor tallies are their ticket to success in budget struggles. Meanwhile, the egalitarian ethic in Washington, D.C., works to undermine the argument that fees should be increased. It is said that such fees would "hurt the poor the most," and so on.*

After a great political struggle, the 1994 Desert Protection Act was approved in Congress by one vote, assuring that the Mojave Desert would henceforth be protected by the National Park Service. But almost immediately, "the new law got bogged down in budget politics," the *Washington Post* wrote.[25] The congressman representing the Mojave district, who had opposed the law's enactment, "persuaded the new Republican majority in Congress last year to withhold Park Service funding for the management of the new preserve, effectively leaving it under the old, less restrictive rules of the Bureau of Land Management." Environmentalists were furious, but the lesson was clear: Live by politics, die by politics.

---

*In the spring of 1996, the House Resources Committee passed an amendment permitting the Park Service and other agencies to set higher fees and to retain them within the agencies. But the likely effect would have been to make the Park Service's most popular attractions, such as Yosemite and the Washington Monument, self-sustaining and therefore independent of the federal budget. The bill did not become law for that reason. The relevant agencies would be deprived of one of their more potent bureaucratic weapons—sometimes called the Washington Monument strategy, in fact. If, at budget time, it seems that appropriations will not be increased sufficiently, agencies are inclined to announce that "budget cuts" will compel them to reduce visitor hours or close outright their most popular facilities. These are precisely the ones that would become independent with a new policy of retained entrance and user fees. House Resources Committee, substitute amendment for H.R. 2107, March 28, 1996.]

WATER IN CALIFORNIA

The problems of government ownership have been well illustrated by water shortages in California in recent years. The casual reader may think that the cause was straightforward: not enough rain for so many people. The real problem was quite different. The water was being wasted. About 85 percent of the available water supply is used by agriculture, which constitutes only 2 ½ percent of the state's economy. Everything else—cities, industry, mining, kitchens, showers, swimming pools—consume no more than 15 percent of the water. In this instance, the property-rights argument has found important support from the Environmental Defense Fund and Bill Bradley, the former senator from New Jersey.

The key difficulty is that the state itself owns the water (some of it is also controlled by the federal government); water in California and other western states is government owned. But the state does not charge for it. "Water in California is free, which doesn't make much sense," said Tom Graff, a senior attorney with the Environmental Defense Fund.[26] Newspaper accounts often say that farmers pay from $7 to $15 per acre-foot for it, but this refers to the cost of building diversion structures. "Farmers receiving water from the Central Valley Project are charged only enough to amortize construction costs over 50 years, at zero percent interest," the *New York Times*'s Peter Passell found in 1991, at the height of the drought.[27] Recipients were paying roughly one-fiftieth of the current cost of water from new sources.

Under the "prior appropriation" doctrine in effect in western states, a user may be granted the right to take water from a stream by seeking permission to do so ahead of anyone else. "While these laws authorize (and indeed encourage) individuals to divert the water and put it to productive use," Marc Reisner and Sarah Bates wrote in *Overtapped Oasis*, "the water itself remains the property of the public [that is, the state]. What each diverter 'owns' is the right to use the water, not the water itself."[28] When the big water projects (dams and aqueducts) were built earlier in the twentieth century, farmers were the most important customers. They acquired rights to it by applying to the State Water Resources Control Board for a permit. The system works in a first-in-time, first-in-right manner.

The farmer's continued right to water depends on his continued use of it. If he stops doing so, he must go to the back of the queue to regain that right—the use-it-or-lose it system. The strong incentive is to keep using it. Once a farmer has received a permit, the last thing he will do is let the state know that he won't be needing water next year. Farmers therefore have a powerful incentive never to stop using what has been for them an almost free commodity. As a result, water in California is used to turn arid fields into rice paddies. (The price of the rice is subsidized as well. Another option is to flood the land, grow nothing, and receive $260 per idle acre from the Department of Agriculture.) At the height of the drought, rice growers in California were using more water than all the households of Los Angeles and San Francisco combined.[29]

By 1991, a serious crisis seemed imminent. Journalists at last began to scrutinize the farmers' incentives to waste water:[30] they didn't have to pay for it in the first place; if in a burst of public spiritedness they decided not to use it, they would lose it; but most important of all, they were not allowed to sell it to others who were willing to pay a high price—the city of Los Angeles, for example—because it was not theirs to sell. They had only use rights, not property rights.[31]

Faced with an emergency, Governor Wilson formed a state "water bank," empowered to buy water from the farmers and resell it to urban users.[32] The price the farmers found acceptable tells us the value of the water to them at the time. At one point, $125 per acre-foot was considered "too low to compensate for the possible effects" on the farming community. Even at $200, some still said no. The city of Santa Barbara showed how valuable water can be. At the height of the drought, residents paid for a desalination plant, although the pure water so generated cost $1900 per acre-foot. The city had good reason to worry. In earlier years, no-growth enthusiasts had blocked construction of new reservoirs, and had even stymied a pipeline connecting the city to the state water supply. So the desalination plant was built.[33]

Why don't government agencies charge more for water? The answer is that they have been captured by their clients. "Without the farmers, the government agencies would never have been able to get the political support they needed to build the dams in the first place," said the economist Gordon Tullock.[34] Along with James Buchanan, he pioneered the field known as "public choice," in which economic analysis is applied to politics in general. (In 1986, Buchanan won the Nobel Prize for his contribution to the field.) The relevant dam-building agencies were able to expand from small beginnings by actively seeking out customers who "demanded" their services. These agencies—the Bureau of Reclamation and the U.S. Army Corps of Engineers, primarily—then enjoyed political support from farmers and could rely on them to lobby on their behalf when budget appropriations were debated.

Normal economic incentives are reversed in the public sector. "If the agency raises its price for the water," Tullock said, "the bureaucrats don't get to keep the additional revenue." They are not paid out of profits. Neither revenues nor expenditures are "theirs." So they have no incentive to economize. "At the same time," Tullock added, "if price increases are under discussion in the political arena, the farmers will be alerted and will put up strong resistance." And this will be conveyed to the politicians contemplating the changes. The result is that reform will probably be blocked. If an agency does raise its prices, not only will demand for water drop, but the agency may even start to show a "profit." Its claims on the general budget may then seem less pressing to the budget director, and its future allocation of tax revenues may decline. Government-supplied goods are usually underpriced for this reason.

In normal times, such officials don't think of the general public as their constituency. The belief that they are guided by an abstract concern for the "public interest" was one of the great unexamined assumptions of all economic analysis until the 1970s. Actually, public officials have their own, more narrowly focused, interest, which is discerned by consulting the beneficiaries of their policies. "In normal times," notice. Normally, the general public doesn't have any idea what is going on in obscure government agencies. California's Water Resources Control Board doesn't normally get into the papers at all. But in the drought years, the press focused on the arcane subject of water pricing. Under these circumstances both the farmers and the bureaucrats were put on the defensive: caught in the act of collaborating with one another, one might say.

Before he became an economist, Gordon Tullock worked for the State Department in China, and there he noticed the same thing. In odd ways, the bad incentives that animate bureaucracies became apparent. Messengers not only had summer and winter uniforms, but spring and autumn uniforms as well. And 40 typewriters were stored in cabinets in the visa office. "It was so easy to order new ones and so difficult to get rid of old ones," Tullock recalled.[35] Perhaps from that observation, public choice theory was born.

With California's population growing rapidly, and water being poured into the ground for farming, the water agencies saw shortages ahead. They weren't concerned, however. As before, they would build more dams and canals. The additional water was there. It only had to be captured before it ran into the Pacific. Everyone would be better off. The farmers would still get cheap water, cities would be able to expand, and the new construction projects would fatten up agency budgets. By the 1970s, however, there was a new variable in the political equation: environmentalists. They believed there were already too many dams and didn't want more. So they set about discovering endangered species, and they sued in the courts. The turning point came in 1982, when they blocked a new project known as the Peripheral Canal. Ever since, they have been a major force in the political allocation of resources in California.[36]

The lack of new dams and canals soon put a strain on the system. Then, with several years of below-average rainfall, the problem became an emergency. By the 1990s, something had to change—and soon. The Environmental Defense Fund became interested and saw the problem: the farmers had "captured" the bureaucracies that nominally controlled them. They then came up with an ingenious solution: Give the water to the farmers! Permit them to own outright what, under the existing system, they were merely allowed to use. Give them property rights in the water. The farmers would be permitted to sell water for a profit, and so would not want to waste it; the cities would be assured of ample supplies; and less water would be used everywhere. More would then be left over to protect the environment—the Sacramento River delta, in particular.

Some environmentalists didn't like the idea, believing they could get all they wanted without compromise; for example by saying "no more growth" to the cities and suburbs. But others saw that the political arena could become hazardous to environmentalism if faucets one day stopped delivering water. That would get everyone's attention very quickly. Better to devise a harmonious solution, letting everyone win, than to go for a divisive political victory.[37] Establishing property rights in the water was the key. It is also paradoxical, because it involves giving what is being wasted to the very people who are wasting it. But, of course, they are wasting it because they don't own it; because they are not allowed by law to do anything other than use it wastefully or lose their right to use it at all. The minute it is owned, the water is "appreciated." The farmer experiences what economists call the "opportunity cost" of failing to put it to profitable use.

Difficulties arose nonetheless. Many farmers resisted the marketing of water. They opposed changing an arrangement that currently benefited them; once in the political arena, their privileged position could only weaken. They preferred their subsidies to the vagaries of change and the uncertainties of markets. Also, if they sold the water, they would in effect cease being farmers and become water entrepreneurs. Individual farmers might do well, but farming communities as a whole would suffer. The suppliers of seed and farm equipment might no longer have anyone to supply them to, as had happened when a similar plan was put into effect in Colorado. For that reason, the California Farm Bureau opposed the plan.

Nonetheless, one or two water-transfer experiments were permitted— one in the Palo Verde Valley, for example, close to the Arizona border.[38] And once again, the Endangered Species Act was brought to bear. Farmers' allocations were cut in order to allow more water to remain in the Sacramento River, where fish are believed endangered. By 1994, it was reported that the price of some farmland in the San Joaquin Valley had fallen to one-third of its 1988 level.[39] By then, it was beginning to look as though the farmers would have done better to accept the water-marketing solution when it was first offered.

The need to allocate some goods by markets is not immediately apparent. At first, water was free because demand was small in relation to the supply that could be developed by building dams and reservoirs. It didn't seem to matter that it was used wastefully. "But as its scarcity increased and the economy using it shifted, the advantage of markets became clear," said Richard Howitt of the

University of California at Davis. Agriculture in the state was once far more important than it is today, proportionately, and the water was abundant enough that farms were the best place to put it. "Now," he said, "perhaps we're better off making microchips out of it." Land also started out as common property in the West, and efficiency wasn't an issue with it either, because it was so plentiful compared to the number of people. "One day, though, someone said: 'Why don't we buy it and sell it here just as we do elsewhere?'" Now, the same thing is happening with water.[40]

ELEPHANTS AND RAIN FORESTS

The same ideas apply with even greater force to Third World countries where property rights, and consequently markets, are less well protected. The World Bank made the case in its *World Development Report* (1992): "When people have open access to forests, pastureland, or fishing grounds they tend to overuse them. Providing land titles to farmers in Thailand has helped reduce damage to forests. The assignment of property titles to slum-dwellers in Bandung, Indonesia, has tripled household investment in sanitation facilities. Providing security of tenure to hill farmers in Kenya has reduced soil erosion. Formalizing community rights to land in Burkina Faso is sharply improving land management. And allocating transferable fishery resources has checked the tendency to overfish in New Zealand."[41]

The large animals that have become endangered in recent decades—elephants, tigers, rhinos—live in countries where private property is rarely secure. Their habitat tends to be on land that is either communal or state controlled. At the same time, their skins and tusks command high prices. Poachers may be armed with high-powered rifles, and the human population is expanding. As long as people were sparse in relation to terrain, and lightly enough armed, there was little need to protect animals by establishing property rights. Now, with only about 5,000 to 6,000 tigers remaining in the wild around the world, they will have to be either privatized or given high-priority state protection if they are to survive.[42] Enlightened disapproval of animal skins as fashionable attire will prove insufficient. It cannot be inculcated worldwide.

As for elephants, we are apt to forget that they are not domesticated. "A herd of elephants goes through an area like a slow tornado, snapping off branches and uprooting trees, leaving destruction behind," the journalist Raymond Bonner has written.[43] Conservationists, directing policy from New York, may not notice the price people pay for living with such animals. In parts of Africa, villagers constantly have to fight off hungry lions, elephants or hippos. Lions have been known to kill 25 goats in one night. Elephants, foraging 18 hours a day, can tear the roof off huts and village grain-storage units, and consume an entire season's food supply on the spot.

To the rich on safari, or the rest of us at the movies, elephants are appealing. But what could cause native villagers to want to conserve them? The value of their ivory is the key. A single tusk was once worth $5,000, in countries where per capita income was about one-twentieth that amount. If the villagers owned the elephants, instead of having to fend them off, it would be worth the villagers' while to protect them. Instead of villagers living under the equivalent of house arrest, the animals could be fenced in, and their ivory sold. Such a strategy has been pursued in southern Africa, including Zimbabwe, South Africa and Botswana. Governments turned over to villages "title" to the wild animals that roam over communal lands. Villagers found that, once elephants had owners (namely, themselves), they became assets. The elephant population of Zimbabwe soared to 77,000 in 1992, up from 32,000 in 1960.

A different approach was pursued in East Africa. Elephants crossed communal terrain at will, and governments tried to discourage poachers by banning all commercial use of the elephant except tourism. Sales of ivory and hide were banned. The president of Kenya set fire to $3 million worth of tusks in front of TV cameras. But the East African elephant population declined from 866,000 to 404,000 between 1979 and 1989. The unwise response was to internationalize the ban. At the Lausanne Convention on International Trade in Endangered Species (CITES) in 1989, the United States joined with most of the rest of the world in a general ban on trade in ivory.

This was hazardous to the elephant. If a ban is successful, the animal is deprived of most of its economic value. Trying to preserve it by such methods is like trying to conserve cows by banning the consumption of beef. There are millions of cattle in the United States because they are profitable. Keeping elephants for the benefit of sightseers in protected parks may be a way of preserving hundreds, or perhaps a few thousand of them, but privatized elephants would be preserved in the millions. Indeed, the high value of the ivory is their life insurance policy. Allowing rural people to make money from elephants gives them a strong incentive to protect them from poachers.[44]

An increasing number of journalists and environmental groups understand the argument, and the World Wildlife Fund has supported removing the "endangered species" label from elephants. In 1997, the Secretariat of CITES eased the ban to permit Botswana, Namibia and Zimbabwe to sell stockpiled ivory.[45] The revenues (estimated at $30 million) will be used for fences. Rhinos also have a high price on their heads, mainly because powdered rhino horn is considered by some an aphrodisiac; a single horn fetched $24,000 in Hong Kong in 1990.[46] Privatization rescues the rhino because the horn pays for the (very expensive) fencing needed both to keep the animals in and the poachers out. The idea is catching on. In Zimbabwe, the area dedicated to animal conservation has grown to more than 17 percent of the territory, most of it private; South Africa, which had 3 large private game reserves ten years ago, today has 25 (and hundreds of small ones).[47]

Controlled hunting can also defray costs. Well-protected animals multiply, and they eventually have to be culled to preserve habitat. Hunters will pay as much as $40,000 for the privilege of shooting a single trophy animal.[48] The first park in Africa to sell licenses to hunt the white rhino was established in 1982. "Five or six times a year," Bill Keller reported in the *New York Times,* "an American or German hunter pays about $25,000 for the privilege." When a rhino must be tranquilized, "hunters pay thousands of dollars for the right to shoot the dart and pose with the drugged beast."[49] The species has recently recovered from its earlier decline.

In the case of the destruction of rain forest, the absence of property rights is directly involved. After the forests became a leading concern in the late 1980s, one reporter wrote that Bolivian forest could be purchased "for less than 25 cents an acre."[50] This was not quite true, unfortunately. Buyers in Bolivia, unlike Chile, will find that they have not purchased clear title, but only a short-lived right to use the land. If permanent title to rain forest really could be bought for 25 cents an acre, then its destruction could have been swiftly stopped. With a combined budget exceeding $500 million in 1990, the ten leading American environmental groups could have bought up the entire rain forest of South America with spot cash and put it off limits to all future development.

Real havoc has been wrought in the rain forests, and the underlying cause has been precisely the difficulty of obtaining clear title. Roger Sedjo of Resources for the Future has drawn attention to "the de facto absence of well-defined property rights."[51] Frances Cairncross, environment editor of the *Economist,* agreed. The problem is that "rain forests have no clear owners."[52] Theodore Panayotou of the Harvard Institute for International Development noted in *Green Markets* that "insecurity of land ownership is the single most severe policy failure in developing countries."[53] An inventory of tropical countries, Roger Sedjo added, "would reveal that most of the tropical forests are publicly owned," the responsibility for management and protection residing with the government. "Closer scrutiny would show that in many cases these governments are either unwilling or unable to adequately protect and manage the forest resources." Consider Nepal:

> In the late 1950s the central government "nationalized" the country's forests. Previously, the forests had been under communal ownership, with local villages having the right to the outputs of the forest as well as the responsibility for their management and protection. Nationalization served only to alienate the villagers

from the forest and serious problems of poaching and erosion of forest borders
ensued. The central government lacked the ability to protect the extensive forest
with which it was now entrusted. [This led to excessive exploitation], thus
providing a variant of the "tragedy of the commons" replayed in the Third World
forest setting.[54]

The problem has appeared in many countries. In Indonesia, companies
hired to cut down state forests were given 20-year concessions, insufficient for
proper management. In Liberia, "virtually no private forest property rights are
recognized," according to Robert Repetto of the World Resources Institute. In
Ghana, changes in property rights accelerated deforestation. Rights once
established by tribal custom were, in the 1970s, "stripped from the traditional
communities and assumed by the central government. As a result Ghanaian
forests are now even more vulnerable to the 'tragedy of the commons' than they
were when property rights were vested in tribal groups . . . The transfer of all
forest rights to the national government has meant that access to the remaining
forest is virtually unchecked."[55]

For a while, Brazil captured the world's attention, and is worth a closer
look. The devastation of its forests was "one of the great tragedies of all history,"
Al Gore said in 1989.[56] Although he visited Brazil and is a professional
politician, Gore showed little interest in the political origins of the Brazilian
debacle. In his *Earth in the Balance,* he wrote that it was brought about by the
desire of "large landowners to earn short-term profits," ignoring "long-term
ecological tragedy."[57] Its real cause, however, was not greedy landowners, but
unwise laws governing land ownership.

Brazil's constitution of 1891 gave ownership and political control of all
unclaimed lands to the separate Brazilian states. But, as in so many countries,
government was consolidated and centralized in the twentieth century. The
military government greatly increased its control over the land in the 1960s. In
1971, Brazil's federal government claimed control of 100 kilometers on either
side of all federal roads in Amazonia. (If such a decree were to be applied within
100 kilometers of U.S. interstate highways, most of the U.S. mainland would
be nationalized.)[58]

There followed an unwise road-building project, which would not have
been undertaken without financial support from the World Bank. In his *Decade
of Destruction,* Adrian Cowell showed that the bank's funding of the $400
million Polonoroeste project, including a road from south Brazil to the
Amazonian states of Mato Groso and Rondonia, was carried out despite
opposition from the bank's own ecological officer. "The momentum of the
Bank's financial machine, the need to lend money to Brazil as its debt developed,
had overridden the practical warnings of its specialists," Cowell wrote.[59] Road

construction opened up access to the Amazon region, and a competition for the (state-owned) land ensued. Squatters received the right to 100 hectares if they could show "effective use" of the land for a year.

The problem was that cutting down the trees counted as effective use. Only the traditional "sustainable use" of harvesting rubber and nuts did not count. For those who had already arrived, and had staked their claims, the best way to guard against competition from newcomers was to cut down trees as quickly as possible. This also made it easier to detect and remove squatters, at the same time eliminating the method by which they might be tempted to document their own "effective use." In effect, if not in law, "the land-claiming process itself has required deforestation," the economist Gary Libecap wrote.[60]

In short, the Brazilian rain forests were invaded by newcomers; those who had already arrived knew that they had no legal title, and if they didn't cut down trees to stake their claim, others soon would. This was the formula—the lack of an orderly legal way of obtaining title to property—that created the disaster the world soon deplored. In an unexpected finale, the World Bank realized that something had gone badly wrong and made amends by hiring a flock of environmentalists. Bank working papers, such as Hans Bimswanger's "Brazilian Policies that Encourage Deforestation in the Amazon" and Robert Schneider's "Brazil: An Economic Analysis of Environmental Problems in the Amazon," noted the poor incentives that the Brazilians themselves had created, and when the Bank's 1992 *World Development Report* came out, it was dedicated to environmental issues.[61] As noted above, a few sensible references to property rights were included, showing that the true nature of the problem was beginning to be recognized.

X

ISSUES AT HOME

INTRODUCTION

Although it has recently become acceptable, almost fashionable, for academics to nod in the direction of property rights when discussing questions of economic policy, the political system itself continues to chip away at the prerogatives of private owners, sometimes to the extent of confiscating most of their rights. Nationalization has been discredited, but it has been replaced by a more insidious philosophy. The owner retains title, but is saddled with taxes, impositions and regulations that might in some cases have seemed excessive to feudal tenants. Contract is here and there yielding its crucial gains to status. Individual rights are threatened by the privileges associated with group membership. A revived feudal interpretation of property has been advanced explicitly.

Democracy imposes few limits on the power and reach of the state. Legislators are unrestrained from organizing themselves into predatory majorities; pennies and dimes are taken from an unwary majority and dollars are delivered to alert interest groups. In the economic realm, officials are subject to little or no constitutional restraint. The continued tendency of the Supreme Court is to centralize power. The Court rarely strikes down federal statutes, as it frequently does state enactments. Belatedly, however, the Court has begun to show some interest in the "takings" effect of municipal ordinances.

In the 1980s, the top tax rates were considerably reduced in the United States, and in many other countries. But federal taxes now take a greater percentage of GDP than at the peak of World War II. Tax thresholds unadjusted for inflation, tax withholding, bureaucratic ambition, and above all the vast complexity of government have made it difficult indeed for average voters to grasp how much is taken from their pockets. The consequences of no-growth regulations that prevent economic activity from occurring can hardly be seen at all. The fragility of the legal infrastructure needed to encourage production is not fully understood. Those who chip away at it in the name of reform can unknowingly take a chip too many.

Even as these changes were occurring, the economics departments in a few universities began examining the economic implications of property rights. The starting point appears to have been curiosity about the employment arrangements of the professoriate itself. Armen Alchian suspected that faculty tenure had something to do with the property-rights structure of non-profit institutions. Ronald Coase's much-quoted article on social cost was not ostensibly about property rights. But it did examine what happens at the borderlines of property: the effects of owners' behavior upon the property of their neighbors.

After many diversions, one of the most basic propositions of economics emerged from his study: When rights are exchangeable, they will be purchased by those who value them most highly. As long as they can be easily traded, therefore, resources will be used efficiently. The concept of efficiency in economics is contentious, but ultimately it turns out to describe whatever outcome is chosen by uncoerced private owners. It is therefore a surrogate for property. When he went to Stockholm to receive the Nobel Prize, Coase observed in his acceptance speech that it makes little sense for economists to discuss the process of exchange without first specifying its legal and institutional setting—the starting point of this book.

NINETEEN

THE FEUDAL TEMPTATION

FROM CONTRACT TO STATUS

WRITING IN THE 1930s, a law professor named Francis Philbrick expressed frustration with the idea that private property "pleads payment of taxes as the whole price" of its protection by the state. Taxes paid, it claims immunity from "all social obligations." Philbrick called for a "modernized philosophy of property," but one that harked back to an earlier period. The burdens placed upon owners should be restored to feudal levels.[1] Philbrick's ideas were echoed a generation later by Prof. John Cribbet of the University of Illinois. He, too, thought it regrettable that the older form of ownership, in which "all property was held subject to the performance of duties—not a few of them public," had not been preserved. Somehow, over time, the rights of owners had flourished, but their obligations had been allowed to dwindle away. "It may be that we threw out the baby and kept the bath," Cribbet thought.[2]

But even as these law professors wrote, the law was changing in ways that they desired. In the United States, the slow erosion of private property rights, starting early in the twentieth century, has continued more or less unchecked despite the demise of the Soviet Union, the collapse of communism and widespread privatization in many other parts of the world. The U.S. Supreme Court in the 1980s admittedly began to take a renewed interest in the issue of takings, after a 50-year hiatus, but in other respects public policymakers have retained the old antagonism to fee-simple ownership.

Several commentators have noticed that the word "feudal" aptly describes the direction in which property rights have been evolving in the United States.[3] The state, of course, has replaced the king in the hierarchy of authority. But one important difference has been little noted by those who welcome this exchange of bureaucracy for monarchy. The hereditary transmission of power at least gave monarchs a long-term interest in the future of their realms, and therefore long time horizons. In our own day, the vision of budget-burdened bureaucrats and reelection-seeking politicians is always short.

Landowners have more and more become stewards who hold their property at the pleasure of the state. Over a century ago, the legal scholar Sir Henry Maine saw that the direction of Western law in the eighteenth and nineteenth centuries had been "from status to contract." In the late twentieth century a reversal is underway. Legal privileges associated with group membership have been restored, threatening to undermine the greatest triumph of Western law: the emergence of a single class of citizens, equal before the law. Privilege was thereby abolished. But today, those able to influence policy in America are seeking to restore it. The new status, usually conferred by genes, gender and ethnic origin, has important legal consequences.

The novel feature of the new status is this: legal privileges are awarded to groups on the basis of a supposed hereditary victimhood. This is unlike anything seen in the past, when privileges acknowledged a supposed superiority. The new classification is restorative in intent—it aims to reduce differences and to bring back an imagined status quo ante, the egalitarian Eden that prevailed before Prejudice entered the world. Before that restoration, however, it will bring division, conflict and bitterness, not to mention economic decline. Unless this momentous change is checked, its economic consequences will be serious in the long run. It already affects decision making across the land. Companies spend vast resources achieving a "balanced" work force that will not attract accusations of "disparate impact," hence lawsuits. A 1989 *Fortune* survey found that only 14 percent of Fortune 500 companies claimed to hire on merit alone. Almost three-fourths admitted to quotas, or to euphemistically named "goals."[4]

The law of contract has been undermined along with equality before the law. A prerequisite of contract is that people must be assumed to enjoy roughly the same status and bargaining power if agreements between them are to be enforceable. Contracts signed by minors or the mentally impaired are not valid. If the citizenry is to be divided into classes of unequal legal status, the whole notion of contract is undone almost by definition. It bears repeating that the rise of equality before the law and the rise of the freedom of contract were the crucial legal antecedents to the free-market economy. But many in the West today have repudiated that past, or have failed to grasp its significance.

Considering that economics is largely about the exchange of goods, and that contract is perhaps the most important device facilitating exchange, economic decline is bound to ensue if contract is impaired. By 1974, nonetheless, Prof. Grant Gilmore of Yale Law School was cheerfully proclaiming the death of contract, in a book of that title. "We are told that contract, like

God, is dead," he began. "And so it is."[5] Laissez-faire economics and the freedom of contract had declined simultaneously, he noted in passing. Prof. Patrick Atiyah of Oxford made the same case more extensively in his *Rise and Fall of the Freedom of Contract.*

Traditionally, courts enforced contracts as written. More recently, this sensible doctrine has been replaced by an ambition to "deconstruct" contracts. Judges have felt emboldened to deny that written contracts really represent an agreement of the parties. A landmark along this unwise road was created by the California Supreme Court in a 1968 case, *Pacific Gas & Electric Co v. G. W. Drayage & Rigging Co.* The court ruled that oral testimony could be used to supplement and amend the written contract, no matter how unambiguous its wording. "If words had absolute and constant referents," the court decided, "it might be possible to discover contractual intention in the words themselves and in the manner in which they were arranged. Words, however, do not have absolute and constant referents." Excluding oral clarifications therefore reflected a "judicial belief" in the possibility of "perfect verbal expression." This in turn was borne of "a primitive faith in the inherent potency and inherent meaning of words."[6]

This flight of judicial fancy allowed the intention of the parties to be divined "by partisan witnesses whose recollection is hazy from passage of time and colored by their conflicting interest," as federal appeals court judge Alex Kosinski wrote in 1988. The overall effect of *Pacific Gas* was to cast "a long shadow of uncertainty over all transactions negotiated and executed under the law of California."[7] It also attacked the foundation of our legal system, he added, for the basic principle that language provides a meaningful constraint on private conduct was undermined. If we are unwilling to say that parties to a contract can come up with language that binds them, how can we send anyone to jail for violating written statutes? They, too, consist of mere words lacking "absolute and constant referents."

Kosinski observed in a later (1989) opinion that the willingness of courts to subordinate voluntary contracts to their own sense of public policy and proper business decorum deprived individuals of an important measure of freedom. "The right to enter into contracts—to adjust one's legal relationship by mutual agreement with other free individuals—was unknown through much of history and is unknown even today in many parts of the world. Like other aspects of personal autonomy, it is too easily smothered by government officials eager to tell us what's best for us. The recent tendency of judges to insinuate tort causes of action into relationships traditionally governed by contract is just such overreaching."[8]

An unstated but guiding doctrine of the late twentieth century is that adults, not just minors, must be protected from themselves in their secular, commercial actions. By 1966, Justice John Harlan was dissenting from the Warren Court majority on the ground that enactments that were "simply permissive of private decision-making rather than coercive" were being struck down as unconstitutional, even though the Fourteenth Amendment had originally been adopted to outlaw government coercion, not purely private action.[9]

In his 1971 law review article, "The Demise of Property Law," Prof. E. F. Roberts of Cornell foresaw, enthusiastically, that landlords of residential housing units would soon be governed by codes that they would not be able to avoid, even by "express agreements to the contrary" with tenants or potential tenants. Within little more than a decade, apartment owners in some cities, notably Santa Monica and Berkeley, were indeed left with little more than title deeds and the responsibility to make repairs and to pay taxes. "If the phoenix represented by land-use planning is going to rise from the ashes," Roberts wrote, "we must return to the medieval notions for inspiration."[10] Here was another professor who hankered after the feudal epoch.

THE POLITICIZATION OF PROPERTY

Sometimes it has seemed that every tenured law professor has at some point bid adieu to property. In his "Thoughts on the Decline of Private Property," Prof. Joseph L. Sax of the University of California at Berkeley was surely not exaggerating when he observed that "we are in the midst of a major transformation in which property rights are being fundamentally redefined to the disadvantage of property owners." Sax, more recently a senior official in President Clinton's Interior Department, focused on the *Penn Central* case (1978), in which the Supreme Court had upheld New York City's refusal to allow the railroad to build a high-rise above Grand Central Station.

The owner had not only been prevented from doing something that all its neighbors had been permitted to do, but it had been stopped because it had earlier done something admirable: it had built an architecturally distinguished building. The most accurate way of looking at the case, Sax wrote, was to say that "the owner was required to continue conferring a benefit on his neighbors." He concluded that "we are going to have to come to terms with the prospect that planning (a word that Americans don't much like), rather than property, is going to be a principal engine of social benefit production in the future."[11]

The judges and legislative bodies that have eroded property rights in the United States have rarely been able to anticipate the consequences of their actions. Tampering with property rights has turned out to be costly—especially for the poor, in whose name so many changes have been made. The unfashionable lesson is that only at the public's peril are good intentions enacted at the expense of property. In the nineteenth century the Supreme Court stood as a bulwark against such well-meaning tampering with the law. In the twentieth, legislative bodies were given the green light. Zoning and urban renewal illustrate the point.

One of the earliest and most important legal victories in the war on property was *Village of Euclid v. Ambler Realty Co.* (1926). In that case, the Supreme Court upheld a zoning ordinance in Euclid, Ohio, a Cleveland suburb, thereby subordinating the constitutional protection of property to the legislature's "police power"—its authority to act on behalf of the public safety, health and morals. Vacant lots in a predominantly industrial part of Euclid were included in an area zoned as residential, thus destroying three-fourths of their value. The federal district court had invalidated the ordinance, finding that if the police power was as extensive as claimed, "all private property is now held subject to temporary and passing phases of public opinion, dominant for a day, in legislative or municipal assemblies." The judge added that the "true object" of the ordinance was "to place all the property in an undeveloped area of 16 square miles in a strait-jacket. . . . The result to be accomplished is to classify the population and segregate them according to their situation in life." In consequence, the economic value taken from the plaintiff, and from others similarly placed, would in all probability disappear, "or at best be transferred to other unrestricted sections of the Cleveland industrial area, or at the worst, to some other and far distant industrial area. So far as the plaintiff is concerned, it is a pure loss."

This sensible judge bolstered his opinion by quoting Oliver Wendell Holmes: When the "seemingly absolute protection" of property (conferred by the Fifth Amendment) is abridged by the police power, Holmes had said, "the natural tendency is to extend the qualification more and more until at last private property disappears. But that cannot be accomplished in this way under the Constitution of the United States." The city appealed, however, and the Supreme Court reversed the district judge, viewing the zoning ordinance as an extension of the law of nuisance.

"A nuisance may be merely the right thing in the wrong place—like a pig in the parlor instead of the barnyard," Justice Sutherland wrote for the majority.[12] Of course, a pig in a parlor may not be a nuisance at all, if the owners of pig and parlor like it that way. But henceforth, with zoning laws authorized by the Court, the judgment of city councilmen would routinely be substituted for that of property owners. "Pigs, factories and homes would now be expected to stay where they belonged," commented Dennis Coyle, a Professor of Politics at Catholic University.[13] In the following year (1927), the Supreme Court ruled that in such cases it would no longer second-guess legislatures, and 47 years elapsed before it accepted another zoning case.[14]

The judicial rationale for zoning had nothing to do with wealth and poverty, but the consequences of zoning turned out to have everything to do with it. Zoning laws have worked relentlessly to protect the estates of the rich and to discourage or prevent building that would ultimately serve the poor. Zoning politicizes property, and, of course, the rich have far more clout in the political arena than the poor. But that is only a small part of the problem. Zoning aspires to protect the character of a neighborhood. Once this premise is conceded as a basis for expanding the police power and abridging property rights, the neighborhoods of the rich will in particular recommend themselves for protection. There's a simple economic reason: the poor have every reason to want to move into rich areas, but the reverse is not true. People who can afford to live in nice neighborhoods are not tempted to live in poor ones.

Developers of less expensive, high-density housing will have a strong incentive to build in good neighborhoods if their "freedom of entry" is not controlled by zoning, or by private covenants. Thus, market forces will tend to "average out" all neighborhoods, as more and more low-cost housing is added within a desirable area. Zoning is exclusionary in its logic, and it is hardly surprising that politics followed that logic: zoning became exclusionary. That this was its purpose was understood by 1940, when the planner Hugh Pomeroy wrote: "Low-density neighborhoods occupied by higher income families should not be faced with the danger of intrusion or encroachment by small lot developers."[15]

In fact, Robert H. Nelson of the University of Maryland has suggested that the sudden and unexpected approval of zoning by a conservative Supreme Court in the 1920s was no accident.[16] The mass introduction of the automobile had made comfortable, low-density suburbs possible, and zoning ensured that they stayed that way. The Court even indicated as much in its *Euclid* ruling, in which it opined that an apartment house in a good neighborhood was "a mere parasite, constructed in order to take advantage of the open spaces and attractive surroundings created by the residential character of the district."[17]

With the exception of taxation, zoning restrictions broadly construed are now perhaps the most serious abridgment of property rights in the United States. (Rent control without vacancy decontrol is certainly the most severe abridgment, but it is confined to a handful of cities, notably New York, Berkeley and Santa Monica.)[18] Zoning pits the present against the future, transferring control over property not yet built to city planners and government agencies; many restrictions are also imposed on existing property. Although this transfer of control was intentional, the long-run effects of zoning upon urban and political life were not. Several such effects have been documented by Bernard H. Siegan, a law professor at the University of San Diego.[19]

Above all, zoning has hurt the poor, who are excluded by regulations that mandate large lots or disallow small apartments. A report published by the Department of Housing and Urban Development in 1991 estimated that the repeal of local bans on renting rooms in private homes could add 3.8 million accessory apartments to the nation's housing supply. The journalist James Bovard has noted that this number is more than 20 times the number of apartments built nationwide in 1992.[20]

Zoning contributes to urban sprawl, prevents highly valued land from being put to high-value uses, causes apartment rents and housing prices to increase, hurts those without cars by requiring that stores be distant from homes, and gives big construction firms with legal departments an edge over small ones unable to cope with a maze of regulations. It also invites political corruption. "Corrupt politicians everywhere recognize zoning as a highly lucrative source of graft," Siegan noted. In Washington, D.C., Bovard has written, the city zoning board "auctions off exemptions to the zoning rules like a medieval church selling dispensations to breakers of the Ten Commandments."[21] The city's zoning plan is so rigid that almost every new building requires a variance.

As for the old argument that without zoning, glue factories would be located in residential areas, this has been falsified in cities that for decades avoided zoning ordinances—Houston being the prime example. The land-use maps of five unzoned Texas cities, including Houston, showed that "industry has largely separated itself," Siegan wrote.[22] The vast bulk of businesses are located on heavily traveled, not residential, streets. During the period in which its land-use restrictions were at their lightest, Houston was one of the most dynamic, rapidly growing cities in the United States. A plentiful supply of apartment buildings kept rentals low, and the combined forces of private property and competition effectively achieved what city planners elsewhere found impossible—as we shall see.

THE TRAGEDY OF URBAN RENEWAL

One of the greatest blows ever struck against private property in the United States occurred in the 1950s and 1960s under the auspices of a federal program called Urban Renewal. With federal financing, local government agencies were allowed to condemn "slum" neighborhoods in hundreds of cities all over the country, and then resell the land to private developers at bargain prices. Those who lived in these "blighted" neighborhoods—perhaps two-thirds of them African-American—were to be relocated in "decent, safe and sanitary housing." A stated goal of the program was "a decent home and a suitable living environment for every American family."

In addition to relocating "slum" dwellers, the program was intended to "stimulate large-scale private rebuilding, add new tax revenues to the dwindling coffers of the cities, revitalize their downtown areas, and halt the exodus of middle-class whites to the suburbs," Herbert J. Gans noted.[23] Eventually, the program destroyed five times as many low-income housing units as it created, and evicted over a million people from their homes. By the time the program was discontinued, a cumulative total of more than $12 billion, unadjusted for inflation, had been spent—perhaps $40 billion in 1998 dollars.[24]

The result is all too conspicuous in many American cities today. Hundreds of inner cities were ruined. The blight created was far worse than anything that it replaced. By 1987, *Time* magazine acknowledged that Urban Renewal had been a "well-intended and wrongheaded Federal mission" that had had the effect of tearing down "quirky, densely interwoven neighborhoods of nineteenth- and early twentieth-century low-rise buildings and putting up expensive, charmless clots of high rises. Or even worse, leaving empty tracts."[25] Tearing down buildings turned out to be easier than putting up new ones under political guidance. Charleston, South Carolina, and Savannah, Georgia, were able to resist the program, which accounts for the survival of their much praised historic districts today.

The politics driving the program were well disguised at the time. Federal money was put at the disposal of local politicians, who gave valuable subsidies to builders and developers. Some of that money then retraced its route, in the form of campaign contributions from the builders and developers to the politicians. But readers will not find any such account of the political dynamics in the early literature on the program. All reformist talk of "slums" and "urban blight" was taken at face value.

In fact, the great obstacle to the removal of old inner-city property had been the market itself. Neither owners nor tenants wanted to give it up. "What this meant in reality was that the poor, despite their poverty, still had enough buying power to make it difficult to dislodge them," as William Tucker wrote in *The Excluded Americans* (which links homelessness to government housing policy).[26] A good many of these buildings never were slums in the first place. If kept in place for another decade or so, much of the property would have been "gentrified," and would today be as much admired as other intact inner-city neighborhoods that escaped the federal bulldozer.

The congressionally approved method of clearing these "blighted" areas was the eminent domain power. But this scheme faced a constitutional hurdle: although the Fifth Amendment permitted the taking of private property for *public* use, with compensation, Urban Renewal planned to take the property and resell it to *private* developers. In the early 1950s, an owner in Washington, D.C., who did not want to surrender his property, even with compensation, filed suit. As with zoning in the 1920s, the initial response of the federal judiciary favored the plaintiff. A district court judge struck down the demolition plan for the District of Columbia, observing that there is "no more subtle means of transforming the basic concepts of our government, or shifting from the preeminence of individual rights to the preeminence of government wishes, than is afforded by redefinition of 'general welfare,' as that term is used to define the government's power of seizure. . . . [The program] amounts to a claim on the part of the authorities for unreviewable power to seize and sell whole sections of the city."[27]

This ruling was overturned by a unanimous Supreme Court, in the important case of *Berman v. Parker* (1954). Justice William Douglas "chose the occasion to concoct an expansive thesis," as Professor Roberts of Cornell noted.[28] Douglas's words, written in a time that seems in retrospect to have been a golden age for American cities, have by now acquired ironic overtones:

> Miserable and disreputable housing conditions may do more than spread disease and crime and immorality. They may also suffocate the spirit by reducing the people who live there to the status of cattle. They may indeed make living an almost insufferable burden. They may also be an ugly sore, a blight on the community which robs it of charm. . . . The concept of the public welfare is broad and inclusive. The values it represents are spiritual as well as physical, aesthetic as well as monetary. It is within the power of the legislature to determine that the community should be beautiful as well as healthy, spacious as well as clean, well-balanced as well as carefully patrolled. . . . If those who govern the District of Columbia decide that the Nation's Capital should be beautiful as well as sanitary, there is nothing in the Fifth Amendment that stands in the way.[29]

Martin Anderson, whose book *The Federal Bulldozer* was written as Urban Renewal was gathering steam, speculated that the Court's decision, significantly reducing the protection of private property in the United States, "may have more serious results than many Americans realize."[30] Indeed it did. Anderson's book was criticized at the time for being too critical; read today, it seems if anything to have underestimated the bitter consequences of Urban Renewal. The program "opened the floodgates to confiscation in the name of renewal," as James Bovard wrote in *Lost Rights*.[31]

All along, it was private property rights that had acted as the great protector of poor neighborhoods; with Urban Renewal, property rights were replaced by political control. If we want to preserve neighborhoods, a multiplicity of private owners will do the job infinitely better than an office full of urban planners. Their incentives are quite different. What city planners do not anticipate is that their best-laid plans must continually give way to pressure from politicians with short time horizons. On the other hand, private owners—in poor neighborhoods as in rich—have a direct, vested interest in seeing that their properties are well maintained, and so remain attractive to potential buyers.

The Urban Renewal Program was discontinued in 1973. It did its damage in the 1950s and 1960s—just as land reform was being imposed abroad. It is not entirely misleading to think of Urban Renewal as equivalent to a "land reform" that Americans imposed on themselves. Property was undermined so that the poor would be helped. One difference between the two programs is that very much more money was spent bulldozing away the core of American cities than redistributing foreign land. Recovery from the damage that was inflicted abroad will probably be more rapid than that at home, where the politicians will not easily relinquish the control that they gained.

Housing for the poor is now widely thought of as something that politicians must provide, because the unaided market will not. What is forgotten in this view is that it was the market that provided housing for people of low incomes in the past. When new housing was built, it would be occupied by those of middle and upper-middle income. The apartments and houses that they vacated then became available for those who earned less. This process is known as "filtering" in the housing business. William Tucker points out that in the years 1900-1930, "developers put up a stunning 80,000 housing units per year in New York," perhaps the greatest level of housing construction in American history, perhaps in world history.[32] The tremendous expansion of New York at that time was easily accommodated with little role for the government beyond mainte-nance of the rule of law.

Today, thanks to no-growth and slow-growth laws, intense regulation, rent control and the general suspicion with which free-market housing is viewed in the cities, all that has changed. In San Francisco in 1995, for example, a mere 532 new units were built, a good many of them set aside for low-income residents. (This in practice means the politically connected, because the demand for such units is vastly greater than the supply.) Housing prices in San Francisco are double the national average, occupancy rates at a historic high.

A parallel development is occurring with automobiles, and once again the poor will be the losers. Automobile manufacturers never made cars for poor people, but poor people bought cars nonetheless, thanks to the used-car market. Even migrant workers and Mexican immigrants could afford a rusty Datsun or an old Buick. Thanks to the 1990 amendments to the Clean Air Act, however, such cars are likely to be labeled "gross polluters" or "smog belchers," words that play the same role for cars, and may lead to the same outcome, as "slums" and "urban blight" did for housing in the 1950s. Over 90 percent of automobile emissions have already been eliminated, but the stricter standards often will be too costly for the poor to meet, and their cars could be removed from the road. The wealthy will have no problems, but the poor in many cases may be consigned to mass transit.

ENVIRONMENTAL TAKINGS

After a while, policy intellectuals understood that zoning and slum clearance were not achieving their intended results. But their desire to control the development, use and exchange of property—to feudalize it—remained as strong as ever. As criticism of urban planning mounted, "a savior in the form of the environmental movement arrived," Bernard Siegan noted. A new rationale was established for achieving much the same goal. Since the air was polluted, resources were running out and species were endangered, even stricter regulations would be needed. "Whereas formerly the argument was about the kind of project that should be permitted, it now often became a question whether there should be any development at all," Siegan added.[33]

In its effect on property, the most important thrust of the environmental movement has been the Endangered Species Act, which became law in 1973 without a dissenting vote in Congress. Good intentions and a popular misconception of what was afoot eventually transferred vast powers from private owners to the federal government. In the popular imagination, thriving and beautiful species had been extinguished by mere carelessness: sportsmen had blazed away at swarms of passenger pigeons, until the last one was alone in a cage. That shouldn't happen again. "They thought they were protecting bald eagles, grizzly bears and whooping cranes," commented Ike Sugg of the Competitive Enterprise Institute. "Little did they know that they would be protecting distinct population segments of cockroaches and flies."[34]

The Endangered Species Act does not distinguish between species, subspecies and "distinct populations."[35] Peterson's *Field Guide to Mammals* notes that some authors recognize as many as 74 species of grizzly bear, while others recognize only 1. By siding with the splitters rather than the lumpers, environmentalists were able to multiply the number of "species" said to be endangered. With a little searching and digging, it became possible to find a local variety of almost anything, and to claim that any economic activity in that spot would disturb its nesting or mating. Through August, 1994, 1,452 species have been listed as endangered or "threatened." They can be found in every state, and most do rely on private land for some or all of their habitat. One of the best known was the Tennessee snail darter, which delayed construction of the Tellico

Dam. Later, the small fish turned up in many places and it became clear that it never had been endangered.

Biologists believe that in the history of life, 99.9 percent of all species have become extinct, the vast majority before *Homo sapiens* arrived on the scene. In no instance is the cause definitely known. Recent claims that human activity has caused a rapid increase in the rate of extinction have never been documented. Harvard biologist Edward O. Wilson said that large numbers of species are "apparently vanishing before they can be discovered," and, citing "independent studies" and "anecdotal reports," he projected a 50 percent reduction of rain-forest species by the middle of the next century.[36] He and Paul R. Ehrlich of Stanford University have used such projections to urge that governments everywhere "cease 'developing' any more relatively undisturbed land."[37] (Their argument was based on the belief that world population would double by 2050, which is no longer considered likely.[38])

Using laws that go back to Justinian, governments have long claimed sovereignty over wild (unowned) animals. In the United States, this "public trust" at first resided with the states, but, like so much else, it was transferred to the federal government step by step. At first the law said it was a crime to "take" listed species. "Harm" was then added to "take," and through court rulings "harm" was interpreted more and more freely. In 1984, a federal judge ruled that "habitat modification" could constitute "harm" and therefore a taking of the animal, and could be construed as a crime, even without any decline in numbers.

At that point, "habitat" became a word that land owners dreaded to hear. If a listed species landed on your property, or near it, it was as though it brought its own property rights with it, just as Garrett Hardin had earlier recommended. In *U.S. v. Anderson Logging Co.*, the federal government enjoined a private landowner from clearing 72 acres of timber on private land because one pair of northern spotted owls were nesting one and a half miles away on government land.[39] Substitute people for owls, and this would have been considered intolerable. "If a homeless person finds his or her way onto an individual's private property," Jonathan Adler of the Competitive Enterprise Institute noted, the owner would not have to forfeit the use of that property and let the homeless person remain.[40]

Richard Stroup of the Political Economy Research Center added: "The Constitution explicitly forbids the U.S. Army, even in the name of national defense, from requiring that a citizen quarter a soldier (that is, provide food and shelter for a soldier). Yet the government can require the same citizen to quarter a grizzly bear, a spotted owl, or any other member of a threatened or endangered species, at the landowner's expense." He added the following significant point: If the army had the same power to billet soldiers that the Fish and Wildlife Service has to billet animals, "we could expect to see soldiers feared, despised and perhaps even ambushed, as listed species reportedly are today."[41]

Indeed, the Endangered Species Act was putting in danger the very animals it was supposed to protect. The law (as expansively interpreted) had radically altered the incentives of owners, but this, of course, was not understood by the animals that might stray onto the property now set aside for them. "'The incentives are wrong,' the former Fish and Wildlife Service Administrator for the state of Texas admitted. 'If I have a rare metal on my property, its value goes up. But if a rare bird occupies the land, its value disappears.'"[42]

Listed species on private land brought with them the prospect of severe penalties, and owners saw them as a threat to their livelihoods. An undeclared defense doctrine was formulated: "Shoot, shovel and shut up." Good conservation practices became actually imprudent. A family in Riverside County, California, fallowed their fields every four years, letting brush and weeds grow, creating a wildlife habitat for meadowlarks and sparrows. But one day the kangaroo rat appeared, and the kangaroo rat is endangered. Now, the family was denied the use of its land. Ploughing would constitute an illegal "take" of the rat, and would subject the owner to a $50,000 fine and/or a year in prison per rat disturbed. Over three years, the family incurred over $400,000 in lost income and expenditures on kangaroo rat regulations.[43]

Two years later, officials disallowed a request for firebreaks on the land, and in October, 1993, a fire devastated over 25,000 acres and 29 homes, burning nearly all of the rat study area and surrounding lands. The regulations "have placed ourselves and the species and habitats in adversarial roles," the owner testified. "We are no longer pleased to see an eagle, or a hawk or a previously unnoticed flower on our land. Sights like these now cause us great concern that our livelihood and our heritage will be stripped away from us."[44]

An owner of 8,000 acres in Greensboro, North Carolina, was put in the same predicament, and he did something about it. For years, he managed his land for the benefit of wildlife. By 1991, however, he was playing host to 29 red cockaded woodpeckers—listed as endangered. His careful management, with controlled burns and preservation of "old growth," was just right for them. But Fish and Wildlife Service guidelines stipulated that a circle with a half-mile radius was the habitat of each bird colony (since reduced to a quarter mile). The human owner thereby lost one-fourth of his property to the woodpecker—and as a direct result of his good stewardship. (One is reminded of owners who lose control of their architecturally distinguished properties to historic preservation laws.) To forestall a total loss of the use of his property, he has since been clear-cutting rapidly where the woodpecker has not yet taken over. The clear-cut area "looks like ground zero of a nuclear explosion," according to a visitor.[45]

It is worth briefly contrasting the environmental regulation of property with the taking of it by eminent domain. In the latter case, the property is frankly taken and the owners are compensated (even if insufficiently, and in circumstances not anticipated by the framers of the Constitution). In the former, owners retain title, but their rights are sharply circumscribed. Untold thousands of Americans have been prevented from building homes, plowing fields, filling in ditches, clearing brush and repairing fences, all on their own land. Private land is thereby taken for public use, but without compensation. Thus, the open socializing of property by planners has been replaced by the more subversive "feudalizing" of it by environmentalists. Humans retain a nominal title that is encumbered by many duties, mostly negative; not for the benefit of higher lords, but mostly for animals, vegetables and minerals. If the condition of our city centers is any guide, the costs of the former appear to have been higher. But only at first sight is this true. The major cost of environmental regulation of property does not show up visibly at all, because it consists mostly of foregone value; of houses and amenities not built that otherwise would have been.

Many other environmental rules have greatly expanded federal power and undermined the rights of property owners. Wetlands regulations provide a dramatic example. In 1900, the Supreme Court had characterized wetlands as "the cause of malarial and malignant fevers," and opined that "the police power is never more legitimately exercised than in removing such nuisances."[46] Today, however it is the preservation of wetlands that is used to undermine private property rights. Amazingly, no wetlands law has ever been passed by Congress. Instead, the Clean Water Act of 1972 was more and more expansively interpreted by the Environmental Protection Agency and the U.S. Army Corps of Engineers, even though the act does not mention wetlands. Applying first to navigable waterways, the act was stretched until it finally covered mudflats, sandflats, sloughs, prairie potholes, wet meadows and large puddles. Law-abiding Americans were sent to prison for the crime of filling in ditches on their own land. Lands could be classified as wetlands even if they were dry for 350 days of the year and as small as puddles. The Corps of Engineers official who had helped write the "Federal Manual for Identifying and Delineating Jurisdictional Wetlands" declared that "for regulatory purposes, a wetland is whatever we decide it is."[47] Here, indeed, was the feudalism that the law professors of an earlier generation had hankered after.

Federal jurisdiction was claimed in ways that could have been written by the satirists of *Saturday Night Live*. Prairie potholes could affect interstate commerce, it was argued, because geese flying from one state to another could glance down and spot a waterhole—the "glancing geese" test. Federal judge Daniel Manion of the seventh circuit argued that "the commerce power as construed by the courts is indeed expansive, but not so expansive as to authorize regulation of puddles merely because a bird travelling interstate might decide to stop for a drink."[48] He was overruled *en banc*. Private property, viewed by this time with growing respect in China and the former Soviet Union, was under mounting attack in the United States, with the help of regulatory contrivances that could only be described as bizarre.

The most important unintended consequence of all this has been the emergence of an explicit property-rights movement in the United States. By 1995, it was said to comprise over a thousand groups, many of little more than household size, but some, like Peggy Riegle's Fairness to Land Owners Committee, with over 15,000 members in all 50 states. They have played a major role in alerting legislators and in giving legal assistance to beleaguered landowners.[49]

The Supreme Court held in 1922, in *Pennsylvania Coal v. Mahon,* that "if regulation goes too far, it will be recognized as a taking," but by the time of *Lucas v. South Carolina Coastal,* just 70 years later, respect for private property had declined so far that the Court left open the possibility that landowners were due no compensation as long as the regulation left them with *some* economic value. By 1994, however, the property-rights movement had became powerful enough to ensure that the Republican Party's Contract with America included a call for revised legislation on this point. In the House of Representatives, the "Private Property Protection Act of 1995" passed by a vote of 277 to 148. It provided for compensation when agency action diminished the value of a parcel of land by more than 20 percent (but was limited to endangered species, wetlands and water-rights regulations). Later, the bill died in the Senate. (In May, 1998, 29 animals and plants listed as endangered or threatened were removed from the list, including the bald eagle, the gray wolf and the peregrine falcon. This was "intended in part to blunt criticism from congressional opponents who complain that endangered-species laws don't work."[50])

THE MORE GENERAL PROBLEM

It is not just private control over land and real estate that has become far more circumscribed. Salary and wages are subject to imposts that know no theoretical limit. Because some level of taxation is legitimate, the assault on this crucial "stream" of property—income—has been little remarked by the defenders of property rights. We hardly notice how remarkable it is that today vendors must keep a record of every voluntary exchange of goods and services, and be prepared to report the total to Washington and surrender, under penalty of prison, whatever fraction the state decrees. At times in the twentieth century, the federal income tax has demanded over 90 percent at the margin. At the same time the erosion of savings by inflation has been more than tolerated by policymakers. The taxation of interest on the shrinking residue has made it difficult for the middle class to preserve its independence from the state.

Shortly after the Berlin Wall fell, Milton Friedman calculated that spending by governments at all levels amounted to about 45 percent of national income, and by that test, "government owns 45 percent of the means of production that produce the national income. The United States is now 45 percent socialist," he wrote. But regulations and controls of the kind detailed above are not counted in the figure, which therefore "underestimates the degree of socialism in the U.S., perhaps appreciably."[51]

War has historically been the great enemy of liberty and source of central control over economic life. What is unprecedented in the United States and western Europe is the continued growth of government at a time of protracted and almost uninterrupted peace. At 21.5 percent of GDP at the end of 1997, federal tax revenues in the United States were higher than they were at the peak of World War II (20.1 percent), and in fact than at any time in the history of the United States.[52] (Total revenues collected by federal, state and local governments reached the highest level ever in 1995). As for western Europe, the average share of state spending in the countries of the European Union was 51 percent of GDP in 1995, up from 34 percent in 1961. In Sweden, the figure is now fully two-thirds of GPD.[53]

Nonetheless, the United States has retained its economic lead in the world. This only shows that the situation has been worse elsewhere. But if these numbers are not reduced, and a greater freedom is not given to wage earners and the owners of private property generally, we may predict the decline of the West, relative to more dynamic economies elsewhere, in the next century. It is a good sign, at least, that since the demise of the Soviet Union, it has become respectable to discuss the problem of economic growth in terms of private property. But there is as yet little sign of let-up in the struggle by Western intellectuals to gain more and more political control.

It is difficult to explain these developments as anything other than a counterrevolution on the part of the intellectual classes who saw the rise of contract, the security of property and exchange by consent as depriving them of power. The Glorious, Industrial, American and French Revolutions had distributed property and power more equally than ever before, and so had set the stage for capitalism. Before that, monarchs, nobility and clergy had enjoyed vast power over the common people. Modern intellectuals, surely, have been striving to recapture that kind of power for themselves in our day. Private property, freely exchanged, has been their greatest obstacle. In the late nineteenth century, the goal was to abolish that obstacle. But when abolition was actually achieved in some countries, all without exception became impoverished. The new struggle is no longer to abolish property, but to encumber it with many restrictions: fines and fees, taxes, takings, regulations, impositions.

Under the older plan, the socialists at least undertook responsibility for production. True, they were unable to produce the goods, but it can be said in favor of the early socialists that they had every intention of doing so. The socialization of property would transform production, they believed. Consumer goods, Nikita Khrushchev said, would "gush forth abundantly" under communism. But they had not studied what they had destroyed, and so they did not understand that its replacement was unworkable.

The feudalization of property, on the other hand, is both a more workable reform and a more openly parasitical one. Private owners are expected to go on producing the goods even as their rights are converted into legal obligations. Their overlords in the redistributive classes and the state apparatus repudiate all responsibility for production, taxing away what they can, keeping a portion for themselves and channeling the residue to privileged recipients, who will vote them back into office. This (we are led to believe) will bring into being a more virtuous, more just, more egalitarian and more secure world. The true goal would seem to be the maintenance of an orderly control over a people who are conceived of as unable to see what is in their own best interest and who, if left to their own devices, will produce little more than anarchy, vulgarity and injustice.

Even as the political war on property was intensifying, however, a welcome change was slowly occurring in the academy. By the 1960s, the subject of property and its relationship to economic activity at last began to attract the attention of economists. One or two of them would go on to win the Nobel Prize.

TWENTY

THE
REDISCOVERY OF
PROPERTY

IN ROUNDABOUT FASHION, economic theory slowly made its way back towards its essential foundations in property. The economist often credited with having started this movement is Armen Alchian, the coauthor of a well-respected textbook, *University Economics*.[1] He taught at UCLA for many years, and he wrote the articles on "Property Rights" for the *New Palgrave Dictionary of Economics* and for the *Fortune Encyclopedia of Economics*. In a 1981 discussion with a number of prominent economists about recent developments in their field, he said at one point: "I feel like a monkey who sat at the typewriter and typed out $E=mc^2$ or something like that, and along came Einstein a little later on and interpreted it. I am constantly amazed at the idea that somehow, and it's always nice to hear, I've played a role in establishing a new field called property rights."[2]

It's remarkable that as recently as 1981, "property rights" was thought of as a new "field" in economics. In fact, property is not so much a field as it is a foundation for all the fields of economics. Alchian's first exploration of the topic had come earlier, in an article about academic tenure published in 1958.[3] He and another economist at UCLA, William Meckling, had been discussing the problem of tenure for university professors. It was an "entirely stupid" system, Meckling commented. But Alchian responded that "it's been around," its survival suggesting that it played a useful function, even if it was not immediately apparent.[4] After going back and forth, Alchian concluded that "it was the result of the kind of property-rights structure in the university, as contrasted with private, for-profit enterprise." Universities, of course, are nonprofit institutions.

In the course of their discussions, the "well known Nobel Prize winner came in one day and said, 'Property rights have no effect on people's behavior.'" Alchian was "taken aback by that," although he believed that the economist later changed his mind. "But at least it gave me an idea at that time that maybe there is more in this whole area than I thought there was," Alchian added.[5]

Academic tenure, a contract giving professors job security until retirement, in the absence of offenses involving moral turpitude or loss of mental competence, is normally explained by the need to protect "the search for truth." This did not satisfy Alchian, however, because competition— between schools, and between teachers themselves—should itself be sufficient to promote truth over falsity. A better explanation seemed to be that tenure was connected to "the absence of the ordinary kind of property rights that exist in profit-seeking businesses."[6]

Many for-profit educational establishments do exist—schools of accounting, art, music, foreign languages and so forth. But universities are almost always non-profit institutions, with no clear-cut owner in the conventional sense. There are merely trustees and managers and administrators, who are unable to appropriate as profits any net gains in wealth. But money that cannot easily be taken out of an enterprise in the form of profits will be consumed within it, in ways that give satisfaction to employees and administrators. And administrators have their own incentives. Unproductive workers who would be fired in a profit-seeking business "will be more readily kept" in a nonprofit, Alchian concluded. There, administrators will accept employment practices that yield a more peaceful life. One such policy is greater job security; in short, tenure. The tendency of nonprofit institutions to dissipate income in the form of comfortable working conditions is reinforced in universities by institutional endowments and "noncustomer income sources," Alchian added.[7] Alumni gifts fall into this category.

"The whole issue [is] in Adam Smith's famous section on the University," Alchian said. In Book 5 of *The Wealth of Nations,* Smith noted that the endowments of universities had "necessarily diminished" the industry of the faculty. At some institutions, the teacher was even prohibited from receiving a fee from his pupils. In such cases, the teacher's interest was "set as directly in opposition to his duty as it is possible to be," Smith wrote. Since it is in everyone's interest "to live as much at his ease as he can," the teacher whose salary is unaffected by his performance will be disposed to neglect his duties. Smith, who had been disappointed in his own teachers at Oxford, wrote that professors "are likely to make a common cause, to be all very indulgent to one another, and every man to consent that his neighbour may neglect his duty, provided he himself is allowed to neglect his own. In the University of Oxford, the greater part of the publick professors have, for these many years, given up altogether even the pretence of teaching."[8]

Not found in Smith's analysis, however, was the explicit joining of the issue to the property rights of administrators. Armen Alchian's analysis was too abstract, and it says something about the nature of discourse within the modern academic world that economists evidently didn't think much about so important an issue as the economic consequences of property rights until they considered their own employment arrangements. Nonetheless, the novel and important feature of Alchian's article was the explanation of an economic anomaly (tenure) by reference to the underlying structure of ownership.

After writing his essay on tenure, Alchian became more interested in property issues and began to examine books on law. What did they have to say about the distinctions between private, public and communal property rights? He could find hardly anything illuminating these crucial distinctions. He looked into Pollock and Maitland's *History of English Law before the Time of Edward I,* which seemed to show that when human institutions are subjected to competition, they "evolve over time," with property rights becoming better defined. Here was the theory that Douglass North would later criticize. And Alchian himself was not able to get very far with it. Why didn't these same pressures, in the direction of better defined property rights, operate in countries all over the world?

A paper of Alchian's, "Some Economics of Property Rights," circulated in manuscript for a number of years without finding a home. Finally, in 1965, a publisher in Italy accepted it.[9] Again, Alchian noted the surprising neglect. Search through the fields of economics classified by the American Economic Association, he wrote, and you find "no mention of the word 'property'."[10] He tactfully allowed that this oversight might be because economists were already familiar with "the pervasiveness of the effects of various forms of property." But that seemed unlikely. More probably, he wrote, economists had "forgotten about the possibility" of undertaking a systematic analysis of the subject. Another possibility was that they had overlooked the subject entirely.

Alchian also analyzed the relationship between property and competition, seeking to refine the observation that owners may do what they want with their own property as long as they don't harm anyone else's. Competition does its own "harm," of course. If I open a restaurant and win away your business, he noted, you may be as hurt as if I had burned part of your building. Then again, "If I open a restaurant and pour smells and smoke over your neighboring land then I have changed the physical attributes of your property; I have violated your private property rights."[11] The former is permissible, the latter may not be. The protection of property, therefore, does not shield one owner from the competition of others. The free-market system therefore depends crucially not just on "private property," but on a particular interpretation of that phrase.

A key difference between private and public ownership is not simply that profit is permissible with the former, Alchian observed. The point is that we can own and sell "shares" in private property but not in public property—a municipal auditorium, let us say.[12] Town residents are its "owners," but cannot receive the capitalized value deriving from the sale of shares in it. Such an auditorium might nonetheless be run at a profit, if its administrators charged a rental fee that more than covered the costs.*

Alchian made a number of other points. He liked to stress that property rights are not always enforced by police power. More frequently, we rely on prevailing ethical and social standards, on custom, etiquette and on the fear of ostracism.[13] Individuals usually "will not stand idly by while some other person's property is stolen," he noted. What he wrote was by no means the last word on property—as he acknowledged—but it was an important first step, and one that had been too long delayed. Alchian "played the leading role in the development of a theory of property rights," the economist Ronald H. Coase has written.[14]

For a continuation of the story, we must now turn to Ronald Coase. He was the "Einstein" who "came along later," in Alchian's account. A contemporary of Alchian's (Coase was born in 1910, Alchian four years later), he helped to pioneer the field that became known as law and economics. Indirectly, and almost inadvertently, this field further helped reunite economic analysis and the structure of ownership. Coase was at the University of Chicago, and the irony is that the economists of the Chicago school who promoted law and economics seldom wrote about property. Frank Knight, a Chicago economist of an earlier generation, had published an influential 1924 paper, "Fallacies in the Interpretation of Social Cost," highlighting the social function of ownership.[15] But the prominent Chicagoans George Stigler and Milton Friedman paid little attention

---

*But they are unlikely to do so because the incentives of managers and town residents will discourage such a policy. Elected managers can curry favor with the voters by charging a minimal fee. The users would prefer to get the auditorium for nothing. The only residents who would prefer "economical" management would be non-politicians with no interest in using the facility— precisely the group with an attenuated interest in such an outcome. They are unlikely to spend time thinking about the issue or lobbying for "economic" rental practices. The historic Seventh Regiment Armory building in New York City illustrates the problem. It houses a multimillion-dollar art collection, yet it is in serious disrepair, with crumbling ceilings and leaky walls. *New York Times* reporters noted the paradox that, "while repairs and maintenance have been postponed for lack of money, the obscure state agency that runs the building has rented out the armory's huge former drill hall for exhibitions at what amounts to bargain-basement prices to a small group of show sponsors. Exhibition promoters clamor for dates that many experts say can produce $1 million in profits for a show running a week to 10 days. But the state rents the space without competitive bidding for less than $7,000 a day." Selwyn Raab and Carol Vogel, "Neglected Urban Armory Battles for Survival," *New York Times,* March 6, 1998.

to the subject. As for Coase's most famous article, it was not ostensibly about property rights at all.

THE COASE THEOREM

Earlier in this book, an attempt was made to distinguish between the influence of law on the economy, and the reciprocal influence of economic outcomes on the body of the law. Typically, law and economics has been more interested in the latter; so much so that Morton Horwitz of Harvard Law School said that, like "vulgar Marxism," it treats law as "superstructure," merely reflecting "what is 'real' in the 'base' of economic rationality."[16] To be sure, it has also noted the ways in which the law affects behavior, predicting "how rational individuals will respond to [legal] rules," as the economist David Friedman put it.[17] The law, whether made by legislatures or by courts, is viewed as "a system of incentives intended to affect behavior."

Examples are familiar, but sometimes the economic consequences of the law are not anticipated. Minimum-wage laws raise the rate of unemployment. Rent-control laws are supposed to benefit tenants, but their long-run effect is more complex: those with apartments when the law is enacted are rewarded, but future tenants, who may not be able to find an apartment at all, will be penalized. Builders will be discouraged, and the city itself may slide into ruin if the law is left unchanged for long enough. Such analysis dates back at least to Adam Smith's discussion of the economic effects of mercantilist legislation. Milton Friedman included a fair measure of "law and economics," so defined, in his *Capitalism and Freedom* (1962).[18] In pointing out the unintended consequences of farm price supports, compulsory Social Security and minimum-wage laws, he was, quite simply, applying economic analysis to changes in the law. Hundreds of such examples could be given.

In 1959, Ronald Coase wrote an article about the Federal Communications Commission, arguing that it was not necessary for the government to allocate radio and television licenses to applicants; market processes could do so, by first establishing property rights in the airwaves and then selling licenses to the highest bidders. In response to those, such as Justice Felix Frankfurter, who said that regulation was essential because there is "a fixed natural limitation upon the number of stations that can operate without interfering with one another," Coase replied that airwaves were in this respect no different from other economic goods. And those who said that competition would lead to chaos had it all wrong. The real problem was that "no property rights were created in these scarce frequencies." He continued:

If one person could use a piece of land for growing a crop, and then another could come along and build a house on the land used for the crop, and then another could come along, tear down the house and use the space as a parking lot, it would no doubt be accurate to describe the resulting situation as chaos. But it would be wrong to blame this on private enterprise and the competitive system. A private-enterprise system cannot function properly unless property rights are created in resources, and when this is done someone wishing to use a resource has to pay the owner to obtain it. Chaos disappears: and so does the government except that a legal system to define property rights and to arbitrate disputes is, of course, necessary.[19]

As to interference between signals, he concluded that the market would take care of this, too, just as it does with real property. Houses do not have to be set so far apart that *no* noise from one reaches others. Expensive houses can be well separated, inexpensive ones huddled together. Analysis of this "spillover," or externality effect, from one property to another then increasingly preoccupied Coase, and it became the basis for his next and most influential article, "The Problem of Social Cost."[20] When Coase won the Nobel Prize in 1991, this article was cited by the Swedish Academy. Steven Cheung, a student of Armen Alchian's, speculated that it "may well be the most cited economic paper of our time," with almost 700 citations between 1966 and 1980.[21]

Coase's article was published in *The Journal of Law and Economics*, which was started in 1958 at the University of Chicago; Aaron Director, another founder of law and economics, was its first editor. The journal was intended as an alternative to the strongly statist tendency of economics departments at that time. No outcome, it seemed, could then satisfy the determined critic of markets. It was joked that economists attributed rising prices to monopoly, falling prices to predatory producers, and unchanging prices to collusion. Director also taught an economics course at the University of Chicago Law School. Some of those who took it went through "what can only be called a religious conversion," said Robert Bork, who was among that number. "It changed our view of the entire world."[22]

Coase's article took issue with A. C. Pigou's claim, in *The Economics of Welfare*, that the "followers of the classical economists" had been too optimistic in suggesting that "the free play of self-interest," without government interference, was sufficient to maximize economic performance. [23] Even Adam Smith had not realized the extent to which the system of natural liberty must be "guarded by special laws" if it is to promote the most productive use of a country's resources, Pigou thought. Pigou illustrated his argument with the familiar examples of externalities. Smoke in towns, for example, "inflicts a heavy uncharged loss on the community, in injury to buildings and vegetables, expenses for washing clothes and cleaning rooms," and so on. The point is that the cost of living with this smoke is borne not by the factory, but by the surrounding community: the cost is "socialized."

Coase replied that in such cases of "negative externality," government intervention is often not necessary, because nearby owners can themselves negotiate mutually satisfactory solutions. His analysis became known as the Coase theorem, and this illustration of it has been repeated in almost every exposition of law and economics. A railroad runs beside a farm, and the engine emits sparks, damaging adjacent crops. No matter who has the legal right (to emit or to be free from sparks), Coase pointed out, the use of resources would be the same, because whoever valued that right most highly would buy it from the other. If, for example, the railroad values the right more highly than the farmer, and the farmer has the right to be spark free, the railroad will buy that right from the farmer.

"Whichever way the legal right is assigned," as Richard Posner wrote in his *Economic Analysis of Law,* "the result, in terms of resource use, is the same: the railroad emits sparks and the farmer moves his crops."[24] There is a difference in that in one case a sum of money is transferred from the railroad to the farmer, in the other case not. But the use of resources is the same, whoever has the property right. This outcome was thought paradoxical, and was disbelieved at first. "There were these intimations to me that my views were wrong," Coase said. Then teaching at the University of Virginia, he was summoned to Chicago to defend his position. A group gathered at Aaron Director's house for what George Stigler called "one of the most exciting intellectual events of my life." Milton Friedman was among the doubters. But Coase "refused to yield to all our erroneous arguments," Stigler recalled. "Milton would hit him from one side, then from another, then from another. Then to our horror, Milton missed him and hit us." By the end of the evening, everyone agreed that Coase was right.[25]

His original goal had been to show that problems that arise between adjacent owners do not have to be resolved by state intervention; the parties affected can themselves negotiate a solution. Then he realized that no matter which party had the right, the use of resources would be the same. The finding may be summarized as follows: When owners are in a position to resolve a "border" conflict by negotiation, the use of resources will be unaffected by the initial allocation of the "property right." It was George Stigler who named it the Coase theorem.

Obliquely, the Coase theorem drew attention to one of the key contentions in this book: that transferable (exchangeable) property rights are the key to economic efficiency, to amity between neighbors and to peaceful relations in society more generally. Coase's insight has since been reformulated as one of the most basic principles of economics: When goods are owned in a well-defined way, and the rights to them are exchangeable, they will be purchased by those who value them most highly. Resources will be put to their highest-valued use. This conclusion could have been arrived at directly, of course, without going through the rigmarole of externalities. But Pigou had brought the subject up, and essentially what Coase did was return economic analysis to the "optimistic" position of the classical economists. Problems arising at the "borders" of property can be solved by private negotiation, and are not in themselves sufficient to overthrow market economics.

At a time when formerly socialist countries are faced with the task of privatization, the Coase theorem suggests a preliminary answer to the question: to whom should public property be sold? Economically, Coase implied, it doesn't much matter, as long as *someone* becomes the owner. "It doesn't matter who owns what," as Coase put it in a more recent interview.[26] If someone else values the good more highly than the existing owner, then he can buy it from the first.

This conclusion contrasts with earlier conceptions of property, showing that, in an important respect, free-market property does differ from its feudal prototype. In ages past, as the word implies, property was thought to be "proper to" its ancient owner and his lineage. Feudal property was so static that transferability was not usually thought of as one of its incidents. The owner of the medieval castle was well known. But who knows who owns the modern skyscraper? The economist's insight is that it does not matter very much who does (and therefore we don't need to know), but it does matter a great deal that the legal system permits *someone* (or some corporation) to own it—and to be free to sell it to the highest bidder.

A DETOUR INTO TRANSACTION COSTS

At this point we must introduce a complication that played an influential role in the development of law and economics. It may also have been misleading. Coase added that his argument was true only on the assumption that there are "no costs of making transactions." We are familiar with the idea of transaction costs, if not the name. They are the costs of making an exchange—over and above the price of the goods themselves. Going to the grocery store involves costs of time and transportation; in a snowstorm, those costs could be high. If you don't know where the store is, the cost will be higher still. In view of the need to stand in line, transaction costs in Communist countries were always very high. When they are high, then, exchange, or the transfer of property rights, becomes an expensive business in itself.

In the case of the smoke-emitting factory, for example, the costs involved in negotiating with those affected may be very high because there probably are many such. The factory owners cannot proceed with negotiations, then, because the cost of negotiating with all the homeowners would be higher than the benefits receivable. In such cases, an economically "inefficient" state of affairs is said to exist, and the private solution becomes impossible. The simplest solution may be a pollution tax, or something like it.

Coase, however, felt emboldened to suggest that such inefficiencies could be eliminated by reassigning the rights (to pollute, to emit sparks) to the party that values it most highly. He argued that courts "should, insofar as this is possible without creating too much uncertainty about the legal position itself, take these [economic] consequences into account when making their deci-sions."[27] Here he had arrived at something quite different from a mere economic analysis of law. He was offering a criterion whereby legal disputes could be adjudicated in particular cases. Justice itself should be subordinated to efficiency—to economics. Economists were for the most part delighted with this bold foray. In slipping past border guards into the contiguous discipline of law, he had begun to colonize a new field, bringing with him the economist's supposedly value-free methodology—cost-benefit analysis.

It was Richard A. Posner, a professor at the University of Chicago Law School, and later a judge on the U.S. Court of Appeals for the Seventh Circuit, who most prominently made the case for Coase. In his influential book *The Economic Analysis of Law,* he argued not only that the criterion of efficiency could be used to determine the law, but that it often had been so used in the past. Common-law judges had been closet economists, apparently, and in making their rulings had often been guided by efficiency as a surrogate for justice. And if only modern-day judges would learn a little economics (as Posner had), the "efficient" solution to legal problems would become clear, and age-old quandaries of the law would be resolved.

To those who said he was demeaning justice, as traditionally understood, Posner replied that "perhaps the most common" meaning of justice simply *is* efficiency.[28] When people say that it is "unjust" to convict people without trial, for example, or to take property without compensation, "they can be interpreted as meaning nothing more pretentious than that the conduct in question wastes resources." Posner later watered down this equation of justice and efficiency to the weaker claim that there appears to be "no fundamental inconsistency" between the two.[29] Then he weakened it again, saying (no doubt correctly this time) that such moral principles as honesty, trustworthiness, charity and the avoidance of negligence and coercion "serve in general to promote efficiency."

Here, then, was a curious sequence of events. First, an imaginary locomotive (or factory) was portrayed as showering sparks (smoke) on enough farmers (or households) to render compensatory negotiations with them difficult. This might perpetuate an inefficient state of affairs (meaning that the railroad or the factory would be willing to pay compensation, were it not for the cost of working out the deal). Then, by 1973, Posner was arguing in print that judges should decide their cases on the basis of efficiency, which was really the same thing as justice. And within a few years, law and economics courses were teaching this strange doctrine in the leading American law schools.

Some legal minds were intrigued by the bracing possibilities of a value-free approach to the law. Perhaps cases really could be decided by ruling for the party who valued a right most highly; or, in cases of liability, for the party who could avoid the fault at the least cost. Perhaps the complexities of right and wrong really could be finessed by substituting this apparently neutral calculus of cost and benefit. Other legal scholars were not so pleased, however. They suspected that Coase and Posner had between them contrived a conjuring trick. But what was it, exactly?

Posner had written that "it may be possible to deduce the basic formal characteristics of law itself from economic theory."[30] To which Arthur Leff of Yale added: "And then do it in a two-page chapter. What bliss."[31] A dismayed Morton Horwitz of Harvard Law wrote that "science," which he put in quotation marks just as Posner had put "justice," had given the "cloak of legitimacy" to the "Posnerian school."[32] It's worth noting that these Ivy League skeptics were themselves halfway disarmed by Posner's positivism—his repudiation of conventional moral norms. He seemed to have found a way of validating market outcomes without actually advocating anything. There had to be a trick. Arthur Leff hunted for the "smuggled normative." Frank Michelman of Harvard saw (correctly) that there was something "tautological, non-empirical, or non-falsifiable" about the whole enterprise.[33] Ronald Dworkin of Oxford perhaps came closest to seeing what was going on. The whole notion of efficiency was a "consequence," not a "cause," of individual rights, he wrote.[34]

PROPERTY AND EFFICIENCY

According to Vilfredo Pareto's definition, efficiency is the economic state that is arrived at by mutually consensual exchange. This means (neglecting transaction costs) that whatever owners voluntarily do with their property is by definition efficient. Efficient is as property does. The following (real-life) case illustrates the point. In 1994, a Japanese-American farmer owned a 58-acre strawberry farm across the street from Disneyland. He sold his fruit for a dollar a bag from a roadside stand. His work involved rising at 5 A.M., turning on windmills in the middle of the night when frost threatened, and so on. The *Los*

Angeles Times reported that he was at one point offered $2 million an acre by Michael Eisner, who took him to lunch in Disneyland. "I couldn't see it," the farmer told a reporter. "I'm not what you call business-oriented people."[35] Economists nonetheless readily agree that his land is being used efficiently. Cost-benefit analysis must include nonmonetary satisfaction on the "benefit" side, and this reduces economists to saying merely that Disney did not offer him enough money to induce him to sell. Thus efficiency is in practice subordinate to property. This was the "smuggled normative" that Professor Leff sought. In economic discourse, therefore, efficient simply means "property-respecting." As a result efficiency has a built-in bias toward the market and the existing distribution of property. Prof. Dworkin was therefore right to see efficiency as a "consequence" of (property) rights. The generally accepted definition of efficiency made this unavoidable.

Another great problem is that the level of inefficiency resulting from marginal impositions upon neighbors has never been established in practice. But it is surely low. It is what happens *within* the boundaries of property that determines whether much, little or no wealth at all is created. Because both Disney's and the farmer's activities count as being "efficient," the one creating a tiny fraction of the monetary wealth of the other, it would seem that any discipline that pays so much attention to cross-boundary externalities—which are as likely to be positive as negative—is a venture in triviality. It subordinates the usual to the exceptional, and distracts us from the general rule.

The claim that "inefficient" situations sometimes exist within a private property system, thanks to high transaction costs, seemed (in Coase's initial formulation) to legitimize the rearrangement of all property rights by efficiency experts—a notion that most free-market economists looked upon with dismay. It would render all property insecure and destroy the entire basis of the free-market system: exchange by consent. Thus an exercise that began with Coase weakening the Pigovian rationale for government intervention went on to raise the possibility of a far more serious intervention.

Posner's and Coase's claim that judges have in the past used economic criteria in deciding cases may be only trivially true. Coase cited a case from English legal history, *Sturges v. Bridgman* (1879), in which noise from a confectioner's machinery disturbed a neighboring doctor. Its "solution," Coase wrote, depended on "whether the continued use of the machinery adds more to the confectioner's income than it subtracts from the doctor's."[36] A.W. Brian Simpson, a law professor at the University of Michigan, recently investigated this case more closely, visiting the record office in London and even the doctor's premises, still standing on Wimpole Street. He found that the important legal question in the case was not who valued the noise making right most highly, but whether the confectioner was entitled to continue his noise making "through having over the years acquired a right to do so under the fictitious doctrine of lost grant."[37]

If you cause a nuisance, in other words, but your neighbor only complains after a few years' delay, you acquire by default a "right" to continue the behavior. The neighbor's "grant" (to sue) is lost if he complains too late. But in *Sturges v. Bridgman* the judge ruled that no such right had been lost by the doctor, whose consulting room at the back of the garden (next to the noisy machinery) had only recently been built. This explained why the noise in earlier years had caused no trouble and was not actionable. As a result, the judge granted the doctor an injunction, bringing the noisy machinery to a halt.

Professor Simpson found Coase's rationale for the ruling unconvincing:

> The judicial opinions in the case make not the least attempt to investigate the economic or social value of the activities or either the doctor or the confectioner; legally speaking, such specific questions were quite irrelevant, as they must in general be in a capitalist system which respects the right of private property. It is not the business of the courts to substitute their despotic dominion for that of the litigants. As occupiers of property the parties must be treated equally, respecting their rights to do what they like on their property, however inefficient, so long of course as this does not violate some legal prohibition. . . . Even today, and certainly not in the nineteenth century, courts do not enter into general open-ended investigations of the efficient use of adjacent tracts of land and allocate rights accordingly. To do so would be the end of the right of private property.[38]

In general, Posner's claims about the "economizing character of the common law" suffers from the grave defect that economic costs and benefits include the subjective and unmeasurable element of "satisfaction" (as the Disney-spurning strawberry farmer showed). This means that it is always possible to look back at any judicial decision and decide that its basis was one of "benefits" outweighing "costs." A famous trespassing case discussed by Posner, *Ploof v. Putnam* (1908) illustrates the point. The plaintiff, caught in a storm, attempted to moor his boat at a convenient dock. An employee shoved the boat away and it was wrecked by the storm. The boat's owner then sued for damages, and the dock's owner was held to be liable. This is how Posner continues the story: "The value to the plaintiff of being able to trespass on the defendant's property during the storm was great and the cost to the defendant of preventing the wreck of plaintiff's boat small. And negotiations for landing rights were, in the circumstances, hardly feasible. The court properly held the defendant liable for the wreck."[39]

The problem is that costs and benefits have been distributed (by Posner's guesses) to create the presumption that the case was decided by the method he discerns. If the judge had ruled the other way, finding for the dock's owner, it would again have been possible to argue that benefit trumped cost. The judge might have argued that the benefit to society of securing property against the temptations of trespassing was higher than the cost of one boat; it was therefore necessary to "make an example" of the boat's owner and find for the dock's owner. (No doubt judges did rule this way in sterner times.)

The common law has long held that people may be entitled to trespass on others' rights in emergencies. And no doubt the case was properly decided. Property rights should give ground when time is short. What is less clear, all the same, is that the judge in this case was guided by economics. He could simply have adopted the rule: "Owners should be charitable in emergencies." To economists of a later era, or to judges trained in economics, this moral rule could be reclothed in the value-free attire of cost-benefit analysis. The case helps us to see why Posnerian analysis has dismayed lawyers of the critical legal studies movement. Posner's method is conservative, in that it will almost always be used to argue that cases in the past were correctly decided, and to create an "economic" rationale for such rulings. The only alternative would be to claim that old cases were incorrectly decided, and this would oblige Posner to impute a different, counterfactual set of costs and benefits to the parties. The arbitrary nature of such an exercise would be conspicuous.

The problem of the subjective nature of costs and benefits had famously arisen in the 1930s, in a debate between Pigou and Lionel Robbins of the London School of Economics. Pigou argued that as an individual's income rises, each additional dollar is worth less to him than the previous dollar. If this were true across the population, the value of one more dollar to a millionaire would be less than its value to a pauper. The state could therefore increase the overall welfare of society by taking dollars from high earners and transferring them to low. The poor would value these transferred dollars more than the rich would miss them. This claim was later used to justify the progressive income tax and income transfers in general.

Robbins said that the argument was not valid because we lack the information needed to make "interpersonal comparisons" of utility. An added dollar may well be of little interest to me, but valuable to you, even though we both have exactly the same wealth. Interestingly, in this debate about income transfers, Posner sided with Robbins, although his argument could be used against his own analyses of legal rules. "The shape and height of people's marginal utility curves are unknown and probably unknowable," Posner said, supporting Robbins.[40] In fact, Posner added, it's plausible to assume "that the people who work hard to make money and succeed in making it are on average those who value money the most." But when the issue was the economic analysis of law, he found it opportune to dismiss as "rather sterile" the argument that comparisons of value between people are impermissible.[41]

Transaction costs cannot be measured, and it is a defect of the law and economics approach that it seeks to circumvent this by "assuming" benefits and costs at a given level. It is the assuming itself that is the error. To be sure, there are situations in which we can say that transaction costs are high (even if we cannot measure them directly). Paul Heyne of the University of Washington has drawn our attention to the difficulty of transferring goods from one place to another in a country (such as the Soviet Union) where, in addition to other costs, it was not clear who owned the goods in the first place.

As the Soviet Union disintegrated, he pointed out, news reports mentioned unharvested food rotting in rural areas, while grocery stores stood empty in cities. Why didn't somebody transport the food to the cities? Arranging the transfer was not so easy: "Who owned the food that was going to waste? Who had authority to harvest it? Who owned harvesting equipment? Who could authorize the use of the equipment? Who owned trucks to transport the food to the cities? Who had fuel for the trucks? How was the food to be distributed once it arrived in the cities? The mere fact that food is going to waste in the fields while people are hungry in the cities is not enough to get food actually moving from farms to urban pantries. The right people must first acquire the appropriate information and incentives."[42]

Compare this with the United States, where fields, food, warehouses and grocery stores are privately owned. "Under a system of clearly defined property rights," Heyne continued, "people with information about the situation would have strong incentives to acquire control of whatever resources were needed to move the food from where it had no use to where it did. And within a system that allows for free exchange among property owners, the necessary resources will quickly and at low cost come together under the control of those who can put them to valuable uses." Thus, transaction costs are minimized in an economy where property is privately owned and where rights are easily transferred.

Once we see that "efficient" should be read as "property-respecting," a different interpretation of Posner's claim (that judges have ruled on the basis of efficiency in the past) suggests itself. If they ruled in ways that made property more secure, and more easily exchangeable, and made free riding more costly, and encouraged competition (all of this out of a respect for common-law rules of property and contract), they would also (incidentally) have enhanced economic efficiency. They would have done so not because they were unconscious economists, but because those rulings were thought to be consonant with justice. For this reason, then, Posner may have overlooked the real explanation for "the economizing character of the common law."

By the time Ronald Coase arrived at Stockholm in 1991, nonetheless, something valuable had emerged from his lengthy meditation on the relationship between law and economics. It led him, ultimately, to a conclusion that might have been too obvious to mention, except that economists had somehow overlooked it for so long. The rights and duties that people possess, he wrote, will be what the law determines, and, as a result, "the legal system will have a profound effect of the working on the economic system and may in certain respects be said to control it." After a few more lines, he made this remark— one that underlies almost everything in this book:

> Until quite recently, most economists seem to have been unaware of this relationship between the economic and legal systems except in the most general way. . . . It makes little sense for economists to discuss the process of exchange without specifying the institutional setting within which the trading takes place, since this affects the incentives to produce and the costs of transacting.[43]

Marx had placed the cart of economics before the horse of law. Superficially, it looked to some legal scholars that the discipline called law and economics was trying to find new rationales for doing the same thing. Certainly there were attempts in that direction. But in the end, the most important result of law and economics was that it drew attention to the fundamental point that when goods are owned, they can be used efficiently, and when they are not, they are used wastefully, and the cost of transferring them to others who value them more highly becomes prohibitively high. Coase, in the end, put the horse back in its proper place. The need to specify the institutional setting "is now beginning to be recognized," he added, "and has been made crystal clear by what is going on in Eastern Europe today."[44]

XI

A NEW BEGINNING

TWENTY-ONE

CHINA, PROPERTY AND DEMOCRACY

THE RECENT CHANGES IN CHINA have no precedent in the twentieth century. It is as though the ruling class and the Chinese people resolved jointly to become the leading power in the world. To do so, the country would have to grow rich, markets would have to be allowed, and the disabling effects of state ownership and collectivization overcome. Private property would have to be permitted, in fact if not in name. The remarkable thing, unforeseen by Western elites and political theory, was that the country began to move in this direction under a nominally Communist government. The Party understood that democracy was not essential, and perhaps was an impediment, to this transformation. In this respect, the Chinese of Hong Kong, Singapore and Taiwan had already pointed the way.

The country remained Communist in name and in official ideology, but practice changed considerably. A far-reaching decentralization of authority—the antithesis of socialism—was called "socialism with Chinese characteristics." Later it was called the "socialist market economy." Words like "privatization" and "private property" were shunned. But at the Fifteenth Party Congress, in September 1997, Social Darwinism itself was not far from view. State enterprises were warned that Herbert Spencer's "survival of the fittest" might apply to them. This was capitalism "at its rawest," warned the *Washington Post*.[1] In France, Communists attending a rally booed the suggestion that they might even think about following the Chinese example.[2]

The retention of power by Communist officials, and their ability simultaneously to participate in, profit financially from, and shape the course of business activity, poses hazards for China's economy in the years ahead. But when the great transformation began 20 years ago, the key role of the government seems to have been to acquiesce in changes that were initiated at the grass-roots level. That in itself was no mean achievement for a Communist government. It was as though the leadership had grasped the truth of Samuel Johnson's maxim: "There are few ways in which a man can be more innocently employed than in getting money."[3] Able now to buy consumer goods, perhaps even an automobile or a small tractor, the people would relish the novelty of prosperity. So, for the most part, they would be content to live without politics. And the party would be able to remain in power.

Intellectuals, of course, would be madly frustrated. Democracy, it has been said, is government by publicity, and intellectuals have learned how to dominate the organs of publicity. So they would beat the drums of protest. But the people would pay them little heed. Valuable powers had already been ceded to the people—above all the right to work, to earn a living, to retain the fruits of their labor. Those who scorn "trade" and value political rights more highly than economic rights have failed to appreciate that point.

The changes began in the countryside. Farmers, not Party members, were the prime movers. Private property or its equivalent was first restored to the rural areas in 1978. In the 20 years since, the country has proceeded toward a market economy with unprecedented speed. In that same time, China enjoyed the largest tax cuts in history, according to Alvin Rabushka of the Hoover Institution.[4] The economy has grown five times faster than the economy of the United States in the nineteenth century. If such changes are sustained for the next decade—and that is a big if—the consequences will be felt around the world. How did this happen?

After the Communist Revolution of 1949, land was allocated to farmers in recognition of their support of the revolution. But they were never given ownership or control. Then, in the name of the revolution, the government began to take the land back. Private grain sales were forbidden. In effect, the state laid claim to the farmers' entire crop. The dwindling farm produce was seized by the state to support life in the cities. Outright collectivization followed. Communist cadres displaced the farmers, who by now were called "peasants."* Independent proprietors became rural proletarians earning "work points" under the command of local cadres, most of whom had no understanding of farming. The desire to work hard disappeared.

---

* "Through the transformation of 'farmers' into 'peasants,' 'tradition' into 'feudalism,' and 'customs' or 'religion' into 'superstition,' there was invented not only the 'old society' that had to be supplanted, but also the basic negative criteria designating a new status group, one held by definition to be incapable of creative and autonomous participation in China's reconstruction." Myron L. Cohen, "Cultural and Political Inventions in Modern China: The Case of the Chinese 'Peasant'," *Daedalus* 122 (spring 1993): 154 ("China in Transformation").

Ten years after the revolution, all the land and productive property had been re-expropriated without compensation. At the same time, regulations and identity cards prevented "peasants" from moving from the country to the city. They were both bound to the land and prevented from making decisions as to its use. A goal of the revolutionary government had been to destroy "feudal elements" in the countryside. "This private economy is the economic basis of feudal regimes, which impoverishes farmers," Mao Tse-tung had written in 1943. "The only way to overcome this problem is gradual collectivization."[5]

There followed the famine of the years 1959-62, caused by the disastrous program of crash industrialization that Mao called the Great Leap Forward. Perhaps as many as 40 million people died of starvation, almost all in the countryside. Ration cards distributed to urban dwellers had been denied to the peasants, who saw that the ideology of equality did not apply to them. When they began to go their own way, the state's threat of withheld benefits was of little avail, because by then farmers weren't receiving any.

After the famine, the central government relinquished some control. Farmers were again allowed to produce on small private plots. But another government-engineered catastrophe followed—the Cultural Revolution. Red Guards, fanatically loyal to Mao, were turned loose on intellectuals and party officials, many of whom were exiled to the countryside. Deng Xiaoping found himself assigned to a tractor-repair factory in Jiangxi Province. His son, a physics student, was thrown from a fourth-floor window and left paralyzed. Perhaps a million people were killed in the ensuing years of so-called permanent revolution. But it created such anarchy that farmers ultimately were able to benefit from it. The chain of command within the party was broken.

Collective farms had their production quotas, and some production teams were permitted to retain any surplus over that quota. Teams subdivided themselves into smaller working groups. In many cases, such groups consisted of family members. In Western terms, private retention of the surplus was equivalent to a highly regressive tax; an arrangement that encourages people to work long hours. In some prefectures, to encourage farmers still more, the party secretary promised that the policy would not be changed in the near future.[6] So began the system of family contracting. As a result, production increased dramatically. The Harvard sociologist Andrew G. Walder saw that this was a "reassignment of property rights" by another name:

> One of the most important latent principles of economic reform in China has been the widespread downward reassignment of use rights within government hierarchies, and at the grass roots, from government agencies to households and individuals. The most dramatic reassignment took place in the dismantling of collective agriculture. Collectively owned village land formerly

cultivated under the direction of production team leaders was reassigned to
households under long-term contracts. While quota-contracts for staple grains
were commonly retained, peasant household attained new rights to make
cropping, management and marketing decisions on their own."[7]

The farmers had long-term leases, not fee-simple ownership. The land
remained formally the inalienable property of the state. Economically, however,
it was the equivalent of a system in which private property was restored. Farmers
now had the reassurance of long time horizons; family members could engage
in production for their own benefit. Once the quota had been met, the marginal
tax rate (on additional production) was zero. The surplus could be traded.

In late 1977, "farm families began to 'bribe' their way out of collective
chores by making deals with local cadres," Kate Xiao Zhou wrote in *How The
Farmers Changed China*. "The head of a family would promise to fulfill the
production quota and gave the cadres a bit over."[8] Private deal making and
contracting gradually spread across farm production and beyond it.

Factional struggles distracted the leadership at the time of Mao's death
in 1976. At first, according to China's Ministry of Agriculture, "the decision-
makers did not acknowledge the family contract responsibility system." It was
considered "a move that opposed the system of socialism."[9] The reform of
China's agriculture is usually credited to the Eleventh Party Congress in
December, 1978. The Party leadership did, on that occasion, improve incentives
by raising farm prices. And they encouraged family production on the side. But
all these measures, Kate Zhou wrote, "were ways to mend the fences of the old
collective system."

Earlier, Deng Xiaoping had supported a pragmatic view of rural
institutions with the famous observation that the color of a cat didn't matter, "as
long as it can catch mice."[10] The 1978 resolution, which he had helped draft,
nonetheless specified that the system of family contracting was illegal.[11] Three
months later, in March, 1979, a letter in the *People's Daily* denounced
decollectivization as a threat to socialism. Eventually, however, pragmatism
prevailed. A government adviser named Chen Yizi, who had returned from years
of exile in the countryside wrote a report favorable to the reforms, and it was
circulated among the top leaders. Whenever farmers practiced the family
responsibility system, he wrote, production increased far more rapidly than
under any other system.[12] Whatever its color, this was a cat that did catch mice.
In the end, the Party institutionalized the system that they had initially opposed.

Kate Xiao Zhou's book is one of the most interesting yet written about
the remarkable developments in China. Born in the industrial city of Wutan in
1956, she was herself caught up in the Cultural Revolution as a child. Her father,
a professor of English, was denounced and imprisoned as a bourgeois

intellectual in 1966. She was later assigned to a poor family in a rural village. Life was primitive: no electricity, running water or toilets. But she made many friends and eventually returned to the city in 1972. There she worked in a factory, and soon learned to save her energy to stand in food queues for hours after work. After the system in the countryside changed and de facto private property was restored, the food lines disappeared as farmers brought their surplus to sell in the cities. "When I in turn visited the village in 1982, it had changed beyond recognition," she wrote. "Almost everyone was building a new house. Every family was engaged in market exchanges. Dinner conversations focused on making money. Linked with moneymaking was the rise in consumption. There was at least one bike in each family. Talk of buying a TV and a small tractor preoccupied villagers."[13]

She argued that what happened in China was a "spontaneous, unorganized, leaderless, non-ideological, apolitical movement."[14] It is not clear that she had heard of Friedrich Hayek's "spontaneous order" of the marketplace.[15] But he could not have put it better himself. Hayek, who died in 1992, probably did not realize that something resembling that spontaneous order may have appeared in the world's most populous country, and a nominally Communist one at that. If the farmers had shown any sign of organizing, or of political opposition to Communism, the state would have responded as ruthlessly as it did later in Tiananmen Square. The farmers only seemed to be organized, because all were searching for comparable opportunities and compatible niches. They shared a common enemy, the state and its operatives, many of whom could be co-opted because they were themselves feeling the pinch of the state's impoverishing policies.

The new policy spread beyond farming. Although two-thirds of China's 1.2 billion population still live in rural areas, a rapidly declining percentage works in agriculture.[16] Between 1978 and 1996, that figure fell from about 75 percent to 50 percent. A similar transformation in Japan took 60 years. The area devoted to farming has also declined, as housing and offices have expanded. Thanks to its long-postponed industrialization, the country has been able to take advantage of new technology that permits low-cost, family-scale production. Local enterprises and light industries began to develop under the umbrella of local governments. Many of them evolved out of the Mao-era repair and communal workshops. There are now about 2.5 million of these enterprises in China, employing over 125 million people. For the last 15 years, their output has grown at the rate of 20 percent a year, twice the national average.

The demarcation between public and private is not as clear-cut in China as it is in the West. The senior official who sponsors a company's transit through the maze of Communist prohibitions in exchange for a slice of equity is "corrupt," but usually only to Westerners. What are we to make of the

"Communist Party member," identified by name in the *Wall Street Journal*, "whose Shanghai interior-decorator company has exploded from 9 employees to 1,200 in three years," and who was quoted as saying in 1997: "Once it hits a certain point, the market will open like a floodgate."[17] The many firms owned by the People's Liberation Army, some of them efficient enough to sell consumer goods marketed through Nordstrom, K-Mart and Wal-Mart, including toys, exercise weights, and fish for fast food restaurants, are also hybrids unknown in the West.[18]

The system has allowed government officials to use their own political clout and pursue their own financial interest simultaneously. At first this had the good effect of encouraging, within the government, the incentive to overcome the torpor induced by Communist restrictions and regulations. The problem now is that the hybrid businessmen-officials are able to use their influence to stifle competition. It is as though the head of the Food and Drug Administration could go into the cigarette-making business, and then apply FDA regulations to his competitors while exempting his own company. It is hard to see how such a system can avoid becoming one of inefficient monopolies.

China's recent experience also forces us to revise our understanding of local government. Local government enterprises are said to be the closest thing to a market economy in China. Unlike traditional state-owned enterprises, they don't survive if they can't meet expenses from their own income. Often they have business partners in Hong Kong or Taiwan, and their products must compete on the world market. As to their lack of environmental controls, Steven Mufson wrote in the *Washington Post*: "Local governments face conflicts of interest as regulators and principal shareholders."[19] In short, regulations are costly, and profits from these enterprises must often finance roads, clinics and primary schools. To "peasants" so recently poor, these amenities have a higher value than an environmental agency's seal of approval.

At the national level, traditional state-owned enterprises remain, employing anywhere from 75 million to 100 million workers. By 1997, however, they were producing a sharply declining percentage of the country's output and absorbing billions of dollars in subsidies. As jobs centers, they are the source of much of the Communist Party's remaining power. Privatizing them involves the politically hazardous step of putting millions of people out of work. At the Party Congress in 1997, nonetheless, President Jiang Zemin announced that the number of such enterprises would be dramatically reduced. The word "privatized" was avoided. Shares would be distributed and the companies would henceforth be "publicly owned."[20]

No doubt many difficulties lay ahead. The *New York Times* noted that when an old factory, with a manager appointed by local officials, is converted to a shareholders' corporation, "the new bosses may want to lay off workers and retool an inefficient operation into one that can be competitive." If so, "will the local Communist Party chief sit by idly as hundreds of workers are sent home?" Or will he say that unemployment is already too high and that "layoffs threaten 'stability' since China has no social security net?"[21]

But the country has already done many things previously thought impossible, and it seems determined to remain on the path to prosperity. If this most recent sale of state assets proceeds as planned, it will be the largest privatization in history, dwarfing anything carried out in England in the 1980s, for example. The contrast with simultaneous developments in Europe is striking. A few days before the announced privatization of almost 130,000 state firms in China, the French government could not muster the political will to privatize part of one company, Air France, even though this was needed to comply with the budgetary criteria for admission to the European Monetary Union.

PROPERTY AND DEMOCRACY

One of the leading Chinese dissidents, Wei Jingsheng, had for years been writing from his jail cell that economic modernization was impossible without democracy. The authorities responded by letting let him out of prison briefly in 1993. They took him on a tour of Beijing, which he had not seen since 1979. "The changes are enormous," Wei admitted. "They made an old Beijinger like myself feel like a tourist—a stranger in his own hometown."[22]

The dramatic changes in China in the last 20 years have demonstrated conclusively that economic growth is not dependent on democracy, at least as we have known it in the twentieth century. China has admittedly had some democracy at the village level since 1988. The *China Strategic Review* called this a "major institutional breakthrough," with elections in two provinces occurring without formal adoption by the Communist Party.* But the important point is that radical economic reform, including the de facto restoration of private property, became a reality in China without benefit of the institutions that define a democracy: universal suffrage, free assemblies, freedom of

---

* "The village elections are no herald of real democracy," Seth Faison reported. "They are held without exception under the control of the local Communist Party organization." But Thomas L. Friedman reported that they are a sign "that China is in a transition from brutal authoritarianism" to one that is "a little less brutal." He quoted Larry Diamond, an observer of the local elections held in March 1998, as calling them an indication "that China is entering a phase in which individuals, groups, villages and enterprises" are more able to "express their interests and concerns." Seth Faison, *New York Times*, March 29, 1998; Thomas L. Friedman, *New York Times*, March 14, 1998; and see X. Drew Liu, "A Harbinger of Democracy," *The China Strategic Review* (May/June 1997): 50.

speech, political competition and organized constituency groups armed with votes.

In fact, the reforms in China took place in the teeth of Western dicta that nothing good could come from a regime deprived of such institutions. No doubt Wei Jingsheng learned his political theory from Western texts. Post-Communist Russia followed Western advice more closely. It had political parties and elections and a hyperactive parliament with redistributive powers before there was much of an economic pie to divide. This suggests that instituting democracy ahead of economic freedom, or simultaneously with it, may be little more than a formula for conflict. Perhaps we do not realize this because we have forgotten so much of our own economic and political history.

China was following the course already successfully charted by the Chinese-populated territories of Taiwan, Singapore and Hong Kong. They, too, had achieved great prosperity and the world's highest economic growth rates in recent decades without benefit of democracy. Hong Kong's experience was generally misrepresented at the time of its transfer from British rule, in 1997. The democracy that was portrayed as so abruptly coming to an end had commenced only in 1995. For more than 140 years, as former U.S. assistant secretary of defense Charles W. Freeman, Jr., pointed out, the British had shown "no inclination to temper their benevolent autocracy by letting Hong Kong Chinese have a role in the politics of the place. The colony's governor appointed the members of Hong Kong's legislative council, insisted on his right to approve public gatherings, scrutinized the press for evidence of lese-majesty, and sometimes threw editors in jail for objecting to British rule."[23]

A high correlation between democracy and prosperity has long been observed by political scientists, but the direction of causation is important. Prosperity tends to bring democracy in its wake—as recently has been shown in Chile, Taiwan and South Korea. It does not follow that regimes will prosper if people are given the vote; especially not if the vote has been imposed by international institutions or by the custodians of foreign aid. In such cases, democracy will be simulated, and almost certainly short lived. "Democracies that arise in poor countries (sometimes because they are imposed from the outside) usually do not last," Robert J. Barro of Harvard has written.[24]

A more sophisticated understanding of the relationship between democracy and wealth was described in 1959 by the sociologist Seymour Martin Lipset. "From Aristotle down to the present," he pointed out, "men have argued that only in a wealthy society in which relatively few citizens lived in real poverty could a situation exist in which the mass of the population could intelligently participate in politics and could develop the self-restraint necessary to avoid succumbing to the appeals of irresponsible demagogues."[25] Democracy is a consequence of prosperity, in other words, not its cause.

Using mathematical techniques, Professor Barro has recently shown that economic growth tends to increase when levels of democracy are "low," but the relationship with growth turns negative once a moderate amount of political freedom is reached. The explanation, he suggests, is that incipient democracy may restrain the tyrannical exercise of power, but when a moderate level of democracy has been reached, a "further increase in political rights impairs growth and investment because the dominant effect comes from the intensified concern with income redistribution." In places such as Chile, Taiwan and South Korea, he argues, political liberalization has probably already gone "beyond the point of growth maximization."[26]

The relationship between economic growth and democracy is confused because nondemocratic regimes can go either way. On the one hand, they can respect property rights and encourage economic growth. The absence of organized constituency groups will make that path easier to take than it would be in a full-fledged democracy. Furthermore, growth will increase public contentment and, for a while at least, defang political challenges from those who are denied access to power. On the other hand, nondemocratic regimes can spurn all considerations of growth. Rulers can enrich themselves by plundering wealth and depositing it in Swiss bank accounts, without worrying about the next election. This is the path that many Third World countries have taken. Can we predict which path a nondemocratic regime will take? "The theory that determines which kind of dictatorship will prevail seems to be missing," says Barro.[27]

In foreign-policy circles today, there is a tendency to think of democracy as a magic tent that can be set down on the rough terrain of tyranny, making good things happen. The U.S. view resembles that of the released Chinese dissident: The Western democracies are prosperous; therefore, only democracy can bring prosperity. To four generations of Americans, a *New York Times* reporter noted in 1996, the promotion of democracy was "the foreign policy equivalent of apple pie."[28] The State Department uses democracy as an important criterion of human rights. The department's survey of human rights in 1995 denounced China as an "authoritarian state," in which the Communist Party "monopolizes decision-making authority." This was inaccurate, inasmuch as considerable decision-making authority—the decisions that people make in earning a living; the decisions to sow, reap, harvest, barter and exchange—had been largely delegated to the people. Only if life is viewed as a life of politics is the State Department's view correct.

Now and then, we hear a dissenting voice from someone in the field. Having completed a three-year tour of duty in Africa for the *Washington Post*, Keith Richburg wrote *Out of America: A Black Man Confronts Africa* (1997). He noted that democracy was the "much-hyped" solution touted by the

academics and Africa specialists who briefed him before he went abroad. But
in covering election after election in that continent, he saw how often they did
more harm than good, allowing "dictators to wrap themselves in a new aura of
legitimacy." Before elections are held, he concluded, constitutions must be
rewritten, the role of imperial presidencies reduced, security and police forces
brought under neutral control, parliaments and judiciaries strengthened.[29]

"Democracy" is often used as shorthand for the Western form of government. But the framers of the U.S. Constitution knew that voting is far from a
sufficient guarantor of good government. Nor does it forestall dictatorship. From
Azerbaijan to Benin, from Serbia to Sudan, tyrants have learned how to get
themselves elected. Arafat legitimized his Palestinian rule with an election for
which he did not have to campaign, and was duly rewarded by the international
community. In favor of democracy, it is true that power is best divided and checked
by a popular chamber. But democracy should be viewed as a means, not as an end,
and voting as an official act, not a universal right. The claim that the ends of
democracy can only be served by universal franchise is modern and suspect. It was
not made by the parliamentary reformers of the nineteenth century.

In Britain, until 1832, only 1 in 12 adult males could vote. This was
expanded to 1 in 7 between the years 1832 and 1867. In the period of Britain's
greatness, then, democracy was restricted. Voting was considered a privilege,
not a right. A voter was, temporarily, an officer of the state. The conservative
opponents of parliamentary reform understood that the universal franchise could
put all property in peril. They worried, reasonably, about the shared linguistic
root of "democrat" and "demagogue." David Ricardo, briefly a member of
Parliament, appreciated the point. Although he favored expanding the franchise,
he wrote in 1818 that property rights were so essential to good government that
he would agree to "deprive those of the elective franchise against whom it could
be justly alleged that they considered it in their interest to invade [property
rights]."[30]

Although universal voting may well be desirable for other reasons, it is
not likely to help secure property, or material prosperity. The opponents of
parliamentary reform saw that the logic of reform pointed toward the curtailment
of economic liberties. Britain duly slipped down that slope in the twentieth
century. In the United States, it would seem that a backward step was taken in
the 1960s. The wording of the 1965 Voting Rights Act would have shocked not
just the conservatives, but also the liberals, of the nineteenth century. The act
outlawed any requirement that voters shall "demonstrate the ability to read,
write, understand or interpret any matter," or shall show "knowledge of any
particular subject." Because literacy tests had been wrongfully used for purposes
of racial discrimination, outlawing the tests was considered the best method of
abolishing the discrimination.

It is questionable whether we should try to impose on other countries a system—full adult franchise—that we ourselves did not have at the outset. In countries where economic liberties are recent and wealth still a novelty, universal suffrage is as likely to lead to conflict as to peace and prosperity. And imposing it validates the complaint of Lee Kuan Yew of Singapore, who said that Westerners "foist their system indiscriminately on societies in which it will not work."[31] Hernando de Soto pointed out that when the correct laws are not in place in the Third World, and people cannot get title to land, the construction of informal housing will take place in reverse order: furniture first, walls last. By the same token, the correct constitutional architecture requires that political steps be taken in the right sequence. Instant, fully enfranchised democracy will almost certainly disorder the political economy. It is encouraging that many of these arguments have recently been made in *Foreign Affairs*, by the managing editor of that august journal, suggesting that the conventional wisdom on this subject is shifting.[32]

To a greater extent than is recognized, China may have more closely replicated the political ordering of events that unfolded in western Europe: An autocratic regime at first tolerates those economic relationships that are conducive to prosperity, and then uses its powers to preserve the gains in wealth from disruption and organized plunder. As the people grow more prosperous, democracy matures. If economic liberties and property rights are to be well respected, a little democracy may well be preferable to the full-fledged variety. Democracy is not like pregnancy; it is possible to be a little bit democratic. Arguably a little bit can be better than going all the way. The right to vote will in any event avail the people little if they are deprived of the right to own and exchange property. With that property right held securely, voting will add but little to the sum of human happiness.

PROPERTY AND (SOME) PROGRESS

The World Bank has begun to discuss property rights in its reports, particularly in reference to environmental problems. So there has been progress since I spoke at their lunch gathering. The fundamental role played by property rights in development is now a more widely accepted proposition. It is better understood that economic performance depends not just on "inputs" (of abstract "factors of production") but on a political structure that preserves individual economic liberty.

In the last decade—and not before then—a concerted attempt has been made to construct an index of economic freedom and then measure the extent or lack of it in countries around the world. The most important such project was undertaken by the Fraser Institute of Vancouver, British Columbia, and published in 1996 with the title *Economic Freedom of the World, 1975-1995*. It was a ten-year project, undertaken with the assistance of dozens of economists, including three Nobelists (Milton Friedman, Gary Becker and Douglass North). By the time its 1997 supplement was published, 47 institutes worldwide were participating. The index measured economic freedom in 115 countries. In an "introduction and overview," the authors wrote: "In an economically free society, the fundamental function of government is the protection of private property and the provision of a stable infrastructure for a voluntary exchange system. When a government fails to protect private property, takes property itself without full compensation, or establishes restrictions (and follows policies) that limit voluntary exchange, it violates the economic freedom of its citizens."[33]

The Heritage Foundation and Freedom House in New York have also published indices of economic freedom, using somewhat different criteria. But the most detailed and exhaustive study was that of the Fraser Institute. In it, a striking correlation was found to exist between the level of economic freedom in various countries and both per capita wealth and the rate of economic growth. In economic freedom, Hong Kong came out top of the list in both the Fraser and Heritage studies, Singapore was second, and both are also near the top in gross domestic product per capita. At the bottom of the list, some of the most economically repressive countries of the world (Algeria, Croatia, Syria, Burundi, Haiti) were also found to be among the most impoverished. (Cuba, Laos and North Korea, at the bottom of the Heritage list, were not included in the Fraser survey; nor were Somalia or Sudan.)

It is now fairly well established among economists and policymakers that the institutional framework "has significant and large effects on the efficiency and growth rate of economies," as the economist Gerald W. Scully has written.[34] So rapidly has the conventional wisdom changed that it seems remarkable that the research on which that claim was made was published in the *Journal of Political Economy* only ten years ago. Societies that "subscribe to private property, and to the market allocation of resources, grow at three times the rate" of societies in which "these freedoms are abridged," he wrote. Summarizing his research in a later book, he wrote, "To my knowledge, this was the first empirical confirmation of such a link." The Berlin Wall fell one year later. Indeed, it does seem extraordinary that a relationship so fundamental to economics and politics was not established until President Reagan was in his last year in office.

The alert reader may have noticed that, if the key principle set forth earlier in the book is correct, China seems to have done the impossible. The principle was that *law* is antecedent to *economy*; that if the right laws are not in place, productive economic activity most probably will not occur. In China, however, the rule of law certainly did not exist when the reforms began. Rather, the law was adjusted after the fact, in response to the beneficial effects of the economic activity that started independently. To use the earlier analogy of baseball, here was a case in which it seems that the rules of the game were adjusted in response to the play. This is precisely what economists such as Friedrich Hayek and Armen Alchian had long believed would happen, and what others, such as Douglass North, eventually despaired of seeing.

It seems clear enough, though, that what happened in China has been very much the exception. One can find reasons (or excuses) for it. One is that the Cultural Revolution brought anarchy, enabling the farmers to make their own decisions without much interference from anyone. So strong is the impulse to privatize and to work with and for the benefit of one's own family members, to make promises and keep them rather than lose face, that the age-old institutions of property and contract could reassert themselves without any need for constitutional specification or well-trodden pathways of legal precedent.

But this, too, is unsatisfactory. For it seems to argue that anarchy begets efficiency. In most places and times, this is obviously not true. There has been plenty of unproductive anarchy in the world. One only has to think, recently, of Haiti, Sudan and Somalia. Nothing good has come of the institutional near-vacuum in these countries.

Clearly, a militantly enforced Communism was sufficient to prevent most economic activity from taking place in China for 30 years; more than sufficient, for it killed millions of people into the bargain. But once that system broke down, and the great majority of the people stopped believing in it, the absence of the rule of law seemed to be no obstacle to what may have been the most rapid economic advance ever. There was no need for an understanding of the common law, or Roman law—of any particular system of law.

To be sure, the equivalent of private property had to develop and above all be tolerated by the authorities. One needed only to look at photographs of construction activity in Shanghai, where in 1997 it was reported that 18 percent of the world's construction cranes were active, to realize that such costly activity would not be taking place at all if the gains from trade could be arbitrarily expropriated and deposited into state coffers in Beijing.[35] That could happen a few times, perhaps, but if it became a habit, the economic activity would dry up. Whatever name is given to the system in China, it is one in which wealth is allowed to accrue to individual people.

In other countries, notably post-Communist Russia, the same response has not been seen. It was quite clear to policymakers in that country, nonetheless, that private property would have to be reestablished if the economy was to recover, even if they were unable to change the system as they might have wished. One only has to read the comments of Yegor Gaidar, who worked for

Gorbachev as economics editor of the journal *Kommunist*, and as a columnist for *Pravda*, and later became Boris Yeltsin's economics minister.

> Despite all the wars and disasters in Europe, modern civilization became possible there because most European nations had lived a settled life for over ten centuries—there were no great migrations, no conquests made by nomadic tribes, just a long tradition of handing down estates, land lots, and rights to land property to descendants. Hereditary title to land emerged and was reinforced by many centuries of tradition. Europe, inhabited by settled peoples, became the fountainhead of the myriad innovations which formed the basis of its civilization and gave rise to a gigantic upsurge in material and spiritual wealth in the second half of the present millennium. One physically feels the effect of this culture as one takes a stroll through some German or British campus, where the soil has never been bulldozed away, as over here, but cultivated assiduously by countless generations.[36]

Many such comments extolling the virtues of private property have been made by Russian officials, academics and writers in the last decade. In fact, few as perspicacious as Gaidar's have been made in the West itself, where such things have been forgotten if they were ever learned. That they should have been made by a *Pravda* writer and grandson of a Red Army hero is but one sign of the remarkable times that we have recently lived through. "From his reading of Adam Smith and the Western economists," David Remnick writes in *Resurrection*, Gaidar recognized that "the only way to build a strong legal order and a prosperous economy was to make what had once been an anathema to the Bolsheviks—that is, private property—a treasured value of the Russian people."[37]

Gaidar's tenure as Russia's economics minister lasted for only two years. Consumer goods appeared in the shops and queues disappeared, but he was undermined by rampant inflation and uncontrolled politics, and was replaced. The difficulties that Russia has encountered since 1991 show how great can be the gulf that separates the intellectual understanding of what is needed and its political realization. Again the Russian case suggests that the aspiring constitutional architect must learn not just the right moves, but the right moves in the right sequence.

We may anticipate, nonetheless, that Russia will before too long find the "normal path" that Gaidar sought. In other parts of the world, a vast change has quietly taken place. Perhaps we really have seen the "fundamental shift in ideas" that Daniel Yergin and Joseph Stanislaw describe in *The Commanding Heights*; a change in which ideas "decidedly outside the mainstream have now moved, with some rapidity, to center stage, and are now reshaping economies in every part of the globe."[38] From Margaret Thatcher's Britain (left intact by Tony Blair), to the New Zealand of Roger Douglas; from Vaclav Klaus's Czech Republic, to the Peru of Alberto Fujimori and the Chile of Eduardo Frei's son and successor, privatization has taken hold worldwide and cannot easily be reversed.

Mexico still has not recovered from its prolonged bout with socialism, nor does it have a real rule of law. By 1997, the reform of its collective farms had not progressed beyond the talking stage. "In Mexico," wrote Alvaro Vargas Llosa, a newspaper bureau chief in London, "property rights, a crucial institution in any society, can hardly be present under Article 27 of the constitution, which states that 'the nation' is the owner of all the land. The heralded reform of the collectively owned *ejido,* or community farm, has not translated into property rights for the peasant."[39]

Americans who deplore the illegal immigration of millions of Mexicans to this country might consider shifting their attention away from border guards and chain-link fences, to the defective institutions that continue to promote the outward migration of Mexico's poor. The vast majority of them, like people everywhere, would far rather stay in their own country, but they are unable to find work. The most important reason is that they do not have secure private property rights to their own land. This consolidates power in the hands of that country's elite and perpetuates the nation's poverty. Mexico did move closer to real democracy in the legislative elections of 1997, and it will be interesting to see if this succeeds, finally, in transforming the system. More urgently, we must hope that the governing classes come to see the domestic and institutional roots of their own difficulties.

Developments around the world give us hope for thinking that this may not be long delayed. The hundred-year experiment in socialism is over. At the same time, the rest of the world is beginning to appreciate the advantages of the political and legal institutions that the United States inherited, benefited from and preserved—in admittedly growing disrepair—for the better part of 200 years. One can only marvel that in the twentieth century, when America enjoyed its greatest world influence, its governing classes often had only a hazy idea of the workings of those institutions, and were unable to explain them to others or transmit them abroad. But the rest of the world is adopting them anyway. The most hopeful sign, since my talk at the World Bank eight years ago, is that intellectuals everywhere are much more ready to accept that the widespread and secure ownership of property is the sine qua non of prosperity.

NOTES

CHAPTER 1

1. Arnold Toynbee, *Civilization on Trial* (New York: Oxford Univ. Press, 1948), 39.
2. Paul Kennedy, *The Rise and Fall of the Great Powers* (New York: Random House, 1987), 16-17.
3. For suspicion of Locke's defense of property, see Jeremy Waldron, *The Right to Private Property* (Oxford: Clarendon Press, 1988); James O. Grunebaum, *Private Ownership* (London: Routledge & Kegan Paul, 1987); Alan Ryan, *Property and Political Theory* (Oxford: Basil Blackwell, 1984); Alan Ryan, *Property* (Milton Keynes: Open University Press, 1987); and Andrew Reeve, *Property* (Basingstoke: Macmillan Education Ltd., 1986).
4. Dennis J. Coyle, *Property Rights and the Constitution* (Albany, N.Y.: State Univ. of New York, 1993), 3, 4.
5. Richard Pipes, "Human Nature and the Fall of Communism," *Bulletin of the American Academy of Arts and Sciences* 49 (January 1996): 48.
6. See Campbell R. McConnell, *Economics: Principles, Problems, and Policies,* 10th ed. (New York: McGraw-Hill, 1987), 38.
7. Armen Alchian, foreword to *The Economics of Property Rights,* ed. Eirik Furubotn and Svetozar Pejovich (Cambridge, Mass.: Ballinger Publishing Co., 1974), xiii.
8. Steven N. S. Cheung, "The Contractual Nature of the Firm," *Journal of Law and Economics* 26 (April 1983): 20.
9. Robert Barro, interview by author, June 1996.
10. Robert Solow, in Arjo Klamer, *Conversations with Economists* (Totowa, N. J.: Rowman and Allanheld, 1983), 130-31.
11. John R. Commons, *The Economics of Collective Action* (New York: Macmillan, 1950), 43.
12. Leon Trotsky, *The Revolution Betrayed* (New York: Doubleday, Doran & Co., 1937), 76.
13. Milton Friedman, interview by author, February 1988.
14. James Boyle, *Shamans, Software, and Spleens* (Cambridge, Mass.: Harvard Univ. Press, 1996), 47.
15. James W. Ely, Jr., *The Guardian of Every Other Right: A Constitutional History of Property Rights* (New York: Oxford Univ. Press, 1992), 16.
16. Pope Leo XIII, *On the Condition of the Working Classes* (*Rerum Novarum,* 1891) (Boston: St. Paul editions, n.d.), paragraph 23.
17. James Q. Wilson, "A Cure for Selfishness," *Wall Street Journal,* March 26, 1997.
18. Daniel Yergin and Joseph Stanislaw, *The Commanding Heights* (New York: Simon & Schuster, 1998), 377.
19. McConnell, *Economics,* 904.
20. U.S. Department of Commerce, *Statistical Abstract of the United States,* 1989 (Washington, D.C.: G.P.O.), 822.
21. "The Mystery of Economic Growth," *Economist,* May 25, 1996.
22. Hernando de Soto, interview by author, February 1989.
23. Paul M. Barrett, "Influential Ideas: A Movement Called 'Law and Economics' Sways Legal Circles," *Wall Street Journal,* August 4, 1986.
24. Arthur O. Lovejoy and George Boas, *Primitivism and Related Ideas in Antiquity* (Baltimore: John Hopkins Press, 1935), 272-73
25. Richard Pipes, *The Russian Revolution* (New York: Knopf, 1990), 125-27.

26. "First editions of the *Essay Concerning Human Understanding* were on sale in December and of *The Two Treatises of Government* as early as October, 1689, though both were dated '1690', for booksellers then, like magazine publishers today, post-dated their books so that they might look new longer." Maurice Cranston, *John Locke: A Biography,* New York: Macmillan, 1957), 327.

27. John Locke, *An Essay Concerning Human Understanding,* vol. 1 (New York: Dover, 1959), 121.

28. Ibid., 125.

29. M. Grossman, *The Philosophy of Helvetius* (New York: Columbia, 1926), 11.

30. G. V. Plekhanov, *Essays in the History of Materialism* (New York: Howard Fertig, 1967), 162.

31. Pipes, *Russian Revolution,* 126.

32. Locke, *The Second Treatise of Government,* in *Two Treatises of Government,* ed. Peter Laslett (Cambridge: Cambridge Univ. Press, 1963), sec. 30.

33. David Hume, *A Treatise of Human Nature* (1740; reprint, Harmondsworth, Eng.: Penguin Classics, 1984), 536-52.

34. Sir William Blackstone's four-volume *Commentaries on the Laws of England* were published from 1765 to 1769.

35. Michael Holroyd, *Bernard Shaw,* vol. 3 (New York: Random House, 1991), 249.

36. "Gorbachev and Yeltsin Answer Questions from Americans on TV," Reuters dispatch, *Washington Post,* September 7, 1991.

37. Al Gore, *Earth in the Balance: Ecology and the Human Spirit* (New York: Plume, 1993), 274.

CHAPTER 2

1. Sir William Blackstone, *Ehrlich's Blackstone,* ed. J. W. Ehrlich (San Carlos, Cal.: Nourse Publishing, 1959), 113.

2. Tony Honore, *Oxford Essays in Jurisprudence,* ed. A. G. Guest (Oxford: Oxford Univ. Press, 1961). See also, Lawrence Becker and Kenneth Kipnis, eds., *Property: Cases, Concepts, Critiques* (Englewood Cliffs, N. J.: Prentice-Hall, 1984), 79.

3. Rehnquist, *Pruneyard Shopping Center v. Robins,* 447 U.S. 74 (1980).

4. American Law Institute, *Restatement of the Law of Property,* vols. 1-2 (St. Paul: American Law Institute Publishers, 1936), iv.

5. Wesley N. Hohfeld, *Fundamental Legal Conceptions As Applied in Judicial Reasoning* (New Haven: Yale Univ. Press, 1923), 23-114.

6. Roscoe Pound, *Jurisprudence,* vol. 5 (St. Paul: West Publishing Co., 1959), 126-27.

7. Richard R. B.Powell, *Powell on Real Property,* rev. ed. (New York: Matthew Bender, 1968).

8. Richard R. B. Powell and Patrick J. Rohan, preface to Powell, *Powell on Real Property,* xv.

9. American Law Institute, *Restatement of Property* 1: 11.

10. Bruce Ackerman, *Private Property and the Constitution* (New Haven: Yale Univ. Press, 1977), 26.

11. Thomas Grey, "The Disintegration of Property," in *Property,* ed. J. Roland Pennock and John W. Chapman, Nomos, vol. 22 (New York: New York Univ. Press, 1980).

12. Sir William Markby, *Elements of Law,* 6th ed. (Oxford, Clarendon Press, 1905), 158.

13. Richard A. Epstein, *Takings: Private Property and the Power of Eminent Domain* (Cambridge, Mass.: Harvard Univ. Press, 1985).

14. Tony Honore, *Making Law Bind* (New York: Oxford Univ. Press, 1987), 161.

15. Robert Ellickson, "Property in Land," *Yale Law Journal* 102 (1993): 1362-63.

16. Frederick H. Lawson, *Introduction to the Law of Property* (Oxford: Clarendon Press, 1958), 90.

17. Ibid.

18. For more on the three configurations, see Jeremy Waldron, *The Right to Private Property* (Oxford: Clarendon Press, 1988), 37-46.

19. Richard A. Epstein, "On the Optimal Mix of Private and Common Property," in *Property Rights,* ed. Ellen F. Paul, Fred D. Miller Jr., and Jeffrey Paul (New York: Cambridge Univ. Press, 1994), 17-41.

20. Mancur Olson, interview by author, April 1993.

21. Hernando de Soto, "The Missing Ingredient," *Economist,* September 11-17, 1993.

22. Paul Samuelson and William D. Nordhaus, *Economics,* 13th ed. (New York: McGraw-Hill, 1989), 841.

23. Edmund W. Kitch, ed., "The Fire of Truth: A Remembrance of Law and Economics at Chicago, 1932-1970," *Journal of Law and Economics* 26 (April 1983): 229.

24. Douglass C. North, "Economic Performance through Time," *American Economic Review* 84 (June 1994): 359-66.

25. Douglass C. North, interview by author, February 1988.

26. Douglass C. North, *Structure and Change in Economic History* (New York: W. W. Norton, 1981), 8, 17.

27. Douglass C. North, *Institutions, Institutional Change, and Economic Performance* (New York: Cambridge Univ. Press, 1990), 6-7.

28. William Stanley Jevons, *The State in Relation to Labour,* 3d ed (London: Macmillan, 1894), 16.

29. Albert V. Dicey, *Law and Public Opinion in England* (London: Macmillan, 1905), 493-94.

30. Ivor Jennings, *The Law and the Constitution,* 5th ed. (London: Univ. of London Press, 1959), 309, 55, 57.

INTRODUCTION TO PART II

1. Garrett Hardin, "The Tragedy of the Commons," *Science* 162 (December 13, 1968): 1243-48.

CHAPTER 3

1. "George Percy's Account of the Voyage to Virginia and the Colony's First Days," in *The Old Dominion in the Seventeenth Century: A Documentary History of Virginia, 1606 - 1689,* ed. Warren M. Billings (Chapel Hill: Univ. of North Carolina Press, 1975), 22-26.

2. Ibid.

3. "Starving Time," in Billings, *Old Dominion,* 28.

4. Charles Campbell, *History of the Colony and Ancient Dominion of Virginia* (Philadelphia: J. B. Lippincott & Co. 1860), 93.

5. "Starving Time," 28.

6. Campbell, *Colony and Ancient Dominion,* 104.

7. Philip Alexander Bruce, *Economic History of Virginia in the Seventeenth Century,* vol. 1 (New York: Macmillan, 1907), 205.

8. Billings, *Old Dominion,* 9.

9. Bruce, *Economic History,* 212-13.

10. Alexander Brown, *The First Republic in America* (Boston: Houghton Mifflin Co., 1898; reprint, New York: Russell & Russell, 1969), 205.

11. Bruce, *Economic History,* 220.

12. Matthew Page Andrews, *Virginia, The Old Dominion,* vol. 1 (Richmond, Va.: Dietz Press, 1949), 68.

13. Ibid., 59, 61.

14. Ibid., 72.

15. Brown, *First Republic,* 205.

16. "A True and Sincere Declaration," in Billings, *Old Dominion,* 14.

17. Ibid., 27.

18. Andrews, *Virginia,* 67-68.

19. William Bradford, *Of Plymouth Plantation, 1620-1647,* ed. Samuel Eliot Morison (New York: Knopf, 1952), 30, n. 2.

20. Ibid., 25.

21. Ibid., 120-21.

22. Ibid., 38.

23. Ibid., 37, n. 2.

24. Ibid.

25. Ibid., 360.

26. Ibid., 364

27. Ibid., 362-63.

28. Ibid., 363.

29. Ibid., 40.

30. Samuel Eliot Morison, introduction to Bradford, *Plymouth Plantation,* xxiv.

31. George D. Langdon, Jr., *Pilgrim Colony: A History of New Plymouth, 1620-1691* (New Haven: Yale Univ. Press, 1966), 12.

32. Bradford, *Plymouth Plantation,* 120-21.

33. Langdon, *Pilgrim Colony,* 30.

34. Samuel Eliot Morison, *The Story of the "Old Colony" of New Plymouth* (New York: Knopf, 1960) 95-96.

35. Bradford, *Plymouth Plantation,* 121.

36. Jean Bodin, *The Six Books Of A Commonweale,* ed. Kenneth D. McRae (Cambridge, Mass.: Harvard Univ. Press, 1962), 11.

37. Ibid., 12, 707.

CHAPTER 4

1. Andrei Sinyavsky, *Soviet Civilization: A Cultural History* (New York: Little Brown, 1988), 165-68.

2. John Wade, *History of the Middle and Working Classes* (1833; reprint, New York: Augustus M. Kelley, 1966), 429.

3. William Forster Lloyd, "On the Checks to Population," in *Managing the Commons,* ed. Garrett Hardin and John Baden (San Francisco: W. H. Freeman, 1977), chap. 3.

4. Harold Demsetz, "Toward a Theory of Property Rights," *American Economic Review* 57 (May 1967): 347-59; reprinted in Harold Demsetz, *The Organization of Economic Activity,* vol. 1 (Oxford: Basil Blackwell, 1988); Garrett Hardin, "The Tragedy of the Commons," *Science* 162 (December 13, 1968): 1243-48; reprinted in Hardin and Baden, *Managing the Commons.*

5. Hardin, "Tragedy of the Commons," 22.

6. Ibid., 20

7. Ibid., 21

8. Garrett Hardin, "Property Rights: The Creative Reworking of a Fiction," in *Naked Emperors: Essays of a Taboo Stalker* (Los Altos, Cal.: Wm. Kaufmann, 1982), 173-82; see also Garrett Hardin, *Filters Against Folly* (New York: Viking Penguin, 1985), 89-114.

9. Elinor Ostrom, *Governing the Commons: The Evolution of Institutions for Collective Action* (Cambridge: Cambridge Univ. Press, 1990); Glenn G. Stevenson, *Common Property Economics: A General Theory and Land Use Applications* (Cambridge: Cambridge Univ. Press, 1991; Matt Ridley, *The Origins of Virtue* (New York: Viking, 1996), chap. 12.

10. Robert C. Ellickson, "Property in Land," *Yale Law Journal* 102 (1993): 1327-28.

11. See John A. Hostetler, *Hutterite Society* (Baltimore: Johns Hopkins Univ. Press, 1974); Karl A. Peter, *The Dynamics of Hutterite Society* (Edmonton: Univ. of Alberta Press, 1987); William M. Kephart, *Extraordinary Groups* (New York: St. Martin's Press, 1976).

12. Martin Buber, *Paths in Utopia* (Boston, Beacon Press, 1958), 139.

13. Amos Elon, *The Israelis: Founders and Sons* (Harmondsworth, Eng.: Pelican Books, 1983), 20.

14. Joel Brinkley, "Debts Make Israelis Rethink an Ideal: The Kibbutz," *New York Times,* March 5, 1989; Daniel Williams, "Down on the Kibbutz, Israelis Face a Financial Crisis," *Los Angeles Times,* May 19, 1989; Glenn Frankel, "Farewell to the Kibbutz," *Washington Post,* July 9, 1989; Geraldine Brooks, "Saving the Farm: The Israeli Kibbutz Takes a Capitalist Tack to Keep Socialist Ideals," *Wall Street Journal,* September 21, 1989.

15. Author's interview with Jacob Gadish (Tel Aviv), February 1990. See Tom Bethell, "Is the Kibbutz Kaput?" in *Free Minds & Free Markets,* ed. Robert W. Poole, Jr., and Virginia I. Postrel (San Francisco: Pacific Research Institute, 1993), 81-90.

16. James D. Gwartney and Richard L. Stroup, *Economics: Private and Public Choice,* 4th ed. (New York: Harcourt Brace Jovanovich, 1987), 670.

17. Birgir Runolfsson, "Fencing the Oceans," *Regulation* (summer 1997): 57-62; and see "The Tragedy of the Oceans," *Economist* (March 19, 1994), 21-24.
18. Ronald H. Coase, *The Firm, the Market, and the Law* (Chicago: Univ. of Chicago Press, 1988), 23. Coase points out in chapter 9 that, although Samuelson's *Economics* had used the lighthouse as an example of a good that only government could provide, lighthouses in Britain had for centuries been privately built and operated.
19. A. C. Pigou, *Economics of Welfare,* 2d ed. (London: Macmillan, 1924), 162.
20. Elon, *The Israelis,* 141.

INTRODUCTION TO PART III

1. The work was written in Constantinople in the reign of the emperor Justinian and consists of excerpts from 2,000 books of Roman law then extant (the great majority of them have since perished). Remarkably, a full English translation of the *Corpus Juris Civilis* was not published until 1985. In that year the University of Pennsylvania brought out the *Digest* of Justinian in four hefty volumes. Both Latin and English translation are included, the latter alone filling 1875 pages of small print. Alan Watson ed., *The Digest of Justinian,* 4 vols. (Philadelphia: University of Pennsylvania Press, 1985).
2. Ibid.,. 1: xi.
3. Ibid., 1: 24.

CHAPTER 5

1. Perry Anderson, *Passages from Antiquity to Feudalism* (London: Verso, 1974), 66.
2. Edward Gibbon, *Decline and Fall of the Roman Empire,* vol. 40 of *Great Books of the Western World* (Chicago: Encyclopaedia Britannica, 1952), 21.
3. Julius Caesar, *De Bello Gallico* (London: William Heinemann, 1917), vi, 22.
4. Baron de Montesquieu, *The Spirit of Laws,* vol. 38, *Great Books,* 26-28 (book 5 chap.14).
5. Ibid., book 6, chap. 3.
6. Aristotle, *Constitution of Athens* (New York: Hafner Publishing, 1950), 6.
7. Plato, *The Republic,* trans. B. Jowett, book 5 (New York: The Heritage Press, 1944), 265.
8. Aristotle, *The Politics of Aristotle,* trans. E. Barker (Oxford: Clarendon Press, 1946), 1262b.
9. Ibid., 1263a.
10. Ibid., 1261b.
11. Ibid., 1263a.
12. Ibid., 1264a.
13. Ibid., 1263b.
14. Ibid., 1329a.
15. Ibid., 1329b.
16. Ibid., 1263a.
17. Ibid., 1329b.
18. Tenney Frank, ed., *An Economic Survey of Ancient Rome,* vol. 1 (Baltimore: Johns Hopkins Press, 1933), 14.
19. Justinian, *Justinian's Institutes,* trans. P. Birks and G. McLeod (Ithaca: Cornell Univ. Press, 1987), 59.
20. Alan Rodger, *Owners and Neighbors in Roman Law* (Oxford: Clarendon Press, 1972), 1.
21. Justinian, *Codex* vii, 16.1.
22. Numa Fustel de Coulanges, *The Ancient City: A Study on the Religion, Laws and Institutions of Greece and Rome* (1864), reprint (Baltimore: Johns Hopkins Univ. Press, 1980), 52-64.
23. *Ibid.,* 62-63.
24. Aristotle, *Politics,* 1270a.

25. *The Digest of Justinian,* ed. and trans. Alan Watson, vol. 1 (Philadelphia: Univ. of Pennsylvania Press, 1985), 24-25.

26. M. I. Finley, ed., *Studies in Roman Property* (Cambridge: Cambridge Univ. Press, 1976), 2-3.

27. Ibid., 23.

28. Ibid., 89.

29. L. P. Wilkinson, ed., *Letters of Cicero: A Selection in Translation* (New York: W. W. Norton, 1968), 145, 148.

30. Bruce W. Frier, *Landlords and Tenants in Imperial Rome* (Princeton, N.J.: Princeton Univ. Press, 1980), 34-39.

31. Finley, *Roman Property,* 73.

32. Ibid., 128.

33. Frier, *Landlords and Tenants,* 32-33.

34. John A. Crook, *Law and Life of Rome* (Ithaca: Cornell Univ. Press, 1967), 142.

35. Ibid., 148.

36. Tacitus, *The Annals of Imperial Rome,* trans. Michael Grant (Harmondsworth: Penguin, 1974), 364.

37. Ibid., 92.

38. Rodger, *Owners and Neighbors,* 2-10.

39. *Digest of Justinian,* 275.

40. Crook, *Law and Life,* 259, 263.

41. J. M. Riddle, ed., *Tiberius Gracchus: Destroyer or Reformer of the Republic* (Lexington, Mass.: D. C. Heath, 1970), 1-13.

42. Ibid., 61.

43. Frank, *Economic Survey,* 221.

44. Anderson, *Passages,* 71.

45. Cicero, *De Officiis,* book 2, trans. Walter Miller (London: William Heinemann, 1913), 259.

46. Ibid., 255.

47. Ibid., 249.

48. Cicero, *De Re Publica,* trans. C.W. Keyes (London: William Heinemann, 1928), book 3, 211.

49. Cicero, *De Legibus,* trans. C.W. Keyes (London: William Heinemann, 1928), book 1, 329.

CHAPTER 6

1. Henry Hallam, *View of the State of Europe during the Middle Ages,* vol. 2 (1818; reprint, New York: W. J. Widdleton, 1874), 267.

2. Alexis de Tocqueville, *De Tocqueville's L'ancien régime,* trans. M. W. Patterson (Oxford: Basil Blackwell, 1956), 184-85.

3. Alan Macfarlane, *The Origins of English Individualism* (Oxford: Basil Blackwell, 1978), 7, 8.

4. Ibid., 199-200, 206, 170.

5. David S. Landes, *The Wealth and Poverty of Nations: Why Some Are So Rich and Some So Poor* (New York: W. W. Norton, 1998), 200, 217; David S. Landes, *The Unbound Prometheus* (London: Cambridge Univ. Press, 1969), 12, 16-17. In a review of *The Wealth and Poverty of Nations* David Frum notes that Landes "ultimately fails to deliver what he promised: an explanation of why the West is rich and most of the rest is not . . . . [H]e seems uninterested in the legal institutions and social habits that gave eighteenth- century English cotton spinners confidence that the contracts they signed would be honored, the profits they made would not be confiscated, and the money in which they stored their wealth would hold its value. Without altogether meaning to, Landes ends up telling the story of *how* the West got rich, rather than *why*." (David Frum, "As the World Turns," *Weekly Standard,* April 27, 1998.)

6. Vincent T. H. Delaney, ed., *Frederic William Maitland Reader* (New York: Oceana Publications, 1957), 48-62.

7. Frederic W. Maitland, *The Constitutional History of England* (1908; reprint, Cambridge: Cambridge Univ. Press, 1955), 142.

8. Ibid., 142.

9. Ibid., 156.

10. Eileen Power, *Medieval People,* 10th ed. (London: Methuen, 1964), 160.

11. Robert L. Heilbroner and Lester G. Thurow, *The Economic Problem,* 4th ed. (Englewood Cliffs, N. J.: Prentice-Hall, 1975), 17.

12. Karl Marx, *Capital,* vol. 50 of *Great Books of the Western World* (Chicago: Encyclopaedia Britannica, 1952), 354-58 (Chapters 26 and 27).

13. Macfarlane, *Individualism,* 195-96.

14. John G. A. Pocock, *The Ancient Constitution and the Feudal Law* (Cambridge: Cambridge Univ. Press, 1957), 33-34.

15. Hallam, *Middle Ages,* 2: 316.

16. Maitland, *Constitutional History,* 134-35.

17. A. V. Dicey, *Introduction to the Study of the Law of the Constitution* (1885; reprint, London: Macmillan, 1960), 199.

18. Coke, 8 Rep. 118a (1610).

19. Frederick Pollock and Frederic W. Maitland, *The History of English Law Before the Time of Edward I,* 2nd ed., 2 vols. (1895; reprint, Cambridge: Cambridge Univ Press, 1968), 1: 407.

20. Ibid., 408-9.

21. Hallam, *Middle Ages,* 2: 328.

22. Maitland, *Constitutional History,* 125.

23. John E. A. Jolliffe, *Constitutional History of Medieval England,* 2nd ed. (London: A & C. Black, 1947), 334.

24. Frederic W. Maitland, *Selected Historical Essays* (Cambridge: Cambridge Univ. Press 1957), 127.

25. Ibid., 137.

26. Hallam, *Middle Ages,* 2: 329.

27. Charles H. Wilson, *Economic History and the Historian* (New York: Praeger, 1969), 120.

28. Modern survey data show that, where different denominations are subject to the same laws, and where none has either legal privilege or disability, as has been true in the United States, there is no significant difference in income between Catholics and other Christian denominations. This suggests that all along the key lay in the domain of law. Gallup Opinion Index, April 1971, No. 70.

29. John Locke, *Letter Concerning Toleration,* in vol. 35 of *Great Books of the Western World,* 2-3.

30. John Locke, *Two Treatises of Government,* ed. Peter Laslett (Cambridge: Cambridge Univ. Press, 1960), *Second Treatise,* paragraph 222.

31. Ibid., paragraphs 27, 40.

32. Ibid., Laslett introduction.

33. P. S. Atiyah, *The Rise and Fall of Freedom of Contract* (Oxford: Clarendon Press, 1979), 14.

34. Adam Smith, *An Inquiry into the Nature and Causes of the Wealth of Nations* (Oxford: Oxford Univ. Press, 1976, reprint, Indianapolis, Liberty Classics), 392.

35. Wilson, *Economic History,* chap. 7.

36. G. E. Mingay, *Studies in Economic History: Enclosure and the Small Farmer in the Age of the Industrial Revolution* (London: Macmillan, 1968), 18-19.

37. Marx, *Capital,* chap. 26.

38. Atiyah, *Freedom of Contract,* 15.

39. Dicey, *Constitution,* 189.

40. Smith, *Wealth of Nations,* 540.

41. Ibid., 541.

42. David S. Landes, ed., *The Rise of Capitalism* (New York: Macmillan, 1966), 99.

43. Arnold Toynbee, *The Industrial Revolution* (1884; reprint, Boston, Beacon Press, 1956), 58.

44. Phyllis Deane, *The First Industrial Revolution* (Cambridge: Cambridge Univ. Press, 2nd ed. 1979), 219, 220.

45. R. M. Hartwell, *The Industrial Revolution and Economic Growth* (London: Methuen, 1971), 245, 247, 250.

CHAPTER 7

1. John M. Davidson, *Concerning Four Precursors of Henry George and the Single Tax* (1899, reprint, Port Washington, N.Y.: Kennikat Press, 1971).

2. James Boswell, *Life of Samuel Johnson* (New York: Doubleday, 1946), 270.

3. Thomas More, *Utopia,* ed. R. M. Adams (New York: Norton 1992), 34.

4. Rousseau, *Discourse on the Origin of Inequality,* in Jean-Jacques Rousseau, *Basic Political Writings,* trans. and ed. Donald A. Cress, introduction by Peter Gay (Indianapolis: Hackett Publishing, 1987), 60.

5. Ibid., 25.

6. Joan McDonald, *Rousseau and the French Revolution, 1762-1791* (London: Univ. of London Press, 1965).

7. John Rae, Life of Adam Smith (London: Macmillan, 1895), 123-24, 208.

8. Adam Smith, *Lectures on Jurisprudence* (Oxford: Clarendon Press, 1978), 5.

9. Smith, *The Wealth of Nations,* I, i, 3. (Hereafter: book, chapter, paragraph.)

10. George Stigler, "The Successes and Failures of Professor Smith," *Journal of Political Economy* 84 (1976): 1209.

11. A. R. J. Turgot, *The Economics of A. R. J. Turgot,* ed. P. D. Groenewegen (The Hague: 1977), xvii, 43-95.

12. Jean-Baptiste Say, *A Treatise on Political Economy* (1803: reprint, New York: Augustus Kelley, 1971), 127-32.

13. James Steuart, *An Inquiry into the Principles of Political Oeconomy,* ed. Andrew S. Skinner (Chicago: Univ. of Chicago Press, 1966), 24, 20.

14. Thomas R. Malthus, *The Works of Thomas Robert Malthus,* ed. E. A. Wrigley and David Souden (London: Pickering, 1986), 6: 249-50.

15. Adam Smith, *The Wealth of Nations,* V, i, 2.

16. David Ricardo, *Works and Correspondence of David Ricardo,* ed. Piero Sraffa (Cambridge: Cambridge Univ. Press, 1962) 1: 204, 154-55.

17. Adam Ferguson, *An Essay on the History of Civil Society, 1767* (Edinburgh: Edinburgh Univ. Press, 1966), 82.

18. William Blackstone, *Ehrlich's Blackstone,* ed. J. W. Ehrlich (San Carlos, Cal.: Nourse Pub. Co., 1959), 113; Jeremy Bentham, *Principles of the Civil Code,* in *Property, Mainstream and Critical Positions,* ed. C. B. Macpherson (Toronto: Univ. of Toronto Press, 1978), 53.

19. Marcello T. Maestro, *Cesare Beccaria and the Origins of Penal Reform* (Philadelphia: Temple Univ. Press, 1973), 131.

20. In the first edition (1764), Beccaria had described property as "a terrible but perhaps necessary right." This was changed in later editions, including the English translation, to "unnecessary." Beccaria was particularly dismayed that the right to property gave owners the right to cut down their own trees. This is what seems to have changed his mind. (Ibid., 91.)

21. Bentham, *Principles of the Civil Code,* ed. Macpherson, 53.

22. Alfred Marshall, *Principles of Economics* (1890; reprint, New York: Macmillan, 1961), 760.

23. William Paley, *The Principles of Moral and Political Philosophy* (London: R. Faulder, 1785), book 3, chaps 1-4.

24. Edmund Paley, *An Account of the Life and Writings of William Paley* (1825; reprint, Farnborough: Gregg, 1970), 340-41.

25. Henry Homes, Lord Kames, *Historical Law Tracts,* 3rd ed. (Edinburgh: J. Bell and W. Creech, 1776), 153.

26. Thomas Jefferson, *The Life and Selected Writings of Thomas Jefferson,* ed. A. Kock and W. Peden (New York: Modern Library, 1944), 38.

27. Peter H. Marshall, *William Godwin* (New Haven: Yale Univ. Press, 1984), 1.

28. William Godwin, *Enquiry Concerning Political Justice,* 3rd ed. (1798), ed. F. E. L. Priestley (Toronto: Univ. of Toronto Press, 1946), 1: 11.

29. Leslie Stephen, *History of English Thought in the Eighteenth Century,* 3rd ed. (New York: P. Smith, 1949), 2: 264.

30. William Paley, *Reasons for Contentment* (Dublin: J. Milliken, 1793), 5-6.

31. H. S. Salt, *Introduction to Godwin's "Political Justice": A Reprint of the Essay on Property* (1890; reprint, Michigan Scholarly Press).

32. Godwin, *Political Justice,* 2: 528.

33. H. S. Salt, *Godwin's "Political Justice".*

34. John Maynard Keynes, *Essays and Sketches in Biography* (New York: Meridian Books, 1956), 12-14.

35. Malthus, *Works,* 1: 65.
36. Malthus, *Works,* 6: 249-50.
37. John R. McCulloch, *Principles of Political Economy,* 4th ed. (Edinburgh: Adam and Charles Black, 1849), 79-90.
38. Malthus, *Works,* 4: 199.

CHAPTER 8

1. David Ricardo, preface to *Principles of Political Economy and Taxation* (1817) (New York: Dutton, 1973).
2. Karl Marx, preface to *Capital* (1867), vol 50, *Great Books of the Western World* (Chicago: Encyclopaedia Britannica, 1952), 7.
3. George Stigler, *The Essence of Stigler* (Stanford: Hoover Institution Press, 1986), 290.
4. John Stuart Mill, "Principles of Political Economy" (1848); Mill, *Collected Works,* ed. John Robson (Toronto: Univ. of Toronto Press, 1963-1991), 2: 199.
5. Ibid., 2: 200.
6. Mill, "Autobiography," *Collected Works,* 1: 255.
7. Mill, "Principles," *Collected Works,* 2: 175.
8. Mill, "Essays on Economics and Society," *Collected Works,* 4: 225.
9. Mill, "A System of Logic," *Collected Works,* 8: VI, x, 3.
10. Mill, "Principles," *Collected Works,* 2: 213, 214, 210.
11. Ibid., 2: 203.
12. Ibid., 2: 204.
13. Ibid.
14. Ibid., 2: 210.
15. Mill, "Chapters on Socialism," *Collected Works,* 5: 746.
16. Mill, "Principles," *Collected Works,* 2: 209.
17. Ibid.
18. Mill, "Chapters on Socialism," *Collected Works,* 5: 748.
19. Ibid.
20. Ibid., 5: 739, 750.
21. Mill, "Additional Letters of John Stuart Mill," *Collected Works,* 32: 220.
22. Marx and Friedrich Engels, *Manifesto of the Communist Party,* vol. 50, *Great Books,* 425.
23. Pierre-Joseph Proudhon, *What Is Property?* (1840), ed. and trans D. R. Kelley and B. G. Smith (Cambridge: Cambridge Univ. Press, 1994), 211.
24. Karl Marx, *The Poverty of Philosophy* (New York: International Publishers, 1963), 198-99.
25. Jeremy Waldron, *The Right to Private Property* (Oxford: Clarendon Press, 1988), 427.
26. Ibid., 428.
27. David McLellan ed., *Karl Marx: Selected Writings* (Oxford, Oxford Univ. Press), 349.
28. Marx, *Manifesto,* chap. 2.
29. Ibid., chap. 3.
30. Karl Marx, *Poverty of Philosophy,* 192.
31. Marx, *Manifesto,* chap. 2.
32. Ibid.
33. Mill, "Principles," *Collected Works,* 2: 204.
34. Friedrich Hayek, ed., *John Stuart Mill and Harriet Taylor: Their Correspondence and Subsequent Marriage* (London: Routledge & Kegan Paul, 1951), 126.
35. Ibid., 137.
36. Marx, *Poverty of Philosophy,* 147.
37. Bertrand Russell, *A History of Western Philosophy* (New York: Simon & Schuster, 1945), 788-89.
38. Robert Skidelsky, *John Maynard Keynes,* vol. 1 (New York: Viking, 1983), 40.
39. Alfred Marshall, *Principles of Economics* (1890; reprint, New York: Macmillan, 1961), 721-22.
40. Ibid., 764.
41. Russell, *History,* 727.
42. Charles Darwin, *The Descent of Man* (1871), vol 49, *Great Books,* 597.

43. J. B. Bury, *The Idea of Progress* (1932; reprint, New York: Dover Publications, 1955), 346-48.
44. Marshall, *Principles,* 243.
45. John Offer, ed., *Herbert Spencer: Political Writings* (Cambridge: Cambridge Univ. Press, 1994), xviii.
46. Ibid.
47. Keynes, *Essays in Biography,* 71.
48. Ibid., 77.
49. Beatrice Webb, *The Diary of Beatrice Webb* (Cambridge, Mass.: Harvard, 1982), 1: 315.
50. G. B. Shaw, ed., *Fabian Essays in Socialism* (London: W. Scott, 1889), 168, 178, 184-85.
51. Richard T. Ely, *Ground Under Our Feet: An Autobiography* (New York: Macmillan 1938), 154, 140.
52. F.W. Taussig, *Principles of Economics* (1911; reprint, New York: Macmillan, 1939), 2: 523.
53. Mikhail Heller, *Cogs in the Wheel: The Formation of Soviet Man* (New York: Knopf, 1988), 125.
54. "Gorbachev and Yeltsin Answer Questions from Americans on TV," Reuters dispatch, *Washington Post,* September 7, 1991.

INTRODUCTION TO PART V

1. Gregory Claeys, ed., *Selected Works of Robert Owen,* 4 vols. (London: William Pickering, 1993), 2: 51.
2. Ibid., 2: 208.
3. Ibid., 1: lii.
4. Ibid., 3: 328.
5. Ibid., 1: xlvii.

CHAPTER 9

1. See G. D. H. Cole, *The Life of Robert Owen* (London: Macmillan, 1930); Sidney Pollard and John Salt, eds., *Robert Owen: Prophet of the Poor* (Lewisburg, Pa.: Bucknell Univ. Press, 1971).
2. J. F. C. Harrison, *The Quest for the New Moral World* (New York: Scribner's, 1969) 49.
3. Robert Owen, *Life of Robert Owen* (London: Effingham Wilson, 1857), 30.
4. Cole, *Robert Owen,* 56.
5. Robert Dale Owen, *Threading My Way* (New York: G. W. Carleton, 1874), 27-37.
6. Harrison, *New Moral World,* 15.
7. Ibid., 154-55.
8. Owen, *Life,* 146.
9. Cole, *Robert Owen,* 193.
10. George B. Lockwood, *The New Harmony Movement* (New York: D. Appleton and Co., 1905), 7.
11. R. D. Owen, *Threading My Way,* 240.
12. Igor Shafarevich, *The Socialist Phenomenon* (New York: Harper & Row, 1980), 194-201.
13. Gregory Claeys, ed., *Selected Works of Robert Owen,* 4 vols. (London: William Pickering, 1993), 3: 326- 27.
14. Cole, *Robert Owen,* 229.
15. Ibid., 230.
16. R. D. Owen, *Threading My Way,* 275-76.
17. Ibid., 286.
18. Morris Hillquit, *History of Socialism in the United States,* 5th ed. (New York: Funk and Wagnalls, 1910), 58.
19. Charles J. Erasmus, *In Search of the Common Good: Utopian Experiments Past and Future* (New York: Free Press, 1977), 144.
20. R. D. Owen, *Threading My Way,* 286.
21. Ibid., 287.

22. Lockwood, *New Harmony Movement*, 120.
23. Ibid., 118.
24. Ibid., 123-27.
25. R. D. Owen, *Threading My Way*, 290.
26. Ibid., 290.
27. Ibid., 293.
28. Charles Nordhoff, *The Communistic Societies of the United States* (1875; reprint, New York, Dover Publications, 1966), 79-80.
29. Lockwood, *New Harmony Movement*, 35.
30. Owen, *Life*, 363-64.
31. Lockwood, *New Harmony Movement*, 40; and see Nordhoff, who devoted long chapters to the Shakers and the Oneida Perfectionists. By 1874, 2415 Shakers lived in 58 separate communities, most in New England. The Oneida Perfectionists, founded in 1848, deemed "exclusiveness in regards to women" as objectionable as "exclusiveness in regards to money." Their religion was fuzzy, and their social experiment, including "complex marriage," or free love, lasted for a generation. (Nordhoff, *Communistic Societies*, 117-301.)
32. Pollard and Salt, *Robert Owen*, 177.
33. Cole, *Robert Owen*, 311.

CHAPTER 10

1. Leon Trotsky, *Literature and Revolution* (Ann Arbor: Univ. of Michigan Press, 1960), 19.
2. Richard Pipes, *The Russian Revolution* (New York: Knopf, 1990), 672.
3. Richard Pipes, *Communism: The Vanished Specter* (New York: Oxford Univ. Press, 1994), 53.
4. Ludwig von Mises, *Human Action*, 3rd ed. (Chicago: Henry Regnery, 1966), 695-96.
5. Pipes, *Russian Revolution*, 671.
6. V. I. Lenin, "Left-Wing Childishness and Petty Bourgeois Mentality," *Selected Works* (London: Lawrence and Wishart, 1937), 7: 359.
7. Pipes, *Russian Revolution*, 685.
8. Ibid., 695-97.
9. V. I. Lenin, "A Single Economic Plan," *Pravda*, February 22, 1921, reprinted in *Selected Works*, 8: 299-306.
10. Mikhail Heller and Aleksandr Nekrich, *Utopia in Power* (New York: Simon and Schuster, 1986), 222.
11. Hewlett Johnson, *The Soviet Power: The Socialist Sixth of the World* (New York: International Publishers, 1941), 87-89.
12. Thomas Sowell, *Knowledge and Decisions* (New York: Basic Books, 1980), 215.
13. Ibid., 215, 393.
14. Mises, *Human Action*, 695.
15. Oskar Lange and Fred M. Taylor, *On the Economic Theory of Socialism*, ed. B. Lippincott (1938; reprint, New York: McGraw-Hill, 1964); Robert Heilbroner, "Reflections: After Communism," *New Yorker*, September 10, 1990.
16. Vladimir Bukovsky, *To Build a Castle: My Life as a Dissenter* (New York: Viking Penguin, 1978), 123.
17. Walter Lippmann, *An Inquiry into the Principles of The Good Society* (Boston: Little Brown, 1937), chap. 6.
18. Friedrich A. Hayek, *The Constitution of Liberty* (Chicago: Univ. of Chicago Press, 1960), 450; Friedrich A. Hayek, *The Road to Serfdom* (Chicago: Univ of Chicago Press, 1944), chap. 5.
19. Roy F. Harrod, *The Life of John Maynard Keynes* (London: Macmillan, 1951), 436.
20. "Shortages Spark Gorbachev Fury at Lazy Workers," AP dispatch, April 26, 1989; and see David Remnick, "Soviet Party Chiefs' Speeches Show Anxieties," *Washington Post*, April 29, 1989.
21. V. I. Lenin, *State and Revolution*, in *Selected Works*, 7: 88-9.
22. Leon Trotsky, *Literature and Revolution*, 256.
23. Sidney Webb and Beatrice Webb, *Soviet Communism: A New Civilization*, 3rd ed. (London: Longmans Green, 1944), 759.

24. Julian Huxley, *A Scientist Among the Soviets* (New York: Harper Bros, 1932), 55.
25. Lincoln Steffens, *Letters of Lincoln Steffens* (New York: Harcourt, Brace, 1938), 930, 1003; and see Genevieve Taggard, review of *The Letters of Lincoln Steffens,* "I Have Seen the Future—And It Works," *Soviet Russia Today* 7 (December 1938): 26-27.
26. A. P. Shatter, "Remaking Human Beings," *Soviet Russia Today* 6 (August 1937): 23-24.
27. Thomas Woody, *New Minds, New Men* (New York: Macmillan, 1932), 467.
28. *Communist Party of USSR Program, 1961* (New York: Crosscurrents Press, 1961), 69-70, 119, 123.
29. Mikhail Gorbachev, *To Work in a New Way* (Moscow: Novosti Press, 1986), 99.
30. Karen Elliott House, "Communist Giants Are Too Burdened at Home to Lead Much Abroad," *Wall Street Journal,* February 6, 1989.
31. Jerome Wiesner (1957), 77-78.
32. Norman Cousins, "Psychology as a Key," *Saturday Review,* July 8, 1961.
33. William Benton, *This is the Challenge* (New York: Associated College Presses, 1958), 106, 110.
34. Robert Heilbroner, *The Future As History* (New York: Harper, 1960), 82.
35. Seymour Topping, "Moscow Issues Party Program: Calls Coexistence a 'Necessity': Foresees Vast Economic Gains," *New York Times,* July 30, 1961, p. 1; "Condensed Version of Khrushchev's Speech to Soviet Communist Party Congress," (transmitted by Tass), *New York Times,* October 18, 1961.
36. W. H. Lawrence, "Allen Dulles Sees U.S. Peril in Soviet's Econmic Rise: CIA Chief Tells Chamber of Commerce Russian Growth Is Greatest Peacetime Threat," *New York Times,* April 29, 1958, p. 1.
37. Paul Samuelson, *Economics,* 11th ed. (New York: McGraw-Hill, 1980), 825.
38. Bill Keller, "Soviets Seek a Definition of Property," *New York Times,* October 1, 1989; David Remnick, "Soviets Seek Strike Ban to Prevent Anarchy: Draft of New Property Law Also Presented," *Washington Post,* October 3, 1989; and see Bill Keller, "Gorbachev Says It's Not Time for Soviet Private Property," *New York Times,* November 17, 1989.

INTRODUCTION TO PART VI

1. Kenneth R. Minogue, "The Concept of Property and Its Contemporary Significance," *Nomos XXII, Property* (New York: New York University, 1980), 3.

CHAPTER 11

1. Garrett Hardin, "The Tragedy of the Commons," *Science,* December 13, 1968.
2. Thomas Aquinas, *Summa Theologica,* I-II, Q 64, art 2, in *Basic Writings of St. Thomas Aquinas,* ed. Anton C. Pegis (New York: Random House, 1945), 2: 491.
3. Thomas Hobbes, *Leviathan* (Harmondsworth, Eng.: Penguin, 1968), ed. C. B. Macpherson, 202.
4. John Hospers, *Human Conduct: An Introduction to the Problems of Ethics* (New York: Harcourt Brace & World, 1972), 345.
5. Alan Ryan, *Property* (Minneapolis: Univ. of Minnesota Press, 1987), 80.
6. Thomas Paine, "The First Principles of Government," in *Life and Works of Thomas Paine* (New Rochelle, N.Y.: 1925), 5: 230.
7. David Hume, *A Treatise of Human Nature,* ed. L. A. Selby-Bigge (Oxford: Clarendon Press, 1978), 507-8.
8. John Rawls, *A Theory of Justice* (Cambridge, Mass.: Harvard Univ. Press, 1971), 15.
9. Ibid., 100.
10. M. W. Jackson, *Matters of Justice* (London: Croom Helm, 1986), 30.
11. Rawls, *Theory of Justice,* 530.
12. Friedrich A. Hayek, *The Mirage of Social Justice,* vol. 2 of *Law, Legislation and Liberty* (Chicago: Univ. of Chicago Press, 1976), chap. 9.

NOTES TO CHAPTER 12

13. Aristotle, *Nicomachean Ethics,* book 5, 1130b, trans. H. G. Apostle (Boston: D. Reidel Publ. Co., 1975), 82.
14. Rawls, *Theory of Justice,* 303.
15. J. R. Lucas, *On Justice* (New York: Oxford Univ. Press, 1980), 186-89.
16. Ryan, *Property,* 87.

CHAPTER 12

1. John Locke, *Second Treatise,* ed. Peter Laslett (Cambridge: Cambridge Univ. Press, 1963), #5.
2. George Herbert, "The Church-Porch," *The Poems of George Herbert*, 2nd ed. (London: Oxford Univ. Press, 1961), stanza 68.
3. James W. Ely, *The Guardian of Every Other Right* (New York: Oxford Univ. Press, 1992), 26.
4. *West Virginia State Bd. of Educ. v Barnette,* 319 U.S. 624 (1943).
5. Thomas Hobbes, *Leviathan,* ed. Michael Oakeshott (New York: Macmillan: 1962), ch. 15.
6. Ibid., 162.
7. Locke, *Second Treatise,* #123, #124.
8. Jeremy Waldron, ed., *"Nonsense Upon Stilts"* (New York: Methuen, 1987), 22-27.
9. Garry Wills, *Inventing America* (Garden City, N.Y.: Doubleday, 1978), 237.
10. Stanley N. Katz, "Thomas Jefferson and the Right to Property in Revolutionary America," *Journal of Law and Economics* 19 (October 1976), 467-88.
11. Frederic Bastiat, "Property and Law," in *Selected Essays on Political Economy* (New York: Foundation for Economic Education, 1964), 99. Schumpeter's description of Bastiat occurs in Friedrich Hayek's introduction to this volume, page ix.
12. Waldron, "Nonsense," 96-109.
13. Ibid., 68.
14. Ibid., 127-28.
15. Morton J. Horwitz, *The Transformation of American Law, 1780-1860* (Cambridge, Mass.: Harvard Univ. Press, 1977), chaps. 2 and 4.
16. Andrew Carnegie, "The Gospel of Wealth" in *A Documentary History of the United States,* ed. R. D. Heffner (New York: Mentor, 1965), 174.
17. Charles Adams, *For Good and Evil: The Impact of Taxes on the Course of Civilization* (New York: Madison Books, 1993) 360-64.
18. *Lochner v. New York,* 198 U.S. 45 (1905).
19. Ibid.
20. Theodore Roosevelt, *The New Nationalism* (1910; reprint, Englewood Cliffs, N.J.: Prentice-Hall, 1961), 33.
21. Herbert David Croly, *The Promise of American Life* (New York: Macmillan, 1909). Herbert Croly believed that the institution of private property "stimulates human cupidity," and like his Victorian predecessors was convinced that "a modification of that institution will itself tend to socialize human nature." Herbert D. Croly, *Progressive Democracy* (New York: Macmillan, 1914), 112.
22. Phillipa Strum, *Louis D. Brandeis: Justice for the People* (Cambridge, Mass.: Harvard Univ. Press, 1984), 322.
23. Robert H. Bork, *The Tempting of America* (New York: Free Press, 1990), 53.
24. *West Coast Hotel Co. v. Parrish,* 300 US 379 (1937).
25. *U.S. v. Carolene Products,* 304 US 144 (1938).
26. Sidney Hook, interview by author, May 1989.
27. James MacGregor Burns and Stewart Burns, *A People's Charter* (New York: Knopf, 1991), 263.
28. Antony Flew, "The Artificial Inflation of Natural Rights," *The Freeman* 39 (December 1989): 483-85.
29. Thomas Paine, *Life and Works of Thomas Paine,* ed. William Van der Wyde, vol. 5 (New Rochelle, N.Y.: 1925), 155-57.
30. David Ricardo, *Works and Correspondence of David Ricardo,* ed. Piero Sraffa, vol. 5 (Cambridge: Cambridge Univ. Press, 1962), 501.
31. John Stuart Mill, *On Representative Government* (1861), in vol. 43 of *Great Books of the Western World* (Chicago: Encyclopedia Britannica, 1952), 383.

32. Charles Reich, "The New Property," *Yale Law Journal*, 73 (April 1964): 733.

33. U.S. Department of State, *Country Reports on Human Rights Practices* (Washington, D.C.: Government Printing Office, 1981), 2, 899.

34. Leon Trotsky, *The Revolution Betrayed* (Garden City, N.Y.: Doubleday, 1937), 76.

35. Alex Kozinski, "The Dark Lessons of Utopia," *Univ. of Chicago Law Review* 58 (Spring 1991): 581.

36. Mark L. Pollot, *Grand Theft and Petty Larceny: Property Rights in America* (San Francisco: Pacific Research Institute, 1993), xxvii.

37. Rand, *Capitalism,* 259.

38. Richard A. Epstein, *Takings: Private Property and the Power of Eminent Domain* (Cambridge, Mass.: Harvard Univ. Press, 1985), 19-31; and see Gordon Crovitz, "Is the New Deal Unconstitutional?" *Wall Street Journal,* January 31, 1986.

39. Bork, *Tempting,* 230.

40. I. Gordon Crovitz, "Property and Liberty: Clarence Thomas and the Coming Conservative-Libertarian Split on the Supreme Court," *Presidential Studies Quarterly* (fall 1992): 711-19.

41. Editorial, "Biden Meets Epstein," *Wall Street Journal*, September 12, 1987.

42. *Nollan v. California Coastal Comm.,* 483 U.S. 825, 107 (1987).

43. Oregon case, *Dolan v. City of Tigard* (1994).

44. Edward H. Crane speech, Washington, D.C., May 1993.

45. Nadine Strossen speech, Washington, D.C., May 1993.

46. Henry J. Hyde, *Forfeiting Our Property Rights* (Washington, D.C.: Cato Institute, 1995). For more recent evidence of the unwillingness of congressional Republicans to defend property rights against the encroachment of forfeiture laws, see James Bovard, "The Dangerous Expansion of Forfeiture Laws," *Wall Street Journal,* December 29, 1997.

INTRODUCTION TO PART VII

1. Hernando de Soto, "The Missing Ingredient," *Economist,* September 11-17, 1993.

2. Dean Acheson, "The Peace the World Wants," *U.S. Department of State Bulletin* 23 (October 2, 1950), 523-29.

CHAPTER 13

1. Richard Easterlin, "Why Isn't the Whole World Developed?" *Journal of Economic History* 41 (March 1981): 1-17; Williams College Conference, see Leonard Silk, "New Thinking on Poor Lands," *New York Times,* November 6, 1985.

2. David S. Landes, "Rich Country, Poor Country," *New Republic,* 201 (November 20, 1989): 23-27.

3. John Jewkes, *Ordeal by Planning* (New York: Macmillan, 1948), 2.

4. Henry C. Simons, *Economic Policy for a Free Society* (Chicago: University of Chicago Press, 1948), 279.

5. Shyam Kamath, "Foreign Aid and India's Leviathan State," in *Perpetuating Poverty,* eds. Doug Bandow and Ian Vasquez (Washington, D.C.: Cato Institute, 1994), 214.

6. P. T. Bauer, *Reality and Rhetoric* (Cambridge, Mass.: Harvard Univ. Press, 1984), 20.

7. Albert O. Hirschman, *The Strategy of Economic Development* (New Haven, Conn.: Yale Univ. Press, 1961).

8. John Maynard Keynes, *The General Theory of Employment Interest and Money* (London: Macmillan, 1936), 383.

9. Charles P. Kindleberger, *Economic Development,* 2nd ed. (New York: McGraw-Hill, 1965), 125-26.

10. Ann Hughey, "The Lessons of the Marshall Plan: It Remains a Model 40 Years Later, But Repeating Its Success Outside Europe Has Proved Elusive," *New York Times,* June 7, 1987;

Leonard Silk, "Marshall Plan, As Seen Today," *New York Times,* June 5, 1987; and see Anne Swardson, "Marshall Plan Changed the Face of Europe," *Washington Post,* May 25, 1997.

11. Kindleberger, *Economic Development,* 125-26; and see "Marshall Plan Changed the Face of Europe," *Washington Post,* May 25, 1997.

12. "Text of the President's Inaugural Address," *New York Times,* January 21, 1949.

13. Nicholas Eberstadt, *Foreign Aid and American Purpose* (Washington, D.C.: American Enterprise Institute, 1988), 6.

14. Eberstadt, *Foreign Aid,* 9.

15. Hirschman, *Economic Development,* 29.

16. John Prior Lewis, *Quiet Crisis in India* (Washington, D.C.: Brookings Institution, 1962), 7, 26, 21.

17. Joan Robinson, in C. H. Feinstein ed., *Socialism, Capitalism and Economic Growth: Essays Presented to Maurice Dobb* (London: Cambridge Univ. Press, 1967), 176.

18. Paul A. Baran, *The Political Economy of Growth* (New York: Monthly Review Press, 1962) xl.

19. Jawaharlal Nehru, *Jawaharlal Nehru: An Autobiography* (London: Bodley Head, 1945), 543, 589.

20. Walt W. Rostow, *The Stages of Economic Growth* (Cambridge: Cambridge Univ. Press, 1960).

21. Ibid., 6.

22. Ibid., 33.

23. Walt W. Rostow, ed., *The Economics of Take-Off into Sustained Growth* (New York, St. Martin's Press, 1963).

24. Walt W. Rostow, *Politics and the Stages of Growth* (Cambridge: Cambridge Univ. Press, 1971), 117-25.

25. A leading principle of ujamaa, Nyerere said, is that "all the basic goods" are "held in common." Julius K. Nyerere, *Ujamaa—Essays on Socialism* (New York: Oxford University Press, 1968), 107.

26. S. Rowton Simpson, "Land Tenure: Some Explanations and Definitions," *Journal of African Administration* 6: 51-52; and see David E. Ault and Gilbert L. Rutman, "The Development of Individual Rights to Property in Tribal Africa," *Journal of Law and Economics,* 22 (April 1979), 163-82.

27. Hernando de Soto, *The Other Path: The Invisible Revolution in the Third World* (New York: Harper & Row, 1989).

28. Hernando de Soto, interview by author, February, 1989.

29. De Soto, *Other Path,* 201-9.

30. Hernando de Soto, testimony to U. S. Joint Economic Committee, April 29, 1992.

31. Eugene H. Methvin, "Crusader for Peru's Have-Nots," *Reader's Digest* (January 1989).

32. Hernando de Soto, interview by author, February 1989.

33. Hernando de Soto, interview by author, May 1992.

34. Joel Millman, "The Next Path," *Forbes* 153 (May 23, 1994), 106-10.

35. Dario Fernandez-Morera, "Outlaws and Addresses: An Interview with Hernando de Soto," *Reason* 25 (February 1994), 28-32.

36. Millman, "The Next Path," 106-10.

37. Hernando de Soto speech to American Enterprise Institute, November 16, 1994.

38. Hernando de Soto, "Property Rights: The Way Out for Coca Growers," *Wall Street Journal,* February 13, 1990.

39. Hernando de Soto, interview with author, May 1992.

40. Hernando de Soto, "Peru's Ex-Drug Czar on Cocaine: The Supply Side," *Wall Street Journal,* February 14, 1992; and interview by author, May 1992.

41. Methvin, "Crusader for Peru's Have-Nots."

42. Hernando de Soto, "Some Lessons in Democracy—For the U.S.," *New York Times,* April 1, 1990.

43. De Soto, interview by author, May 1992.

44. Editorial, "Foreign Aid Failure," *Wall Street Journal,* March 2, 1989.

45. Paul Craig Roberts, "Candor in Report from AID," *Washington Times,* March 8, 1989.

46. IRIS draft paper, U.S. Agency for International Development, Washington D.C. May 7 1990.

47. Mancur Olson, interview by author, May 1993.

48. "Development Depends on Institutions," IRIS, unpublished paper, Univ. of Maryland, 1991.

49. Tina Rosenberg, "So-So De Soto," *The New Republic* (October 7, 1991).

50. G. K. Chesterton, *What's Wrong with the World* (New York: Sheed and Ward, 1942), 58.

CHAPTER 14

1.   John Kenneth Galbraith, "Conditions for Economic Change in Underdeveloped Countries," *Journal of Farm Economics* 33 (November, 1951), 689-96.
2.   Barbara Ward, "Recipe for a Victory in the Far East," *New York Times Magazine,* March 25, 1951; and see Wolf I. Ladejinsky, "Too Late to Save Asia?," *Saturday Review* 33 (July 22, 1950): 7-9, 36-38.
3.   Louis J. Walinsky, ed., *Agrarian Reform as Unfinished Business: The Selected Papers of Wolf Ladejinsky* (New York: Oxford Univ. Press [for the World Bank], 1977), 3-7.
4.   Ibid., 579-80.
5.   John D. Montgomery ed., *International Dimensions of Land Reform* (Boulder, Colo.: Westview Press, 1984), 118.
6.   Ronald P. Dore, *Land Reform in Japan* (New York: Oxford Univ. Press, 1959), 172-73.
7.   Walinsky, ed., *Agrarian Reform,* 129.
8.   Ladejinsky, "Too Late to Save Asia?"
9.   Walinsky, ed., *Agrarian Reform,* 12.
10.   Isador Lubin, "Two Patterns for Land Reform: The Free World vs. the Soviet," *U.S. Department of State Bulletin,* December 22, 1952, 990-95; and see Isador Lubin, "Hope of the Hungry Millions," *New York Times Magazine,* February 10, 1952.
11.   "Text of the U.S. Statement on Cuba," *New York Times,* June 12, 1959.
12.   R. Hart Phillips, "Urrutia Criticizes U.S.," *New York Times,* July 14, 1959.
13.   R. Hart Phillips, "Castro Calls U.S. Enemy of Latins," *New York Times,* July 27, 1960.
14.   Jerome Levinson and Juan de Onis, *The Alliance that Lost Its Way* (Chicago: Quadrangle Books, 1970), 66.
15.   Ibid., 64-69.
16.   James R. Whelan, *Out of the Ashes* (Washington, D.C.: Regnery Gateway, 1989), 132.
17.   Juan de Onis, "Chile at Critical Point of 'Revolution,'" *New York Times,* November 7, 1966; Barnard L. Collier, "Land-Reform Law Is Signed in Chile," *New York Times*, July 17, 1967.
18.   Juan de Onis, "Chilean Reforms Pressed by Frei," *New York Times,* May 22, 1966.
19.   Juan de Onis, "Attack by Castro Proves Helpful to Frei in Chile," *New York Times,* March 18, 1966.
20.   De Onis, "Reforms Pressed by Frei."
21.   Whelan, *Out of the Ashes,* 270-71.
22.   Ibid., 152.
23.   Collier, "Law Is Signed."
24.   Editorial, "A Shocker from Chile," *New York Times,* July 18, 1967.
25.   Malcolm W. Browne, "U.S. Prestige Gets Setback in Chile," *New York Times,* February 6, 1968.
26.   Levinson and de Onis, *Alliance,* 239.
27.   Juan de Onis, "Chile's Drought Worsens Strife Over Reforms," *New York Times,* September 18, 1968; and see Malcolm W. Browne, "Frei Facing Political Struggle in Chile," *New York Times,* November 14, 1968.
28.   Ibid.
29.   "A Latin American 'Showcase' Where Reforms Went Sour," *U.S. News & World Report,* March 17, 1969, 68-69.
30.   Whelan, *Out of the Ashes,* 289.
31.   Ibid., 308.
32.   John P. Powelson and Richard Stock, *The Peasant Betrayed* (Boston, Mass.: Oelgeschager, in association with the Lincoln Institute of Land Policy, 1987), 97.
33.   Roy L. Prosterman and Jeffrey M. Riedinger, *Land Reform and Democratic Development* (Baltimore: Johns Hopkins Univ. Press, 1987), 133-34.
34.   "Roy L. Prosterman, "Vietnam's Land Reform Begins to Pay," *Wall Street Journal,* February 5, 1971.
35.   "James P. Sterba, "Land Reform comes to Vietnam—or Does it?," *New York Times,* April 5, 1970; Elizabeth Pond, "How Thieu embraced plan: Viet Land Reform Gathers Speed," *Christian Science Monitor,* June 18, 1969.
36.   Iver Peterson, "Vietnam's Land: A Plank From the Communists," *New York Times,* July 6, 1969.
37.   Jude Wanniski, "The Political Economy in Perspective: El Salvador's Threat to U.S. Revival," *Polyconomics, Inc.,* March 27, 1981, 2-3.

38. Editorial, "Vietnam Land Reform," *New York Times,* April 9, 1970.
39. Max Frankel, "Johnson Plans to Repeat Vietnam Strategy Parley," *New York Times,* March 26, 1967.
40. James P. Sterba, "Land Reform Bill Passed in Saigon," *New York Times,* March 11, 1970.
41. Thomas C. Fox, "Thieu Delivers First Titles In a Big Land-Reform Plan," *New York Times,* August 29, 1970.
42. Roy Prosterman testimony before Senate Committee on Appropriations, August 28, 1970, 167.
43. Thomas C. Fox, "Vietnam Land Reform Advances, But Slowly," *New York Times,* January 4, 1972.
44. Ibid.
45. Prosterman and Riedinger, *Land Reform,* table 4.
46. Ibid., 98.
47. Ibid., 140.
48. Robert Shaplen, "Letter From Indo-China," *The New Yorker,* January 28, 1974.
49. Frances Starner, "S. Vietnam: A Question of Priorities," *Far Eastern Economic Review* 84 (April 15, 1974): 52-53; and see "Report from South Vietnam: One Place Where A Truce Brings No End to Woes," *U.S. News & World Report,* November 5, 1973.
50. William Shawcross, "Report from Saigon: An Economy Near Collapse," *Ramparts,* July 1974; Fox Butterfield, "Farming Is Set Back in Vietnam," *New York Times,* February 10, 1975; "Governments Act on War Refugee Aid," *New York Times,* April 3, 1975.
51. Agence France-Presse, "Saigon Is Pressing Exodus to Farms," *New York Times,* October 5, 1975.
52. Roy L. Prosterman testimony, Senate Committee on Foreign Relations, July 29, 1975, 517.
53. Roy L. Prosterman, "IRI—A Simplified Predictive Index of Rural Instability," *Comparative Politics* 5. (April, 1976): 349-52.
54. David E. Lilienthal, *The Journals of David E. Lilienthal* (New York: Harper & Row, 1964-83).
55. Afsaneh Najmabadi, *Land Reform and Social Change in Iran* (Salt Lake City: Univ. of Utah Press, 1987), 68-72, 216.
56. Azar Tabari [Afsaneh Najmabadi], *Merip Reports,* March-April, 1983.
57. Mohammed Reza Pahlavi, *Answer to History* (New York: Stein and Day, 1982), 22-23.
58. Najmabadi, *Land Reform,* 79.
59. Lilienthal, *Journals,* 4: 132.
60. Najmabadi, *Land Reform,* 4.
61. Barry M. Rubin, *Paved With Good Intentions: Iran and the American Experience* (New York: Oxford Univ. Press, 1980), 109.
62. Ann K. S. Lambton, *The Persian Land Reform, 1962-1966* (Oxford: Clarendon Press, 1969), 91.
63. Ann K. S. Lambton, *Landlord and Peasant in Persia* (London: Oxford Univ. Press, 1953), 393.
64. F. Bostock and G. Jones, *Planning and Power in Iran* (London: Frank Cass, 1989), 174.
65. George B. Baldwin, *Planning and Development in Iran* (Baltimore: Johns Hopkins Press, 1967), 95.
66. Eric J. Hooglund, *Land and Revolution in Iran: 1960-1980* (Austin: Univ. of Texas Press, 1982), 50, 53-54.
67. Reuters, "Shah Gives Away Caspian Estates," *New York Times,* October 8, 1961; Harrison E. Salisbury, "Shah Bids U.S. Help Make Iran A Showplace in Fight on Reds," *New York Times,* November 5, 1961; Harrison E. Salisbury, "Premier of Iran Warns Wealthy to Change Ways: Dr. Amini Asks Sacrifices to Avert a Revolution," *New York Times,* November 9, 1961.
68. *Merip Reports,* December 1975.
69. Eric Pace, "Iran's Shah Crowns Himself and Queen," and "Mohammed Reza Pahlavi: A Reform-Minded Ruler," *New York Times,* October 27, 1967; and see Editorial, "On the Peacock Throne," *New York Times,* October 28, 1967.
70. Eric Pace, "Oil Boom Is Aiding Reform Plans of Shah of Iran," *New York Times,* September 25, 1967.
71. David E. Lilienthal, *Change, Hope and the Bomb* (Princeton, N.J.: Princeton Univ. Press, 1963), 6.
72. Lilienthal, *Journals,* 6: 312.
73. Ibid., 314.
74. Ibid., 325.
75. Grace E. Goodell, The *Elementary Structures of Political Life: Rural Development in Pahlavi Iran* (New York: Oxford Univ. Press, 1986), 24-26; and author's interviews with Goodell.
76. Goodell, *Elementary Structures,* 146.

77. Lee Griggs, "Oil and Water Rebuild an Ancient Land," *Fortune* 82 (November, 1970): 88-97, 128.

78. *Merip Reports,* December 1975.

79. Lilienthal, *Journals,* 5: 137.

80. Ibid., 7: 448, 451.

81. Goodell, *Elementary Structures,* 31.

82. Lilienthal, *Journals,* 7: 627.

83. Prosterman and Riedinger, *Land Reform,* 151.

84. Roberto Aguilar, interview by author, March, 1988.

85. U.S. Agency for International Development, Inspector General's audit, Jan 18, 1984.

86. Prosterman and Riedinger, *Land Reform,* 159.

87. William Thiesenhusen, "Agrarian Reforms in El Salvador," paper, Land Tenure Center, Madison, Wisconsin, September 1, 1993.

88. Elliot Abrams, interview by author, March 1989.

89. Prosterman and Riedinger, *Land Reform,* 158.

90. John Bruce, interview by author, November 1993.

91. Shirley Christian, "Chile Develops 'Stockholders' Culture," *New York Times,* July 20, 1987; Shirley Christian, "An Unlikely Lab for Free Markets," *New York Times,* June 21, 1987.

CHAPTER 15

1. B. F. Stowasser, ed., *The Islamic Impulse* (London: Croom Helm, 1987), 235.

2. Edward Said, "A Tragic Convergence," *New York Times,* January 11, 1991.

3. Bernard Lewis, "Islam and Liberal Democracy," *Atlantic Monthly* 271 (February 1993): 89-98.

4. Ken Ringle, "Activists Call for Action on North African Slavery," *Washington Post,* March 14, 1996; and see Steven A. Holmes, "Slavery Is an Issue Again," *New York Times,* March 24, 1996.

5. *Claiming the Future* (Washington, D.C.: The World Bank, 1995), 4.

6. Ibid.

7. Arnold J. Toynbee, *Between Niger and Nile* (London, Oxford Univ. Press, 1965), 82-84.

8. Ann E. Mayer, ed., *Property, Social Structure, and Law in the Modern Middle East* (Albany, N.Y.: State Univ. of New York Press, 1985), 206.

9. David Pryce-Jones, "Self-Determination, Arab Style," *Commentary* 87 (January 1989): 39-46.

10. David Pryce-Jones, *The Closed Circle: An Interpretation of the Arabs* (New York: Harper & Row, 1989).

11. Daniel Doron, "Without Prosperity, Peace Has Little Chance," *Wall Street Journal,* September 26, 1995.

12. Joel Bainerman, "Why Palestine Can't Grow: Under Arafat's Rules, There's No Business as Usual," *Washington Post,* January 28, 1996.

13. World Bank, *Claiming the Future,* 3.

14. Tony Horwitz and Geraldine Brooks, "Market Mosque Contradictions Stifle Iran," *Wall Street Journal,* August 11, 1989.

15. A. A. Mawdudi, *The Islamic Law and Constitution* (Lahore: Islamic Publications, 1980), 252.

16. Bernard Lewis, *Islam in History* (New York: Library Press, 1973), 267.

17. Ann E. Mayer, *Islam and Human Rights* (Boulder, Colo.: Westview Press, 1991), 49-50.

18. Ibid., 62-65.

19. Joseph Schacht, *An Introduction to Islamic Law* (Oxford: Clarendon Press, 1964), 2, 205.

20. Norman Anderson, *Law Reform in the Muslim World* (London: Athlone Press, 1976), 161.

21. Lewis, "Islam and Liberal Democracy."

22. Clifford Hallam, "Execution Day in Riyadh," *Commentary* (February, 1986).

23. C. F. Volney, *Travels Through Syria and Egypt in the Years 1783, 1784 and 1785,* 3rd ed. (London: G. Robinson, 1805), vol. 1, 5-8, 92-93, 175-79.

24. Albert Hourani, *A History of The Arab Peoples* (Cambridge, Mass.: Harvard Univ. Press, 1991), 250.

25. Marshall G. S. Hodgson, *The Venture of Islam,* vol. 3 (Chicago: Univ. of Chicago Press, 1974), book 6, chap. 1.

26. Will Durant and Ariel Durant, *The Story of Civilization,* vol 8, The Age of Louis XIV (New York: Simon and Schuster, 1963) 425.

27. Arnold Toynbee, *A Study of History,* 2nd ed., vol. 3 (London: Oxford Univ. Press, 1935) 42, 44, 47.

28. Adam Smith, *Wealth of Nations* (Oxford: Oxford Univ. Press, 1976), 422.

29. Thomas R. Malthus, *The Works of Thomas Robert Malthus,* ed. E. A. Wrigley and David Souden (London, Pickering, 1986), 2: 110.

30. C. F. Volney, *Travels.*

31. Elie Kedourie, *The World of Islam* (London: Thames & Hudson, 1976), 325.

32. James B. Fraser, *Narrative of a Journey into Khorashan in the Years 1821 and 1822* (1825, reprint Delhi: Oxford Univ. Press, 1984), 166, 190.

33. John R. McCulloch, *Principles of Political Economy,* 4th ed. (Edinburgh: A. and C. Black, 1849) 84-86.

34. Nassau Senior, *A Journal Kept in Turkey and Greece in the Autumn of 1857 and the Beginning of 1858* (1859; reprint New York: Arno Press, 1977), 152-53.

35. Francois Bernier, *Travels in the Mogul Empire, A.D. 1656-1668,* rev. ed., trans. Irving Brock (Delhi: S. Chand & Co., 1891), 227-28, 232.

36. Karl Marx, Friedrich Engels, *Collected Works* (New York: International Publishers, 1983), 39: 333-34.

37. Ibid., 339-40.

38. Karl Wittfogel, *Oriental Despotism* (New Haven, Conn.: Yale Univ. Press, 1957), 228-29.

39. Lewis, *Islam in History,* 270.

40. *Ibid.,* 271.

41. John Barker, *Syria and Egypt Under the Last Five Sultans of Turkey* (1876, reprint, New York: Arno Press, 1973), 1: 305, 318.

42. Maxime Rodinson, *Islam and Capitalism,* trans. B. Pearce (Austin: Univ. of Texas Press, 1978), 14.

43. Daniel Pipes, interview by author, February 1993.

44. John Thomson, interview by author, November, 1993.

45. Anderson, *Law Reform,* 7.

46. Taha al Alwani, *American Journal of Islamic Social Sciences,* 8 (1991), 130, 319, 514.

47. Ibid.

48. Yusif di Lorenzo, interview by author, February, 1993.

49. Sohrab Behdad, "Property Rights in Contemporary Islamic Thought," *Review of Social Economy,* 47 (summer 1989).

50. Volney, *Travels,* 2: 402.

51. Raphael Patai, *The Arab Mind* (New York: Scribner's, 1973), 307, 322, 115.

52. Claude S. Jarvis, *Three Deserts* (London: J. Murray, 1936), 143.

53. Ibn Khaldun, *An Introduction to History,* vol. 1, trans. Franz Rosenthal (New York: Pantheon Books, 1958), 303, 304-5.

54. John L. Wright, *Libya* (London: E. Benn, 1969), 54.

55. J. Burton, epilogue to Steven Cheung, *The Myth of Social Cost* (London: Institute for Economic Affairs, 1978).

56. William R. Polk, *The Arab World* (Cambridge, Mass.: Harvard Univ. Press, 1980), 82.

57. Daniel Doron, interview by author, February 1990.

58. *Mission to Earth: LANDSAT Views of the World* (Washington, D.C., Scientific and Technical Office, National Aeronautics and Space Administration, 1976), 8.

CHAPTER 16

1. Nicholas Watt, "Blair Blames Britain for Irish Famine Deaths," *The Times* (London) June 2, 1997.

2. Clyde Haberman, "NYC: The Irish Finally Stop to Remember," *New York Times,* March 18, 1997.

3. Joel Mokyr, *Why Ireland Starved* (London: Allen & Unwin, 1983), 1-3, 275-76.

4. T. W. Guinnane, "Ireland's Famine Wasn't Genocide," *Washington Post,* September 17, 1997; and see Letters: "The Irish Famine: Complicity in Murder," *Washington Post,* September 27, 1997.

5. Mokyr, *Why Ireland Starved,* 294.

6. Paul Johnson, *Ireland: Land of Troubles* (London: Eyre Methuen, 1980), 84.

7.   Thackeray, quoted in ibid, 83.

8.   Nicholas Mansergh, *The Irish Question: 1840-1921* (London: Allen & Unwin, 1975), 43.

9.   Thomas M. Gallagher, *Paddy's Lament: Ireland, 1846-1847, Prelude to Hatred* (New York: Harcourt Brace Jovanovich, 1982), 68-71.

10. James O'Connor, *History of Ireland, 1798-1924* (New York: G. H. Doran Co., 1926), 279.

11. Mansergh, *Irish Question,* 109, 119.

12. David Ricardo, *Works and Correspondence of David Ricardo,* ed. Piero Sraffa (Cambridge: Cambridge Univ. Press, 1962), 7: 174-75.

13. Thomas R. Malthus, *Principles of Political Economy,* 2nd ed. (1836, reprint, New York: A. M. Kelley, 1951), 349-50.

14. Mokyr, *Why Ireland Starved,* 42.

15. O'Connor, *History of Ireland,* 1: 278.

16. Mokyr, *Why Ireland Starved,* 278.

17. House of Commons, Devon Commission, *Parliamentary Papers,* 1845, vol. 19, 15-16.

18. John Stuart Mill, *Principles of Political Economy* (1848), book 2, chaps. 9 & 10.

19. John Stuart Mill, *John Stuart Mill on Ireland,* ed. R. N. Lubow (Philadelphia: 1979), 7.

20. Mokyr, *Why Ireland Starved,* 83.

21. Ibid., 86.

22. Mansergh, *Irish Question,* 119.

23. Anna George de Mille, *Henry George: Citizen of the World* (Chapel Hill: Univ. of North Carolina Press, 1950), 98.

24. J. A. Fox, *A Key to the Irish Question* (London: Kegan Paul, 1890), 149.

25. Cecil Woodham-Smith, *The Great Hunger* (London: Hamish Hamilton, 1962), 19.

26. John Stuart Mill, *England and Ireland* (London: Longmans Green, 1881), 21.

27. William F. H. Lecky, *A History of Ireland in the Eighteenth Century* (1892, reprint, Chicago: Univ. of Chicago Press, 1972), 43-46.

28. Godfrey Locker-Lampson, *A Consideration of the State of Ireland in the Nineteenth Century* (London: Constable, 1907), 596.

29. R. B. O'Brien, *The Parliamentary History of the Irish Land Question* (London: Sampson Low, 1880), 161-65.

30. Isaac Butt, *The Irish People and the Irish Land: Letter to Lord Lifford* (Dublin: J. Falconer, 1867), 103.

31. Isaac Butt, *Land Tenure in Ireland: A Plea for the Celtic Race* (Dublin: J. Falconer, 1866), 50.

32. O'Connor, *History of Ireland,* 2: 27.

33. Butt, *Letter to Lord Lifford,* 40.

34. Mill, *England and Ireland,* 18-19.

35. Butt, *Letter to Lord Lifford,* 91.

36. Mill, *England and Ireland,* 20.

37. Butt, *Letter to Lord Lifford,* 188-89.

38. Ibid., 103-4.

39. Fox, *Key to the Irish Question,* 154.

40. Ibid., 149.

41. Ibid., 298.

42. Ibid., 298.

43. Butt, *Letter to Lord Lifford,* 90.

44. John E. Pomfret, *The Struggle for Land in Ireland, 1800-1923* (1930; reprint, New York: Russell & Russell, 1969), 43.

45. Leonce de Lavergne, *The Rural Economy of England, Scotland, and Ireland* (Edinburgh: Blackwood and Sons, 1855), 386.

46. Roy W. Jastram, *The Golden Constant* (New York: John Wiley, 1977), 41-48, 113-14.

47. Lavergne, *Rural Economy,* 383.

48. Ibid., 387.

49. Pomfret, *Struggle for Land,* 81-96.

CHAPTER 17

1. Lysander Spooner, *Collected Works of Lysander Spooner,* vol. 3, ed. C. Shively (1884; reprint, Weston, Mass.: M&S Press, 1971).

2. D. J. McConville, "Intellectual Property Gains Respect: Patent Holders Have Never Had It So Good," *Industry Week,* March 7, 1994.

3. Andrew Pollock. "The New High-Tech Battleground: Patent Litigation Can Be a Better Way of Making Money Than Selling Products. But Will It Squelch Innovation?" *New York Times,* July 3, 1988.

4. Philip Wittenberg, *The Protection of Literary Property* (Boston: The Writer, Inc., 1968), 12-20.

5. Ernst P. Goldschmidt, *Medieval Texts and Their First Appearance in Print* (London: Bibliographical Society, 1943), 112.

6. Elizabeth L. Eisenstein, *The Printing Press as an Agent of Change* (Cambridge: Cambridge Univ. Press, 1979), 235.

7. John Perry Barlow, "A Framework for Rethinking Patents and Copyrights," *Wired,* March 1994.

8. Wittenberg, *Protection.*

9. Mark Pendergrast, *For God, Country, and Coca-Cola* (New York: Scribner's, 1993), 421-25.

10. Bentham, quoted in Arnold Plant, *Selected Economic Essays and Addresses* (London: Routledge and Kegan Paul, 1974), 44.

11. Senate Committee on the Judiciary, Subcommittee on Patents, report prepared by Fritz Machlup, *An Economic Review of the Patent System,* 1958, Committee print 15.

12. Constitution of the United States, Article 1, Section 8, no. 8.

13. Mark Twain, The *Autobiography of Mark Twain,* ed. Charles Neider (New York: Harper, 1959), 281.

14. Joel Mokyr, *The Lever of Riches* (New York: Oxford Univ. Press, 1990), 248.

15. John Jewkes et al., *The Sources of Invention* (London: Macmillan, 1958), 45; Mokyr, *Lever of Riches,* 248.

16. P. Challu et al., *World Competition,* 15 (1991).

17. E. Mansfield, *Management Science,* 32 (1986).

18. Mokyr, *Lever of Riches,* 247.

19. Ibid., 248.

20. Fritz Machlup, "Patents," *International Encyclopedia of the Social Sciences* (New York: Macmillan. 1968), 11: 463-65.

21. *The Writings of Thomas Jefferson,* A. Lipscomb, ed. (Washington, D.C., Thomas Jefferson memorial association of the United States, 1904), 7: 93-99.

22. Ibid., 7: 444-53.

23. Ibid., 13: 326-38.

24. *Computer Software, Intellectual Property and the Challenge of Technological Change* (Washington, D.C.: Office of Technology Assessment, GPO, 1992), 185.

25. Plant, *Essays and Addresses,* chaps. 3-5.

26. Friedrich Hayek, *The Fatal Conceit* (Chicago: Univ. of Chicago Press, 1988), 6.

27. Tom Palmer, "Intellectual Property: A Non-Posnerian Law and Economics Approach," *Hamline Law Review,* 12 (Spring 1989): 261.

28. John Perry Barlow, "A Framework."

29. Bill Gates, *The Road Ahead* (New York: Viking, 1995), 120.

30. National Research Council (U.S.), *Intellectual Property Issues in Software* (Washington, D.C., National Academy Press, 1991), 44.

31. Nancy Rutter, "The Great Patent Plague," *Forbes ASAP,* March 29, 1993.

32. Simson Garfinkel, "Patently Absurd," *Wired,* July 1994.

33. James Boyle, *Shamans, Software and Spleen: Law and the Construction of the Information Society* (Cambridge, Mass.: Harvard Univ. Press, 1996).

34. U.S. Information Infrastructure Task Force, *Intellectual Property and the National Information Infrastructure* (Washington, D.C., Commerce Department, 1995), n. 204; and see, Bruce Lehman response to Open Letter from Law Professors, Feb 28, 1996.

35. Jessica Litman, "Revising Copyright Law for the Information Age," *Oregon Law Review,* 75 (Spring 1996): 27-28.

36. *Sony Corp. v Universal City Studios,* 464 US 417 (1984); and see Peter Passell, "Why the Best Doesn't Always Win," *New York Times Magazine,* May 5, 1996.

CHAPTER 18

1. Stephen Budiansky, "Giving Green a Bad Name," *U.S. News & World Report,* June 22, 1992.
2. Murray Feshbach and Alfred Friendly, Jr., *Ecocide in the USSR: Health and Nature under Siege* (New York: Basic Books, 1992); and see Douglas Stanglin, "Toxic Wasteland," *U.S. News & World Report,* April 13, 1992, 40-52.
3. Richard L. Stroup, interview by author, March 1994.
4. Alston Chase, "A Scribe's Guide to Scientific Correctness," *Washington Times,* November 29, 1994; and see Alston Chase, "Behind the Environmental News Curve," *Washington Times,* December 16, 1993.
5. Bureau of Land Management, Public Land Statistics, Table 1-3: "Comparison of Federally Owned Land with Total Acreage of States, Fiscal Year 1995." Louisiana and Minnesota have been counted as west of the Mississippi.
6. Jon Bowmaster, "Take This Park and Love It," *New York Times Magazine,* September 3, 1995, 24-27.
7. John Baden and Richard L. Stroup, "Saving the Wilderness: A Radical Proposal," *Reason* 13 (July 1981), 28-36.
8. Pamela Snyder and Jane S. Shaw, "PC Oil Drilling in a Wilderness Refuge," *Wall Street Journal,* September 7, 1995.
9. Robert O'Toole, *FREE Perspectives* (Bozeman, Montana), Autumn 1993.
10. Lester C. Thurow, *Washington Post,* April 7, 1996.
11. Tim Wirth, "The Importance of Wild Lands," *San Francisco Examiner,* June 24, 1992.
12. Gifford Pinchot, *The Fight for Conservation* (1910; reprint, Seattle: Univ. of Washington Press, 1967), 3.
13. John Baden, "Destroying the Environment: Government Mismanagement of Our Natural Resources," National Center for Policy Analysis (Dallas, Tex.), *Policy Report* 124 , October, 1986, 9.
14. Robert O'Toole, *Reforming the Forest Service* (Washington, D.C.: Island Press, 1988), 20-21.
15. Perri Knize, "The Mismanagement of the National Forests," *Atlantic Monthly* (October 1991), 98-112.
16. O'Toole, *Reforming the Forest Service,* 2-4; and see Stephen Budiansky, "Sawdust and Mirrors: The Forest Service's Unusual Book-keeping Is Costing the Environment and the Public Plenty, " *U.S. News & World Report,* July 1, 1991.
17. Knize, *Atlantic Monthly.*
18. John Lancaster, "Tallying Cost of Logging National Forests," *Washington Post,* October 20, 1990.
19. Timothy Egan, "Citing Space Photos, Scientists Say Forests in the Northwest Are in Danger," *New York Times,* June 11 1992.
20. John Lancaster, "Under Attack, Forest Service Chief Is Silent," *Washington Post,* September 21, 1990.
21. Timothy Egan, "Dissidents Say Forest Service Shifts Its Role," *New York Times,* March 4, 1990.
22. Tom Kenworthy and Dan Morgan, "Panel Would Allow Massive Logging on Federal Land," *Washington Post,* March 3, 1995.
23. Alston Chase, *Playing God in Yellowstone: The Destruction of America's First National Park* (Boston: Atlantic Monthly Press, 1986), 6.
24. Park Service visitor numbers: Jane S. Shaw and Richard L. Stroup, "How to Improve Our Parks," *Forum for Applied Research and Public Policy,* n.d.
25. William Claiborne, "Mojave Caught in Dispute Over Man's Relationship with the Desert," *Washington Post,* May 28, 1996.
26. Tom Graff, interview by author, April 1992.
27. Peter Passell, "Economic Scene: Greening California," *New York Times,* February 27, 1991.
28. Marc Reisner and Sarah Bates, *Overtapped Oasis* (Washington, D.C.: Island Press, 1990), 60-61.
29. Jane Gross, "Cast as Villains in Drought, Rice Farmers Defend Water Rights," *New York Times,* April 7, 1991.

30. Elliot Diringer and Lori Olszewski, "Running Dry," parts 1-5 ("Why Water Crisis Won't End"; "Workplaces Starting to Share the Pain of Shortages"; "Thirsty Cities Covet Water Used by Farms"; "Nature Gaining Clout in Battle Over Water"; "How to Solve Crisis Over Scarce Water"), *San Francisco Chronicle,* April 15-19, 1991.

31. Marc Reisner, "Kept from Selling Water, Farmers Naturally Waste It," *Los Angeles Times,* February 28, 1991.

32. Elliot Diringer, "Rival Groups Seek End to State's Water Wars," *San Francisco Chronicle,* February 13, 1991; Lori Olszewski, "California Drought Bank Ends Search for Water," *San Francisco Chronicle,* April 5, 1991.

33. Michael McCabe, "Santa Barbara's Drought Fight Over," *San Francisco Chronicle,* April 2, 1992.

34. Gordon Tullock, interview by author, April 1991.

35. Ibid.

36. Marc Reisner, *Cadillac Desert* (Harmondsworth, Eng.: Penguin Books, 1986), 379.

37. Tom Graff, interview by author; and see Robert Reinhold, "U.S. Says Scarce Water Supplies Won't Go to California Farmers," *New York Times,* February 15, 1992.

38. Robert Reinhold, "Farmers in West May Sell Something More Valuable than Any Crop: Water," *New York Times,* April 6, 1992.

39. Jonathan Marshall, "State's Water Shortage Threatens Farms' Future," *San Francisco Chronicle,* October 24, 1994; and see David Margolick, "As Drought Looms, Farmers in California Blame Politics," *New York Times,* June 24, 1994.

40. Richard Howitt, interview by author, April 1991.

41. *World Development Report* (Washington, D.C.: World Bank, 1992), 12.

42. John Ward Anderson, "Poachers Felling World's Tigers Rhinos," *Washington Post,* November 29, 1994; and Michael 'T Sas-Rolfe, "How to Save the Tiger," *Wall Street Journal,* February 17, 1998.

43. Raymond Bonner, "Crying Wolf Over Elephants," *New York Times Magazine,* February 7, 1993; and see Raymond Bonner, *At the Hand of Man* (New York: Knopf, 1993).

44. Richard C. Morais, "Save the Elephants!" *Forbes,* September 14, 1992, 338-345.

45. Suzanne Daley, "Ban on Sale of Ivory Is Eased to Help 3 African Nations," *New York Times,* June 20, 1997

46. Jane Perlez, "Rare White Rhino Avoids Extinction in Preserve in Zaire," *New York Times,* June 5, 1990; . and see Jane Perlez, "Rhino Near Last Stand, Animal Experts Warn," *New York Times,* July 7, 1992.

47. Ken Wells, "Animal Farm: The Hot New Slogan in African Game Circles Is 'Use It or Lose It'; Private Ranches Proliferate, Villages 'Sell' Elephants and Favor Ivory Sales," *Wall Street Journal,* January 7, 1997.

48. Ibid., and Wendy Marston, "The Misguided Ivory Ban and the Reality of Living with Elephants," *Washington Post,* June 8, 1997.

49. Bill Keller, "Africa Thinks about Making Wildlife Pay for Its Survival," *New York Times,* December 27, 1992.

50. Nathaniel C. Nash, "Bolivia's Rain Forest Falls to Relentless Exploiters," *New York Times,* June 21, 1993.

51. Roger Sedjo, "Tropical Forests, Property Rights," unpublished paper, Resources for the Future, Washington, D.C., April 15, 1991; and see Roger Sedjo, "The World's Forests: Conflicting Signals," Washington, D.C.: Competitive Enterprise Institute, February 1995.

52. Frances Cairncross, *Costing the Earth* (Boston: Harvard Business School Press, 1992), 142.

53. Theodore Panayotou, *Green Markets: The Economics of Sustainable Development* (San Francisco: ICS Press, 1993), 77.

54. Sedjo, "Tropical Forests."

55. Robert C. Repetto, *The Forest for the Trees?: Government Policies and the Misuse of Forest Resources* (Washington, D.C.: World Resources Institute, 1988), 87, 44, 82.

56. Eugene Linden, "Playing With Fire: Destruction of the Amazon is 'One of the Great Tragedies in History,'" *Time* 134 (September 18, 1989): 76-85.

57. Al Gore, *Earth in the Balance: Ecology and the Human Spirit* (New York: Plume, 1993), 287.

58. Gary Libecap, paper, "Property Rights, Rent Dissipation and Environmental Degradation in the Brazilian Amazon," Karl Eller Center, Univ. of Arizona, November 1991.

59. Adrian Cowell, *The Decade of Destruction: The Crusade to Save the Amazon Rain Forest* (New York: H. Holt, 1990), 132.

60. Libecap, "Property Rights."

61. Hans Binswanger, "Brazilian Policies that Encourage Deforestation in the Amazon," World Bank Environment Dept., paper no. 16, 1989; Robert Schneider, "Brazil: An Economic Analysis of Environmental Problems in the Amazon," World Bank, 1990; World Bank, *World Development Report*, 1992; William Magrath, "The Challenge of the Commons: The Allocation of Nonexclusive Resources," World Bank Environment Department, working paper no. 14, February 1989.

CHAPTER 19

1. Francis Philbrick, "Changing Conceptions of Property In Law," *Univ. of Pennsylvania Law Review* 86 (1938): 691.

2. John Cribbet, "Changing Concepts in the Law of Land Use," *Iowa Law Review* 50 (1965): 245.

3. Dennis J. Coyle, *Property Rights and the Constitution* (Albany: State Univ. of New York Press, 1993), chap. 7.

4. Alan Farnham, "Holding Firm on Affirmative Action," *Fortune* 119 (March 13, 1989): 87-88.

5. Grant Gilmore, *The Death of Contract* (Columbus: Ohio State Univ. Press, 1974), 3.

6. *Pacific Gas & Electric Co. v. D. W. Drayage & Rigging Co.*, 69 Cal. Reptr. 651 (1968).

7. *Trident Center v. Connecticut General Life*, 847 F.2nd 654 (9th Cir. 1988).

8. *Oki America, Inc. v. Microtech International*, 872 F.2nd 312 (9th Cir. 1989); and see D. B. Rivkin and L. A. Casey, "How Binding Are Contracts?" *American Enterprise*, November/December 1993.

9. 387 U.S. 391.

10. E. F. Roberts, "The Demise of Property Law," *Cornell Law Review* 57 (November 1971): 1.

11. Joseph L. Sax, "Some Thoughts on the Decline of Private Property," *Washington Law Review 58* (1983): 481.

12. *Village of Euclid v. Ambler Realty,* 272 U.S. 365 (1926), and Bernard H. Siegan, *Land Use Without Zoning* (Lexington, Mass.: Lexington Books, 1972), 203-5.

13. Coyle, *Property Rights,* 41-42.

14. *Zahn v. Board of Public Works,* 274 U.S. 325 (1927).

15. Robert H. Nelson, *Zoning and Property Rights* (Cambridge, Mass.: MIT Press, 1977), 13.

16. Nelson, *Zoning,* 14.

17. Ibid.

18. An attempt to bring rent control in New York City to an end, after 54 years, was defeated by the state legislature in the spring of 1997. In California, the state legislature partially rescued landlords in Berkeley and Santa Monica in 1993, with a provision that brought rents closer to the market-clearing level.

19. Bernard H. Siegan, *Other People's Property* (Lexington, Mass.: Lexington Books, 1976), chaps. 1 and 3.

20. James Bovard, *Lost Rights: The Destruction of American Liberty* (New York: St. Martin's Press, 1994), 26.

21. Ibid.

22. Siegan, *Other People's Property,* 43.

23. Herbert J. Gans, "The Failure of Urban Renewal," *Commentary* 39 (April 1965): 29-37.

24. John C. Weicher, *Urban Renewal: National Program for Local Problems* (Washington, D.C.: AEI, 1972).

25. Kurt Anderson, "Spiffing Up the Urban Heritage," *Time* 134 (November 23, 1987): 72-83.

26. William Tucker, *The Excluded Americans: Homelessness and Housing Policies* (Washington, D.C.: Regnery Gateway, 1990), 179.

27. Martin Anderson, *The Federal Bulldozer* (Cambridge, Mass.: MIT Press, 1964), 190.

28. Roberts, "Demise of Property Law," 16.

29. *Berman v. Parker,* 348 U.S. 32-33.

30. Anderson, *Federal Bulldozer,* 13.

31. Bovard, *Lost Rights,* 42.

32. Tucker, *Excluded Americans,* 254.
33. Siegan, *Other People's Property,* 38.
34. Ike Sugg, interview by author, June 1995.
35. "Endangered Species Act: Information on Species Protection on Non-Federal Lands," (Washington D.C., U.S. General Accounting Office, 1994).
36. Edward O. Wilson, "Is Humanity Suicidal? If Homo Sapiens Goes the Way of the Dinosaur, We Have Only Ourselves to Blame," *New York Times Magazine,* May 30, 1993, 27, 29.
37. Paul R. Ehrlich and Edward O. Wilson, "Biodiversity Studies: Science and Policy," *Science* 253 (August 16, 1991): 758-762.
38. Nicholas Eberstadt, "World Population Implosion?" *The Public Interest* 129 (Fall 1997): 3-22.
39. Written statement of Ike C. Sugg before the Endangered Species Act Task Force Committee on Resources, House of Representatives, May 18, 1995, 8.
40. Jonathan Adler, "Property Rights, Regulatory Takings, and Environmental Protection," Washington, D.C.: Competitive Enterprise Institute (April 1996), 4.
41. Richard L. Stroup, "The Endangered Species Act: Making Innocent Species the Enemy," *PERC Policy Series* PS-3 (April 1995), 9.
42. Betsy Carpenter, "The Best Laid Plans," *U.S. News & World Report,* October 4, 1993, 89.
43. Testimony of Cindy Domenigoni before the Endangered Species Act Task Force, Riverside, California, April 26, 1995.
44. Ibid., see also Ike C. Sugg, "California Fires—Losing Houses, Saving Rats," *Wall Street Journal,* November 10, 1993.
45. Adler "Property Rights," 20.
46. *Hoffman Homes Inc. v. Administrator, U.S. E.P.A.,* 999 F. 2d 256 (7ᵗʰ Circuit 1993), 262.
47. Bovard, *Lost Rights,* 34; and see Robert J. Pierce, National Wetlands Newsletter, November/December, 1991.
48. *Hoffman Homes Inc. v Administrator, U.S. E.P.A.,* 999 F. 2d 256 (7ᵗʰ Circuit 1993), 263.
49. Peggy Riegle, interview with author, June 1994.
50. Joby Warrick, "Babbitt Sets Plan to Pare Endangered Species List," *Washington Post,* May 6, 1998.
51. Milton Friedman, "We Have Socialism, Q. E. D.," *New York Times,* December 31, 1989.
52. Information from Bruce Bartlett, who compiled GDP and federal-receipts data from *the Survey of Current Business* (January/February, 1996) and from *Economic Indicators* published by the Joint Economic Committee of Congress.
53. Terence Roth, "The Outlook: Europeans Are Moving to Overhaul Welfare," *Wall Street Journal,* June 3, 1996.

CHAPTER 20

1. Armen A. Alchian and William R. Allen, *University Economics* (Belmont, Cal.: Wadsworth Pub. Co., 1964).
2. Edmund W. Kitch, ed., "The Fire of Truth: A Remembrance of Law and Economics at Chicago, 1932-1970," *Journal of Law and Economics* 26 (April, 1983): 163, 228.
3. Armen A. Alchian, "Private Property and the Relative Cost of Tenure," in *Economic Forces at Work* (Indianapolis: Liberty Press, 1977), 177-202.
4. Kitch, "Fire of Truth," 228-29.
5. Ibid, 229. A participant told the author that the Nobelist was Kenneth Arrow, who won the prize in 1972.
6. Alchian, "Tenure," 186-87.
7. Ibid., 201.
8. Adam Smith, *Wealth of Nations* (Oxford: Oxford Univ. Press, 1976), 760-61.
9. Armen A. Alchian, "Some Economics of Property Rights," in *Economic Forces,* 127-49.
10. Ibid., 128.
11. Ibid., 132.
12. Ibid., 137.
13. Alchian, "Property Rights," 129.
14. Alchian, introduction to *Economic Forces,* 9.

15. Frank H. Knight, "Fallacies in the Interpretation of Social Cost," in *The Ethics of Competition* (New York: Harper & Bros, 1935), 217-36.

16. Morton Horwitz, "Law and Economics: Science or Politics?" *Hofstra Law Review* 8 (1980): 905.

17. David R. Henderson, ed., *Fortune Encyclopedia of Economics* (New York: Warner Books, 1993), 694-95.

18. Milton Friedman, *Capitalism and Freedom* (Chicago: Univ. of Chicago Press, 1962), 178-89.

19. Ronald Coase, "The Federal Communications Commission," in *The Economics of Property Rights*, eds. Eirik Furubotn and Svetozar Pejovich, (Cambridge, Mass.: Ballinger Publishing Co., 1974), 81, 82.

20. Ronald H. Coase, "The Problem of Social Cost," *Journal of Law and Economics*, 3 (October 1960): 1-44.

21. Steven N. S. Cheung, "The Contractual Nature of the Firm," *Journal of Law and Economics* 26 (April 1983): 20.

22. "Fire of Truth," 183.

23. A. C. Pigou, *Economics of Welfare*, 4th ed. (London: Macmillan, 1960), 127-28, 184.

24. Richard A. Posner, *Economic Analysis of Law*, 2nd ed. (Boston: Little Brown, 1977), 35.

25. Kitch, "Fire of Truth," 220-21.

26. Thomas W. Hazlett, "Looking for Results: An Interview with Ronald Coase," *Reason* 28 (January 1997): 40-48.

27. Ronald H. Coase, *The Firm, the Market and the Law* (Chicago: Univ. of Chicago Press, 1988), 119.

28. Posner, *Economic Analysis of Law*, 22.

29. Ibid., 184.

30. Posner, *Economic Analysis of Law*, 393.

31. Arthur Allen Leff, "Economic Analysis of Law: Some Realism about Nominalism," *Virginia Law Review*, 60 (1974): 459.

32. Horwitz, "Science or Politics?," 905.

33. Frank Michelman, "A Comment on 'Some Abuses and Abuses of Economics and Law,'" *Univ. of Chicago Law Review* 46 (1979): 310.

34. Ronald Dworkin, *Taking Rights Seriously* (Cambridge, Mass.: Harvard Univ. Press, 1977), 98.

35. William F. Powers, "Strawberry Fields Forever? One Man Digs in Against Disney," *Washington Post*, March 9, 1994.

36. Coase, *The Firm*, 105-7.

37. A. W. B. Simpson, "*Coase v. Pigou* Reexamined," *Journal of Legal Studies* 25 (January 1996): 53-97.

38. Ibid., 90, 91

39. Posner, *Economic Analysis of Law*, 128-29.

40. Ibid., 345-46.

41. Ibid., 11.

42. Paul Heyne, *The Economic Way of Thinking*, 7th ed. (New York: Macmillan College Publishing Co., 1994), 75.

43. Ronald H. Coase, "The Institutional Structure of Production," *The American Economic Review*, September 1992, 717-18.

44. Ibid.

CHAPTER 21

1. Editorial, "China's Reach for Greatness," *Washington Post*, September 21, 1997.

2. Roger Cohen, "To Deplore Capitalism Isn't Always to Fight It," *New York Times*, September 21, 1997.

3. *The Oxford Dictionary of Quotations*, 3rd ed. (New York: Oxford Univ. Press, 1979), 276.

4. Alvin Rabushka, "The Great Tax Cut of China," *Wall Street Journal*, August 7, 1997.

5. Kate Xiao Zhou, *How the Farmers Changed China: Power of the People* (Boulder, Colo.: Westview Press, 1996), 37.

6. Ibid., 49.

7. Andrew G. Walder, *China's Quiet Revolution* (New York: St. Martin's Press, 1994), 7.

8. Zhou, *Farmers Changed China,* xxi.
9. Ibid., xii.
10. Ibid., 51.
11. Ibid., 63.
12. Ibid., 64.
13. Ibid., preface.
14. Ibid., chap. 1.
15. Friedrich A. Hayek, *The Fatal Conceit* (Chicago: Univ. of Chicago Press, 1988), 37. In February 1998, Hayek's *Constitution of Liberty* sold out immediately after publication in China. "We have the direct experience of what Hayek is writing about," said the book's translator, Deng Zhenglai. A forum on the book, organized by an economist named Mao Yushi, was attended by "a veritable Who's Who of Chinese progressives." ("China's Road from Serfdom," *Wall Street Journal,* May 12, 1998).
16. World Bank report on China, September, 1997.
17. Kathy Chen, "Opening Doors: China Is Encouraging Private Home Buying, And It Is Rising Fast," *Wall Street Journal,* July 16, 1997.
18. Lena H. Sun, "U.S. Is Big Market for Firms Owned by Chinese Military; Huge Amounts of Goods Linked to PLA," *Washington Post,* June 24, 1997.
19. Steven Mufson, "China's Fields Yield to Factories," *Washington Post,* July 22, 1996.
20. Steven Mufson, "China to Cut Most State-Owned Firms: Planners Declare They Will Practice 'Survival of the Fittest,'" *Washington Post* September 15, 1997.
21. Seth Faison, "A Great Tiptoe Forward: Beijing Talks of More Private Enterprise But Seems Unlikely to Stay Out of Its Way," *New York Times,* September 17, 1997.
22. Fred Hiatt, "The Skyscraper and the Bookstore," *Washington Post,* June 1, 1997.
23. Chas. W. Freeman, Jr., "Hong Kong and False Alarms," *New York Times,* June 22, 1997.
24. Robert J. Barro, "Democracy: A Recipe for Growth?" *Wall Street Journal,* December 1, 1994; and see Robert J. Barro, "Pushing Democracy Is No Key to Prosperity," *Wall Street Journal,* December 14, 1993.
25. Seymour Martin Lipset, "Some Social Requisites of Democracy: Economic Development and Political Legitimacy," *American Political Science Review* 53 (1959): 69-105.
26. Robert J. Barro, *Determinants of Economic Growth: A Cross-Country Empirical Study* (Cambridge, Mass.: MIT Press, 1997), 59.
27. Ibid., 50.
28. Judith Miller, "At Hour of Triumph, Democracy Recedes As the Global Ideal," *New York Times,* February 18, 1996.
29. Keith B. Richburg, *Out of America: A Black Man Confronts Africa* (New York: Basic Books, 1997), 238; and see Robert D. Kaplan, "Democracy's Trap," *New York Times,* December 24, 1995.
30. David Ricardo, *Works and Correspondence of David Ricardo,* ed. Piero Sraffa (Cambridge: Cambridge Univ. Press, 1962), 5: 501. For discussion of the hazards of Parliamentary reform, see Walter Bagehot, *The Collected Works of Walter Bagehot,* ed. Norman St. John Stevas (London: The Economist, 1974), 6: 181-379.
31. Fareed Zakaria, "Culture Is Destiny: A Conversation with Lee Kuan Yew," *Foreign Affairs* (March/April 1994), 108.
32. Fareed Zakaria, "The Rise of Illiberal Democracy," *Foreign Affairs* (November/December 1997): 22-43.
33. J. Gwartney, R. Lawson, and W. Block, *Economic Freedom of the World, 1975-1995* (Vancouver: Fraser Institute, 1996); and see the subsequent 1997 *Annual Report,* by Gwartney and Lawson; and B. T. Johnson and T. P. Sheehy, *The Index of Economic Freedom* (Washington D.C.: Heritage Foundation, 1995, 1996).
34. Gerald. W. Scully, "The Institutional Framework and Economic Development," *Journal of Political Economy* 96 (1988): 652; and his later book, *Constitutional Environments and Economic Growth* (Princeton, N. J.: Princeton Univ. Press, 1992). See also Stephen Knack and Philip Keefer, "Institutions and Economic Performance: Cross-Country Tests Using Alternative Institutional Measures," *Economics and Politics* 7 (November 1995), 207-227.
35. Robert G. Kaiser, "China Rising: Is America Paying Attention?" *Washington Post,* October 26, 1997. Orville Schell wrote in *The Nation* that driving in from the Shanghai airport "is like being in one of those American children's workbooks in the thirties that boastfully limned futuristic

landscapes filled with belching smokestacks, trains barreling down tracks toward distant horizons, planes zooming overhead and freeways coursing through thickets of skyscrapers." Orville Schell, "Twilight of the Titan: China—The End of an Era," *The Nation,* July 17/24, 1995, 84.

36. David Remnick, *Resurrection: The Struggle for a New Russia* (New York: Random House, 1997), 44-45.

37. Ibid., 45.

38. Daniel Yergin and Joseph Stanislaw, *The Commanding Heights* (New York: Simon & Schuster, 1998).

39. Alvaro Vargas Llosa, "To Give Latins Real Reform, Start With Property Titles," *Wall Street Journal,* January 3, 1997.

INDEX